PROFESSOR R. W. FOGEL
HARVARD UNIVERSITY
1737 CAMBRIDGE ST., RM. G-7
CAMBRIDGE, MA. 02138
4/1/81

THE WORLD OF LABOUR

THE WORLD OF LABOUR

G.D.H. COLE

Edited with an introduction and notes by
JOHN LOVELL
Lecturer in Economic and Social History,
University of Kent

BOOKS
10 East 53d St., New York 10022
(a division of Harper & Row Publishers, Inc.)

Published in the U.S.A. 1973 by:
HARPER & ROW PUBLISHERS, INC.
BARNES & NOBLE IMPORT DIVISION

'The World of Labour' first published in 1913 by G. Bell, London and revised in 1915, 1917 and 1919

This edition with 1919 text first published in 1973 by The Harvester Press

'The World of Labour' © executors of the late G. D. H. Cole
Introduction © John Lovell 1973

ISBN: 06—491257—4

Typesetting by Campbell Graphics Ltd., Newcastle upon Tyne
Printed in England by Redwood Press Limited, Trowbridge
Bound by Cedric Chivers Limited, Portway, Bath

All rights reserved. No part of this publication may be reproduced, stored in a retrieval system or transmitted in any form or by any means, electronic, mechanical, photocopying, recording or otherwise without prior permission.

Contents

Introduction by John Lovell	page vii

THE WORLD OF LABOUR

Notes to the Text	page xxxv

Introduction

G. D. H. Cole's *The World of Labour* was published on 6 November 1913. It was his first major publication. The book was an undoubted success, and new editions appeared in 1915, 1917 and 1919. A reviewer in the *Economic Journal* described it as 'the most important book on trade unionism since Mr. and Mrs. Webbs' *Industrial Democracy*',[1] and this opinion was repeated in other quarters. *The World of Labour* was, however, a book whose mood differed strikingly from that of the Webb's *Industrial Democracy,* and it was no doubt partly this contrast which accounted for the book's appeal.[2] The contrast was no coincidence. In 1913 Cole, as a young member of the Fabian Society, was in revolt against the Webbs' dominance of that body, and the publication of the *The World of Labour* has to be seen against the background of the politics of the Fabian Society.

Cole had joined the Oxford Fabian Society in 1908 shortly after his arrival at that University (he was still at Oxford in 1913, as a Fellow of Magdalen College, when the *The World of Labour* was published). The young university socialists were extremely active at this period, and played an energetic part in the Webbs' Poor Law campaign of 1909—11.[3] Impressed by this activity, the Webbs were anxious to draw the young men from the universities into the work of Fabian research. During the summer of 1912 they set up a Control of Industry Committee, composed of about eighty members of the Society, together with numerous consultative members drawn from the trade unions and co-operative societies. The object of the Committee was to conduct an exhaustive enquiry into the methods by which industry should be controlled and administered in a socialist state. It was in effect the Webbs' response to the development of syndicalist ideas in Britain at this period, ideas which cut right across their own collectivist blueprint for society.⁴ The Committee, as they hoped, would produce an authoritative statement denouncing syndicalist schemes for direct workers' control of industry, and upholding their own vision of an industry owned and controlled by the elected representatives of the people and administered by expert bureaucrats. The Committee divided itself into four sub-committees, dealing respectively with associations of consumers, associations of producers, public services, and associations of wage earners. In the event the Webbs' project misfired. It certainly attracted the young university socialists. William Mellor, one of Cole's close associates at Oxford, became full-time secretary of the Committee, and Cole himself joined the project in May 1913. During the course of that year the Committee transformed itself into a permanent organisation—the Fabian Research Department. Various reports were produced as planned, but the sub-committee on associations of wage earners ran into serious difficulty. The draft report produced by the Webbs was completely unacceptable to Cole and Mellor, who in turn were unable to force through their own proposals. The deadlock reflected fundamental differences between the Webbs on the one hand and the younger generation of Fabians on the other. As Margaret Cole has written, these differences were to a considerable extent simply a matter of contrasting temperaments and intellectual backgrounds, but, as she also points out, there was nonetheless a real clash of principle.⁵ The fact was that Cole and Mellor had been deeply influenced by the very ideology that the Webbs were so anxious to discredit—syndicalism.

It was not in Cole's nature to accept without reservation any ideological package, least of all one imported from abroad.⁶ But the syndicalist emphasis on the workers' right to control their own industrial destiny seemed to him to offer the prospect of a more truly democratic society than the one foreshadowed by the undiluted collectivism of orthodox Fabians. It was, however, a particular version of syndicalism which especially appealed to Cole, as it did also to Mellor and many others of their generation. The theory in question was Guild Socialism, a theory which, as we shall see, attempted to incorporate the syndicalist demand for workers' control within a much modified collectivist framework. Guild Socialism was, however, much more than an attempted compromise between syndicalism and collectivism. It had intellectual roots of its own which stretched back to the work of William Morris.[7] It was in fact a disciple of Morris—Arthur J. Penty—who first definitely formulated the idea of Guild Socialism, in his book *The Restoration of the Guild System*, (1906). Guild Socialist ideas made their impact upon Cole and Mellor by way of the columns of the *New Age*. The editor was A. R. Orage, an associate of Penty's, and its most important contributor, after 1908, was S. G. Hobson. Hobson, in collaboration with Orage, produced a series of articles for the *New Age* which, in Cole's words, 'gave the National Guilds movement a definite shape, and made it for the first time a practical and constructive force'.[8] The articles were certainly a constructive influence upon Cole's thinking, and his indebtedness to them is carefully acknowledged in the Preface to the first edition of *The World of Labour*.

Cole became an ardent supporter of Guild Socialism during the course of 1914, but in the two preceding years, while he was writing *The World of Labour*, he still hesitated to commit himself fully to the new doctrine. As he was to write later: 'I was not, however, at this stage definitely a Guildsman, both because I then disliked the name and because the movement seemed to have too little touch with industrial realities'.[9] Later books by Cole were to be explicitly Guild Socialist in approach,[10] though this was not the case with *The World of Labour*. But the influence of the Guild Socialist writers is strong nonetheless. Their essential attraction for Cole was that they appeared to have hit upon a scheme of workers' control or industrial self-government which could be applied to the specifically British industrial situation. Hobson and Orage had visualised the transformation of the existing British trade unions into a series of National Guilds which would control industry on truly democratic lines. They had in fact forged the vital link between existing trade unionism and a new order in industry, and it was this association which more than anything else fired Cole's imagination.

To view British trade unions in this way was to view them from a standpoint entirely different from that adopted by the Webbs in their *Industrial Democracy* (1897). The greater part of that work is devoted to an analysis of trade union function—'the methods used, the regulations imposed, and the policy followed by Trade Unions' (1920 edn., Preface, pp.

xx—xxi). This analysis was intended to stand independently of any judgements concerning the consequences of trade unionism for society in its then existing form, or concerning its role in the society of the future. Judgements of this nature the Webbs did make, in the latter part of the book. When they came to considerations of this kind, or, more specifically, to the question of the role of trade unions in the socialist society of the future, they were not inclined to accord to the unions a position of central importance. The latter were to be excluded from industrial decisions affecting what was to be produced and the manner in which production was to take place, leaving them essentially confined to matters relating to conditions of employment. Even in this last sphere the Webbs envisaged increased legislative intervention, and saw the function of the unions, at least in part, as that of assisting the state in the formulation and enforcement of legally binding national minimum standards.[11] This was still essentially the position of the Webbs in 1913.

In *The World of Labour* there is no attempt at an objective analysis of trade union function, and the whole momentum of the book derives from the assumption that the trade unions, so far from having a subordinate role to play in the society of the future, are in fact the key factor in the process of social change. It was this assumption of course which accounted for the conflict on the Fabian Control of Industry Committee, mentioned above. The standpoint of Cole and Mellor in relation to the trade union movement was closely linked to the situation in British industry during the period 1910—14. *The World of Labour* appeared at a time when the great Dublin transport strike was in full swing, and the period immediately preceding the book's publication was one of acute industrial unrest.[12] The activities of the small Parliamentary Labour Party, the political arm of the labour movement, must have seemed trivial indeed in comparison with the industrial conflict in which the trade unions were then involved. It was therefore natural enough for socialists of Cole's generation to focus their hopes for the future on the industrial organisations of the workers. Cole was, however, a realist. He was convinced of the vital importance of the unions, he was fascinated by the Guild Socialist vision of the path which union development should take, but he was very well aware of the distance which the British trade union movement would need to travel, both in terms of organisation and ideology, if it was to fulfil its real mission as he saw it. It was this realism which accounted for the reservations he still had concerning Guild Socialism in 1913. The movement had 'too little touch with industrial realities', it was more concerned with theorising about the character of the society of the future than with considering how the transition to this society might be achieved, and its propaganda was confined to the columns of the *New Age*, a journal with no influence outside the ranks of middle class intellectuals (pp. 51—2). *The World of Labour* was the first attempt to relate the new theories of industrial democracy, Guild Socialism included, to the realities of the trade union situation in industry. As a result it caused some offence to the purists on the *New Age*,[13] but it was to become a landmark in the evolution of a workers' control movement in Britain.

In order to place *The World of Labour* in its proper perspective, it is necessary to pay some attention to the development of this movement and, in particular, to Cole's part in this development. At the beginning of 1914 Cole decided to commit himself to Guild Socialism. For him, however, commitment did not mean simply taking one's place in a little circle of like-minded intellectuals; it meant instead the active propagation of Guild Socialist ideas. Together with William Mellor he began a series of articles on these ideas in the *Daily Herald*. As he wrote later, 'our object in these articles was at the same time to popularise Guild propaganda and to bring it into the closest possible relation to the everyday work of the Trade Union Movement'.[14] The next step was the formation of a specifically Guild Socialist propagandist organisation, and at a conference held in London during Easter 1915 the National Guilds League was launched, with Mellor as its first General Secretary. Prior to this development Cole had been involved in an attempt to capture the Fabian Society for Guild Socialist research and propaganda.[15] The attempt had failed, but the Guild Socialists were successful in winning control of the Society's Research Department, which developed eventually into the Labour Research Department. Although Beatrice Webb did not lose interest in the work of the organisation, its activities came to be entirely dominated by the leading Guild Socialist spirits— Cole, Mellor, and also R. Page Arnot, the future historian of the Miners' Federation. Cole was the Honorary Secretary of the Department during the war period, with Page Arnot as the paid secretary.

The establishment of the National Guilds League and the capture of the Fabian Research Department gave to the Guilds movement an impetus it had not possessed in its early years. The League was never a large body but it was immensely active, producing pamphlets and sending out speakers to various parts of the country. Its propaganda was of course mainly directed towards the unions. The role of the Research Department was, however, perhaps of greater significance. Its primary function was to carry out intensive research into existing trade unionism, and much work of this kind was in fact done. Basic research into trade unionism became, however, only one part of the Department's work. The outbreak of war in 1914 had confronted the trade unions with a highly complicated industrial situation, and one with which they were ill-equipped to cope. They lacked staff to provide the background information and research essential in a rapidly changing environment. So it was that the Research Department came to function as a service institution for the trade union movement, with numbers of trade unions and trades councils affiliating directly to it. The Department's *Monthly Circular,* started in 1917, provided the unions with the general information and statistics which they needed. Margaret Cole described its function as that of 'a kind of left-wing *Ministry of Labour Gazette*'.[16] Beyond this, the Research Department produced a great range of pamphlet literature dealing with industrial issues, it acted as a general inquiry bureau for the unions, and it prepared detailed briefs for individual unions involved in collective bargaining. All this activity, of course, bore no direct relation to Guild Socialist propaganda or to the workers' control movement in any form, but it had an important indirect relation. It brought prominent Guild Socialists—Cole, Mellor, Arnot—into close contact with trade union officers at workshop, branch and national level. In Cole's case this was especially true, since in 1915 he became research adviser to the Amalgamated Society of Engineers, a position he retained until the end of the war. It is perhaps going too far to say that by making themselves indispensable to the unions during the abnormal conditions of war the Guildsmen of the Research Department had created for themselves a position of special advantage when it came to propagandist activity. Nonetheless, they did acquire some influence in the trade union world, and they used that influence to promote policies in accord with their Guild Socialist ideology.

Guild Socialist permeation of the trade union world during the war years was by no means inconsiderable.[17] The engineering industry, being the focal point for the production of munitions, was naturally the most beset with wartime problems. During 1915 it is likely that Cole was able to exert some influence over the policy of the engineering unions, encouraging them to demand from the government a share in the administration of the dilution schemes then being introduced in munitions plants. However, the government rejected the proposals put forward by the unions, and official union interest in questions involving control in this industry then subsided for the remainder of the war. Furthermore, it has been argued that the brief interest shown by the engineering unions in such questions arose wholly out of a concern for the protection of craft interests. Although there were some Guildsmen among the official trade union leaders in the industry at this period, there is apparently no evidence to suggest that the demands put forward in 1915 were seen by the unions as a first step towards the industrial democracy advocated by the Guild Socialists.[18] The influence of the Guildsmen over official union policy in this industry was therefore slight—at workshop level the position was altogether different, as we shall see below.

In other industries greater progress was made. Syndicalist influence had been present in both the railway and coal industries before the war, but during the wartime period the influence of the more moderate Guild Socialist approach began to make itself felt. This approach suggested a compromise between the syndicalist objective of complete workers' control to be achieved by direct action, and the official union policy of straightforward nationalisation. The Guild Socialists advocated a system of joint control, under which the industry concerned would be taken into public ownership, but where control would be shared between the state and the trade unions.[19] By 1917 the National Union of Railwaymen and the Railway Clerks' Association had both come to support the idea of joint control of the railway industry, and when the war ended they put this demand to the government. It was, however, in the coal industry that the greatest headway was made with joint control. At the 1918 conference of the Miners' Federation this policy was officially adopted, and the Executive was instructed to draft a Mines Nationalisation Bill that would provide for it. The resulting scheme was submitted to the 1919 Royal Commission on the Coal Industry. It was worked out in considerable detail and has been described as 'the most important document produced by the British workers in their struggle for workers' control'.[20] The influence of the Guild Socialists in all this was paramount. Frank Hodges, Secretary of the Miners' Federation after the war and the man who moved the adoption of the joint control policy at the 1918 conference, was a Guildsman. The Secretary of the Northumberland Miners, William Straker, who acted as the miners' spokesman on nationalisation and joint control at the sessions of the 1919 Royal Commission, was also a Guildsman. When it is remembered that the future of the coal industry was the central issue in the post war confrontation between Capital and Labour it will be seen that the part Guild Socialism had come to play in the trade union world was by no means negligible.

Guild Socialist influence extended beyond engineering, mining, and railways, although these were obviously the critical industries. In particular, the building workers and postmen were influenced by their propaganda. The Union of Post Office Workers produced a detailed scheme for the transformation of the Post Office into a self-governing National Guild, and a number of its leaders were members of the National Guilds League. In the building industry an attempt was actually made after the war to put Guild Socialism into practice, starting with the setting up of a building guild in Manchester in 1920, an experiment launched by local trade unionists with the help of S. G. Hobson. Building guilds in other areas quickly developed following Manchester's initiative, and the movement culminated in the setting up of a National Building Guild in 1921. These are only the most prominent examples of Guild Socialist influence upon the official trade union movement.

Cole himself came, in the immediate post-war period, to occupy a position at the very centre of the industrial movement. In 1918 he left his post with the Engineers and moved over to the Labour Party, becoming its secretary for research.

He retained, however, his position in the Labour Research Department and became actively involved during 1919 on the Labour side of the National Industrial Conference.[21] As a result of this latter activity he became a member of the Trade Union Co-ordination Committee set up after the 1919 railway strike. The objective of this Committee was to produce a scheme which would enable the Trades Union Congress to really function as a co-ordinator of trade union activity in industry. The outcome of its deliberations was, of course, the setting up of the TUC General Council in 1921. The detailed drafting of the scheme which produced the General Council was done by Cole. It was a unique opportunity for him to attempt to put into practice his ideas concerning the need for a centralisation and rationalisation of trade union structure, ideas that had been expressed before the war in *The World of Labour*.[22] For it had been clear in 1913 that theories concerning the future government of industry which based themselves on the trade unions were only credible in so far as those institutions were seen to be capable of reforming their own chaotic structure. An interest in the problems of trade union structure was something that, of necessity, went hand in hand with serious advocacy of workers' control.

One of the most significant spheres of Guild Socialist influence during the war and immediate post-war period remains to be mentioned. The Guildsmen's propaganda derived its power to a large extent from the fact that it was working with the grain—it was rationalising and reinforcing attitudes and tendencies that had developed independently and had a life of their own. The focal point of these developing tendencies during the war period was the workshop movement in the engineering industry. The forces which gave rise to this movement—largely unofficial, and developed around the power of the shop stewards at the place of work—were described by Cole himself in his book *Workshop Organisation* (1923). Suffice it here to say that the shop stewards' movement as it developed became very much a workers' control movement. In the case of the Clydeside engineering workers there were pre-war influences that worked in this direction, for the Socialist Labour Party with its Industrial Unionist ideology had been strong in this region. The shop steward's movement, however, while its earliest and most vigorous development occurred on Clydeside, came to include the other major centres of engineering production. In any case its attitudes and policies, even on Clydeside, were never simply those of the SLP. The Guild Socialists attached great significance to the emergence of this movement. Cole wrote in his *Workshop Organisation:* 'as the Guild Socialists had seen clearly even before the war, any movement by the workers towards democratic control in industry would have to be rooted in the workshops, and would largely depend for its growth on the capacity of the workers' organisations to assume control over the operations of production' (p.89). For a time the Guild Socialists were able to exert considerable influence upon the shop stewards movement. The first provincial branch of the National Guilds League, established in 1916, was, in fact, composed of Glasgow shop stewards, whose journal *The Guildsman* was subsequently adopted by the National League as its official organ. Outside Glasgow the influence of Guild Socialism was less apparent, but by no means negligible; it was for example of some significance in Sheffield, an important centre of the movement.[23]

The shop stewards certainly took up one aspect of the Guild Socialist programme, namely, the idea of 'encroaching control'. Unlike the more extreme versions of syndicalism, the approach of Guild Socialism was essentially gradualist in character. In some industries, such as mining and railways, it envisaged the realisation of its programme by way of nationalisation, with a scheme of joint control in the early stages being gradually transformed into a complete system of industrial self-government on Guild lines (see ch.XII below, esp. p.391). In other industries, of which engineering and also building stand as the main examples, it was realised soon enough that no prospect existed of achieving workers' control via the route of nationalisation. It was here that the concept of 'encroaching control' came into its own. The idea was that the trade unions would gradually wrest from the employers more and more of the functions of management, until the latter could be finally ousted. When *The World of Labour* was first published this idea had not yet emerged with any clarity. There is some notion regarding the way in which the union might gradually push back the frontier of managerial prerogatives, but this is seen as something which would operate in both privately and publicly owned industries indiscriminately (pp.385—6). At this date Cole had not at his disposal the idea of 'encroaching control' as a strategy to be applied specifically to those industries where progress towards workers' control via the route of nationalisation was impossible.

The scheme was in fact first propounded in detail at a conference of Guild Socialists at Storrington, Sussex in December 1914. An essential ingredient was a device that subsequently came to be called the 'Collective Contract'— whereby the workers in a given unit would undertake the organisation of the whole process of production in return for a lump sum payment to the union on the basis of output. In this way a whole range of managerial functions would be transferred to the workers. The notion held considerable appeal for the militant shop stewards in the war-time engineering industry. It was taken up and developed by John Paton, a shop steward and founder of the Glasgow Guild Socialist branch. In 1917 Paton together with William Gallacher, the President of the Clyde Workers' Committee, produced a pamphlet in which they attempted to apply the general idea of the Collective Contract to the workshop movement in engineering.[24] The appeal of the Guild Socialist conception of 'encroaching control' was, however, it must be admitted, somewhat short lived. It was in many ways an unrealistic policy and came to be seen as such by the shop stewards' movement. Furthermore the Russian Revolution, which had a tremendous impact upon the movement was a powerful factor discrediting the gradualist approach. In the immediate post war period the policy was repudiated and the shop stewards' organisations came more and more under the influence of Communism. By 1921 it was possible for Gallacher to regard as 'a piece of infantile sickness' the scheme of Collective Contract which he and Paton had produced in 1917.[25]

Guild Socialism had its limitations, and these were to be revealed soon enough, but it did make a considerable impact upon the trade union world—official and unofficial—in the years that followed 1914. Trade union interest in the question of workers' control was certainly roused during this period, and while it is true that this was mainly due to the abnormal situation in industrial relations that arose out of the war, it is also true that the Guild Socialists were more successful than any other group in providing the unions with a theory to match their new found interest.[26] The shift in trade union opinion that took place in this period naturally affected Cole's whole interpretation of the labour situation in Britain. In 1913, when he was writing *The World of Labour*, it had seemed to him that the will to control being generated from within the trade union movement was strictly limited. This feeling emerges clearly in the following passage:

> If we are to wait for producers' control till the Unions have directly expropriated all employers, and extended their power over all industrial conditions and processes, we shall wait till doomsday—and a little after. *Trade unionists do not, in the main, desire to control industry nowadays, and, unless those who do actually control it help them to realise their power, it may be long before they desire it very much more.* It is the function of the State, here as elsewhere, to liberate and stimulate energy, to give the worker the fullest measure of control that he is capable of, in order that he may be got to desire more (pp.381–2, *italics mine*).

Cole did feel that there were some signs of progress at this time, and he referred to the 'nascent demand for control of industry which is springing up within Trade Unionism' (p.382). In particular, he saw the increased proportion of strikes concerned with 'discipline' and 'management' (as opposed to strictly economic issues) as indicative of this 'nascent demand'. But this tendency appeared to him to be largely unconscious: 'There are signs that the Unions are making demands for the enlargement of their sphere of control; but there are no signs that the meaning of those demands is being realised' (p.382). By 1919 the position had changed, and support for workers' control in some form or another was widespread. It was possible for Cole to write in the Introduction to the 1919 edition of *The World of Labour*, that so far as the labour movement was concerned, 'the internal battle for the idea of workers' control has been fought and won' (p.xiii).

The transformation in the outlook of the unions was all the more significant in view of their enormously enhanced numerical strength, a result of wartime full employment and inflation, and in view also of their apparently militant post war mood—1919 and 1920 witnessing a quite unprecedented level of strike activity. In this situation it is not difficult to see why Cole felt immensely strengthened in his Guild Socialist convictions. He believed, along with many others, that the days of the capitalist system in this country were now definitely numbered. The question in 1919 seemed to be less whether fundamental changes in society would take place, as what form they would take. The organisations of the workers appeared to have definitely staked out their claim for, at the least, a share in control. Guild Socialism seemed to be a way of realising this demand gradually and peacefully, avoiding the violent upheavals that were then shaking the Continent. The contrast in mood between 1913 and 1919 is well brought out by a comparison between Cole's *The World of Labour* and his *Chaos and Order in Industry* (1920). In the one, labour is represented as at best groping forward towards the ideal of industrial self-government; in the other, it is a question of investigating how this ideal might be applied, industry by industry.

The Guild Socialist movement was always a movement of the few rather than of the many, like the Fabian Society from which it sprang. Its influence was, however, out of all proportion to its numerical strength. The membership of the National Guilds League was never more than a few hundred, but its output of propaganda was prolific. An American observer, Arthur Gleason, in 1920 wrote this of the Guild Socialists:

> In the last five years, the Guildsmen have done a service akin to that done by Blatchford for a former generation. They don't write as simply nor as vigorously as Blatchford did in "Merrie England", but they, like him, are evangelists. They have carried on excellent Salvation Army work in popularizing the idea of a British brand of syndicalism. They have domesticated that immense dynamic. But for them, the Central Labour College, the Socialist Labour Party, the I.W.W., French ideas, the phrases of Tom Mann, and the tracts of Daniel De Leon would have perhaps been the only deposit of syndicalism and industrial unionism. The result would have been a small minority of workers over-stimulated with a doctrine that omitted one-half the truth. But Orage, Cole, Mellor, Hobson, Bechhofer, Reckitt, and a few others rendered the alien vocabulary into a British blend which pleased the palate like Lipton's tea. (op.cit., p.262).

Gleason's observations were very much to the point. Only the Guild Socialists had succeeded in extracting from syndicalism a programme which had a chance of acceptance inside the British trade union movement; they had, as he said, 'domesticated that immense dynamic'. Unfortunately for them, however, they did not succeed in domesticating the influences that sprang from the Russian Revolution. It was the example of Russia which, as we have noted, increasingly attracted the leaders of the war-time shop stewards' movement, and before long advocates of the Soviet system and the dictatorship of the proletariat were to be found within the National Guilds League itself. The latter body was increasingly wrent by internal conflicts between right and left, so that as early as 1920 Cole foresaw the likelihood of a split.[27]

The conflict was one that concerned both priorities and practicalities. There were those, either members of the League or associated with it, for whom the smashing of the capitalist system was the one great and urgent objective; considerations as to the nature of the democracy that was to succeed capitalist society were secondary. This viewpoint was naturally sympathetic to Russian Communism, and the sympathy was not undermined when the Bolsheviks abandoned their earlier workers' control schemes and, in the interests of efficiency, substituted a far more authoritarian regime in industry. But, for Guildsmen like Cole, the implementation of workshop democracy and the avoidance of totalitarianism were of the very essence; they were not to be sacrificed at any price. In the pursuit of these objectives, furthermore, they were able to envisage the possibility of a long drawn out period of transition between capitalism and socialism; Frank Hodges, for example, was prepared to think in terms of "ten, fifteen, twenty years".[28] Violent, catastrophic change held little appeal.

The truth was, however, that the pro-Communists had pin-pointed obvious weaknesses in the position of the moderate Guildsmen. The latters' notion of 'encroaching control' for one thing, was simply unrealistic. British capitalists were not going to sit back and allow the workers to expropriate them step by step.[29] In any case, after 1920 economic developments worked decisively against the proponents of 'encroaching control'. In 1921 there was a severe depression, and although things had improved a good deal by 1924, the level of unemployment was to remain high for the remainder of the inter-war period. In such a climate as this it was impossible to sustain anything approaching the level of workshop organisation and influence that had been built up during the wartime; the shop stewards' movement simply ceased to have any real *industrial* significance. Any doubts that remained were resolved by the 1922 lock-out in the engineering industry. The changed economic climate also led to the collapse of the building guilds, so that by 1922 also progress in this field had come to a definite halt. 'Encroaching control' presupposed as a minimum requirement a vigorous workshop organisation, and in this regard the depression constituted a major setback indeed. The alternative gradualist route to workers' control, via nationalisation, proved to be equally illusory. It quickly became clear in post-war Britain that the state was not going to pave the way for the National Guilds by nationalising key industries, with or without joint control. Superficially therefore, the argument that the smashing of capitalism and the capitalist state was a necessary prerequisite for any progress towards workers' control appeared to carry some conviction. Certainly progress on the lines that had been envisaged by most Guildsmen became progressively more difficult to believe in, until in 1922 the movement finally gave up the ghost.

There had been other weaknesses in the Guild idea that manifested themselves in the post-war years. As Cole himself later admitted, little detailed thought had really been given by Guildsmen to the problems of democratic industrial management. In particular, Cole felt in retrospect that the preoccupation of Guild Socialists with industrial democracy at the workshop level had been at the expense of serious consideration of the problems of higher control and planning.[30] Certainly the vagueness and imprecision of the Guild Socialist blueprint for industry to some extent undermined its credibility, and Arthur Gleason strongly criticised the Guild Socialists from this point of view in 1920 (op.cit., p.272).Gleason felt that Cole and his associates had left unresolved too many questions of this kind. When Cole made his statement on workers' control to the 1919 Royal Commission on the Coal Industry he failed, in Gleason's view, to carry his arguments because 'promising facts, he gave none, and generalizing on "aspiration", and "inspiration", he did not reveal knowledge of instincts in industry.'[31] In making this last point, however, Gleason was introducing a criticism of a rather different kind to that noted above. He was suggesting that not only were the Guild Socialist schemes for the future of industry insufficiently detailed in themselves, they were also imperfectly founded on the realities of the existing industrial situation. 'It would be profitable', he suggested, 'to supplement the large paper programs of control with a fact study of how far actual control has proceeded, and what functions the workers are now willing and ready to take over'.[32] A preliminary study along these lines was indeed published in 1920, but it was the work not of a Guildsman, but of another American observer of the British labour scene—Carter Goodrich's, *The Frontier of Control*.

It may be argued, of course, that the criticisms of Gleason do the Guild Socialists less than justice, especially in view of their activity in the Labour Research Department. In any case the fact is that no matter how carefully the Guild Socialists had researched their schemes, the latter would still have foundered in the economic and political climate of the early 1920s. The forward thrust of trade union power, which had begun in 1910 and been sustained by the war and post-war boom, came definitely to a halt in the depression of the early 20s. Thereafter trade unionists were concerned above all with the defence of the wage and hour standards which they had won; the onslaught on managerial prerogatives had to be postponed indefinitely.

This review of Guild Socialism and the workers' control movement may seem to have carried the discussion some distance from *The World of Labour* itself, but the digression was a necessary one. I have drawn attention to the way in which some reviewers of Cole's book in 1913 bracketed it with *Industrial Democracy*. Yet there was a vital difference between the two. The Webbs were careful in their book to separate their analysis of trade union function from their speculations as to the appropriate union role in the socialist society of the future. For this reason, their work was able to survive until the present day as a classic in the interpretation of trade unionism. In *The World of Labour*, however, Cole's discussion of the state of existing trade unions, perceptive as it is, is nonetheless coloured throughout by his conception of their role in the society of the future. The objectivity for which the Webbs strove is to a large degree lacking in *The World of Labour*, and of course is entirely lacking in some of Cole's later books, such as *Self-Government in Industry*, and *Chaos and Order in Industry*. It is not suggested that this is of itself a defect, since Cole made no secret of his commitment. It does mean, however, that one must regard *The World of Labour* as being very much a product of a particular time and a particular movement.

It remains to introduce the reader to the lay-out of the book and something of its substance. On the former Cole had this to say: 'the plan on which I built up my book was that of proceeding from the simpler to the more complex, from the indefinite unrest to the definite reconstruction'.[33] The first two chapters are very general in character, and deal with what Cole described as the 'double Labour Unrest'. The first and immediately obvious aspect of the contemporary labour unrest was the strike wave that had been sweeping through industry since 1910. The causes of this industrial militancy, and its stated objectives, were, as Cole recognised (pp.35—6), primarily of a straightforward economic character. It is interesting that Cole rejects as an explanation of this unrest the theory that people had become disillusioned with the Parliamentary Labour Party and were therefore more or less deliberately switching from political to industrial action (pp.36—8). This explanation was canvassed at the time, and has been used a good deal by historians since. It would seem to have little to recommend it.

The focus of *The World of Labour* is really on the second aspect of the labour unrest, which was of an intellectual character—'the labour movement in search of a philosophy' (p.1). There had set in a revulsion against Collectivism. People were looking for a more truly democratic ideal which placed some limit upon the growth of state power; hence the increasing interest in Syndicalism. To what extent were the two unrests related? Cole wrote: 'These two stirrings of popular will and imagination have acted and reacted on each other continually, and we have often been tempted to believe that their combination was imminent; but in the main, each has taken its own course and managed to inspire the other with no more than a phrase or an illustration' (p.1). Throughout the book he does, on the whole, successfully resist the temptation to believe that the mass of the workers were significantly influenced by the wave of new ideas circulating amongst the labour intellectuals. On the other hand, it emerges clearly enough in the first two chapters that he believed the two unrests to be working in the same direction.

The militancy of the workers, while directed towards short term gains in material living standards, was also, in Cole's view, symptomatic of a more deep seated rejection of the existing industrial system (pp.33—4). Furthermore, the militancy was to some extent assuming new forms and raising new issues. Workers were demanding more say in the running of their own unions, and they were demanding curtailments in managerial prerogatives which would allow them more control over their working lives. The status of the trade unions relative to political labour was being enhanced, and increased interest was being taken in ways in which trade union structure and organisation could be improved. These new interests and problems corresponded to some extent with the developments taking place in the realm of ideas, and in particular with the growth of the syndicalist challenge to collectivism. There was therefore, Cole felt, a 'central unity' underlying all the various issues and problems confronting the world of labour in 1913 (p.56). Although he recognised that serious interest in syndicalist ideas as such was confined to relatively few, he felt that the concept of syndicalism could be stretched to cover the whole range of new impulses passing through the labour movement at this time. He wrote:

> Of all these various and yet homogeneous matters we have been outlining is made up the vague and indefinite movement we are learning to call Syndicalism. Those who fear vagueness in terminology more than they love a new idea will shun the word; but by those who really understand that there is something new in the air needing a name, it will be welcomed. Such a label must of necessity begin by being indefinite: it took Socialism more than half a century to get its definite connotation, and its doing so was not in the end clear gain. Syndicalism is a word which means something and something important, though what it means is at present ill-understood. Its meaning is, in fact, something the future has to decide by its manner of facing the present crisis in the industrial world (p.55).

The first two chapters, therefore, are concerned to suggest that a central unity of a syndicalist character underlay the 'indefinite unrest' of the period. Before proceeding on the path of 'definite reconstruction', Cole turned to a comparative analysis of trade union movements, whose purpose was really to get beyond what he regarded as dogmatic theorising about syndicalism and to trace the idea back to its roots in specific economic and cultural contexts. The two chapters on France were especially important from this point of view. Here Cole was able to show that a good deal of what passed as syndicalist theory was in fact simply a rationalisation of the specifically French trade union situation. The absence of collective bargaining agreements between employers and unions and the violent and disorderly character of industrial conflict in France should, Cole suggested, be seen as arising not so much from adherence to syndicalist dogma on the theory and practice of direct action as from the weakness and instability of French trade union organisation. 'Theory', he commented, 'always distorts the truth by rationalising it' (p.108). Cole's aim was not of course to discredit syndicalism in France—indeed he thought that the French trade union movement might well become the finest in Europe (p.105)—but he did wish to show that much of what was thought of as syndicalist doctrine could not be taken at face value and was not in the least applicable to the British situation. Having made this point, Cole was ready enough to recognise that, as a general idea, French syndicalism might have something of value to offer to other countries. At this level he felt that the theory was strong 'where it affirms and weak where it denies' (p.126). As an assertion of the rights of the producer, and of the value of his organisations, Cole felt that syndicalism was valid. But in carrying the producer's point of view too far, to the extent of denying the role of the state as representative of the consumers—and of the national culture—he felt it was 'led into extravagance and perversity' (p.126).

Cole's treatment of America is a good deal less satisfactory than his treatment of France, since he greatly oversimplified the situation across the Atlantic. The contemporary American writer, Carter Goodrich, commented: 'American students should not judge this by its chapter on American Labor, which is not a fair sample'.[34] It might be thought surprising that Germany should be relegated to the general survey in chapter

6 instead of receiving the same detailed treatment as France and America, since Cole admitted that the German labour movement was reckoned at that time to be the strongest in the world and the efficiency of its organisation commanded much respect in Britain (p.173). Yet it was not, however, associated with syndicalist ideology and therefore it was of less interest to Cole. In his discussion of the concept of the 'general strike' Cole returns to a theme first sounded in the opening chapter of the book—the strength of national sentiment among the working class (p.27). He had then criticised those syndicalists who purported to believe that nationality did not matter, and he now drove the point home by arguing against those who thought that an international general strike would prove to be an effective device for preventing the outbreak of war. 'But there is nothing so certain', he wrote, 'as that at the first breath of a war-scare, all the peaceable professions of the workers will be forgotten, and jingoism will sweep like a scourge over the country' (p.196). This comment was, of course, made in 1913—without the advantage of hindsight. The importance of nationality was a vital consideration for Cole. It was not merely that it undermined hair-brained schemes like the international general strike, or even that it rendered unrealistic a view of society constructed solely around the position of the worker in industry. The point was that it also meant that each national labour movement had to a large extent to work out its own salvation, and this was the fundamental lesson which Cole drew from his comparative survey. Valuable insights might be gained from a knowledge of other labour movements, but it was not possible to transplant a labour philosophy wholesale from one country to another. On this Cole was emphatic: 'The greatest service that can be done us by the intelligent study of foreign Labour movements is to save us at least from becoming cosmopolitans' (p.165).

The outline of Cole's argument has emerged clearly enough by the end of Chapter 6, about halfway through the book. The resurgence of trade unionism in contemporary Britain is seen as the major hope for social progress, and in this sense he endorses the syndicalist viewpoint. Two reservations have, however, been introduced. In the first place there is a rejection of the more extreme versions of syndicalism which deny to the state any role in the society of the future. Secondly, there is an insistence on the need for each nation to work out its own path to the new society. These two reservations lead, in the concluding chapter, to an affirmation of the Guild Socialist position. This is seen as a home grown philosophy of labour capable of reconciling the extremes of syndicalism and collectivism: 'The Guild Socialism of the *New Age* is a proposal for the co-management of industry by the State and the Trade Unions. Ownership of the means of production is to rest with the community, but the Unions are to be definitely recognised by the State as the normal controllers of industry' (p.363). This, then, was to be the role of the trade unions in the long run. However, before Cole turns to consider these long term objectives he devotes four chapters (7—10 inclusive) to the immediate issues facing the trade union movement.

The long and the short term were of course intimately related. Cole was perfectly aware that the British trade unions in their existing state were utterly unfitted in all respects to play their part in the creation of this future society. In fact he regarded the existing movement with contempt: 'The strivings of a few restless spirits have made little impression on the mass of Trade Unionists. The apathy is still profound, the stupidity incredible' (p.208). Referring to the structure of the movement he remarked that Britain 'has evolved a Trade Union structure that is the merest chaos' (pp.210—11). On the other hand, the strivings of which he spoke gave some hope of change, and he therefore devoted much thought to ways in which the movement could be reformed so as to fit it for the higher tasks ahead. He realised well enough that without these reforms the larger vision was doomed. Chapters 7 and 8 are, therefore, devoted to a careful and detailed analysis of the problems of existing trade union structure and government and the ways in which these problems might be resolved. So far as structure was concerned Cole recognised (as the TUC itself was later forced to recognise in the 1920s) that it was no good devising some ideal system, based for example on the principle of industrial unionism, and then attempting to induce the various unions to conform to it (p.250). The way forward was to examine the situation in different industries and identify the most likely avenues along which progress could be made towards a more rational and effective structure. Ideally, Cole wanted a trade union structure based on industry, with the activities of the various industrial unions co-ordinated from the centre by a strong central organisation.

This was an objective he shared with most trade union radicals of the period. The value of his analysis, however, was that it recognised the inevitability of a piece-meal and incomplete adaptation of the movement to this ideal form, and was full of well thought out suggestions of ways in which progress might be made. The sections dealing with the shipbuilding and engineering industry and with the problem of the general labourer are of particular interest.

The chapter dealing with trade union government is of the same high standard as that on structure, and taken together they constituted a programme of reform far in advance of anything else that was put before the trade union radicals of the period. Cole summed up this programme under the phrase 'the Greater Unionism'. He saw progress towards this as entailing essentially three things (p.284): a reform of structure aimed at consolidating and co-ordinating the trade union forces, a reform of the internal government of trade unions with a view to making them more truly representative of their various constituent groups and, the overhaul of the administrative arrangements of the unions with a view to greater efficiency. This programme is something which, to some extent, stands independently of the rest of the book. Although it was seen by Cole, at this time, primarily in terms of a precondition of progress towards a system of National Guilds, the validity of its arguments does not depend upon Guild Socialist or Syndicalist assumptions and it could well have been endorsed by a wide spectrum of opinion. Indeed, the problems of trade union structure and government discussed by Cole were to be of continuing interest long after Guild Socialism and Syndicalism had faded well into the background.

Chapters 9 and 10, which follow upon the survey of structure and government, deal with a variety of issues causing immediate concern in the world of labour: for example, discussion of the public attitude towards industrial conflict, which brings in the question of the role of the state in industrial relations under the existing system. In Chapter 10 consideration is given to the various panaceas put forward by employers and others as a cure for industrial unrest. Co-partnership and profit-sharing schemes are discussed—and, of course, rejected—by Cole as workers should not settle for anything less than the complete transformation of society.

In Chapter 11 Cole moves from the immediate problems of the trade union movement to what he regards as its long term objectives, and this remains the focus of his interest for the rest of the book—although in Chapter 13 the contemporary Parliamentary Labour Party comes in for a good deal of adverse comment. In this last part of the book Cole is taking up again his early themes. He felt that the syndicalists had diagnosed correctly the general direction in which society was headed, although their analysis erred in its negative attitude towards the future role of the state. Cole's notion of a Guild Socialist compromise between the extremes of syndicalism and collectivism emerges clearly in this concluding part of the book,[35] and there is an extensive discussion of the whole question of the relationship between the trade unions and the state. In my view this is not the most satisfactory part of the book. It is marred by a good deal of repetition and a certain vagueness. Cole was at his most effective in dealing with the concrete problems of contemporary trade unionism, and it is at this point that *The World of Labour* is at its strongest. The further he was removed from the immediate and tangible issues, the less sure was his touch.

It is, however, not my wish to conclude on a note of criticism. For anyone wishing to understand the impulses passing through the British Labour movement during one of the most crucial periods of its history Cole's book remains indispensable. It has also a further significance. Since the Second World War, in conditions of full employment, interest in the question of control in industry has revived. Thus the debate on workers' control, which Cole did so much to initiate in *The World of Labour*, continues still.

BIBLIOGRAPHICAL NOTE

Later books by G. D. H. Cole dealing with trade unionism and industrial democracy:

Labour in Wartime, London, Bell, 1915.

Trade Unionism on the Railways (with R. Page Arnot), London, Fabian Research Department, 1917.

Self-Government in Industry, London, Bell, 1917.

The Payment of Wages, London, Labour Research Department, 1918.

Chaos and Order in Industry, London, Methuen, 1920.

Guild Socialism Re-stated, London, Parsons, 1920.

Labour in the Coal Mining Industry, Oxford University Press, 1923.

Trade Unionism and Munitions, Oxford University Press, 1923.

Workshop Organisation, Oxford University Press, 1923.

Organised Labour, London, Allen and Unwin, 1924.

The Next Ten Years in British Social and Economic Policy, London, Macmillan, 1930.

Workers' Control and Self-Government in Industry, (Ed. with W. Mellor), London, The New Fabian Research Bureau, 1933.

The Case for Industrial Partnership, London, Macmillan, 1957.

Works by Margaret Cole which relate to G. D. H. Cole's interest in trade unionism and industrial democracy:

Growing up into Revolution, London, Longmans, 1949.

The Story of Fabian Socialism, London, Heinemann, 1961.

The Life of G. D. H. Cole, London, Macmillan, 1971.

'Guild Socialism and the Labour Research Department' in Asa Briggs and John Saville, *Essays in Labour History 1886–1923*, London, Macmillan, 1971.

Notes to the Introduction

[1] *Economic Journal*, No.93 Vol. XXIV, March 1914, p.100. See also *New Statesman* review, 29 November, 1913.

[2] I am indebted to Dame Margaret Cole and the late Raymond Postgate for drawing my attention to the way in which contemporaries were struck by this contrast in mood.

[3] M. Cole (ed.), *The Webbs and their Work* (1949) p.152.

[4] Ibid., pp.152–4. See also M. Cole, *The Story of Fabian Socialism* (1961), pp.150–1.

[5] *The Webbs and their Work*, pp.154–6 and p.160. Also *The Story of Fabian Socialism*, pp.147–9.

[6] Syndicalism and the associated doctrine of Industrial Unionism were evolved in France and the United States of America respectively. The essential elements of these doctrines are well summarized (from the point of view of their impact upon Britain) in Branko Pribićević, *The Shop Stewards' Movement and Workers' Control* (1959), pp.10–21.

[7] The inspiration which Cole drew from Morris' work may be seen clearly in *The World of Labour*, pp.9–13 and 419–20. It is even more evident in Cole's later book, *Self-Government in Industry* (1917), pp.119-22. Not all prominent Guild Socialists were at one with Cole in laying emphasis upon the need to restore to the worker his 'joy in labour'—a concept derived of course from Morris' idealisation of the medieval craftsman. Frank Hodges, the Miners' Secretary and a Guild Socialist, saw workers' control in rather different terms, and his views are worth quoting at some length: *'Workers' control is a means, and not an end.* Work in the modern industrial world is unpleasant for the majority of workers. They will find their expression as human beings outside the working hours—in the use of leisure for family life, education, a hobby. Control they will use to get efficient management and machinery, with which to shorten hours to the minimum which is consistent with the essential work of high production. Control, they wish, to save them from the waste and insecurity and long hours of the present system, which leaves no secure and creative leisure. A minimum of work consistent with a production which will give sufficient commodities for a good life for all workers: they will use control to obtain that. *But control will never of itself be an answer to the instincts thwarted by standardised machine industry. The answer will be found outside of working hours'.* Quoted by Arthur Gleason, *What the Workers Want* (1920), p.182.

[8] Cole, *Chaos and Order in Industry*, (1920), p.49.

[9] Ibid., p.51.

[10] For example, *Self-Government in Industry, Chaos and Order in Industry*, and *Guild Socialism Re-stated* (1920).

[11] Ibid., Part III, Chapter 4. In *The World of Labour*, Cole, while disagreeing with the conclusions reached by the Webbs as to the future role of the unions in the control of industry, nonetheless accepted their framework of argument (pp.353—62). However, in his later book, *Self-Government in Industry*, Cole was a good deal more scathing in his handling of the Webbs' work.

[12] The strike in Dublin aroused tremendous interest in labour and socialist circles: see the extensive coverage of the conflict in the *Daily Herald*, September and November, 1913. For a contemporary account of the general industrial unrest during the period prior to the publication of *The World of Labour* see J. Watney and J. A. Little, *Industrial Warfare* (1912).

[13] See the review of the book in the *New Age*, 20 November 1913 and Cole's letter in reply, 4 December 1913. The review in the *Daily Herald*, 5 December 1913, tended to take the same line as the *New Age*.

[14] *Chaos and Order in Industry*, p.52. Cole and Mellor had collaborated before in the production of the pamphlet *The Greater Unionism*, published in 1913—before *The World of Labour*.

[15] M. Cole (ed.), *The Webbs and their Work*, pp.157—8, *The Story of Fabian Socialism*, pp.151—4, and *Growing up into Revolution* (1949), pp.63—4.

[16] *The Story of Fabian Socialism*, p.179.

[17] It was actually in about 1913 that they really replaced the strict Syndicalists as the leading advocates of workers' control in this country. See Pribićević, op.cit., p.2.

[18] Ibid., p.49.

[19] An excellent example of the impact which this kind of approach had upon some prominent unionists is to be found in the statement made by C. T. Cramp, president of the National Union of Railwaymen, to Arthur Gleason; see that author's *What the Workers Want*, pp.212—14, and the summary of Robert Smillie's views in the same book, p.215.

[20] Pribićević, op.cit., p.8. In the brief account of Guild Socialist influence upon the trade unions that follows, I have drawn largely upon the above work, especially pp.9—10, and Cole's own *Chaos and Order in Industry*, especially pp.52—4.

[21] This was, of course, a conference of the two sides of industry convened by the Lloyd George government, ostensibly with a view to improving the climate of industrial relations after the war. Cole acted as secretary to the trade union side, and was in part responsible for the drafting of the *Memorandum on the Causes of and Remedies for Labour Unrest* which was produced by the trade union representatives. The *Memorandum*, reproduced as Appendix I in *Chaos and Order in Industry*, concludes: 'The widest possible extension of public ownership and *democratic control* of industry is therefore the first necessary condition of the removal of industrial unrest' (italics mine).

NOTES TO THE INTRODUCTION

[22] In 1913, however, Cole had envisaged the General Federation of Trade Unions, rather than the TUC, as the future central co-ordinating body for the trade union movement (pp.242–6).

[23] J. T. Murphy, the most important figure amongst the English shop stewards, was, according to Cole, at one time connected with the Guild Socialist movement. Ibid., p.86. The most important formative influence upon Murphy, however, as in the case of many English wartime shop steward leaders, was the Amalgamation Committee Movement. Pribićević, op.cit., p.86 and Ch. 4.

[24] See *Workshop Organisation*, pp.133–7 and Appendix H. See also *Chaos and Order in Industry*, pp.154–6.

[25] Pribićević, op.cit., p.154.

[26] Ibid., pp.163–4.

[27] *Chaos and Order in Industry*, p.49. Cole's fear at this time regarding the damage that might be done to the whole workers' control movement as a result of internal ideological warfare was powerfully expressed in another part of the above book. 'Let us', he wrote, 'at all costs avoid becoming narrow doctrinaires and applying our theories in the spirit of the Inquisition' (p.196).

[28] Gleason, *op.cit.*, p.260. I have drawn here primarily upon Pribićević's analysis, op.cit., pp.133–46, and Cole's own Foreword to this work—completed only a few months before his death. See also Cole's *Workshop Organisation* pp.101–2.

[29] Pribićević, op.cit., pp.149 and 151.

[30] Foreword to Pribićević op.cit., p.vii.

[31] Ibid., p.265, and Appendix III, Ch. III.

[32] Ibid., p.269.

[33] *New Age*, 4 December 1913, p.155.

[34] Carter L. Goodrich, *The Frontier of Control* (1920), Note on Sources.

[35] A more outspoken statement by Cole as to his position on this general issue is to be found in his *Self-Government in Industry* (1917): 'If we had to choose between Syndicalism and Collectivism, it would be the duty and the impulse of every good man to choose Syndicalism, despite the dangers it involves. For Syndicalism at least aims high, even though it fails to ensure that production shall actually be carried on, as it desires, in the general interest. Syndicalism is the infirmity of noble minds: Collectivism is at best only the sordid dream of a business man with a conscience. Fortunately, we have not to choose between these two: for in the Guild idea Socialism and Syndicalism are reconciled'. (p.122). Cole became increasingly hostile to the Collectivism of the Webbs after 1913.

THE WORLD OF LABOUR

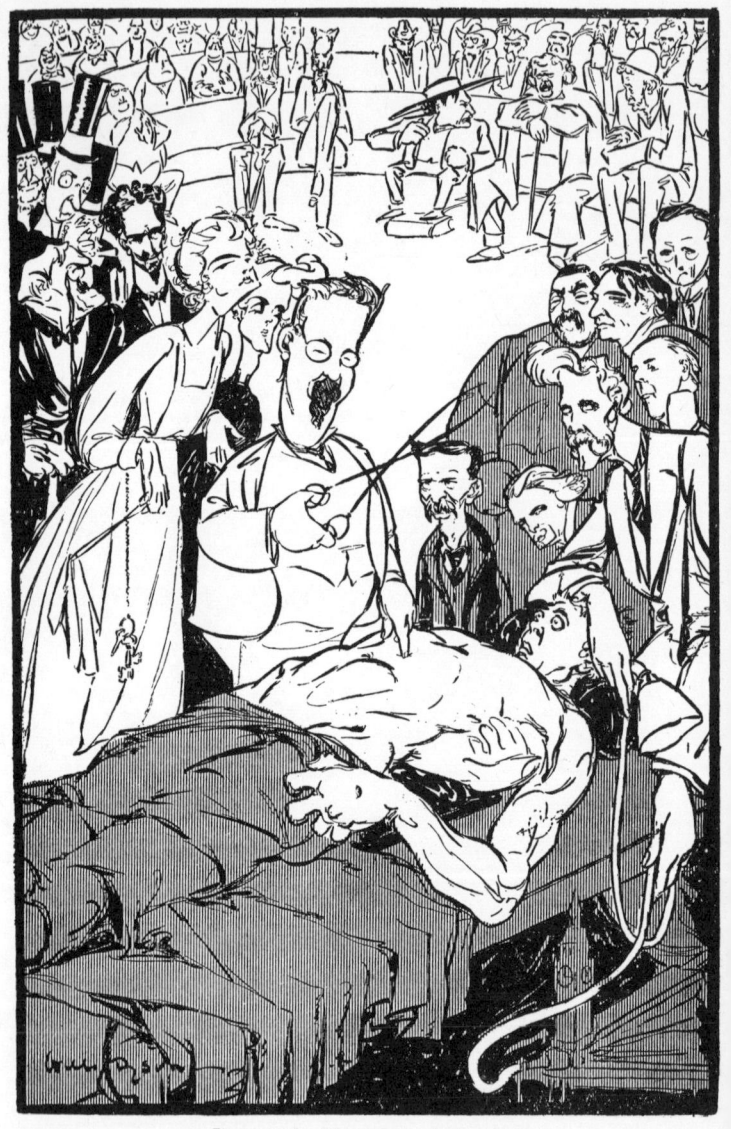

LABOUR'S MEDICAL ADVISERS
A DEMONSTRATION IN THE NEW STATESMANSHIP

THE WORLD OF LABOUR

A DISCUSSION OF THE PRESENT AND FUTURE OF TRADE UNIONISM

BY

G. D. H. COLE

WITH A FRONTISPIECE BY WILL DYSON

FOURTH EDITION, WITH NEW INTRODUCTION

LONDON
G. BELL AND SONS LTD.
1919

First Published, 1913
Reprinted 1915, 1916, 1917, 1919

INTRODUCTION TO THE EDITION OF 1919

ANY book about the Labour Movement written before 1914 must necessarily date itself to a considerable extent. The position of Trade Unionism both at home and abroad has been fundamentally changed by the war. When I wrote in 1913, there was no Trade Union movement in Russia, apart from secret and persecuted political societies. To-day, Trade Unionism and Co-operation are almost the only live forces, except purely political and military organisations, in Soviet Russia. When I wrote, German Trade Unionism was the submissive handmaid of German Social Democracy, pursuing strictly constitutional courses under a militaristic and autocratic Empire. To-day, it is swinging from left to right and from right to left, under the alternating impulses of Spartacism and unrepentant Imperialism. Since I wrote, the Belgian movement has been shattered by the war, and to-day, amid the ruins of Belgian industry, the work of rebuilding it has hardly begun. In France, without violent change, Trade Unionism has gained greatly in stability and power ; but in the process it seems to have shed a great deal of its earlier Syndicalist idealism, so that it appears at least possible that it has taken permanently a form far more nearly resembling that of British Trade Unionism than when I wrote In America, where the Government has been busy imprisoning the leaders of the Industrial Workers of the

World, there is a growing movement of unrest, and new forces seem to be arising inside the American Federation of Labour to challenge the ascendency of Mr. Samuel Gompers. Lastly, in this country, the economic and industrial situation has fundamentally changed, and, even in the midst of the political triumphs of reaction, Labour is revealing in the economic field a new sense of power against which political forces are too weak to stand.

We are living in a world of rapid change—a world in which new forces are constantly coming to light. It is a world which defies summary or analysis, and makes interpretation very difficult. Its events from day to day are an object-lesson in the vanity of human wishes and the shallowness and impotence of human leaders. The powers of the world to-day are not great men or even great nations, but the elemental forces of hunger for food, hunger for blood, hunger for land, touched everywhere with a touch of idealism, high or low, but determined principally by sheer economic compulsions. The movements which count to-day are mass movements, originating—no one knows how—among undistinguished people, and creating their own prophets and interpreters as they spread. Soviets, Workers' and Soldiers' Councils, Workers' Committees and all the rest of the new forces have come into being not so much because idealists (still less because politicians) have created them, as because they arose naturally and inevitably out of the social situation in which men found themselves. They are neither created nor begotten, but proceeding; and that is the firmest guarantee of their vitality.

Before the war, the tendency towards association was growing rapidly throughout our own and other communities. It grew, because slowly men and women

INTRODUCTION TO THE EDITION OF 1919 ix

were feeling their way towards the common expression of their common purposes and desires. For a while the war, by breaking up normal groups and creating artificial ones, seemed likely to check its progress; but before long the associative impulse asserted itself inside the new groups. Shop stewards and shop committees in this country, sailors, soldiers and workers in Russia became organised; and the perceptible quickening of the spirit of association has extended not only to the working class, but to salary-earners and professionals of various sorts and degrees of social status.

The political Revolutions in Russia and Central Europe, and still more the actual and attempted economic and social Revolutions which have followed in their train, are only the tops of the universal waves of democratic organisation. The time has not yet arrived at which the new orientation of the Labour Movement on the continent of Europe can be described; and I do not propose to attempt an impossible task. Not only are the conditions still changing so rapidly and dramatically as to make analysis impossible; the operation of the various censorships and the disturbance of international communications have made it a hopeless task even to get reliable news about actual events. I must, therefore, perforce leave to some future occasion any attempt to revalue the forces of European Labour in terms of post-war economic power.

In a recently published book, *An Introduction to Trade Unionism*, I have tried to describe the present organisation and policy of the Labour Movement in this country; and to that book I must refer readers who desire to know how the actual structure and methods of Trade Unionism have changed during the last few years. They will find that a beginning, but only a small beginning, has been made of dealing with some of the problems discussed in this book. In general, however, they will find that it is true to say that, despite the great increase in Trade Union membership and power, most of the unsolved problems of 1913 remain unsolved in 1919. Only in two or three directions has real progress been made towards the solution of internal difficulties, and even in these cases the new forces making for progress are still at the stage at which they seem rather to be creating new problems than to be solving old ones.

To some extent, I have already dealt in other books with some of the most important of these new forces. Thus, both in *Self-Government in Industry* and in *An Introduction to Trade Unionism* I have tried to describe the growth of the Shop Stewards' movement in the engineering and kindred industries, and of the similar ' rank and file ' movements among other sections such as the railwaymen. These new movements are attempts to solve the problem of internal democracy in the organisation of Trade Unionism. Based mainly upon the workshop or other place of work, they endeavour to build up on that basis a more responsive and democratic type of organisation than has been secured by the accepted forms of Trade Union structure—the branch, the District Committee of branches, the National Executive and the Delegate Meeting. They have arisen naturally and spontaneously among the workers in the shops and other places of work, and their growth has been fostered by the huge aggregation of complicated problems which has arisen in the workshops out of war-time conditions, such as dilution of labour. They have been for the most part unofficial bodies, often quite unrecognised by the Unions to

INTRODUCTION TO THE EDITION OF 1919 xi

which their members belong, and often falling out with the National Executives and the constitutional procedure of the Unions. I believe that they will not remain permanently unofficial, but will succeed in bringing about such changes in Trade Union methods of government as will ensure to them an important position in the constitutional machinery of the more democratic Trade Unionism of the future.

Writing in 1913, I dwelt with some emphasis upon the increasing rift between the official and the ' rank and file ' elements in the Trade Union world. The permanent official of a Trade Union tends under modern conditions at once to concentrate more and more power in his own hands and to get more and more out of touch with the feeling of his members. The branch organisation of Trade Unionism, built on a basis which fails to ensure any close community of active interest among its members, has too often very little life, and in these circumstances fails to act as an effective instrument of democratic government by expressing constantly the will of the members on matters of industrial concern. Thus, the democratic basis of Trade Unionism becomes unreal ; and a lack of democracy in the smaller unit inevitably carries with it an even greater lack of democracy in the larger units of organisation. As already appeared clearly in 1913, the only way of securing real democracy in the national Trade Union movement is by building it up on a basis of real democracy locally.

The importance of the shop stewards' movement lies in the fact that it does pave the way for a solution of this problem. Although hitherto it has seemed to be creating new difficulties by widening the rift between members and officials and by taking power unconstitutionally into its own hands, all these tendencies have really been paving the way for a new form of Trade Union organisation. I believe that the future lies very largely with a form of Trade Unionism based upon the workshop and built up throughout its structure on the foundation of the workshop.

The reasons for the growth of these new forms of organisation are to be found not only in the desire to re-establish democracy in Trade Union government, or in the peculiar conditions of war-time industry, but even more in the new direction and orientation of Trade Union policy. The desire to secure a measure of direct control over industry was already becoming marked in the British Labour Movement before the war, and the interest which I felt in its development was indeed the chief motive which first led me to write this book. But what was only an inchoate tendency before the war is already in some of the principal industries a definite and consciously formulated demand. The miners have coupled with their demand for mine nationalisation an equally insistent demand for a half-share in the control of the nationalised mines, both nationally and locally, and in the particular pits. The railwaymen are putting forward an almost identical demand in the case of the railways, and the demand for control is also being strongly pressed in the Post Office and the Civil Service. Nor is the demand confined to State-owned industries or to industries in which State ownership is imminent : it is also being pressed in rather different forms in many other industries, and more particularly in the engineering and shipyard group.

This change or development in policy has affected the various Socialist bodies as well as the Trade Unions. The National Administrative Council of the Independent Labour Party has now expressed its economic policy in the following resolution:

" This Conference affirms its belief that the public ownership of the means of production, distribution, and exchange is an essential object of Socialist effort and propaganda, and declares that industrial democracy can only be established through the workers securing control of the means of production and of the organisation and administration of industry."

It is safe to say that such a resolution would have been strenuously opposed by most of the national leaders of the I.L.P. a few years ago.

In view of the growing acceptance among Socialists of the idea of direct control of the industry by the workers through their Trade Unions or Guilds, some things that are written in this book may seem by this time to be mere " floggings of a dead horse ". I do indeed believe that, so far as the Labour Movement is concerned, the internal battle for the idea of workers' control of industry has been fought and won. There are still unregenerate Collectivists, left in the world; but even they are compelled to moderate their language and conceal their dislike of industrial democracy and their distrust of human nature. There are also, of course, still plenty of Trade Unionists and of Trade Union officials who are not even now as advanced as the Collectivists, and still believe in a purely reformist Trade Unionism working permanently within the structure of the capitalist system. But these ' Great Boygs ' have ceased to be more than temporary and occasional obstructions, and there can be no doubt that the active sections in both the Trade Union and the Socialist Movements are now definitely seeking industrial democracy

This is far, of course, from meaning that industrial democracy is actually being achieved or is actually in prospect of achievement. The protagonists of Capitalism and the professional politicians are fully alive to the menace of what they regard as ' industrial Bolshevism ', and are doing their best to counter it by every means in their power. Failing of success by the use of force and repression, they are casting about for some method of turning away the wrath of Labour by soft words and specious concessions. It is now generally recognised that, in the words of the Trade Union Memorandum on Unrest submitted to the Industrial Conference of 1919, " Labour can no longer be controlled by force or compulsion of any kind ". As an alternative to compulsion, proposals are now being put forward for some sort of partnership between Capital (or rather Capitalists) and Labour in the control of industry. By these means it is hoped that the existing organisation of industry for private profit can be not only preserved, but also strengthened by the granting to Labour of an apparent interest in its maintenance.

This is no mere revival of the old and discredited schemes of profit-sharing and Labour Co-partnership with which I have dealt in this book. It is a proposal, in certain cases at least, for a sort of ' Trust ' organisation of industry under huge capitalistic combines, with Labour admitted as a sort of junior partner in the Trust. A proposal on these lines was certainly put about on behalf of the mineowners by the Mining Association of Great Britain as soon as the miners' claim for national ownership and a share in control seemed to be on the point of success. Less ambitious schemes have also been put forward in other cases ; and it is clear that these schemes are a new factor to be reckoned with in the industrial situation.

INTRODUCTION TO THE EDITION OF 1919 xv

Moreover, the Whitley Report, with its proposal for Standing Joint Industrial Councils in the various industries, may easily be interpreted as a step in the same direction. I do not mean that this was consciously the aim of all, or even a majority, of the members of the Whitley Committee ; but it is plain that in certain cases the Whitley Councils are being used to promote a sort of partnership between Capital and Labour. This is especially marked in the case of those Councils—the Pottery Council is one instance— in which the maintenance of selling prices is one of the declared objects. For this object is justified as a means of maintaining profits on the one hand and wages on the other, without the provision of any safeguard for the interests of the consumer.

Of course, not one of these schemes contemplates the real admission of Labour to its proper place in the control of industry. When capitalists to-day offer a share in control, what they really mean is a share in profits and a voice in the ascertainment and maintenance of profits. There could be no better commentary than this on the attitude of the employer in regarding industry as existing for the purpose of making profits. But, when Labour asks for control, it is not with profits or profit-sharing that it is primarily concerned, but with the democratisation of the actual management of industry, and the securing for the organised workers of a real measure of control over the conditions under which they work. Labour's remedy for the curse of profiteering is not a share in profits for itself, but the public ownership of industry combined with a system of democratic control.

It may be that the capitalists are so nervous about the industrial future that they will even be willing to concede to the workers a substantial share in management, on condition that the profit-making system is preserved and the continuance of dividends ensured. This, indeed, seems to be taking place in Germany as the capitalists make their last throw against the democratic attempts to enforce measures of socialisation. The attitude of the workers to such proposals will depend on the conditions accompanying them. They will be ready to assume all the control which they can secure; but, in doing so, they will carefully guard themselves against giving any guarantee of dividends to the capitalists. They will refuse to be entangled in the profiteering system, and will press on their demand for the national ownership of industry together with the demand for democratic control.

This is clearly the attitude adopted by the Miners' Federation of Great Britain towards the proposals put forward by the mining capitalists. These proposals have only caused the miners to reiterate, with increased emphasis, their demand for national ownership and joint control with the State. Mr. Straker's proposals for national ownership and joint control [1] are the miners' reply to the coal-owners' suggestion of an anti-social profit-making Trust of capitalists and Labour.

The social situation in relation to industrial control has not so much changed since I wrote this book in 1913 as advanced in a manner that was foreseen, but with unexpected rapidity. The measures necessary for a solution of the industrial problem remain the same; it is only that the solution seems far nearer and more immediately possible. There is still no way out of the economic dilemma of modern Society except by the establishment of a system of public ownership combined with democratic administration of industry.

[1] In evidence before the Coal Commission on March 14th.

This change has come about, or this advance has taken place, both because Labour has grown stronger and more conscious of its strength, and because Capitalism, especially in the sphere of finance, is confronted with a situation of extraordinary difficulty. The war has not only impoverished nearly all nations in terms of real wealth ; it has fundamentally altered the distribution of purchasing power among the nations of the world. It has upset markets, and involved international and national finance in complications from which it is very doubtful whether they will succeed in making their escape. They might do so, if nations were Christian enough to forgive one another their debts, and if Governments had the courage to adopt a drastic policy of reducing war debts by the conscription of wealth. But where is the nation or the Government that is likely to pursue such a course ? Vested interests oppose at every turn, even though, in opposing, they are really digging the grave of the whole system on which their continuance depends. I do not mean that Capitalism in this country or in America is about to undergo a sudden and dramatic collapse. It will not do that, except under the impulse of crashes abroad or of Labour at home. But I do mean that the whole structure of Capitalism, imposing as it still seems, has been undermined, and that it will no longer take a very strong push to tumble it over altogether.

Clearly, the most likely force to give it this push is Labour. Apart from the new spirit that is animating the organised workers to-day, the Labour Movement has become, since I wrote, more inclusive and more representative. One of the most important developments of recent years is the progress of organisation among the less skilled workers. This was beginning in the years before the war, from 1911 onwards ; but the war has greatly accelerated the movement towards Trade Union organisation among these sections. This has meant, not only greater strength to these workers in their bargaining with employers, but also a great change in their position within the Labour Movement —a change hastened by dilution and the blurring of the lines of demarcation between skilled and unskilled, which has gone on far more rapidly during the war than at any previous period.[1]

Before the war, there were approximately 400,000 workers organised in the general labour Unions, which include the majority of the less skilled Trade Unionists. At present these Unions have a membership of more than a million, and are joined together in a powerful Federation of General Workers which serves as a means of co-ordinating policy until amalgamation can be brought about. There have been numerous discussions on the question of amalgamation, and a number of the smaller Societies have actually been swallowed up ; but complete amalgamation has not yet been accomplished among the larger Societies. There is, however, already a close working arrangement between three Societies,[2] which have joined to form a sort of confederation under the name of the National Amalgamated Workers' Union. This combination has over half a million members. The two largest Societies remaining—the National Union of General Workers and the Dock, Wharf, Riverside and General Workers' Union—have for some time been discussing amalgamation ; but no actual scheme has yet been issued. The National Federation of Women

[1] See Ch. VII.
[2] The Workers' Union, the National Amalgamated Union of Labour and the Municipal Employees' Association.

Workers, which now represents about 50,000, is not connected with the National Federation of General Workers.

Considerable progress has thus been made towards the consolidation of forces among the less skilled workers. Nothing, however, has been done to adjust or alter their relationship to the craft Unions representing the skilled workers. The difficulties described in Chapter VII. of this book remain very much where they were in 1914, except that the war has greatly aggravated the problem, and at the same time greatly increased the strength of the less skilled in comparison with that of the skilled. There is no doubt that the ' industrial Unionist ' movement, which desires to have skilled and unskilled organised together in the same Unions, has made great headway as a theory ; but there is still little sign, except in the various ' rank and file ' movements, of its application in practice.

In general, comparatively little progress has been made in the practical task of consolidating Trade Union forces. The majority of the Trade Unionists in the iron and steel industry have joined forces in a single combination — the Iron and Steel Trades Confederation—and an effective Federation has been formed in the building industry between the various National Unions ; but in the majority of cases unity is still to seek. The engineering trades and others are discussing amalgamation projects, and the Trades Union Congress has appointed a Committee to consider the whole question of Trade Union structure ; but these are mere projects, and their conversion into facts is still confronted with the same obstacles as in 1913. It is safe to say that the movement towards effective combination has made far greater strides among Employers' Associations than among Trade Unions during the war period.

Perhaps the biggest change that has come over the organisation of the Labour Movement since 1913 is on the political side. The Labour Party in Parliament, even after the Election of 1918, is still very much the same Labour Party as before, except that all the prominent I.L.P. members have been defeated; but the organisation of the Labour Party as an extra-parliamentary body has undergone big changes and very great expansion. The constitution has been broadened so as to admit individual members, and an attempt has been made on a considerable scale to build up a real Party of "workers by hand and brain" with a constructive programme covering the whole ground of national and international policy.

I do not mean to imply that this new policy has yet been carried out in any thoroughgoing way, or that a universal *rapprochement* of manual and brain workers has taken, or is taking, place. Far from it. The results of the change are only slowly becoming manifest, and a considerable section in the Trade Union movement has still to be convinced of the *bona fides* of the brain workers. If the suggested alliance is ever fully consummated, it will certainly not be as the result of a compromise on conservative lines, designed so as not to offend the susceptibilities of either party : it will come only when and because the workers by hand and brain are conscious of an essential unity of economic and social aim. The way to unity is not for the Labour Party to become *bourgeois*, or to adapt its programme to suit the *bourgeoisie* : it is for Labour as a whole to adopt a constructive attitude towards the industrial problem.

Thus, the new Labour Party is really only the political expression of new forces which are at work in the economic field. Its chances of ultimate success depend on the success of the movement of industrial and professional organisation which is steadily sweeping the brain workers into the net of Trade Unionism and voluntary association. If manual workers and brain workers can achieve a beginning of economic unity, the success of the movement towards political unity will be ensured.

Doubtless, the immediate spur to organisation among the brain workers, as among the manual workers, has been largely the need for, and the hope of, larger remuneration and more satisfactory conditions. These alone will certainly not suffice to create a stable fellowship of workers by hand and brain. But, caught alike in the 'vicious circle' of wages (or salaries) and prices, the wage-earners and the salariat will, I believe, be forced to seek a common solution by taking the control of industries and services into their own hands.

Thus, the events of the last few years have greatly confirmed my faith in Guild Socialism as the only real solution of the industrial and economic problem. The theory and practice of Guild Socialism are indeed confronted with many unsolved problems of their own, and much hard thinking and actual experience are still required before they reach maturity. But, whatever the obscurities and ambiguities of Guild Socialism may be, I am convinced that the idea of functional democracy has abundantly proved its rightness and its relevancy to the present situation. The application of the principle of democratic self-government, not merely to political organisation, but to every sphere of social activity—to every social function of the community—is the vital social concept of the new age.

In this brief introduction, I have been able to do no more than point to some of the larger changes which have come about since this book was first written. Those who desire to go more fully into the nature of these changes I must refer to other books in which their various aspects have been more fully worked out. Of my own books, *An Introduction to Trade Unionism* is an attempt to set out briefly the main facts and tendencies of Trade Union organisation at the close of the war. *Trade Unionism on the Railways*, in which I collaborated with Mr. R. Page Arnot, is a sketch of the organisation and attitude of the workers in one of the ' key ' industries of the Labour Movement. *The Payment of Wages* is an attempt to describe the methods of payment by results under the wage system which have led to so much controversy in recent years, and to bring out their close relation to the problem of industrial control by the workers. *Self-Government in Industry* is a development of the ideas contained in the later chapters of this book, and an attempt both to expound the philosophy of the Guild Movement and to face some of the difficulties raised by its opponents. *The Meaning of Industrial Freedom*, in which I collaborated with Mr. W. Mellor, is a very short statement of Guild principles viewed from the angle of Trade Unionism. Lastly, *Labour in the Commonwealth* is a general study of the big economic forces at work in the new world, and an attempt to interpret the attitude of the younger generation towards the social problem.

Of books written by other writers, there are a few which I must commend to the notice of readers. Mr. A. J. Penty's *Old Worlds for New* is an extraordinarily live and vigorous study of the Guild problem from the standpoint of a craftsman with a fine appreciation of mediæval conditions. Messrs. Reckitt and Bechhofer, in *The Meaning of National Guilds*, have put together the first complete outline and statement of the theory and practice of National Guilds, with a specially good section dealing with Trade Unionism. Mr. Bertrand Russell's *Roads to Freedom* is a most attractive study of the various theories of control, viewed from a standpoint which leaves its author somehow outside each and all of the theories which he describes. Lastly, Mr. L. S. Woolf's *Co-operation and the Future of Industry*, written with a quite remarkable lack of understanding of Guild Socialism, presents from the Co-operative point of view a challenge which Guildsmen have still to take up. The relation of the great Co-operative Movement of consumers to the theory of Guild Socialism is perhaps the most immediate of the unsolved problems before us. It is a problem which will be solved, I believe, by a fuller admission of the functional aptitude of Co-operation within the Guild community, and to that extent by a revision of Guild Socialist theory in its attitude towards the State. That is too large a question to be dealt with here; but it is a question to which I shall return in the near future.

G. D. H. COLE.

LONDON, *April* 1919.

PREFACE TO THE 1917 EDITION

THAT two new editions of this book should have been called for in time of war is a fact remarkable enough to call for comment. Published in the autumn of 1913, it had been before the public less than a year when war broke out. The immediate effect of the war was to stop its sale. Men's minds were engaged by very different issues, and, for a time, they neither thought nor read about Labour. This, however, was not for long. In the autumn of 1915 a new edition appeared; and now, a year from the date of its publication, that edition too is exhausted.

The explanation is, of course, simple. We have been told, over and over again, that this is an engineers' war. This is to put a narrow interpretation upon the facts; but it is safe to say that in the present war Labour has counted for far more than any other section of the community. Not only has Labour furnished the soldiers: Labour in the workshop has been, and remains, a decisive factor. At every stage of the war's progress we have been dealing with Labour problems: the engineer, the miner, the transport worker, and the agricultural labourer are the most vital groups in a Society organised for war. Labour questions, which in 1914 seemed to have been shelved till after the war, have been with us more than ever. One by one they have risen again, urgently demanding solution or at least temporary adjustment. With the early part of this history of Labour in war-time I have dealt in a separate book, and I hope, at some time in the future, to take up the tale again and carry it through to the end. In this Preface my purpose is only that of stating in quite general terms how what I wrote about Labour before the war looks under the searchlight of two years' war-time experience.

Some time ago, a well-known newspaper published a series of articles under the title " My Changed Opinions ". Various writers were asked to search their souls and explain how their attitude to life had changed as a result of the war. The general upshot of the series was that the writers had, for the most part, changed their opinions very little. I too am very much in that position. The past two years seem to me to have furnished striking confirmation of the general view put forward in the later chapters of this book. Driven, by the hard necessity of modern war, to intervene in industrial matters to an unprecedented extent, the State has proved itself, in the words of M. Lagardelle, " a tyrannical master ". Experience of State intervention has doubled my assurance that the only solution of the industrial problem that is compatible with personal liberty is the control of the industries by the workers engaged in them, acting in conjunction with a democratised State.

It may be said that it is unfair to generalise from the abnormal experience of war-time; but I do not think that this is altogether true. In war-time, the State takes on a shape which makes manifest the characteristic merits and defects of State control. Something must be allowed for purely abnormal legislation designed solely to meet war emergencies; but if we make these allowances, we are, I think, entitled to argue from the State at war to the State at peace.

If war has taught us nothing else, it should at least have made us heartily ashamed of our industrial system. After two years of war, we have still an industrial machine which is fundamentally inefficient, and moreover liable at any time to serious breakdown. The rotten fabric of capitalist control has been stayed and girdered by emergency legislation; but this has not served to conceal its rottenness. The pre-war organisation of industry has failed us; and the fundamental question is not how it is to be restored, but what is to be put in its place.

With this general indictment many schools of critics of present-day conditions will agree. But there are at least three different schools animated by different philosophies and putting forward different suggestions for industrial reconstruction. One school will tell us that the only solution lies in the definite assumption, once for all, by the State of direct responsibility for the conduct of industry, and that industry must be nationally owned and controlled in the interests of the nation. This school includes Socialists and anti-Socialists, or at least Labour men and anti-Labour men. The aims and claims of bureaucracy have expanded immensely during the war : the Collectivist tendency has become, not simply more marked, but more definitely hostile to Labour. Everything, therefore, that was said against the Collectivist solution before the war seems to me to need saying with double emphasis to-day.

There is, however, a new school of thought in the field which is, fundamentally, far more dangerous than Collectivism. This school is no less firm in its insistence that industry must be organised on a national basis; but the method by which it proposes to accomplish this is indirect. Taking, usually, as its special province the economic "war after the war", it demands the mobilisation of national resources in order that British industry may dominate the world market and British capitalism triumph. To national ownership and administration of industry it is opposed; but it demands in their place the national recognition and organisation of private capitalism. The war has brought into existence a plentiful crop of mammoth capitalist organisations such as the British Empire Producers' Organisation and the British Industries' Federation; it has kindled in the minds of many class-conscious advocates of capitalism the hope of a new era of capitalist expansion, in which private profiteering will be carried on more than ever under State license and State protection. We have been told by a writer in the *Times Trade Supplement* that "we must munitionise all our industries". Surely, if words have a meaning, this can only signify that we are to give to private employers State protection and State recognition, and a new power over the community based on the assumption that production for profit is a public service. Fine phrases about the co-operation of Labour in this new organisation of capitalist exploiters does not serve to disguise the ideal behind. State recognition for the private employer, State subventions for research and expansion in the interests of the capitalist, State provision for the training of efficient wage-slaves, probably State regimentation of Labour by repressive legislation—these are the ideas which, openly or in disguise, seem to be animating the advocates of national capitalism.

It may be said that, without open recognition, the

State, as far as it has done anything, has done all these things in the past. That is true enough; but full recognition and conscious organisation of such a system would make a great difference. They would, in fact, give a new lease of life to capitalism when it is already discredited by its failure even to do its job efficiently.

Perhaps the most typical example of this new form of State-aided capitalism is to be found in the methods, adopted or projected, of State control of mines and shipping. Instead of nationalising these services outright, our politicians have preferred to adopt methods of control which leave the capitalist structure of industry untouched, and, while claiming from the owners something by way of excess profits, practically assure to them more than their pre-war rates of profit, and, in addition, very greatly extend their control over the workers whom they continue to employ. When the Government took over the South Wales coalfield, it assumed, not "ownership", but "possession", and its first and significant instruction to the coalowners was to "carry on as usual". Broadly speaking, it is true to say that the only real change introduced by control was that the coalowners acquired a new security for their ownership and their profits, while the men were subjected to a new and more severe discipline to be exercised through their employers. The vicious principle of the Insurance Act, by which the State endows the employer with disciplinary and responsible powers over his workers, has been carried many stages further during the war. A new feudalism is being created, in which the capitalist stands between the State and the workman as the lord stood between King and villein. State control based on a guaranteed capitalism is a more complete form of the Servile State than seemed possible in this country before the war.

I have said that there are three schools of thought struggling to secure the realisation of their respective ideals of industrial reconstruction. The two schools so far described are both prophets of social and industrial reaction—the second infinitely more dangerously reactionary than the first. The third school alone can claim the allegiance of those who believe in human freedom and in the widest possible diffusion of responsibility and self-government. It is not a new school, and its tenets are expressed too clearly in this book to call for restatement here. I want only to see whether the events of the war have in any way served to modify the point of view advanced before the war.

For the ideal of National Guilds, the war has meant a material set-back and a moral advance. Trade Unionism has been weakened materially by the surrender of rights and powers which are in some cases essential to its fighting strength. On the other hand, increasingly the events of the war have led those who care for freedom, whether in the Trade Union movement or outside, to a clearer understanding of the need for a division of the supreme power in Society. They have seen, with fear and mistrust, the overwhelming claims advanced on behalf of even a capitalist State in every sphere of life; and many of them are looking eagerly for some form of social organisation capable of holding the State in check. This, under the conditions of a modern industrial Society, they can find only in the Trade Union movement.

How, then, is Trade Unionism to be strengthened? This should be the first consideration for every man and woman who desires the preservation and advancement of civil and industrial liberty. The answer must be that Trade Unionism can only assume the rôle of equality with the State if it takes on a new purpose, and comes to be animated by a unifying and constructive idea. The lamentable flabbiness, the fatal indecision, the childlike gullibility of Trade Unionism during the war have all arisen from the fact that the Trade Unions have, as a whole, neither ideas nor policy. There are weakness and lack of science enough in the machinery of Trade Unionism ; but the fundamental weakness is not in the machine, but in the manning of it. If there were in the minds of Trade Unionists a constructive programme for Labour, defects in Trade Union structure and government could soon be remedied, and the potential power of Labour would express itself in terms of actual achievement. The idea of capitalism in industry can be overthrown only by a rival idea : a Labour movement that is dominated by capitalist ideology or by no ideology at all cannot stand.

Those who imagine the profiteer in the guise of a "fat man lifting the swag" are often too little awake to the real character of the class-struggle as a conflict of ideas. They do not realise that the capitalist mind is permeated with the idea of " divine right ", and that the capitalists do in truth believe themselves to be indispensable servants of the public. In their eyes, the relation between master and workman is a natural and inevitable relation : they believe profoundly that their "enterprise" is the foundation of national prosperity and a good title to autocracy in industry. If, then, they are to be overthrown, the conception of industrial autocracy must be off-set by that of industrial democracy, and there must be in the minds of Trade Unionists no less clear a conception of " divine right ", the right of self-government in industry as well as in politics.

How profound is the clash of ideals in industry becomes yearly more manifest. The growth of the demand for control on the side of the workers is now receiving a good deal of attention from both friends and foes : but the parallel attempt on behalf of capitalism to systematise and make scientific the autocratic conception has not as a rule been seen in its proper perspective. Scientific Management is the last state of a capitalist autocracy turned bureaucratic in self-preservation. In its infancy as yet in the country, it represents a deliberate attempt not merely to shut out the majority of the workers from all self-direction and responsibility, but also to make more absolute the cleavage between the classes of directors and directed. It is the diametrical opposite of National Guilds : the one would diffuse responsibility and authority throughout the industrial population ; the other would concentrate these things in the few " most capable " hands. To advocates of Scientific Management, democracy in industry appears as the cult of incompetence; to National Guildsmen, Scientific Management is a natural manifestation of the Servile State.

It is in Scientific Management that State-aided capitalism would find an instrument of oppression to its hand. The name may be absent ; but there will certainly be an attempt to introduce the reality. Already this is being manifested in the cry against " restriction of output " which never ceases to be heard in the capitalist press. It is a specious cry ; for " restriction of output " has an ugly sound, and it is obvious that, other things being equal, the greatest possible output is to be desired. It is a popular cry ; for it is represented to the consumer that he is hurt by a policy which forces up prices and means that there is less to go round. But what the critics of " restriction of output " seldom say in so many words is the meaning they attach to the phrase. Do they confine it to definite " ca' canny," *i.e.* going slow as a deliberate policy, or do they include under it any practice which the employer in his wisdom may regard as " restrictive "—for instance, the refusal of a Trade Union to allow unlimited child labour, or the operation of a machine by labour of an inferior grade, or a refusal to adopt piece-work or the premium bonus system? Such practices have often been denounced as restriction of output ; and under the pretext of freeing industry from the restrictive action of Trade Unions, attempts have been made to sweep them away. These attempts will undoubtedly be renewed after the war, when the day comes for the restoration of Trade Union conditions, and they will be reinforced by the argument that only freedom from all restrictions can enable British trade to secure the mastery and Great Britain to pay for the war.

Against such blandishments it is to be hoped that Trade Unionism will stand firm ; for a wholesale abrogation of Trade Union restrictions would mean the triumph, not of British industry, but of industrial autocracy. The Trade Union customs which the employer calls " restrictions " are not, of course, uniformly wise ; but, taken as a whole, they are the bulwark of Trade Unionism and the beginning of a new industrial order. The negative control over industrial management which they constitute is a foundation on which the structure of positive control must be built.

What, then, are the prospects for Trade Unionism after the war ? In one sense, there may, or may not, be a period of industrial conflict : in another sense, a great conflict is inevitable. There may, or may not, be huge strikes and upheavals in the world of Labour : there is bound to be a great struggle for mastery between the two ideas of democracy and autocracy in industry. There are too many people, both Trade Unionists and others, who can conceive industrial conflict only in terms of strikes and lock-outs. I am not so sure that the conflict of ideas will be fought mainly in this way, though no doubt many strikes, successful and unsuccessful, will mark its progress. That depends on the economic situation after the war, and, still more, on the steps taken to prepare for the after-the-war situation.

No one wants strikes for their own sake ; but every friend of Labour sees the need for the preservation, and use at times, of the strike weapon. To waste strikes upon unimportant issues is to fritter away the power of Trade Unionism ; to keep them as far as possible for great questions of principle should be the object of Trade Unionists. The better, then, the means of adjusting differences as they arise, the greater is the chance of doing this, and to secure the best possible methods of negotiation with employers without sacrificing any principle or yielding to any coercion would surely be the best policy for Trade Unionism after the war. This should be the Trade Union attitude in approaching suggestions for " better relations " with employers or for a share in " workshop control ". They should aim at securing the fullest possible machinery of joint negotiation ; but they should refuse absolutely to accept any suggestion for joint control which would involve even the smallest sacrifice of Trade Union independence and freedom of action. Under this test, most suggestions for " work-

PREFACE TO THE 1917 EDITION xxxv

shop control" or "joint control" will certainly fail; but no less rigorous test ought to be applied. The most fatal thing would be for Labour to be in such a hurry to get control as to accept some form of control which would block the way for a further advance.

After all, there is no such hurry. There is every need for haste in strengthening and perfecting Trade Union organisation, and in securing the general acceptance among Trade Unionists of a constructive policy; but a too great anxiety for immediate results may well be disastrous. If industrial democracy is the end in view, Labour has a long way to go, and it must set its own house in order before it can hope for any great success. Internal reorganisation, and hard thinking by Trade Unionists are, then, as much the needs to-day as they were when this book was written: indeed, the need has become greater as the plans of capitalism and bureaucracy have developed and expanded. The war has been the season of neo-capitalist experiment; and only a vigorous and instructed Trade Union movement can have any hope of prevailing. If Trade Unionism cannot find an ideal and develop a policy, all our industries will be "munitionised", and all our workers will be enslaved.

G. D. H. COLE.

December 1916.

PREFACE TO THE 1915 EDITION

In the two years that have passed since this book first appeared, I have found out many of its faults. In the changes made in the present edition, I have aimed not so much at bringing it up to date, as at correcting what I now see to have been definite mistakes and false conclusions. The greater number of the changes occur in Chapters VII. and VIII., in which the structure and government of Trade Unionism are dealt with. I have also corrected my account of National Guilds in Chapter XI., which was, in the earlier edition, misleading.

The present-day problems arising out of the European war, which make it impossible to bring this book up to date just now, I have surveyed in another book—*Labour in War Time*.

G. D. H. COLE.

MAGDALEN COLLEGE, OXFORD,
July 1915.

PREFACE TO THE FIRST EDITION

No book on Trade Unionism can avoid being very largely a book about books. It is impossible for me to acknowledge, save in the form of a bibliography, the immense amount of unacknowledged borrowing this volume contains. I can only mention here, what any reader will soon see for himself, that I, like all students of Trade Unionism, owe a great deal to Mr. and Mrs. Webb for their standard works on the subject. I mention this debt because I very often disagree with their conclusions; but, whatever view I took, I could not help going to their *History of Trade Unionism* and *Industrial Democracy* for admirably arranged and accurate information. A second debt which I cannot leave unrecorded is to the *New Age*, which too seldom gets, from writers on Socialism and Trade Unionism, the credit it deserves. I am far from agreeing with all the views expressed by the *New Age*; but I find in it and nowhere else a sense that theory and practice are not naturally separable, and an attempt to face the problems of Trade Unionism in the light of a whole view of life. I believe the series of articles on *Guild Socialism* and the *Wage System*, which have appeared in the *New Age* during the last two years, are shortly to appear in book form. The large class of persons that has for so long persistently neglected the *New Age* will then have another chance to bring itself up to date, and my obligation will become still more manifest.

I owe very much to my friends also. Much that I have gained from scattered conversations and discussions I cannot well acknowledge; and especially for a great deal of information that I have got from various Trade Unionist friends I can only render general acknowledgment. My greatest debt is to Mr. W. Mellor, of the Fabian Research Department, to whom I owe many valuable suggestions embodied in Chapters VII. and VIII., and with whom I am now collaborating in a series of penny pamphlets designed to expound, in relation to specific problems, the Greater Unionism for which this book also is a plea. The first of these *Pamphlets of the Greater Unionism*, itself called *The Greater Unionism*, has recently been issued by the National Labour Press.[1]

I must also thank Mr. W. Stephen Sanders for allowing me to use, in Chapter VI., unpublished information relating to German Trade Unionism, and Mr. A. E. Zimmern for a very interesting letter concerning the Labour movement in America.

G. D. H. COLE.

MAGDALEN COLLEGE, OXFORD,
September 1913.

---

[1] Only the first pamphlet of this series appeared; but I hope soon to replace it by a new series of larger studies dealing with Trade Unionism in each of the principal industries.

CONTENTS

CHAP.		PAGE
I.	MEANS AND ENDS	1
II.	THE LABOUR UNREST	30
III.	LABOUR IN FRANCE	58
IV.	COMMENTS ON THE FRENCH LABOUR MOVEMENT	101
V.	LABOUR IN AMERICA	128
VI.	FURTHER LESSONS FROM ABROAD—THE GENERAL STRIKE	166
VII.	TRADE UNION STRUCTURE—INDUSTRIAL UNIONISM AND AMALGAMATION	205
VIII.	TRADE UNION GOVERNMENT—CENTRALISATION AND LOCAL AUTONOMY	259
IX.	SOCIAL PEACE AND SOCIAL WAR—CONCILIATION AND ARBITRATION	285
X.	LABOUR'S RED HERRINGS—THE FUNCTION OF CO-OPERATION	320
XI.	THE CONTROL OF INDUSTRY—SYNDICALISM AND COLLECTIVISM	344
XII.	THE FUTURE OF TRADE UNIONISM	370
XIII.	ECONOMICS AND POLITICS	393
XIV.	HOPES AND FEARS	413
	BIBLIOGRAPHY	427
	INDEX	437

THE WORLD OF LABOUR

CHAPTER I

MEANS AND ENDS

It is not too much to say that, during the past two or three years, we have been in the midst of a double Labour Unrest. There has been, first and most recognisably, the new New Unionism, an awakening of the fighting spirit in the ranks of organised labour; but there has been at the same time, both as cause and as consequent, an intellectual unrest which may be called the Labour movement in search of a philosophy. These two stirrings of popular will and imagination have acted and reacted on each other continually, and we have often been tempted to believe that their combination was imminent; but in the main, each has taken its own course and managed to inspire the other with no more than a phrase or an illustration. Thus we find the word Syndicalism used loosely by New Unionists as a name for their point of view, and, on the other hand, the Coal Strike used, by real Syndicalists, as an example of the national awakening of the Syndicalist spirit in England. But in fact, the New Unionists are not Syndicalists, and the Coal Strike was not an experiment in Syndicalism.

We are about to use the history of these two unrests to define our attitude both to the more immediate future and to the remoter possibilities of the situation of the

Labour movement in Great Britain. It is difficult to do this without betraying a double impatience; both Utopian revolutionaries and Social Reformers are hard to suffer gladly, and it is no less hard to find anywhere a combination of idealism and a readiness to recognise that facts are facts. It is not the purpose of this book either to define the perfect society *in vacuo*, or to flounder vaguely in the Serbonian bogs of social 'betterment'. The question is, ' What can be made of the Labour movement, taken as it is ? ' or still better, ' What is the Labour movement capable of making of itself ? ' What, in fact, are its practicality and its idealism respectively worth ?

It is the tidier method to begin with the theorists. It is the most striking contrast between the British and the continental Labour movements that here the intellectuals seem to have so little influence as to be almost negligible. Socialist theory, so fruitful of quarrels abroad, has been in England, at least till quite lately, unimportant. There have been plenty of differences in the ranks, but they have been on practical rather than on theoretical questions. It might seem, then, that theory should be, in this country, very much an open matter. But in reality we have been saved from important divergences within the Labour movement [1] not because our intellectuals have had no influence, but because a single and very practically-minded body of them long ago carried the day. The first leaders of the Fabian Society, and in particular Mr. and Mrs. Sidney Webb, were able so completely, through the Independent Labour Party, to impose their

---

[1] The Social Democratic Party has indeed been all along in opposition, but it has seldom caused serious embarrassment to its opponents. Only in the last few years has there been really strong division among the theorists, *e.g.* the Fabians and the *New Age*.

conception of society on the Labour movement that it seemed unnecessary for any one to do any further thinking. On such a view, the intellectual problem of Labour was solved, and only the practical problems remained: the Labour movement therefore became intensely 'practical', and, so far as the end in view was concerned, as fantastically fatalistic as the worst of the later followers of Marx. The progress of Labour was beautifully resolved into the gradual evolution of a harmony divinely pre-established by the Fabian Society in the early nineties. The history of the recent intellectual unrest is, in great measure, the sign that Labour has at last used up the inspiration of the early Fabians, and is turning elsewhere for light—to what is vaguely called Syndicalism from what Mr. Punch has named 'Sidneywebbicalism'.

In the Socialist theory of the eighties and the early nineties, no doubt vagueness and muddle were the weaknesses and dangers. Fabianism and Collectivism triumphed just because they were able to offer the worker something definite, tangible and intelligible, an elaborate scheme of social reconstruction which was universal without being blurred, and which was, further, recognisably taking the direction in which industry was, of its own accord, tending continually more and more. For the moment this scheme was satisfying; it seemed to offer a 'State-Providence' which was an assurance of ultimate success; it looked both reasonable and practicable in the highest degree. Yet nowadays all the papers, from the *Morning Post* to the *Daily Herald*, are full of the 'collapse of Collectivism', and behind so much smoke there must be, at any rate, some fire. On the other hand, what can no longer be taken for the whole truth may well be an important part of the truth, and there has clearly been too much readiness to throw the baby out with the bathwater, and make away with the whole Collectivist theory. What is wanted is not annihilation and a new start, but revaluation and a new synthesis.

In face of the growing distrust of the State in all its forms, of representative government and the 'House of Pretence',[1] in face of Mr. Belloc's very French *Servile State* bogy, in face of the rising tide of the force of revolt the newspapers call Syndicalism, is it not necessary to admit that what Fabianism gained in definiteness it, at any rate partly, lost in breadth? Its very success was the result of its limitations, and its limitations are in turn making its inadequacy felt. So we have the vague uprising of Syndicalism, which is in itself much more an instinctive protest than a new philosophy. The wage-earner crying for freedom refuses to believe that the General Will of a bureaucratic Cabinet "leaves him as free as before": he exclaims against the tyranny of democracy, but is at a loss at present to point the way to a new freedom. Just at this point philosophy, in the course of a somewhat similar evolution, offers him her aid: the Anarchism of Nietzsche's 'revaluation of all values' gives place to the *élan vital* of the Bergsonians, and M. Bergson's assertion of instinct as the equal of reason takes on a political aspect which he certainly did not foresee. M. Sorel, the philosopher of Syndicalism, in his *Réflexions sur la Violence*, takes up the parable, and the free-will controversy becomes a political question. In England, a Conservative like Mr. Fabian Ware, in his book *The Worker and his Country*, is found acclaiming the Syndicalist movement as an assertion of instinct against reason.

What, at bottom, does all this worship of instinct

[1] The *Daily Herald's* regular name for the House of Commons.

mean ? It is clear that there is a widespread breakdown of the old reverence for law and order, a readiness not merely to disobey, but to give theoretical justifications for disobedience. There is a feeling that the great State has got out of touch with the people, and that no mere democratic machinery at elections will be able to bring it back again. There is a new individualism, an assertion that the individual, as the only sentient being, is after all ultimate, a reassertion in a new form of Herbert Spencer's argument against Socialism that " the State has no common sensorium ". And there is a claim, on behalf of the individual, for a greater measure of effective self-government than can be given by the ballot-box and the local constituency.

All these protests, however, are mainly negative : they point to something wrong, without directly indicating the remedy. The worship of instinct is in form a worship of the indeterminate, when what is wanted is a new determination. Unrest requires direction, but at present there is no clear lead given save that of the old Collectivism itself. An advance to a new positive theory can only be hoped for when Collectivism is put in its place, when the gaps in its theory are more adequately understood, and when the materials at hand for reconstruction have been more fully examined.

Parliamentary Labour, Fabianism and Trade Unionism have been at one with Radicalism in regarding the social problem as first and foremost a question of distribution, of the division of the national income. Marx did not originate, but only formulated clearly and consistently from a particular standpoint, the view that, in modern society, industry tends continually to further concentration. Production on a large scale is assumed to be cheapest and most efficient, and it is therefore assumed that political reform must take the course of furthering and completing the transition to it by handing over to State Monopoly (or State Capitalism) the industries which are already being gathered rapidly into the hands of private monopolists. This process, being regarded as inevitable, settles the question of production, and the dominant fact of the industrial situation becomes a three-cornered fight between masters, men and consumers for the appropriation of the national dividend. In this warfare of profits, wages and prices, one at least is recognised as beyond the control of legislation. Where the private trader can put up his prices to meet his wages bill—and who shall stop him?—it is inevitable that the public and semi-public employer should be allowed to do the same. So the result of the Railway settlement is the Railways Bill. Nor has the consumer, except as a Co-operator, succeeded in organising to resist the increase in prices: a universal boycott is even less conceivable than a General Strike. In the main, therefore, the industrial war becomes one between masters and men, both combined, over the division of the product of industry. And, at present, the masters seem to have the advantage in organisation. The Employers' Federation, with infinite resources behind it, fights the Trade Union or Federation of Trade Unions, and round the contest the whole social problem is centred.

Between these two, the main question is one of wages. The worker tries to make his wages increase faster than prices rise; the master tries to guard himself from competition by resisting the demands of the workers. And in the midst of their contests, the State is alarmed by the cry that the rich are growing richer and the poor poorer, and that the purchasing power of the workers is not increasing as rapidly as the national wealth. This clearly is the point of view from which the social problem is customarily regarded, and we can safely prophesy that when nationalisation comes, as come it must, in one or other of our great industries, it will come mainly as the result of the deadlocks and bickerings with which we are familiar in industrial life. Even for most adherents of Labour, this has been almost the whole. They have looked forward to an impartial State, controlling and organising industry, securing for the worker an adequate share in the wealth he produces, laying charges on industry for benevolent State services for the benefit of the weak and incapable, probably competing with similar States in the world-market, and in other respects carrying on production much as it is carried on now, with a State Department in place of a Trust and a bureaucrat in place of a managing director.

Collectivism then has been mainly a theory of distribution : like the Co-operative Wholesale Society, it has looked on production from the consumer's point of view, and has envisaged a grand national organisation of consumers, the State, employing workers just as the Co-operative Wholesale and the Municipalities now employ workers in production. Syndicalism, on the other hand, is a very ill-thought-out and vague assertion of the producer's point of view. Syndicalism claims for the worker not merely higher wages, but also something which it terms generally the 'control of industry'. It demands that men be regarded not as 'citizens' or 'consumers', but as 'producers', that their work be recognised as the central fact of their lives, and that industry be reorganised in their interest rather than in that of the consumer. These are no doubt extravagant claims ; but if they are to be granted any validity, they will involve at least a re-examination of the Collectivist theory. Mr. Sidney Webb, the arch-Collectivist, was distinguished all along by his insistence that, even in a Socialist State, strong Trade Unions would be a necessity. While he was doing more than any other man to build up the Labour Party, he was, in his writings, insisting on the paramount importance of Trade Union action. But, unfortunately, this part of his doctrine found less expression in Fabian propaganda, and even he seemed, till only the other day, to have forgotten much of the best of his earlier teaching. The Labour Party, the child of Fabianism, has been too ready to regard the Trade Unions as a mere electioneering device for making the working-classes seem more Collectivist than they are.

But within Trade Unionism itself, there have been signs of the half-conscious awakening of the new spirit. Wages are still the central question of dispute with employers; but along with wage-disputes, there have been growing up more and more disputes about conditions of labour, and about what the employers call 'discipline.' Workshop conditions, limitation of hours, and the non-unionist question have all grown in importance till they threaten in future to dwarf wages as the cause of disputes. Experience of collective bargaining has given the Unions confidence in their powers, and the tendency is continually to extend the sphere of such bargaining. It is being realised that the method of collective bargaining can be applied, not only to wages and hours, but to every point of difference that can arise in the workshop between employers and employed. Not only can it safeguard the standard of living for the workers collectively; it can also be used for the redress of individual grievances. Moreover, it can be used as a means of getting a share in the actual control of management. Discussion of wages inevitably leads on to discussion of management, and the right to discuss can be turned into the right to interfere. In the recent unrest the workers are demanding the extension of their industrial jurisdiction to cover new fields. Autocracy in the workshop is already breaking down, and this, together with the great increase in disputes over the non-unionist question, seems to lend plausibility to the Syndicalist ideal.

There is clearly much in this new attitude which represents a return to the older Socialism of men like Robert Owen and the Christian Socialists, or again to the teaching of Ruskin and Morris. William Morris, with his demand that everything made should be " a joy to the maker and the user ", was only putting in an idealised form, the demand which Labour is beginning to make on society of its own accord. With his thoughts fixed on the skilled crafts, Morris was led to put this demand in a form that is, within a measurable space of time at least, unrealisable. But his ideal is grand enough to be worth a moment's investigation. Pleasure, joy, interest, expression in the works of a man's hand, taken from the worker by Capitalistic Production and the Industrial Revolution, are what Ruskin and Morris desired to restore to the world. There is a great difference between the common-sense ideal of high wages, and the other ideal of enabling men somehow to express, in the daily work of their hands, some part of that infinitely subtle and various personality which lives in each one of them, if we can but call it out, a birthright which not even Capitalism has done away with, though it has often maimed and perverted men's whole lives and works.

But here generally comes a blank negative. The Industrial Revolution, whether we regard it as the greatest of calamities or as the greatest of man's victories over nature, is a fact which cannot be gainsaid, and Collectivism does seem at least to be able to make its incidence less unjust and burdensome. The project of restoring man's joy in labour too often ends in baseless aspirations, in false mediævalism and impossible regrets of the advent of machinery. We cannot, if we would, set back the hands of the clock; we cannot dispense with the so-called superfluities of civilisation; we cannot take any step to increase the quality of what we produce, if in doing so we are actually decreasing the quantity. There is no hope in solutions of the social problem which end in a false æstheticism, as they began in a false reading of history. Even if machinery is ultimately to be driven from the more skilled crafts, there must, as Morris himself said, be more machinery before there can be less. It is no use, when we are working for the future, to be for ever lamenting the past; facts are facts, and it is on facts that we have to build.

The great industry, then, has to be accepted as inevitable: the Middle Ages have gone past wishing for, and if the producer is to have pleasure in his work, the pleasure cannot in most cases be that of the individual craftsman working in his own home or workshop at something which shall be entirely the work of his own hands. The factory has come to stay, and the machine has come to stay. Are we then to say that it is better to abandon the hopeless task of giving men pleasure in their work, and concentrate instead on giving them adequate wages? Is the 'Leisure State', rather than the 'Work State', what we ought to aim at? It is part at least of the service of Syndicalism to have corrected an ambiguity in this question. In demanding the control of industry for the worker, the Syndicalist has not as a rule demanded an impossible return to out-of-date methods of production. He has asked liberty for the worker to determine the conditions of his labour, without stating any intention of destroying machine-production. There is, in fact, no reason why the workers should not control a modern factory as well as a mediæval workshop. Under modern conditions the producer may still be taken into account as a producer, and the social problem may still be more than a question of distributing incomes. It is only possible to deny this offhand by asserting that the conditions of efficient industry must be so revolting that no body of men will voluntarily accept them; but to maintain this is openly and unashamedly to advocate the Servile State. For the world of Labour, the problem of the control of industry lies within a sphere in which modern conditions of production are assumed.

It is evident that such a view emphasises the central importance of Trade Unionism to the Labour movement. Regarded merely as the instruments of collective wage-bargaining, the Unions are the most powerful weapon in the hands of Labour; if they are in addition the germs of the future organisation of industry as a whole, their importance becomes at once immeasurably greater. It will therefore be the main business of this book to study the achievements and possibilities of Trade Unionism both in itself and in its relation to other working-class movements, and to draw what conclusions are possible with regard both to the policy to be pursued here and now, and to the remoter future. It is at least indisputable that if the worker can in any way control industry, it will be through his Trade Union alone, and not by the development of new 'Guilds' outside them, modelled, probably wrongly, on what is supposed to have been the organisation of industry in the Middle Ages.

There is no doubt, for many people, an extraordinary fascination in the proposals of such a book as Kropotkin's *Fields, Factories and Workshops*. This appeal for the 'redintegration' of industry catches us all, as Morris caught us, in a weak place, and we are willing to give it any amount of sentimental sympathy. That, in the skilled crafts at least, there will be some such return is certain: as the standard of taste improves and the standard of living goes up, there will be a demand that at least such personal possessions as furniture and clothing shall be well and artistically made, and, with the development of electrical power, it will become easier to restore the integrity of such smaller crafts. But whether such a restoration is possible, or even desirable, over the whole of industry is quite another question. In the great factory at any rate, to say nothing of all the workers engaged in distribution, large-scale production will continue, and the release of the worker will come only by a gradual improvement in working conditions. Employers are even now beginning to find out that, in some trades at any rate, high wages pay, and they will come to find that it pays to devolve a great measure of workshop control on the employee.[1] Workshop committees and

[1] There are indications that such a devolution is beginning in Mr. Edward Cadbury's recently published *Experiments in Industrial Organisation*. 'Shop' piece-work (*i.e.* paying the whole workshop for all it produces) is a beginning. See, however, p. 324.

pleasant working conditions will gradually become the rule in industry, and, as factories move out of the towns, there will be realised some approximation to what William Morris called, in the best of his tracts, 'A Factory as it might be'. And, when matters have got so far, the Trade Unions will certainly have a strong case for demanding that they shall go further.

Agriculture has been omitted altogether from this book, because it offers so many special problems for solution that it cannot be treated merely incidentally ; but we may say a word about it here, where we are dealing with Prince Kropotkin's proposals. Whatever we may think of the possibility of 'redintegration' in the factory, the case for it in agriculture is clearly made out. The new agricultural co-operation in Ireland and elsewhere is quietly creating in the fields the conditions that it will take long and patient endeavour to realise in the factory and the workshop.

For Collectivism and the Labour Party, we have seen, the central problem is one of wages ; Syndicalism demands the control of industry. It would seem that on either showing the Trade Unions must be of primary importance ; for in both cases the natural method seems to be that of Collective Bargaining. If it is no use to nationalise industry without obtaining real control over it, it is of equally little use for the workers to control industry without getting more out of it. The methods seem to presuppose each other, and equally to presuppose the Trade Unions. If industry is to be nationalised, only strong Trade Unions can prevent bureaucracy, which it is fashionable to call the Servile State ; if industry is to be syndicalised, only strong Trade Unions will be capable of running it. On either showing, Trade Unionism should be the first concern of Labour.

Mr. G. K. Chesterton once wrote, in the *Illustrated London News*, that nowadays we were getting all the disadvantages of Socialism without any of its advantages, the interference without the control, the servility without the comfort. Either, he urged, the State must stop interfering, or else it must go the whole way and really undertake management. It is now some years since those words were written, and everything that has happened since has gone to show on the one hand that the State is not at present good at running industry, and on the other that, even under the most old-fashioned of Whig Premiers, it cannot help interfering with industry more and more. The State is in the dilemma of fearing to nationalise, because it mistrusts its own capacity, and yet of being wholly unable to interfere successfully without nationalising, as well as utterly impotent to refrain from interference. Syndicalism and Labour Unrest are the result as well as the cause of this dilemma. The State that cannot save itself is not likely at present to save the worker, who is therefore driven back upon himself, and forced to find his salvation in the development of his own institutions. Strong and intelligent Trade Unions are the condition of an effective Labour Party in Parliament, just as surely as they are the condition of good wage-bargaining with the employers.

The Anti-Socialists of all times, from Herbert Spencer to Mr. Hilaire Belloc, have seen in Socialism the instrument for turning the nation of shop-keepers into a nation of shop-assistants. And it is clear that State Socialism alone can do nothing to prevent this. Neither popular control from without nor democratic control from within is a distinguishing feature of the existing Government Departments. In the industry of the future, we clearly need both forms of control, and both can be secured only by methods that are mainly educational. First, there is the method of educating the workers through their Trade Unions, and on the industrial field. Every strike, every demand made by the Unions, is a contribution to the education of the worker, as well as an attack on the capitalist system. Secondly, there is education by means of the Parliamentary Labour Party, which tends more and more to attempt to justify its existence at present rather as an educational institution than as an actual means of expropriation. Here the Labour Party has at least one weakness in comparison with the Trade Unions. Trade Unions do win victories, and such victories have a great effect on their membership—the Dock Strike of 1911 is a notable instance. But, broadly speaking, the Labour Party does not win victories. It depends for its appeal on promises to be redeemed when it is in a majority; and to anyone who knows its prospects, such promises are so many cheques postdated to the Greek Calends. The present Labour Party can never become a majority and would be sadly at a loss to know what to do if it did become one. It is therefore difficult for it to make any but an obscurantist appeal except to the already converted; and an obscurantist appeal is hardly likely to be educative in its influence. The Labour Party reflects Trade Unionism and cannot surpass it.

But in industrial questions the plight of Liberalism is no better. The social legislation of the Liberal Government, whether it was ever meant to raise wages or not, has not done so, except in the solitary instance of the Trade Boards Act. For the average worker, whatever its power to alleviate sweating,

Liberal legislation has no message. Social Insurance, which is there to maintain the reserve of labour for industry, leaves employer and employed just as they were, to determine, by trial of force, which shall in the end pay the piper. Here again the effect on the worker depends on the strength of his Trade Union. The State provides the machinery; if the worker is weak, he will pay for it: if he is strong, he will make his masters pay. On every hand then we are driven back on the belief that the hope of the worker lies in Trade Unionism, and that as the Unions are strong or weak, Labour will expropriate or itself be spoliated.[1]

Trade Unionism, then, is the most powerful weapon in the workers' hands and, for that very reason, the greatest educational influence at their command. But Trade Unionism itself demands of its members a certain standard of intelligence, and requires, for effective working, a large proportion of members with a keen understanding of the situation in which they are placed. There is therefore a very real place in the Labour movement for education in a more restricted sense, for the great movement of working-class education whose beginnings we are watching at the present day. Indeed, there are some who go so far as to place all hope of a change for the better in the new educational movement. In his inspiring book, *What is and what might be*, Mr. Edmond Holmes presented a survey of the actual and the possible in Elementary Education, and offered, by way of introduction, some general remarks on the place of educa-

---

[1] Even if prices are raised to cover the increased wages bill, Labour makes some gain; for prices are spread over the whole community and wages over only a section. This favours organised against unorganised Labour, and for sweated trades the State must step in.

tion in national regeneration. Briefly, he takes the view that it is impossible, by means of legislation, to bring about any approach to a state of society to which the motto 'Each for all and all for each' will have any application. With this ideal of the Socialists, he tells us, he has the deepest sympathy; "but", he goes on, "in trying to compass their ends by legislation, before the standard of reality has been changed, they are making a disastrous mistake". Our schools are, as he puts it, "hotbeds of individualism", and he holds that Socialism without a spiritual revolution would be the worst condition into which society could fall. Even if we cannot fully agree with Mr. Holmes, we can no longer have the confidence that a mere change in the machinery of the State will of itself carry spiritual regeneration. We have learnt that Collectivism and Trade Unionism have both their business aspect, and that either State Socialism or Syndicalism might be brought about by the tyranny of a majority, or even a minority, without any realisation of the General Will. Even if education is not everything, it is at least a very great deal.

No doubt much of this education in a wider outlook is obtained by the workers through their political societies and their Trade Unions. We have already insisted on the educational value of Trade Unionism, and there is no need to draw back here. But that there is need for a wider culture, for something which is not in any way measurable in pounds, shillings and pence, not even the most ardent advocate of the economic interpretation of history need be at pains to deny. Such a movement is just coming into existence: the Workers' Educational Association is gradually spreading over the country, and offering to adult workers the chance of real education which has always been withheld from them in the past. It is a society aiming at bringing within the reach of all who desire them tutorial classes and lectures on any branch of higher education which the students themselves may select. It has now over a hundred regular Tutorial Classes, mainly in industrial centres, with over three thousand students pledged to a three years' course. Over thirty-five thousand men and women of the working-classes, it is estimated, were reached by its lectures in the course of the past year. For seven years there have been Summer Schools in Oxford, where the students have met one another and come into contact with good tutors on their various subjects, and had in addition a very enjoyable time. The importance of this movement is that it does not and cannot have the result of lifting men and women out of their class : this was a fault often legitimately found with earlier efforts at working-class education—for where a man is asked to give up his whole time to the business of being educated, he is inevitably removed from his work and his class—but to the W.E.A. such a complaint has no application. Students are not asked to leave their work and seek education ; education is brought to them, and they are asked to select their own subjects. Naturally industrial history and economics are the most often chosen, as well as the easiest to teach such students ; but general history is also on the increase, and a great variety of other subjects occurs.

That this movement is gradually having its effect, and that this effect will be progressive, cannot be doubted. It is growing, and men do not come out of the classes just as they went in. Little groups of intelligent and informed workers are springing up all over the country ; it is not that the W.E.A. is discovering a few geniuses, but that the average of intelligence is high. These groups will in the future prove as powerful a leaven as the first Trade Unionists, or the groups of enthusiasts who followed the lead of the Rochdale Pioneers. The problem of education will thus begin to solve itself, and the awakening will come mainly not by Act of Parliament (though Parliament can help with money and encouragement), but by the spontaneous act of the workers themselves. Only by such growth can a truly popular education arise.

Everywhere, in fact, we are faced by the uprising of the group. Everywhere we have before us a new group-psychology, group-ideal, and group-action. Here it is in the Trade Union, there in the Co-operative Society, here again in the new educational grouping; but everywhere we are witnessing the creation of new individualities within the State. All over Europe the situation is the same: the last estate is realising that, in the words of Marx, " its liberation must be its own act ", and that it can find power to act only by the creation of its own institutions, its own corporate individualities. The group-principle, it is being seen, is the true principle of working-class solidarity, and is alone able to substitute, for the disorderly discontent and unrest of the mass or mob, the organised protest and formulated demand that are essential to all movements that Society need recognise. As a French Syndicalist has said, " Democracy ", the bare ballot-box democracy of the great State, " mixes the classes ": it confuses all ideas and aspirations in one great mass, in which all coherence and cogency are lost; it can grasp only the shadow while the substance eludes it, only the mechanism whose informing spirit it cannot hold.

It is the struggle of reaction against this new power that we are now witnessing everywhere, but especially in the industrial field. For the new ideas have come most forcibly to the front in the case of Trade Unionism, with which all the supporters of things as they are have recently been waging open or secret warfare. All the denunciations of the 'tyranny of Trade Unions', all the Taff Vale decisions and 'Osborne' judgments, of which we in this country have heard so much, find their parallels on the Continent, and are only the outward and visible signs of the determination of the old order to resist the new by every means in its power. The workers in their natural groups are asserting a new right; and as this right is seen to be fatal to the established codes of law and 'Manchester School' equity, there is no want of fighters to die in the last ditch for a cause that is already past saving. The repeal of the Combination Acts was already the first breach in the wall: the Trade Union Act of 1876 placed the Unions in a position strong enough to be safe from every danger, however exposed to petty judicial annoyances. The State has conceded the right to combine, and when that is granted, in the end, everything follows. The workers have "nothing to lose but their chains, and a world to win"; and, finally, they cannot help winning it.

From this new fact of social structure must come a reconstruction of political and social theory. We have long been accustomed to hearing, as much from Socialist and Labour theorists as from any other school, that Society is an organism and possesses a life-principle and will of its own, transcending the will of all the individuals composing it. On this question probably Mr. Balfour and Mr. Ramsay Macdonald would be found in perfect accord: both would agree that Society is an indivisible whole and possesses a common life. I fear that both would agree further that it must follow from this fact that the organisation of a class is in itself anti-social, in that it breaks up the Commonwealth, which is one, into unreal divisions on a basis of self-interest. The class-struggle is in fact said to be anti-social, to be merely the selfishness of one man writ large in the group, incapable alike of idealism and of self-devotion. A political party is supposed on this showing to have the advantage over a class that it organises upon an intellectual basis of belief and not upon an appetitive basis of self-assertion. But it should be observed that such an argument only holds good in a Society which is itself without classes. The class-struggle is preached, not on the ground that it is desirable, but on the ground that it is a monstrous and irrefutable fact. The class-structure is established in our social institutions, and it is only by means of the class-struggle that we can escape from it. The argument against the class-struggle presupposes that both classes are equally in the right, or that there is actually no such thing as right.

What then, since the class-struggle is to be accepted as an awful fact of social structure, is the relation between the class and the group? To possess any sort of unity or individuality, the group must have some common interest and aim, capable of binding its members together. It must be striving to realise something which is of importance, collectively and individually, to all its members, or else it will possess neither stability nor value. Such a bond may be found, in different times and places, in the most various spheres of human activity. Its unity may be religious, as in a Church; or political (in the narrower sense in which the word is applied to State institutions) as in Chartism; or educational, as in a University; or again industrial and economic, as in a Trade Union. It may be either material or spiritual (it is more often both), self-seeking or altruistic, instinctive or rational, blind or intelligent. It may, in short, have any of the attributes of human will, from which it differs, for the present purpose, only in being social instead of individual. The group therefore, or the class organised as a group, whose aim is in the main self-seeking, can only be condemned where an individual would be condemned for seeking his own advantage; that is, where the advantage sought is in itself unjust. Every group that is articulate with a common aim and a common demand has a claim to be heard just as cogent as the claim of the individual citizen. It is the right of such groups, called in France the new '*droit prolétarien*', that the philosophy of Syndicalism (which is after all in origin only the French name for Trade Unionism) has arisen to assert. In this it is not too much to say that we have the germ of the political philosophy of the future.

It is the aim of the chapters that follow to present a study of one side of this new development. In making the attempt, we shall be in the true line of evolution alike of the facts of history and of the theory of politics. The direct contribution of the French Revolution to political institutions was no doubt a legalisation of *laissez-faire* individualism, the denial of all particular associations within the State; but it is not difficult to show that this denial was an accidental result of historical environment rather than a correct interpretation of revolutionary theory. The *Loi le Chapelier* of 1791 abolished all particular associations, not because all associations had been shown to be wrong, but because the associations which then existed in France, from the *compagnonnages* to Marat's revolutionary clubs, were dangers to the prosperity and safety of the State. The gradual restoration of particular associations during the nineteenth century was not only an answer to the logic of facts, but also a direct fulfilment of true revolutionary principles. The case of Rousseau is generally quoted in opposition to this view, and reference is freely made to his pronouncement in the *Social Contract*. It is worth while to look at the actual passage—

" It is therefore of importance, if the General Will is to find expression, that there should be no particular society within the State, and that every citizen should express opinions only in accordance with it. . . . If there are particular associations, they should be as numerous and as equal as possible " (*Social Contract*, Book II., ch. iii.).

It must be remembered, first, that Rousseau is thinking of his ideal State, the small city community; and secondly, that he is considering a State free from inequality between individual and individual. Where there is such inequality, a substitute can be found only by getting the weak to combine : where the State is large, Rousseau himself holds that the General Will is lost, and it is only a step from this to the endeavour to recreate it by means of particular wills balanced as evenly as possible. In recognising that where there must be particular associations, they should be evenly matched, Rousseau admits the group-principle to be inevitable in the great State. We may then legitimately regard the new philosophy of groups as carrying on the true egalitarian principles of the French Revolution.

The particular phase and aspect of this evolution which we are about to study is but a part of the greater movement. In the world of Labour, as in Society as a whole, there are abroad two great principles, the spirit of solidarity and the spirit of devolution. The problem of democratic government is not being worked out merely in the vexed questions of our Parliamentary institutions, Home Rule all round, devolution of Parliamentary procedure by means of committees, decentralisation and popular control in Government Departments and the like; it is arising with equal insistence within the Trade Unions themselves, as a battle of officialdom against the rank and file, the branch or craft against the Union, the Trade Union against the Industrial Union or the Federation. And in this sphere it is peculiarly instructive, because here at least the democracy is being given some chance to solve its problems for itself and in its own way. With the exception of the Co-operative movement, which has had no such important difficulties to face, Trade Unionism is the first instance of a democracy really governing itself and dictating its own methods of government. For the first time, the three powers, legislative, executive and judicial, are effectively united in the same hands.

There is then at least this much justification for the Syndicalist attitude which sees in the Trade Unions the germ of the whole future organisation of society. The only true democracies of the present might well, it may seem, go to constitute the State of to-morrow. Cannot the Unions, the Syndicalist asks, so build upon the foundations they have laid as to be able in the end to supplant the capitalist State and all its works, take over not merely the running of industry but the whole of Society, and be themselves the State of the future? Stress has been laid in this opening chapter mainly upon the merits of Syndicalism, because we have been speaking of positive ideas, and, like all popular movements, Syndicalism is strong in what it asserts and weak in what it denies. Its weaknesses there will be ample opportunity to observe later, as its particular claims are discussed : the general weakness of its denial need alone be insisted upon here. Syndicalists are never tired of telling us that the strength of Syndicalism lies in taking man as a producer, at his daily work, as the victim of capitalist exploitation and the industrial system : but this claim carries along with itself its own limitation. It is a demand that the worker shall control the conditions of his own industry, or it is nothing. It is proud for the present to claim that it associates men, outside all political parties and religious sects, in the industrial sphere ; but if this is so, it can claim no competence beyond the domain of industry. No doubt its weakness is that of the economic reading of history ; the worker has become under Capitalism so much a worker and so little anything else ; and industrial questions have come to absorb so much of his energies, that he can hardly regard himself as concerned with the State or Society in any save industrial relations.[1] The State has become for him an external power that may or may not intervene in his industrial disputes, and which he always expects to interfere or refrain at the wrong moment: for the worker, the State has come to represent merely a ' justice ' which either holds its hand or miscarries. It has done so little either to give him control over his life or to raise his standard of living that he must be pardoned if he cannot concede to it functions which are in no sense industrial, if his perception of the true

[1] It would be difficult to overestimate the stimulus given to this attitude by the predominant place taken by the Tariff controversy in modern party politics.

sphere of politics—all too seldom the sphere with which the Houses of Parliament busy themselves—is dulled, and if, in his preoccupation with the concerns of his daily life, he fails to see that, outside all industrial questions, there is a sphere for the State in which, by great educational reforms, and by promoting and stimulating by every means in its power the finer expressions of the national life, it may remain in reality the first expression of the national will and the depository of the national greatness. Syndicalism is ready to deny all this because it has its eye on the man at his work, because it rightly regards the fact that he is a producer as the most important thing about him, and because, in so doing, it has not been content to assert the truths it has grasped, but has gone on to deny those which lie beyond its reach.

Syndicalism in the form of which we have just spoken will not become important in this country. It is in France, the home of ideas done to death, but always the home of ideas, that this point of view has made real headway. The different temper of English Trade Unionism was seen only last year [1] at the Annual Congress, which rejected the topic of Secular Education and for the future refused it a place on its agenda. If Trade Unionism is to fit itself for the control of industry, it must stick to its last, and, if it is to meddle with politics at all, it must create for that purpose a special organ with a separate existence. The control of industry may be the future destiny of the Trade Unions; the direct control of the whole national life is most emphatically not for them. A purely economic theory must neglect all sorts of things that are of the greatest importance in the national life; but it must do more than that: it must neglect nationality also. Mr

[1] 1912.

Fabian Ware's recent book,[1] which was in many respects an eloquent appreciation of Syndicalist ideals, was at pains to point out this error. For industry, for the economic man, nationality is unimportant : capital is organised internationally, and Trade Unions are gradually building up an international solidarity. There is consequently a frequent assertion that nationality does not matter : " the country of the worker is his belly ", says one French Syndicalist leader. But however little nationality may matter economically, it still enormously matters morally, socially and politically. The very ease with which the international solidarity of Labour can be swept away by the faintest breath of a war-scare is an illustration of this fact. Nationality can only cease to affect a man sentimentally in the moment when it is not affecting him practically ; let his country be threatened, and capitalist exploitation becomes in an instant of secondary importance. Nationality is still the strongest bond which can join men together, and so long as it retains its strength, there will remain a great and fruitful province for the national State. Syndicalism can only deny patriotism by representing industry as the whole of life ; but, however oppressive its conditions may be, however urgently the exploitation of labour may demand revolution, industry can never be the whole social problem. It is the greatest question of the day, but it is not the only question.

It will be the aim of this book to take the social problem at its most urgent, and the theory of Syndicalism at its strongest point, and to endeavour to follow out, as clearly as possible, the forces that are going to the making, out of the mere fighting organisa-

[1] *The Worker and his Country.*

tion of the Trade Unions, of something that has a claim to more than sympathy with its uphill fight. We shall be examining Trade Unionism in the light of the theory we have outlined, seeking in it the realisation of the new group-personality which is the central fact of modern society. We shall do this in the belief that the Trade Unions are tending to establish a sovereignty of their own, limited no doubt in its sphere, but real and absolute within its proper competence. For this new sovereignty we can find no other name than Economic Federalism, a gradual grouping of Unions into a single great Federation of Industry. The methods of realising this organisation and the manner of its action we shall be investigating throughout : it is important here merely to state a general intention, the purpose which is behind the writing of this book. The State must be set free from the impossible task of regulating all the details of industry ; it must be liberated for the work that is worthy of the national dignity, and it must leave to those who alone are competent to deal with them, the particular tasks of industrial organisation and management. Devolution is the order of the day, and we must have devolution, not merely by localities, but also by purposes. Even if the State cannot be wholly detached from industry, the problem is to free it as far as possible, and not, as some people seem to think, to concentrate all possible tasks in its hands. No doubt the ultimate power must reside in the democratic State ; but it does not at all follow that the State should do all the work. It should allot tasks to the members of the national family, and not do all the work by means of hired servants. Responsibility is the best teacher of self-reliance : self-government in the Trade Union has done wonders for the workers, and the Co-operative Societies have taught democracy many useful lessons. But with the gradual extension of Trade Union competence to cover more and more of the industrial field, the lessons it will be able to afford will be of infinitely greater value. In controlling industry, democracy will learn the hard lesson of self-control and the harder lesson of controlling its rulers, and, in so doing, it will become actual instead of nominal. With such institutions, we may hope to improve upon Rousseau's ideal, and even in the great State, to secure the realisation, in large measure, of that elusive but fundamental reality which he named the General Will.

CHAPTER II

THE LABOUR UNREST

'UNREST' is, as we have said, a vague term. It denotes in the first place a consciousness that all is not as it should be, and a dissatisfaction with present conditions; but it does not point to the possession of a panacea, to a widespread knowledge among the workers of what is necessary to remedy their grievances. Pure unrest is grievance without argument, dissatisfaction with the present without an ideal for the future. But though the very use of the word points to an absence of formulation and understanding by the worker of what he really wants, unrest could in fact find no possible outlet unless it in some measure materialised itself and asserted definite demands allowing of acceptance or refusal. The unrest therefore found determinate expression in the recent series of strikes, and will continue, as long as it remains, to find similar expression. In the strike a definite claim is made; and though there may be, behind the particular demand, a wider ideal and even a whole theory of social revolution, it is not necessary, for the purpose in hand, that this ideal background should be at all generally recognised. Every Labour movement will always have these two aspects: it will be at once a present claim for better conditions, and, in the minds of some at least of its advocates, an inroad on the present constitution of Society and an advance in the direction of social reconstruction.

Clearly these two demands, the ideal and the immediate, may both be formulated in either of two ways. The one is Socialism, in the widest sense of the word : the other is Social Reform, in so far as it is a real modification of the society of the present. Both of these spirits, singly or together, may appear either in the industrial or in the political field. The Parliamentary Labour Party may be regarded as an ameliorative influence, a means of getting certain reforms out of Parliament ; or, again, the Labour Party or an independent Socialist Party may be looked upon as the expression of the ideal aspirations of the workers, as the means of overthrowing capitalistic Society as a whole. Of course, the view usually and reasonably taken is a combination of these two views : neither revolutionism nor reformism is found in all its purity ; but, broadly, these two conceptions of the function of Labour in Parliament stand in perpetual opposition. On the other hand, there has long been in France, and there is rapidly growing up in this country, a similar cleavage of opinion within the Trade Union movement itself. The older Unionism was purely an instrument of collective bargaining and mutual insurance, aiming at the realisation of 'a fair day's wage for a fair day's work' by progressive modifications of present conditions : but in face of this, there is now abroad in the Trade Unions a new spirit, whose motto is 'the abolition of the wage system', aiming at a Trade Union revolution and the reconstruction of society to some extent on an industrial basis. Within the Labour movement, Syndicalism, in the widest sense, and the old Unionism confront each other in the industrial field just as Social Democracy and Labourism are opposed in the sphere of politics.

We have seen that, when the Labour Party got into politics, it soon became to the last degree Reformist. It was found impossible, even apart from the actual 'moderate' composition of the Labour Party, to continue for ever " holding up the torch of the ideal " in face of the perpetual detail of Parliamentary procedure. But whereas, with a party more thoroughly imbued with idealism, it might have been possible to secure at once practicality and attention to detail and a really idealistic point of view, the narrow vision of the majority of Labour members easily adapted itself to the Parliamentary situation, and the Parliamentary Labour movement ceased to fulfil the ideal needs of Labour, which was compelled, in pursuit of its wider conception of social reconstruction, to turn back once more to the Trade Union movement, and endeavour to find in it that very idealism the absence of which had previously done much to call the Parliamentary Party into being. Opportunely, as men's thoughts were swinging back to industrial action, Syndicalism appeared to give the movement a philosophic sanction. The philosophy of Syndicalism had been practically full-grown in France ever since 1902 ; it took so long in making the Channel passage, because only when the Labour Party had had its fling was the moment ripe for its appearance. Syndicalism, then, took the restless, the discontented and the extremist for the moment by storm. It in no sense caused the industrial reaction ; but it lent it, through a minority, force and direction. Few accepted it as a whole ; but for one who was ready to take it at its face value, there were thousands, including even its bitterest opponents,

THE LABOUR UNREST

who were influenced by it, and found in it to some extent a sanction for the direction in which their thoughts had been independently moving.

It is therefore often convenient to use the name Syndicalism loosely, to cover with it a wider problem than exact phrasing would warrant, and to assemble under its banner, because of a real resemblance, many leaders and movements that would indignantly repudiate the imputation. Of real Syndicalism there is in England practically none; of an impulse which, unless we consent to the inaccuracy, we must leave nameless, there is a great deal, and it is so important to emphasise the unity that we do not for a moment boggle at the perversion. The labour unrest is real; that will be generally granted. But, over and above its reality, it is more than an inarticulate impulse: it possesses direction and determinateness, and this direction is Syndicalistic much in the same sense as the Minority Report was Socialistic. There is a unity to be disentangled, if we do not exact too great definiteness or too much self-consciousness.

What, then, are the causes of Labour Unrest? The one cause that is real and fundamental is underpayment, or exploitation. The feeling that "all labour is robbed" is by this time pretty general even among the classes which such a discovery by no means persuades to give up the proceeds or even to desist from the process. The "ninepence for fourpence" of the Insurance Act and the still more specious '5 per cent. for nothing on wages' of co-partnership are a clear sign of the growth of this consciousness, even if it were not apparent in the increase of what Mr. Webb trustfully calls "social compunction". This, the one permanent basis of discontent, is what at bottom justifies all revolution, and makes all strikes, however wrong in their particular circumstances, ultimately right and defensible. This is the continual background of all unrest, the wavering but undying aspiration of the dispossessed to recover their lost birthright, and to enter once more into possession of the earth. The abiding discomfort, which is for many destitution, and for the majority poverty, is the one great cause of the insurgence of democracy—a cause that is too often neglected, just because it is always present. The poverty that we have with us always morally justifies every revolution, though it proves no particular uprising to be wise or well-directed.

For the thinker and the revolutionary, as for the real Tory, this will stand out as the really significant cause. The economist, the social reformer, and the befogged and ignorant general public, however, will demand information about the occasional causes; they will always want to know how the rotten structure is to be patched up, how this or that outbreak is to be calmed, and how this or that aspiration can be satisfied without real surrender, or side-tracked without detection. For if there can be a greater dishonesty in envisaging the problem, a greater refusal to face the facts, than that which the aspiring politician has to learn, it is assuredly to be found in the narrowness, egoism, and intellectual indolence that characterise the great British public. If the industrial revolution has turned the worker into a mere producing-machine, it has quite equally turned the public into a mass of mere consumers, with consciences always in their pockets and brains nowhere—or directed to anything rather than the social question. In this country, at least, it is useless to invoke public opinion, because it is selfish, unenlightened and vindictive.

We need not, however, dispute that it is of great

THE LABOUR UNREST

importance to get clear about occasional and temporary causes, so long as the permanent and fundamental cause is kept always in sight. We know why, ultimately, Labour is discontented with its lot—the mystery is rather why it is not infinitely more so than we find it—but this by itself tells us too little. We want to know further why discontent comes to a head at this or that point of time, and why it takes this or that form rather than another. Doubtless, there is much in these particular inquiries that must for ever elude us; but partial answers are both possible and necessary. If then we ask why the Labour Unrest came in 1910 rather than at some other time, the answer will be real and relevant, though incomplete.

First, we may lay much, as is usually done, to the charge of the rise in prices all round. From 1900 to 1910, wages were nearly stationary, while prices went up by leaps and bounds. The reader has only to go to Mr. Chiozza Money's *Riches and Poverty*, or to the official statement just issued by the Board of Trade, to find this abundantly confirmed. Now, it is clear that stationary wages and rising prices mean decreased comfort and increased sense of deprivation; and, though mere under-payment tends to produce acquiescence and servility rather than revolt, the same cannot be said of actual retrogression in the standard of living. The falling off of purchasing power, whether connected in the worker's mind with the rise in prices or merely felt as a hard fact, is calculated to produce revolt and not acquiescence; and this is precisely what has occurred. It is often argued that the poor, buying bad goods below market price, feel the rise in prices less than statistics assume, and that really the shoe has not pinched at all or at least so hard as we suppose; but this would apply in any case only to a small section of the very poor in the great towns ; and it would be far truer to say that vast numbers, living on spasmodic credit from small traders who have to overcharge them to make ends meet, really feel the pinch far more than other classes of the community. Wasteful buyers of necessity at the best, they are also the first to experience the effects of a general rise in prices. They are the worst customers, and they are most at the tradesman's mercy ; and therefore they suffer. It is indeed useless to dispute that, between 1900 and 1910, the condition of the workers as a whole grew steadily worse. It may have made some advance since then ; but we are now investigating the conditions that preceded the unrest. First then, as occasional cause, we have a rise in prices without a corresponding rise in wages ; that is to say, we have a fall in real wages and in purchasing power. This by itself would be enough to account for the outbreak, and probably was, in fact, the main cause. No doubt, the process of reasoning in the worker's mind was seldom so logical ; he merely felt the discomfort and resented it ; and then the social student stepped in to provide him with a theoretical justification for which he probably cared very little, save when it served him as an argument. But, realised or unrealised, this fall in real wages was the main basis of the labour unrest.

A second cause to which, in some quarters, considerable prominence is given, is the supposed failure of the Parliamentary Labour Party. At the 1906 elections, the new party clearly aroused not a little enthusiasm and expectation : the confidence was sustained till after the passage of the Trades Disputes Act, its one real, and, it may be, short-lived triumph ; but from that moment its honour in the Labour world has steadily decreased. It has not really done so much less than those who knew it expected all along ; but it has disappointed extravagant and ill-founded expectations, and it has afforded no basis for newer and more justifiable hopes. We knew all along that the Labour Party consisted for the most part of unimaginative Liberal working-men of the old type, and that, so long as it remained full of such men, it could not be a really independent party ; but this was not so clearly recognised by the Labour movement as a whole, and especially by the Socialist wing, which looked forward to collaring the whole for Socialism. We should have known all along what to expect ; but now that we have got it, many of us are not satisfied. It seems to many that the great Labour movement has been content recently to put too many eggs into one basket, and that, now we have seen how it limps under the weight, it is time to restore a balance.

Doubtless, for their own purposes, various types of people have been ready to make all they can of this ' failure '. The Conservatives, not unnaturally regarding the Labour members as just so many disguised Liberal voters in Parliament, have been quite ready to use the arguments of their extreme opponents to throw discredit on an enemy they regard as, for the moment at least, the more dangerous. Preoccupied with matters parliamentary, they see that the weakening of the Labour Party does not necessarily strengthen any other section of their opponents, and may therefore well be sheer gain. We therefore find them arguing, along with the Syndicalists, that the Labour Party is only the tail of the Liberal dog, and only diverging in the conclusions they desire to draw. On the other hand, there is the attack of the Syndicalist, who either repudiates parliamentary action altogether, or holds that the importance attached to it is, for the present, exaggerated. This attack may take any form, from extreme 'direct-actionism' to modified disillusion with the actual achievements of the Labour Party. We shall have more to say of this aspect of the question later; for the moment we are concerned with it only as a contributory cause of labour unrest.

As such, its importance has certainly been much exaggerated. The Labour Party has indeed ceased to excite enthusiasm, and therefore to make progress; but this is equally the recent position of all political parties. Political interest may not have waned; but political enthusiasm has certainly done so. Most men are, if not disgusted, at least bored with all parties. With the Labour Party there is not so much positive cause for complaint as with the Liberals; and, therefore, men are more bored than annoyed. Further than this most people have not gone; there is nothing like the great and conscious revolt against politics that the Syndicalists and the *New Witness* would have us believe in.

It may be said that a revulsion of feeling need not be highly conscious. Men may revolt, without knowing exactly why, or even that they are doing so. In this sense, the dissatisfaction with politics has no doubt had something to do with the turning of men's minds back to industrial action and the strike. But in the main there is no need to go so far afield in the search for causes. The attack on politics rather profited subsequently by the labour unrest than itself caused it. The reverse would no doubt have been more logical; but the logical order is often reversed in fact. Economic pressure, falling or stationary wages accompanied by rising prices, and a rising standard of expectation are by themselves cause enough for a hundred times as much unrest as we have had, or are likely to get for years to come.

Above all, the *cause* was not the hot weather. The weather was no doubt a favourable accident; it made it easier to get and keep the men out, and contributed something to the success of the strikes. But at most, it only determined the actual moment of the outbreak; it had nothing to do with deciding whether there should or should not be a strike at all.

Agitation, another explanation popular in some quarters, no doubt did something too. But agitation must have something to agitate about; and where it has that, the subject of the agitation takes the place as cause of the agitation itself. The blessed word ' agitator ' is only used to dull the social conscience of the well-to-do. The cause of discontent was that people found they had not enough money, and that money was not going so far as it had gone. The unrest, therefore, was in a great measure not revolutionary: the demand was, in the minds of most of those who made it, for increased comfort rather than for abstract justice. Such a demand has, however, always revolutionary possibilities, and these were present to the minds at least of some of the leaders and not a few of the rank and file. Where there is such a germ, industrial action is the best soil for making it grow; but it must be admitted that there is at present very little real revolutionary feeling in this country. By ' revolutionary ' is, of course, meant aiming at complete social reconstruction and not at mere patching and mending of the existing social system: it is not implied that the method of revolution need be violent and catastrophic.

In denying ' agitation ' as a cause, we should not be understood to deny the enormous influence which certain leaders had over the recent unrest. Tom Mann and Ben Tillett, to mention only two, are names with which the uprisings of 1910–12 will always be associated. Yet even their influence—great as it undoubtedly was—has been, on the whole, exaggerated. Tom Mann did not in any sense cause the strikes or the unrest : he contributed a great deal to the direction they took and to the guiding of the ' unrest ' into definite and constructive channels, but he cannot be said to have caused it. He utilised an existing state of affairs with an eye to a wider future as well as to the present. His career is therefore interesting rather as an account of the enduring results the movement is likely to bring forth, than as the historical explanation of its origin. Tom Mann's success came no doubt largely from his personal qualities, his gift of oratory, and his strong personality and vivid enthusiasm ; but it came much more from the fact that he chose the right moment for his reappearance. The time was ripe, and it was his fortune and privilege to be the spark to set the train alight.

Tom Mann, after many years' absence in Australia, returned to England at the end of 1910. As far back as 1889 he was concerned with John Burns and Ben Tillett in organising the London Dock Strike, and, as a Trade Union theorist, wrote some articles in the journal of the Amalgamated Society of Engineers, of which his recent views are only a development. In those articles he favoured closer unity by means of Federation ; events since then have proved that bare Federation is, in most cases, of very little use, and that Amalgamation alone can give unity with the strong financial basis that is absolutely essential. In Australia and New Zealand he studied the working of the complicated systems of arbitration which are

THE LABOUR UNREST

there in force, and gathered an impression highly unfavourable to arbitration as a whole.[1] The industrial battle, he found, must, in spite of all State machinery, finally amount to a trial of strength and organisation between masters and men, a warfare which may be either open or concealed, and which he would sooner have revealed in all its nakedness. He therefore returned to England with views upon the industrial question already strongly formed. He found, as we have seen, the temper of the workers already at boiling point, and was at once invited to play a leading part in the outburst. From the first, he knew his business; he was well aware that the English worker cannot be carried away by mere reasoning, and that the only way to get him to concern himself with an idea is to show it him actually at work. Tom Mann therefore began by organising strikes, and only preached the abstract gospel of the strike when he had already shown how it could be realised in practice. The first Dock Strikes of Liverpool and London were his practical demonstrations of the theory he had to present. They were followed by pamphlets—by no means so cogent in themselves as the actual experiments—by lectures given all over the country, and by an agitation carried on mainly through the Industrial Syndicalist Education League. We shall have more to say of this campaign later on : here we only draw attention to Tom Mann's career because it is impossible, in looking back upon the unrest, to miss so central a figure. Tom Mann, whatever his weaknesses, was, for the moment, the most striking personality in the Trade Union world. The ideas this book is an attempt to advocate are largely

[1] Tom Mann's *From Single Tax to Syndicalism* contains an account of his Australian experiences.

those which seem likely to be permanently conserved out of the rather ill-assorted mass that he has put before the world of Labour. The appeal for solidarity, which is the vital and informing idea of all his propaganda, is precisely the idea which a developed labour organisation is in most danger of neglecting. The egoism of organised groups is no doubt in itself superior to the egoism of isolated individuals, just as a band of thieves, among whom is honour, is better than a single thief, whose hand is against all men. But if egoism is to pass into something higher, organisation must not remain merely sectional : the world of Labour must be made to realise its unity, and to work together for the common good. When it does that, there is more hope that it will realise the existence of an even higher common good which is not that even of Labour as a whole, but of the entire community. It may to some people be a disappointment to understand that such a realisation would at once make the social revolution certain.

Unrest, the unrest of which we have been speaking, is almost purely a national phenomenon. Strong though the bonds that bind the commercial doings of nations together have grown, they have not yet caused either Labour or the employers to organise, or even to feel, to much purpose, internationally. Doubtless there is on both sides a realisation that the interest of either party is at bottom the same in every country, and that national development may often be stimulated or retarded by conditions overseas. Certainly too, feeling in these matters is destined to become, in the near future, far more international ; and international sentiment is certain to be followed, at a respectful distance, by international organisation. But at present such causes are wholly insignificant beside the special industrial circumstances of each particular country ; and it is on these, and not on international feeling, that the ebb and flow of unrest will for some time continue to depend. Such circumstances themselves are indeed far from being wholly independent of similar conditions in other countries ; but these correspondences are as yet largely unsystematised, and, broadly speaking, we may say that ' unrest ' depends almost solely upon national, as opposed to international, circumstances.

What, then, is the value of all the talk we hear about the ' international proletariat ' and the solidarity of the dispossessed in every country on the face of the earth ? It is necessary here to distinguish. Solidarity of this sort is admittedly unrealised and for the present unrealisable. At the most, it is only possible to get occasional co-operation in times of crisis ; and, as we have recently seen in the case of Belgium, even so much is very difficult to secure. The Belgian workers, it will be remembered, preparing for a general strike in support of universal suffrage, asked British workers to help them by refusing to handle coal intended for Belgium. This was referred by the British Miners to the Transport Workers, who did their best, but achieved practically nothing. In fact, any such proposal offers extraordinary difficulties, and in the main, Labour in each country has to be left to fight its own battles. A day may come when more will be possible ; but that day is not yet.

There is, however, another sense in which the international question is highly relevant to our subject. Even if the dispossessed of different nations cannot do much to help one another, they have at bottom the same battles to fight, and the same enemy to overthrow. Everywhere exploiter and exploited face each other in a social system which, more or less complicated in different instances, is always fundamentally the same. Everywhere is found political democracy realised or well on the way to realisation; and everywhere this democracy is illusory because it is accompanied by a tyrannical economic feudalism, which leaves the voter, for all his hard-won democratic liberty, still a wage-slave and a member of the great class of the disinherited.

But this international kinship, however inspiring, does not make much practical difference. There are international questions of a different sort which are hard facts and have, whether we like it or not, to be taken into account. It is unquestionable that, with the world-market as highly organised as it now is, a difference in rates of wages, and consequently in cost of production, between two countries cannot but affect the industry of the country paying the higher rates. Of course, the difference may be neutralised by national character or local conditions, or the higher wages may actually be productive enough in point of efficiency to annul it; but, unless these conditions are present, it is clear that the countries where wages are lower will have an economic pull. This means two things: first, that no country can afford to get too far ahead of its rivals in point of wages and the like, at least under a capitalistic régime; and secondly, that it is to the interest of the Labour movement in any country that other nations shall not lag behind. For, if they do, the countries that are in advance of the rest will be unable to make further progress, in so far as they are rivals of the more backward. The Labour movement must therefore aim everywhere at a corresponding, if not a co-operative, advance; the solidarity of international Labour is more than the idealistic camaraderie of the oppressed; it is even the essential condition of amelioration.

It does not follow from this, as some Syndicalists would have us believe, that the worker must abjure patriotism, and become a citizen of the world of Labour, pure and simple. Just as the individuals who work together in a Trade Union for the bettering of their lot still remain individuals, the national Labour organisations may work together without losing their nationality. However much they may need to co-operate, they certainly do not require to be fused. In point of fact, we find that while, in recent years, Trade Unionism has been making a parallel growth in various countries, its progress and direction have been by no means uniform. The general aspect of industrial organisation is very different indeed in England, in Germany, in France, in Italy, and in the United States; and these differences seem to come partly from the peculiar conditions under which industry is carried on in each case, and partly from differences in national temperament and tradition. In England, we seem to have come to one of the periodical crises in national organisation; and it will be impossible to attempt the task of resolving our present problems without some examination of the national movements of other countries. This will accordingly form part of our task, before we go on to draw conclusions and make provisional recommendations. The influence of other national movements has to be taken into account in respect both of what it has actually accomplished and of the lessons we may profitably learn from it.

For, even if Labour in this country must, in the last resort, provide for its own salvation, it is still clear that, in valuing the various means at its disposal, we have to take into account such modifications in their use and disposition as can be learnt from abroad. These inquiries are therefore necessary as helps towards the resolution of the main question in industry, which faces not merely the worker, but also the public at large. This question is, first, whether strikes have failed; and secondly, if so, whether they must inevitably fail. Is the strike, as an instrument of industrial emancipation, really played out, or have we come to a period in which we may expect to witness its great and successful revival? We can only decide this question when we have looked further into the actualities and the possibilities of Trade Unionism, and, until we have settled it, we cannot hope to settle the vexed problem of the relation between industrial and political action. Here, merely surveying the facts of the unrest, we are directly concerned only to see what is actually taking place. We can expect at best to answer only the first part of the question, and to say whether strikes do or do not fail. Whether they must fail we can only see, if at all, at the end of our inquiry.

Certain superficial facts at any rate are clear. As a general rule, in the past the best paid labour has struck, while the worst paid has been either legislated for, or more often, neglected. Just recently we have seen exceptions to both these rules: the best paid labour, by strikes or threats, has secured legislation; and the worst-paid labour, influenced by the unrest, has begun to strike. The Miners have secured their Eight Hours' Act and their Minimum Wage Act, and so seem to have acted up to the Syndicalist principle that "useful laws can be won by direct action"; and, on the other hand, the Cradley Heath strike of Chain-makers, and the recent strikes in the Black Country are cases of the insurgence of the underpaid and underorganised. But as a whole the rule is still unchanged; and we cannot expect that it will soon be otherwise. Organisation brings higher wages, and, even more, high wages lead to organisation; and therefore those who are best off are always in the best position for getting more. The defect of Trade Unionism as a whole is that it helps the strong more than the weak. This has no doubt its compensating advantages: it is easier in this way to make some slight breach in the capitalist system, and for effective action of any sort it is necessary that the workers in some trades at least should be well organised. But, on the face of it, this inherent defect of our Trade Unionism does seem to leave a wide sphere for the action of Parliament in industrial matters. Labour, as a single great movement, cannot afford to leave the weaker brethren, and more especially the weaker sisters, in the lurch.

It is often urged that this defect would be remedied by the Greater, as opposed to 'craft', Unionism, and, in the sequel, we shall have to examine this claim more narrowly. But it is at any rate clear that any practicable form of Unionism would still leave many of the underpaid as unorganised as now. It would increase the solidarity of all grades in industries already well organised, but it would not mean a sudden organisation of the workers in industries where Unionism is at present weak.

We shall, then, find it necessary to allow a place to parliamentary action for the raising of wages in certain kinds of industry, and, in order to assign briefly the scope of such action, we shall have to examine shortly the Wages Board or Trade Board system as it is found in Australia and, under Mr. Churchill's Act, in England. We shall also have to say something of other sorts of Minimum Wage proposals. In doing so, we shall be dealing with governmental action as raising wages where direct action would be impotent, with committees appointed by Parliament definitely to take sides, and help the weaker sections of the world of Labour.

It is important to realise that this is a wholly different problem from another which we shall be unable to neglect. Such Wages Boards are not instances of conciliation or arbitration. They are State action in the interests of the oppressed, and imply no revolutionary principle, or admission that labour as a whole is underpaid. They merely raise abnormal wages to the standard rate, and do nothing actually to raise that rate.

Conciliation, on the other hand, is founded on an entirely different principle. It aims, not at helping one party to a conflict against the other, but at increasing the chances of industrial peace. It takes no side, and merely tries, by measuring strength, to replace conflicts by peaceful settlements. The peace it presupposes is the peace, not of the two parties, but of the community at large. A settlement by conciliation is, or may be, as much a trial of strength as a strike. It is a method of comparing resources—of which public support may of course form part—in order to avoid a trial of endurance between profits and stomachs—or purses. Such conciliation may be applied to any branch of labour in which a conflict, a trial of strength between the parties, may arise; but not elsewhere. It is the diplomacy of industrialism, and differs only in that it may easily take on permanent forms. This has been stated more strongly perhaps than some of the facts warrant, on the basis of a definite view of the proper scope and methods of conciliation. In the sequel, it will be examined in much more detail, and its tendency to pass over into an artificial binding-down of the employee by long agreements will be further discussed.

Arbitration is the third factor that has to be taken into account. It rests upon a principle differing from both the former. It neither definitely takes sides, and aims at raising wages in the interest of the oppressed, nor is a mere trial of strength a substitute for actual stoppages of work. Arbitration is in fact a vague word, which covers a multitude of meanings.

Conciliation in itself implies merely a meeting of the two parties to discuss terms of peace. This meeting may aim either at preventing or at ending a stoppage, and may be undertaken either on the motion of the parties themselves, or on a suggestion from outside. Both kinds of conciliation are plentifully found in this country, and we shall have to study them apart. A second differentia is to be found in the presence or absence of a neutral Chairman. In pure conciliations, the parties are confronted, and no more; the Chairman, if there is one, has no actual power. The neutral element once admitted, however, conciliation readily changes its character; the Chairman acquires more and more power, and often becomes in the end a pure arbitrator, before whom the two representative sections of the Board merely appear as witnesses. The third and most important factor is whether the decisions of the Board—or of the Chairman—are, or are not, binding. If decisions made by the Chairman alone are binding, it is clear that we have passed over from conciliation to arbitration. Recourse is then to an impartial judge from without, and the parties merely appear, as in a court, to have their case tried.

This still leaves open the question of principle for the Chairman or arbitrator. Is he to be guided by the strength of the parties, or by abstract justice, or by a combination of the two? Or is he to regard himself as there merely to secure peace at any price, and to be guided throughout by the merest opportunism? We seem to have been content, so far, to leave such questions unsettled; and, in doing so, we have made the arbitrator's task very difficult. Arbitration is, in fact, a name for a new method of keeping industrial peace, and it is still so vague and indeterminate mainly because our rulers have not yet decided what to do. Sir George Askwith's visit to Canada and his report upon it, are, in this connection, of the first importance, as they seem both to indicate the line of future development, and to show very clearly that a veiled form of compulsory arbitration is a proposal to be reckoned with by the Trade Unions in the near future. To this they hardly seem enough awake, though an Act on the lines of the Canadian measure would certainly, as has happened in Canada, profoundly modify the whole industrial situation. It will therefore be essential to discuss all these points in more detail.

In this, as in other cases, the general impression left by Labour in this country is that of a feeble intellectual life. There would seem to be little conscious attempt to do the hard thinking which is at present necessary, and an appalling readiness to muddle through on the old ideas. In particular, Labour journalism shows signs of this weakness. Of the two Labour dailies, the *Daily Citizen* seems to be of the old opinion that "to generalise is to be an idiot", and stedfastly refuses to confront big Trade Union questions. It welcomed the coming of the National Union of Railwaymen, but, reflecting the common hostility of the old leaders to most forms of Trade Union amalgamation, carefully refrained from drawing any more general conclusions. On the whole, the *Citizen* reflects the policy of the Labour Party, which is mere opportunism. It is not a journal for soul-searchings, or for the working out of anything new.

Soul-searchings are, on the other hand, the strong point of the *Daily Herald*, which devotes itself to a somewhat indiscriminate revolt against all that is. The *Herald* is delightfully fresh and receptive of ideas, and rushes at a generalisation like a hunter at a five-barred gate; but its power of co-ordination is limited, and it seems to find difficulty in passing from revolt to reconstruction. Mr. Will Dyson's cartoons are splendid, and the *Herald's* violence is refreshing; but it too has failed to formulate a well-defined policy.

The only other Socialist paper, except the *New Statesman*, which stands for Mr. and Mrs. Webb, containing any constructive suggestions, is the *New Age*, the aggressively independent weekly, which may be loved or hated, but never tolerated. The *New Age* also has an almost universal propensity to denunciation; but in its policy of ultimate co-operation between the State and the Unions, which it names National Guilds, it has hold of the only possible solution of the industrial problem. The proposal for co-management between the State and the Unions is unquestionably a forecast of the society of the future; and we shall have much more to say of it hereafter. The weakness of the *New Age* is that its theoretical reconstruction is imperfectly accompanied by suggestions for the actual transition. It is always a little scornful of the present and more than a little scornful of democracy; it does little to teach us how to build the New Jerusalem, of which it has seized the general idea. It is, however, above all a paper with ideas, and the phenomenon is rare enough for gratitude. Its influence is very limited at present, and it unfortunately appeals mainly to the middle-classes.

It is, in fact, exceedingly difficult to get new ideas into the heads of old administrators; and, the first need of the Unions in their everyday life being competent administrators, an official type of mind has been developed and has filled all the posts. The wild fulminations against Syndicalism of Labour leaders, who ought to know better, would be less harmful had not nearly all the legislative, as well as the executive, work of the Unions fallen into their hands. The administrative mind, good at carrying out a policy, is bad at dictating one, and the practical union of the two powers in the Executive Committees of the Unions has brought about the feeling of opposition to leadership which is now running through the Labour movement. Precisely the same problem has arisen in industrial, as in political, democracy; in both, the representative system needs revision, and no one yet knows quite how revision is to be accomplished. The problem of Trade Union government is as great and pressing as that of the Greater Unionism. This, too, is at the back of the unrest, and forms a great part of the ill-digested mass of aspiration which we call Syndicalism.

For the moment, the working-class seems to have shown itself incapable of clear thinking. It has done next to nothing, during the last three years, to introduce order into the chaotic jumble of new ideas by which it has been stirred. It would no doubt be better for it to do its own thinking without help from outside; but, as it is unlikely to do this, it cannot afford to reject any help that is forthcoming. It is difficult for the Trade Unionist, and especially for the leader actually engaged in administrative work, to take a view of the condition of Trade Unionism which transcends the particular problems of his own industry. The administrator as a rule does not generalise, while the member of the rank and file, if he does generalise at all, does so far too broadly. Into this gap middle-class Socialists and sympathisers—those who on the Continent are called the 'intellectuals'—will be forced to step. The work which Mr. and Mrs. Webb began with *Industrial Democracy* nearly twenty years ago has to be taken up anew, and the question has to be studied over again in the light of more recent developments. For the doing of such work this book is a plea. The work itself demands co-operation and long, patient endeavour. But, if there is to be any escape from the present muddle, it is work that must be done.

It is indeed true that, so far, the entry of the intellectuals into the field of industrial politics has been a dismal fiasco. The *Daily Mail's* banal publication, *What the Worker Wants*, from Mr. H. G. Wells's articles to the scattered contributions of most of the distinguished nonentities in Christendom, is a long record of absolute bankruptcy of ideas. Mr. Wells characteristically describes the muddle well, but has no hint of a solution to offer. The rest fail even to understand that anything out of the way is happening. But the 'intellectuals' of the *Daily Mail* need not be the intellectuals of the new philosophy of

Labour. There are real inquirers who, would they but turn their attention this way, could do much to formulate an up-to-date philosophy for the Labour movement. Collectivism is both too fruitful to be allowed to die, and too narrow to be the whole truth. But unless old doctrines are revised, they will perish, and there will be nothing to put in their place.

It must then be realised that the unrest has not merely a cause but a justification. It is the first awakening of a new and positive demand, of a nascent philosophy which needs formulation and interpretation. Behind the new industrialism is the germ of the demand for the real control of industry by the workers, for an 'Industrial Democracy' that shall mean not merely Trade Union management, but the real superintendence of industrial processes and conditions.

It is a sign of this growing demand that, in all the great industrial countries of Europe in which tables are kept showing the various causes of strikes, the proportion due to direct demands for higher wages shows a marked diminution. Disputes tend more and more to centre round questions which, a few years ago, would unhesitatingly have been lumped together as matters of 'discipline' and 'management', clearly outside the competence of Trade Unions. The breakdown of the Brooklands Agreement is one case; but by far the most widespread sign of the new spirit is the increasing prominence of the non-unionist question. Naturally, this question arises only in cases in which Trade Unionism is already strong; but the definite assertion of the refusal to work with non-unionists throughout even one industry would be a tremendous step in advance, and could not fail to have an immense effect on the

Trade Union movement as a whole.[1] For every step the Unions take towards becoming compulsory corporations, preserving free entry, but allowing no non-unionists in their industries, takes them a long way towards attaining the competence necessary for a far higher control over industry as a whole. In the end, the fitness of the Unions to control industry must depend on the will and corporate capacity of their members. They are indeed as yet a very long way off the necessary coherence and capacity; but every move they make in this direction should be welcomed. The delegation of control by the State is the only possible solution; and instead of lamenting the lot of the 'free labourer', more accurately known to the populace as the 'blackleg' or 'scab', those who desire real progress should be concerned in destroying him root and branch. The 'free labourer' is at best a mere ignorant catspaw of the employer, and, as the better employers are finding out, it pays better in the end to play fair.

Of all these various and yet homogeneous matters we have been outlining is made up the vague and indefinite movement we are learning to call Syndicalism. Those who fear vagueness in terminology more than they love a new idea will shun the word; but by those who really understand that there is something new in the air needing a name, it will be welcomed. Such a label must of necessity begin by being indefinite: it took Socialism more than half a century to get its definite connotation, and its doing so was not in the end clear gain. Syndicalism is a word which means something and something important, though what it means is at present ill-understood. Its meaning is, in fact, something the future has to decide by its

[1] The Miners and the Railwaymen are making this demand.

manner of facing the present crisis in the industrial world. At present, it is impossible to do more than pick out the various problems which it has to face without further defining their central unity. Briefly, we may set forth the most important after this fashion :—

1. *Industrial Organisation.*—Should the workers organise on an ' occupational', an ' industrial', or a ' craft ' basis ? (see Chapter VII.).
2. *Industrial Action.*—Are strikes or politics the best weapon for the working-classes ? (see Chapter XIII.).
3. *Trade Union Control.*—How can the internal organisation of the Unions be modified so as to give the rank and file greater hold over the leaders, without making combined action slower or more difficult ? (see Chapters VII., VIII., and XII.).
4. *Strikes and Arbitration.*—What should be the attitude of Labour to proposed methods of industrial peace ? (see Chapter IX.).
5. *The Control of Industry.*—How can the workers be given a greater share in the real control of industrial processes and methods of production ? (see Chapter XI.).

All these problems may seem to lack co-ordination, and to be merely scattered and isolated points round which discussion happens simultaneously to be raging. They pass, however, too readily one into another to admit of such a view. The first four problems are all being faced, at the present time, by Trade Unionists all over the country, and in all countries in which the Labour movement has made much progress. They have, of course, taken on different forms according to the time and place of their appearance ; but, on

THE LABOUR UNREST

the whole, they have offered much the same difficulties for solution. America alone should be excepted; for there the problems have arisen in so peculiar a form that, though it is important to deal with them in order to explain certain industrial phenomena in this country, it is more important to remark differences than resemblances. It is well to begin with Syndicalism in France, both as being the first in time, and as raising the questions in their most general form.

CHAPTER III

LABOUR IN FRANCE

THE evolution of the Labour movement in France reproduces, in the main outlines, the national history since the Revolution of 1789. It is therefore in broad contrast with the English movement, just as English national history is with that of France. The English Trade Union movement has reached its present development because there has at no point been a break; the evolution has been continuous, and dictated in every case by the pragmatic logic of the immediate fact. In France, on the other hand, the ' syndical ' movement has felt the effect of all the successive shocks sustained by the national system : it has built itself up only to fall in the midst of the next national upheaval, and in consequence of this marked discontinuity it has not developed, purely in face of practical considerations, a mass of entanglements and contradictions which, working fairly well in practice, are the despair of the theorist. It may well be, indeed, that this repeated need for rapid re-creation of the movement has caused theory to play a larger part than practice in giving it form; several times over it has been created whole, after a pattern in somebody's mind, and not slowly developed as the facts called it forth. But still more this attention to theory has been the effect of national temperament : the French, still full of revolutionary principles, and concerned to make everything square with the ideas of 1789, have always thought of the syndical problem as a unity, and been concerned to give it logical form and justification. Long before the philosophy of Syndicalism was thought of, long before Pelloutier began his work, the Radicals who, led by Waldeck-Rousseau, legalised the 'Syndicats' in 1884, had worked out for themselves a conception of the place the workers' Unions should occupy in the Society of the present and of the future. The ideas of the Syndicalists are a development—whether justifiable or not, we shall have to consider—of the views of the Radicals who were responsible for the law of 1884.[1]

This theoretical character of the French movement makes it both easier and more difficult to study for our purpose. It is easier to ascertain the ideas that are behind it and to get a general view of its aims; but it is correspondingly difficult to discover how far it succeeds or fails. Doubtless, the impulse it has given to the sluggish mind of English Trade Unionism comes mainly from its theoretical basis, and is therefore more readily estimated; but, before we can pass judgment upon it, we certainly want to know what it has effected, and this is far harder. Not merely is the continuous history of French Labour organisation much shorter and the development in every respect more rudimentary, but also the French have so far been very

[1] For the ideas of the Radicals, see J. Paul-Boncour, *Le Fédéralisme Economique*, which has a preface by Waldeck-Rousseau. For their view of Syndicalism, see M. Paul-Boncour's *Les Syndicats de Fonctionnaires*. The chapter "Les Idées Syndicales de Waldeck-Rousseau" in Victor Diligent's *Les Orientations Syndicales* also gives a good outline. See further, M. Leroy, *Les Transformations de la Puissance Publique*, and L. Barthou, *L'Action Syndicale*.

poor hands at keeping records and statistics. The Government statistics of the Office du Travail are very unsatisfactory, and those kept by the C.G.T. or its constituent parts wholly inadequate. In book after book, where figures are thought worthy of admission at all, the same old statistics are given, and even these are seldom trustworthy. We are therefore driven very much to form our view of Syndicalism in France mainly on the theory, on its professions of what it aims at doing, rather than on the actual record of what it has done. We shall make some attempt at estimating its actual achievement, but in the main we shall be concerned with views more than with facts. After all, it is with views that we are more directly concerned.

It is important, at the outset, to get a general view of the state of Labour organisation in France. Even this is not so easy as it seems to us, with our carefully sorted Trade Union returns and Board of Trade publications. The *Office du Travail* does indeed publish figures showing the aggregate strength of Trade Unionism in France, but these figures do not by any means represent the real fighting force of Labour. They include ' *syndicats mixtes* ', which are mere benefit societies, often attached to particular factories; ' *syndicats jaunes* ', which are more or less ' blackleg ' institutions supported by the masters; and agricultural *syndicats*, which have no part in the general industrial movement. Thus, although the strength of Trade Unionism in France is officially given at more than two millions, this by no means represents the strength of the Confédération Générale du Travail (C.G.T.) or that of the effective fighting force of industrial workers. On the whole, it seems safe to conclude that the strength of the organised workers in French industry is under a million.[1] This number compares very unfavourably with the three millions odd of either England or Germany, even when the numbers engaged in industry, excluding agriculture, in these countries are taken into account. Trade Unionism in France has certainly made nothing like the progress it can show in either England or Germany, and there seems no sign of any rapid advance at present. No doubt, the English Unions have a far longer history behind them, and are therefore naturally more advanced ; but in the case of Germany we find a newer organisation catching up and passing the older movement. On the score of numbers alone, French Trade Unionism has nothing to boast of : it is behindhand, and seems unlikely to move forward more rapidly than in the past. It would not, however, be safe to attribute this weakness entirely to the particular form which the movement has taken in France. It would seem, as we shall see later on, to be far more a result of national character and environment as well as of the actual conditions of French industry.

As all the world knows, the chief power in the French Labour movement is the Confédération Générale du Travail. Here, too, the numbers are by no means easy to determine. The only figures on which reliance can be placed are those of the members actually contributing to the central funds of the C.G.T., *i.e.* those for whom affiliation fees are paid by the societies to which they belong. These, according to M. Jouhaux, General Secretary of the C.G.T., number 450,000.[2]

[1] 977,350 is the figure based by Levine on the official figures for 1910, making the necessary deductions for agricultural workers, etc. But it still includes many *syndicats jaunes*, which are not fighting organisations.

[2] See L. Jouhaux, *Le Syndicalisme Français*, 1913, p. 9.

But contributions are paid very irregularly, and M. Jouhaux reckons that the actual number of members is over 600,000. Mr. Levine, on the other hand, puts it at only 357,814 for 1910.[1] This, however, refers to actual paying members, of whom M. Pouget tells us there were 295,000 actually paying into the section of Federations in 1909.[2] If, then, M. Jouhaux's figures are reliable, and there is little reason for believing that they are not, the C.G.T. has, in the last few years, grown considerably in effective membership, and we shall not be wrong in putting its effective force at quite 500,000. When the non-fighting *syndicats* are deducted from the estimated total of rather under a million, this leaves not very many organised workers outside the C.G.T. It is indeed significant that, in spite of the continual disputes that have divided the C.G.T. into two hostile groups, there has been only one secession, that of the *Cheminots de l'Est* (Eastern Railwaymen), who alone of the dissentient 'Reformist' *syndicats* split off in 1909 after Niel's resignation of the post of secretary. The very fact that the C.G.T. has held together so firmly shows that it is not merely the misguided body of fanatics some detractors would have us believe. But before we pass judgment we must examine its policy, and to do this it is necessary to go back a little.

We have seen that the history of the French movement lacks the continuity which is peculiarly characteristic of our own. Labour organisations were, like all particular associations, wholly suppressed in 1791 by the Loi Chapelier, which, aiming at destroying the old 'campagnonnage' and the revolutionary

[1] L. Levine, *The Labour Movement in France*.

[2] The *Bourses* formerly paid the C.G.T. so much per *syndicat* affiliated, and therefore their membership was often unknown.

clubs headed by Marat, put its ban in a form which
prohibited reconstruction. In this, the revolutionary
leaders no doubt conceived that they were carrying
out Rousseau's ban on particular associations, and
looked forward to liberty, equality, and fraternity
in industry as well as in politics. But theories and
laws were alike powerless against the logic of facts,
and, in spite of prohibitions, trade associations continued to exist and even multiplied. It is unnecessary
here to follow the early struggles of Labour through
the period of repression under Napoleon or through
the subsequent period of the Restoration. The
Revolution of 1848, in Paris, at any rate, made a
clean sweep of the past, and a new start was made.
A wave of co-operation passed over France, and when
it had died down a new 'syndical' movement began
to arise. From 1864, Napoleon III. attempted a
conciliatory policy, and the *syndicats*, though not
legalised, were freely tolerated. The Commune of
1871 in the main affected only Paris, and as soon
as the period of repression was past, the *syndicats*
reappeared, and began to grow in strength. Up to
this time, however, they remained purely local in
character, and no attempt was made to co-ordinate
their scattered activities. There was a stirring of
working-class feeling; but there was no formulated
policy and no national movement.[1]

The history of modern Trade Unionism in France
really begins with the passing of Waldeck-Rousseau's
law legalising the *syndicats* in 1884. This law, which
is to France what those of 1871 and 1876 are to
England, at once gave the *syndicats* a fair measure
of freedom, and left them at liberty to follow the

[1] For the history of the Labour movement in France, see
Levine, *op. cit.*

natural lines of development. Until the question of Trade Unionism among State servants and teachers came to the front a few years ago, the law of 1884 had provided a fair working basis. And, if the matter is now reopened, there is no suggestion of going back on what was then granted. It is inevitable that State servants should in time win the full right to combine. The whole dispute does not touch the principle on which the law rests, and indeed only arises out of an attempt to remove an anomaly.

The law of 1884 prepared the way for a more open form of organisation than had been possible during the period of mere toleration after the Commune. The first Labour Congress had been held at Paris in 1876, and from that time there had been congresses almost annually. The third, held in 1879, had even declared for Socialism; but this had led to a split on the part of the moderates in 1880. Up to 1886 the Congresses had little industrial importance; they were mainly meeting-points of the various schools of Socialist thought headed by Jules Guesde, Brousse, and Allemane. In 1886, however, a general congress of *syndicats* met to express its dissatisfaction with the new law, largely with the clause compelling registration of all unions. It resulted in the foundation of a National Federation of *Syndicats*, which soon fell into the hands of the followers of Guesde, and became a mere tool of the *Parti Ouvrier Français*, a pure Marxist body. It was prevented from gaining industrial importance by its lack of any national organisation by industries or of any effective local unity, and in the eyes of the political leaders it seems to have been mainly a vote-catching device. In 1887 the first really important move was made by the foundation of the Paris *Bourse du Travail* or

'Chamber of Labour', soon followed by the opening of several others. These first *Bourses du Travail*, which were founded by, or with the help of, the municipalities, aimed at being for Labour what Chambers of Commerce are for the employer, general meeting-places and centres of organisation for the locality. Municipal subsidies were secured, partly as election bribes, but far more because the *Bourses* were to serve as Labour Exchanges for unorganised as well as for organised Labour. In 1892 the *Bourses* held their first congress, and in 1893 formed the *Fédération des Bourses du Travail*. Before this, the question of the General Strike had begun to agitate the world of Labour. In 1888, in spite of Guesdist influence, the National Federation of *Syndicats* voted in favour of the principle of the General Strike, and, in the years following, the Allemanists, who dominated the *Bourses du Travail*, also declared for it. In 1893 disputes led to the closing of the Paris *Bourse* by the Government, and working-class feeling became much more bitter. In 1894, in face of the opposition of Guesde, the National Federation of *Syndicats* was amalgamated with the Federation of *Bourses*, while, in 1895, seven hundred *syndicats* formed themselves definitely into the C.G.T. A rival central organisation, founded by the Guesdists, soon perished.

There were thus two separate national organisations in the field: the Federation of *Bourses*, which depended on a purely local bond of union, and made no attempt to organise by industries beyond the local *syndicat*; and the *Confédération Générale du Travail*, which was still little more than a Trade Union Congress with a standing committee. The years that followed were spent in useless bickerings and fruitless reconciliations between the two. The C.G.T. continued throughout to be very weak: it could get no subscriptions from its affiliated *syndicats*, and, without funds, remained impotent. The F.B.T., on the other hand, grew and prospered. In 1892 there were ten *Bourses*; in 1894 there were thirty-four; in 1902 there were already ninety-six, of which eighty-three were in the Federation. Pelloutier, the inspiring director of the movement, went so far as to estimate the membership at 250,000; but this was certainly an exaggeration. At last in 1902 the Federation of *Bourses* and the C.G.T. coalesced, and formed the organisation which is now known to all as the C.G.T.

This early history is important for the understanding of the modern movement, which has been all along very much dominated by its origin. Effective labour organisation in France sprang, in fact, wholly from the *Bourses du Travail*. Attempts to organise nationally had all been signal failures, and it was not until the device of local organisation was hit upon that concerted action became in any degree possible. *Syndicat* in France still means a *local* union—there are at the present day only four national *syndicats*—and the sense of corporate individuality has always been very strong in the localities. The *Bourses* therefore to some extent succeeded, by working on local feeling, in doing what all other forms of labour organisation had failed to do. The *Fédération des Bourses* was, from the very moment of its foundation, the pivot of the whole movement. When, therefore, unity was at last achieved, it was above all important that the work of Fernand Pelloutier should not be wasted, and that the *Bourse*, while joining the C.G.T., should preserve its individuality and its place in the movement. At the same time, concerted and harmonious working had to be secured.

The moment of the union was itself opportune. Between 1899 and 1902, Waldeck-Rousseau's ministry, including the Socialist, Millerand, was engaged upon a programme of social reform. In 1899 a project to amend the law of 1884 by the grant of further recognition to the *Syndicats* was introduced, and the *Conseil Supérieur du Travail* was reorganised. In 1900 came the Councils of Labour and the new arbitration project. All these measures, save the *Conseil Supérieur*, aroused strong opposition, and working-class feeling was stirred up. In 1902, therefore, Labour was more awake than ever before, and the well-meant Radical efforts at ' social peace ' had succeeded in doing more than they bargained for. The long period of probation left Labour with a developed theory of action. It had not grown up merely in the air, and at every point it had created its own instruments of expression. With the completion of the structure in 1902 the time was ripe for testing its power. Thenceforward we have Syndicalism in practice, the conscious attempt to wield the weapon ; there is still need to improve it, but in the main the emphasis passed from organisation to action. Pelloutier, the master-mind of the *Bourses*, had been concerned chiefly with their organisation ; MM. Pouget, Griffuelhes and Jouhaux, the present leaders of the C.G.T., and even M. Lagardelle, its theorist, are interested mainly in encouraging and directing its action. The change is clearest in M. Sorel, who passed from a theoretical work, *L'Avenir Socialiste des Syndicats* to *Réflexions sur la Violence* with their vehement denunciation of theory and insistence on the need for continual and unremitting activity. The history of the last ten years is therefore at once more interesting and less easy to follow than what precedes it : practice never runs so smoothly as theory, and in order to discover the general character of the movement we are forced back upon the more recent statements of the theorists, who, generalising from the facts, present a synopsis of the movement as a whole.

The historical method is further impossible because, in action, the organisation preserves and intensifies its local character. Except in a few clearly national industries, such as mines and railways, the locality remains always the centre of feeling and action. It would therefore be impossible, as well as useless, to trace the history of all the strikes in which the C.G.T. has engaged. There will be cause to mention a few ; but generally it need only be said that the official figures of strikes show a great increase about this time in the numbers involved.

Up to 1902, as we have seen, the C.G.T. had been practically impotent. It had spent its time in financial troubles, in conflicts and temporary reconciliations with the *Fédération des Bourses*, and in hopeless attempts to assert itself as the real head of the Labour movement, but it had been clear all along that the *Bourses* still retained all the power and were the natural organs of labour organisation. The report of the *Comité Fédéral* of the C.G.T. in 1902 frankly confessed its weakness. " It has progressed only very slowly and has existed with difficulty on an income of a few hundred francs. Its propaganda has been practically non-existent, and its results insignificant ". In fact, the lack of an organisation by localities, a *lien local*, was fatal to it not only financially, but in all its work. A local unit is the first necessity of French labour organisation.

During the same period, the *Fédération des Bourses*

had grown and flourished. Internally, the *Bourses* had developed and placed themselves on a sound footing, and mushroom growths had been discouraged by the Federation. They had, indeed, still to weather the financial crises caused by the withdrawal of municipal subsidies ; but the tendency was already to much greater militancy, and the spirit of the modern C.G.T. lived in them before its time.

The amalgamation of these two bodies gave the Labour movement what it needed : a single strong organisation embracing both the local and the occupational units. The old Guesdist *syndicats* and the old C.G.T. had been impotent industrially for lack of local unity; and even the *Fédération des Bourses* had found its range of action circumscribed and its activities mutilated for lack of centralisation in particular industries. It was the purpose of the new organisation to secure twice over the membership of every *syndicat*, to get it to join both its local *Bourse du Travail*, and the Federation of its industry. The Statutes of the C.G.T. (I. 3) put this point plainly : " No *Syndicat* will be able to form a part of the C.G.T. if it is not federated nationally and an adherent of a *Bourse du Travail* or a local or departmental Union of *Syndicats* grouping different associations ". Thus, M. Lagardelle explains, the two sections will correct each other's point of view : national federation of industries will prevent parochialism (*localisme*), and local organisation will check the corporate or ' Trade Union ' spirit. The workers will learn at once the solidarity of all workers in a locality and that of all workers in a trade, and, in learning this, they will learn at the same time the complete solidarity of the whole working-class.

The new C.G.T. therefore organised itself in two sections : it was as important to maintain the distinction as to secure equal and harmonious working. Each section keeps its separate existence and has its own central committee : at regular intervals the committees meet together as a *Comité Confédéral*. Complete autonomy remains with each section ; but as they have been mainly in the same hands, there has been no friction, and, up to the present, the C.G.T. has been the model of a perfectly functioning federal council. It is true that the intention of the Statutes has not been perfectly carried out : many *syndicats* belong to *Bourses* and not to an Industrial Federation, and there are some of which the reverse is true. But all along the tendency has been towards the completing of this double relation, and, so far as action is concerned, the C.G.T. has worked as if the organisation were complete.

It is now time to examine it in more detail. Its intention is, throughout, federal. "At every stage", writes M. Pouget. "the autonomy of the organism is complete. . . . The co-ordination arises naturally, beginning from the bottom. To popular sovereignty syndicalism opposes the rights of individuals". It is very important to realise the emphasis French Syndicalism lays on starting from the bottom. At every stage, it asserts the right of the individual (*syndicat, Bourse* or *Fédération d'Industrie*) to the greatest possible autonomy : and it holds that, in so doing, it is following the line of natural growth. The development by the working-class of institutions of its own, what M. Lagardelle calls ' Socialism of Institutions ', is far more really the central point of its philosophy than any Bergsonian *élan vital*. To the wider aspect of this question we shall have to return later on : at present we need only notice that the federal principle is expressed at every stage of the organisation.

At the bottom, the real and vital foundation of the whole fabric, we have the class-conscious proletarian, who is less the raw material of the organisation than himself its first and most vital organ. He is a member directly only of his *syndicat*, the local association of his trade, within which it is still possible for the members to keep adequate check on their representatives. Beyond membership of his *syndicat*, the workman has no direct ties: the unit at the next stage is the *syndicat* itself, which should become a part locally of its *Bourse du Travail* and nationally or regionally of its Industrial Federation. Here first we encounter the group principle in action. Just as each individual *syndiqué*, whatever his personal character, counted in the *syndicat* as one and no more, so each *syndicat*, whatever its character or membership, counts, in the *Bourse* or Federation, as one and no more. The *syndicat* is now the individual and counts as such. The principle is the same at the next stage: each *Bourse* or each Federation has its representative on its section of the C.G.T. itself or on the combined *Comité Confédéral*. Only in the Annual Congress the *syndicat* becomes once more the unit, and each is entitled to its single representative.

We have already given our reasons for estimating the total strength of the C.G.T. at between 500,000 and 600,000, and made some comment on the apparent smallness of this figure. It should be realised at the outset that this weakness does not mean that the C.G.T. represents only a small section of the really organised workers in France, but that the organised workers themselves form only a small section of the industrial population. In proportion to the whole number of really organised workers, as many adhere in France to the C.G.T. as in England to any of the three central bodies.[1] The weakness then is that of the whole Trade Union movement in France, and not of the C.G.T. within the movement. It may of course still be due to the policy of the C.G.T., but in that case it seems remarkable that a rival organisation has not grown up outside it. The C.G.T. is not yet old enough to make a rival impossible, especially in France, where organisations are born and die with equal facility. It is far more natural to trace the weakness of the French movement first to a national disinclination for combination; secondly, to the tendency to keep 'friendly society' activities outside the Unions, and thirdly to the character of French industry. For French industrial life is not, and still more was not when the modern Labour movement arose, by any means so complicated as ours in England. It preserves a more local character, and, on the whole, the number of small masters is very large. Aggregation in large factories undoubtedly tends to create strong labour organisations; and the scattered nature of much French industry goes a long way towards accounting for the weakness of Trade Unionism. It is a further sign of this that Unionism is strongest and most centralised just where 'trustified' industry has won the day. With the growth of centralisation in French industry the *syndicats* will certainly grow stronger.

However, the Reformist party within the C.G.T. is fond of pointing to its weakness as proving the futility of its revolutionary policy. Jules Guesde has said:

[1] In 1911, the Labour Party had 1,394,402 Trade Union members, the Trade Union Congress 1,645,507, and the General Federation of Trade Unions 750,000. They have all increased since then; the 1913 Trade Union Congress was representative of 2,250,000 workers.

"What classes—and judges—Syndicalism as a part of the world movement is its lack of members"; but a very different view is taken by the actual leaders of the C.G.T. M. Pouget, for instance, writes with satisfaction : "It is just because the *syndicats* possess this purely 'fighting' character that they have not yet attracted the crowds of workers of whom foreign organisations are so proud". Numerical weakness is on this showing itself a source of strength; and the argument might carry more weight were not those who use it always prompt to chronicle their own increases. In this country, where immense numbers of Trade Unionists are attracted merely by 'benefits', it may be, on reflection, a surprise that the French *syndicats* have been able, almost without benefits, to attract half a million members. Very few of our Unions, except in highly skilled trades, could preserve their stability on low contributions, and purely for the purpose of industrial warfare. The figures point to a greater, rather than a less, development of class-consciousness in France than in this country, where the question of separating 'friendly' from 'fighting' contributions is only just beginning, with the rise of the Greater Unionism, to attain to real importance. In France, the dispute is as old as Proudhon.

In 1908, M. Pouget claimed that, out of 5500 real *syndicats ouvriers*, 3500 were in one or other section of the C.G.T., and that many of the rest were *jaunes*; i.e. *syndicats* run by the employers in the interests of industrial peace. At this time only 2600 *syndicats* were included in the Section of Federations, but it was estimated that 900 more belonged only to *Bourses du Travail*. Even this force, however, would be no more than a 'conscious minority', able to succeed in industrial movements only by carrying the unorganised along with it ; and it is because they recognise this that the leaders try to make the best of a bad job, of what one of them calls the "sheepish apathy" of the working-class, and therefore to pride themselves on being such a minority.

We cannot be too careful to make the meaning of this theory clear to ourselves. M. Pouget goes so far as to say : " There is for the conscious minority an *obligation* to act, without paying any attention to the refractory mass, on pain of being forced to bend the neck with those who are unconscious ". Action, class-consciousness in practice, is made not merely a right, but a duty : the conscious minority is represented as creating the society of the future, and therefore as having a right and an obligation to speak for the whole working-class and not merely for itself. The ' tyranny of Trade Unions ' is thus resolved into justifiable and necessary leadership, by which the way is shown to the more backward brethren. That this is in fact the manner in which French strikes are run seems beyond doubt ; for the French, if they organise with difficulty on a permanent basis, are, as M. Griffuelhes[1] says, peculiarly liable to those "passing fits of anger", those *colères passagères*, which seem to suit the temper of the Latin races. The minority does seem, in a large number of cases, to be able to lead the majority ; for instance, it is estimated by M. Lagardelle that in 1905 nearly a million workers joined in the agitation for an eight hours' day. But this power does not justify rejoicing over weakness on the part of the C.G.T. It may be better for some purposes not to have in the Unions a majority intent only on benefits ; but even

[1] In his interesting *Voyage Révolutionnaire*, which gives much the best idea of the real state of the Labour movement in France.

if we grant this enormous supposition, the main thing is still to turn the conscious minority into a majority, and to despair of doing so is to despair of the human race. It is over the sacrifices and changes involved in getting this majority that Revolutionaries and Reformists most often join battle.

This theory of the rights of minorities has had further curious developments in the constitution of the C.G.T. We have seen that its organisers have been at pains in every case to seek out the true 'individual' and make it the unit of action and representation, and that in consequence every *syndicat*, whatever its size, is represented at Congress by a single delegate. By this means, it is urged, the formation of new units is encouraged, and power is prevented from falling into the hands of single large and powerful Federations, as, for instance, the Miners dominate our Trade Union Congress. With that instructive example before us, we can hardly fail to give the French system a measure of sympathy. It was, however, estimated by a writer in the Reformist organ, *L'Ouvrier Textile*, that delegates representing 22,000 voters may command an absolute majority in conferences representing hundreds of thousands. Again, M. Guérard wrote in *L'Humanité* that at Amiens in 1906, where 200,000 *syndiqués* were represented, 45,000 commanded a majority of the votes. Of course, it is not to be supposed that the parties are ever really divided in this fashion: the figures represent merely a conceivable and not an actually possible situation. But the Reformist section is never weary of insisting that, overwhelmingly as it is always defeated in the voting at Congress, it has none the less a majority behind it in the country. Again, the Confederal Committee of the C.G.T. is composed of one representative for each Federation of isolated *syndicat*. Thus, the *Fédération des Blanchisseurs* with 80 members and the *Fédération du Textile* with 20,000 have each one vote, and a local *Syndicat* with 20 members is represented by its delegate just as much as the *Syndicat National des Chemins de Fer*, with 45,000. As this committee elects the General Secretary and has the supreme control, this form of representation is significant. M. Niel, the Reformist Secretary of the C.G.T., wrote of his party in May 1909, when he tendered his resignation, " It is necessary for them to conquer in the Confederal Committee the majority which they already possess in the country ". M. Pouget, on the other hand, estimates that two-thirds of the whole strength of the C.G.T. are Revolutionaries. It is not the case, as we might expect, that all the small *syndicats* are Revolutionary and all the large ones Reformist : at Amiens the Railway Workers with 24,000 and the *Fédération du Livre* with 10,000 members were Reformist ; but the Metal Workers and the Marine Workers with 14,000 and 12,000 were both Revolutionary. Again, the two largest Federations stand on opposite sides, the *Fédération du Bâtiment* with about 40,000 members being among the most Revolutionary, and the Miners, who number over 30,000, Reformist. On the whole, it seems probable that, while the system of voting doubtless favours the Revolutionaries, the change produced by Proportional Representation, which the Reformists demand, would not be great enough to reverse the position of the parties. Reformism may be gaining ground : it has certainly not yet conquered the majority.

It may be indeed that the position of the Reformists

is weakened by the little interest many of them take in federal doings. At Marseilles in 1908 the Miners though entitled to 58, only sent 37 delegates, the Railwaymen only 73 out of 269, the *Fédération du Livre* 50 out of 167. With the single exception of the *Cheminots de l'Est*, they remain members of the C.G.T.; but they are content to take little part, save when it suits them, in a policy they cannot control.

M. Lagardelle has put the case against the Reformists in an epigram. "*Le Réformisme ne voit dans le réformisme que la réforme.*" For him, the 'corporate' or 'Trade Union' spirit is "the end of all idealism"; it denies solidarity, and creates a "working-class aristocracy" which "only makes corporate egoism more bitter". On its own showing, Reformism aims only at the direct improvement of the condition of labour, and not at any catastrophic overthrow of the whole capitalist régime by direct syndical action. It is opposed to the General Strike and Sabotage, and, as it aims at making its own terms with the masters, its policy comes into immediate conflict with that of the Revolutionaries on the question of industrial agreements. The Revolutionaries are as a rule against all *paix sociale*, against anything that is more than a mere suspension of hostilities with their natural enemy, the employer; in theory they repudiate all agreements, and in practice they at least claim that no agreement be concluded for more than a year at the longest, and reserve to themselves the right to break every undertaking on the first favourable opportunity.[1] For the

[1] The motion of Griffuelhes at Amiens in 1906 (carried by 830 votes to 8) puts the official view of the function the C.G.T. has to perform. "In the work of everyday demand,

Reformists, the strike is only a *pis aller* ; for the Revolutionaries, it is at once the method of the Social Revolution and the most powerful instrument of working-class education. Occasionally, as in 1905, the two parties find a satisfactory common programme ; both are equally interested in the shortening of the hours of labour, and accordingly they combined readily in the eight hours' campaign. But even here the concord was short. In M. Pouget's view, " The formula ' Conquest of the Eight Hours' Day ' has not a narrow and rigidly concrete sense ; it is a platform of action which broadens out till it embraces all the conditions of labour ", " an educative formula ". M. Lagardelle is still more explicit and calls it " a perfect platform for extending the notion of the class-war to all workers ". " In the struggle for the eight hours' day ", he writes, " the eight hours were often forgotten, and the class-war alone remembered ". Between two such parties there can as yet be no permanent accord : either the *syndicat* is to be the mere weapon of material advancement within the capitalist system, or it is to be the fighting and organising unit of the whole working-class.

It may seem that in Great Britain we have reached on the question a fair, working compromise, while in Germany the question has not even arisen. But, in this country at least, a cleavage that is not merely between the ' common sense ' and the ' impossibilist ' sections does seem to be springing up, and it is becoming of greater importance to under-

Syndicalism pursues the co-ordination of working-class efforts and the increase of the well-being of labour by the realisation of immediate improvements. . . . But this task is only one side of the work of Syndicalism ; it prepares entire emancipation, which can only be realised by capitalist expropriation ".

stand the practical side of a revolutionary Trade Union programme. As has been the case in France, the conflict is bound to become more bitter between these two sections whenever the question of industrial arbitration comes to the front. It is round the question of ' agreements ' that ' Revolutionary ' and ' Reformist ' are always bound to come to blows ; and it was the social legislation of M. Millerand that first gave rise to the quarrel in France. It is, for the understanding of the actual situation, important to realise that the C.G.T. gives no orders and is a purely advisory body. *Syndicats* that are in disagreement with its policy may therefore continue members of it without conforming to its views, just as Mr. Havelock Wilson, though an advocate of compulsory arbitration, can go as a delegate to the Trade Union Congress here. This course of action is, in fact, freely followed by such Federations as the Textile Workers and the *Livre*, as well as by the National *Syndicat* of Miners. The general view of the C.G.T. on such a matter does not secure a uniform practice. Even the Revolutionary section has not been able to maintain in practice an absolute adherence to the ' No Agreements ' doctrine. It has been forced instead to assert its clear right to break any and every agreement at will ; but, as the policy would be suicidal in practice, it in fact often makes agreements and sticks to them. The ' collective contract ' has in the past few years made considerable progress in France.

Naturally, the Revolutionary or Reformist character of a *syndicat* or Federation reacts as well as depends on its internal organisation. The Revolutionary bodies are, as a rule, guerilla forces, burdened with as little as possible beyond their actual fighting equipment, and not much concerned with the 'friendly' aspect of Unionism. The Reformists, on the other hand, tend to levy higher contributions, and to pay more attention to 'benefits'. The predominance of the Revolutionary section is largely accounted for by the extreme reluctance of French workers to pay high contributions, and, though the recent tendency has been in nearly every industry to raise these, the leaders have always to face the greatest reluctance on the part of the rank and file to accept the slightest increase. Consequently, there is in most *syndicats* very little 'mutual aid', and generally even such as there is, is not obligatory on the members. Sickness and unemployment pay are exceptional, and even strike pay is seldom given regularly. In 1908 there were 1073 strikes, of which 837 were conducted by organised workers; but in 46 only was regular strike pay available. Of course, this deficiency is very often supplied by other means, with which we are rapidly becoming familiar in this country also: voluntary contributions are sent to the strikers from workers in other trades or districts, *soupes communistes*, such as the Taximen had in London, are often started by the *Bourses du Travail*, and the children of strikers are boarded out free in other neighbourhoods; but the poverty of the movement as a whole goes far towards accounting for the vogue of *sabotage* and the sympathetic strike, as well as for the whole idea of the *Grève Générale*. The C.G.T. itself makes no money contribution to strikes, and confines itself to advice and propagandist help. Suggestions are often made for the starting of Co-operative Societies in connection with the Unions, but there seems no likelihood that this will be done, in face of the objection to higher contributions. It is even rendered more unlikely by

LABOUR IN FRANCE

the fusion of the different French Co-operative Societies into a single body, accomplished only this year, which seems to make the final defeat of sectional Co-operation.

Each *syndicat*, we have seen, owes a double allegiance, and this allegiance is financial as well as spiritual. The contribution paid by the workman to his local *syndicat* is never less than 50 centimes (5d.) a month, and may rise as high as 4 francs (3s. 4d.); but it is more often near the lower figure than the higher. The affiliation fee to the National Federation varies from 10 centimes to 75 centimes and even to 2 francs (1d.—7$\frac{1}{2}$d.—1s. 8d.) per member monthly; but it is on an average from 10 to 60 centimes (1d. to 6d.) a month per member. Besides this, the local *syndicat* pays the *Bourse du Travail* an affiliation fee of from 10 to 40 centimes (1d. to 4d.) a month per member. The central organisation in turn exacts a double subscription; from each *Bourse du Travail* it takes 5 centimes ($\frac{1}{2}$d.) a member annually, and from each Federation or National *Syndicat* 60 centimes (6d.) monthly for every hundred members, which works out at nearly $\frac{3}{4}$d. a year per member. Thus the central body, as well as most of the Federations, is very weak financially: in the years 1906-8 the total income of the section of *Bourses* was 16,000 francs (£640), and that of the section of Federations 24,700 francs (£988), and both these sums represented an increase on previous years. It will be seen, then, that for the most part the movement gets along without resources, and depends for its efficiency on anything rather than the money-bags which play so great a part in British Trade Unionism. The workers, in most cases, regard the *syndicat* purely as a fighting organisation, and therefore many of the less adventurous refrain from joining. The mobility of a force that has nothing to lose is obviously much increased, and strikes become very much easier to arouse; but, as a rule, such strikes are short and sharp, and do not extend over very wide areas. In such a case, even if no victory is won, defeat matters comparatively little from a material point of view. It must, however, be admitted that such organisations dissolve as easily as they arise, and that a single disaster may therefore be sometimes more fatal to them than to our long-established Unions with vested interests to preserve.

In a few cases, the position is very different. The members of the *Fédération du Livre* have long paid in two francs monthly, and the contribution has recently been slightly increased. But in return for this they receive strike pay of 3.50 francs a day for thirteen weeks, sick and unemployed benefit at the rate of two francs a day for a maximum of thirty-six days a year, and *viaticum*, or travelling allowance when in search of work. The Textile Workers, again, pay one franc a month and get strike pay at the rate of two francs a day. But these are exceptional cases, and where we find this form of organisation we find also the Reformist spirit. While the C.G.T. agitated for an eight hours' day in 1906, the *Fédération du Livre* spent 600,000 francs on a partially successful campaign for a day of nine hours. A curious case is that of the *Fédération du Bâtiment*, which has the highest dues after the *Livre*, and is none the less of the revolutionary party.

On the whole, we can still say without hesitation that the spirit of French Trade Unionism is against high contributions. The *syndicat* still generally regards itself as a fighting unit, and is prepared to fight without funds. In 1908, out of 5500 *syndicats*, only just over one thousand had ' *Caisses de Secours Mutuel* ' and only 743 unemployment funds. The intrusion of 'friendly' purposes into the *syndicats* is widely feared as the beginning of the end of their fighting spirit. "In France", writes M. Pouget, "we do not scorn mutual aid, which is the primary form of solidarity, but we keep it outside the *syndicat*". "In strikes", he says elsewhere, "the financial support is in great measure due to voluntary subscriptions". The official view is that the *syndicats* should not be overcharged with purposes other than those of resistance, and that '*Mutuellisme syndical*' is "fatal to the forward march of the whole proletariat". On the other side, the '*syndicats mixtes*' of the North do not touch questions of wages, and are solely occupied with *mutualité* ('friendly' activities).

It is disputable how far this fighting character of the French *syndicats*, coupled with their light contributions, has the effect of keeping down numbers. It is certain that in Belgium the effect of raising the contributions was a great increase of members, and that in both England and Germany vast numbers are drawn into the Unions almost solely by the desire to participate in 'benefits'. If we do not argue at once from these analogies to the French case, it is because we cannot be certain that the actual state of affairs is not rather a result than a cause, and does not in fact answer better the real needs of the French character. It is unsafe to argue that, because a method clearly suits England, it must necessarily suit France also. French Syndicalism has its peculiarly national character, and, however much we may be influenced by it in England, its most national characteristics are bound to be left behind. These peculiarities are individual and particular; but, while we may discard them in forming our own national doctrine, it is our business, if we wish to follow the French movement, to understand them in a spirit as little insular as possible.

The quarrel of Revolutionaries and Reformists, which in industrial action centres as a rule around the question of high and low contributions, has another side that we cannot afford to omit. With it are bound up all the varied aspects of the problem of State intervention. In Syndicalist denunciations, 'corporatism' and 'interventionism' are frequently coupled together. Both are, according to M. Pouget, "rampant within the C.G.T. itself". It is, Syndicalists declare, the obvious purpose of the capitalistic State to defeat revolutionary aims by the granting of more or less illusory social reforms, of which the legislation of M. Millerand forms the classical example. Joint boards of employers and employees, it is said, mix the classes, and make for an unreal *paix sociale*, which is the object of bourgeois Radicals like Waldeck-Rousseau. Compulsory insurance and compulsory arbitration are alike opposed on these grounds: the General Committee of the C.G.T., reporting on the arbitration question, said that "in parliamentarising the strike the governing classes would kill the legitimate spirit of revolt which animates the workers". Of other proposals, M. Pouget declares that "the Government is minded to grant the *syndicats* powers of jurisdiction and trading in the hope of drawing them into the capitalist 'sphere'".

This controversy has two aspects. First, the Syndicalists are at war with the regular Reformists, who wish to secure improvements in the conditions of labour by means of legislation. They are also at war with that section which desires closer co-operation between the *syndicats* and the Socialist Party, and looks forward to the conquest of the *pouvoirs publics* as the means of establishing the new society. Against the first, we have seen, they advance the view that peaceful settlement not only leaves the worker no better off materially, but also kills the spirit of revolt which animates him. Against the second, a further line of argument is necessary. " To-day ", writes M. Lagardelle, " men believe less and less in the creative force of the State and the magic power of Parliamentarism ". " *La lutte de classe ne peut être menée que sur le terrain de classe* ". The State is thought of as a bourgeois institution, to which it is vain to look for help. " It is the business of Syndicalism ", M. Lagardelle writes, " to be self-sufficient ".

All the same, the *syndicats* do not wholly repudiate government intervention. They insist rather that it shall intervene under compulsion and as the inferior party. " Useful laws can be won by Direct Action " is their guiding principle, and M. Sorel has written in his *Réflexions sur la Violence* that "the determining factor in politics is the poltroonery of the Government ". This method of compelling intervention we find pursued in a series of agitations. In 1902 begins the agitation for the monopoly of *placement* (Labour Exchange work) and inspection, resulting in 1903 in the closing by the Government of the private Labour Exchanges—which, it is true, were often able to open again under other names. Shortly afterwards, a similar campaign was started in favour of State technical instruction, and the classical example is, of course, the agitation for an eight hours' day in 1905-6. Since the arrest of M. Griffuelhes and others in 1906, relations with the Government have been too strained for a repetition of such tactics, and the line of agitation has been more strictly professional.

A kindred and even more pressing question for the Syndicalists is the definition of the proper relation between the *syndicats* and the Socialist Party. The earlier history of French Unionism is very largely that of its gradual emancipation from undue subjection to pseudo-Marxian State Socialism. The attempts of M. Guesde to make the *syndicats* mere election agencies of the Socialists still rankle in the minds of Syndicalists, and even find their echo in the C.G.T. Congresses, where M. Renard of the Textile Federation regularly proposes reaffiliation with the Socialist Party,[1] and is as often overwhelmingly defeated. " Marx ", says M. Lagardelle, " always set over against the fatalism of capital the liberty of the proletariat. . . . Guesde ", on the other hand, " gave his conception a one-sided and rigid form, taking account only of economic necessity, and failing to recognise working-class freedom ". The Syndicalists interpret Marx's saying that " the emancipation of the workers must be the act of the workers themselves " as meaning that emancipation can only come to them organised as workers, " *en tant que producteurs* ", " *sur le terrain de classe* ". ' Class ', they hold, is a natural division, ' party ' artificial and intellectual. " Democracy mixes the classes ". And they maintain further that any party, ' Socialist ', ' Labour ', or ' Radical ', will equally lose touch with the workers and adopt the character of the *terrain* on which it is compelled to act. They quote with appreciation the works of Nietzsche: " The State, what is that ? Open your ears. The State is the coldest of monsters. It lies coldly. ' I, the State,' it says, ' I am the people '. A lie. Wherever there is a people, it does not understand the State, it detests it."

This determination to destroy the State is combined, in many writers, with a determination to use it while it exists. " Incontestably ", M. Lagardelle writes, " for its constitution and development, working-class democracy has need, a while yet, of political democracy. . . .

[1] The motion was lost by 724 votes to 34 at Amiens (1906).

But it makes use of political democracy only the better to destroy it ". Taking the view that economic power necessarily precedes and conditions political power, he regards the function of a Socialist Party in Parliament as indeed real, but as temporary and subordinate. " The party now seems only an auxiliary organism of which the usefulness is certain, but the power of action restricted." It is exceedingly difficult in reading M. Lagardelle to ascertain what is the nature of the sphere of usefulness he finds for a Socialist Party. " The task of a Socialist Party in Parliament ", he writes, " can only be to aid by legislation the work of the proletariat in organising itself autonomously ". But even to give this help effectively—and we may admit it to be the greatest service possible—seems to involve that very *conquête des pouvoirs publics* which M. Lagardelle is always denouncing so fiercely. In his view, " Syndicalism does not deny parties, but only their ability to transform the world ", and thus, even if the conquest of public power were to be accomplished, the function of a Socialist Government would still be purely auxiliary and could not of itself effect the transformation of society. " If ", M. Sorel wrote in *L'Avenir Socialiste des Syndicats*, " the workers triumphed without having accomplished the moral evolutions which are indispensable to them, their rule would be abominable and the world would be plunged again into sufferings, brutalities and injustices as great as those of the present ". And M. Lagardelle himself says that " Syndicalism has always laid it down as a principle that bourgeois institutions will be eliminated only in proportion as they are replaced by working-class institutions ". The essence of the Social Revolution is held to lie in the creation of a new set of working-class institutions and ideas. M. Lagardelle holds that " for

Marx what always differentiates social classes is to be found in their institutions and their ideology ".

It is clear that, on such a view, any party which is compelled to work within the *cadre* of bourgeois society must take on a bourgeois character and adapt itself to bourgeois institutions. " The rupture between bourgeois society and the Labour movement finds free play only in the sphere of production ". . . . " The Labour movement has no sense-organ except as it develops its own institutions at the expense of capitalist institutions ".[1] If, then, the whole Labour movement is not to be watered down into mere social reform, it is essential that it should keep itself clear of all party divisions, and insist continually on the one real division—the class-war. The efforts of the Socialist Party to recover control over the Syndicalist movement have proved fruitless ; but it is interesting, in France as in Italy, to see how far the Socialists have been prepared to go in the attempt at reconciliation. M. Lagardelle has called the ' Integralism ' of the Italian Socialist, Enrico Ferri, " an attempt to reconcile contraries ", and it is abundantly clear that the Socialist Party has generally attempted to please all parties by juxtaposing, in a single resolution, the views of every section, without any coherent attempt to work out the relations between them. At Limoges in 1906, at the Socialist Conference, M. Jaurès carried a long motion from which the following are characteristic passages :

" The Congress, convinced that the working-class will not be able to enfranchise themselves fully except by the combined force of political action and syndical action, by syndicalism going as far as the general strike, and by the conquest of the whole political power, with a view to the general expropriation of capitalism. . . .

[1] M. Lagardelle.

"Convinced that this double action will be so much the more efficacious as the political and the economic organism have their complete autonomy. . . .

"Invites the militants to do their best to dissipate all misunderstanding between the C.G.T. and the Socialist Party".

Already, the old Guesdist attempt at complete subordination of the *syndicats* to the Party is given up, and the Socialists are willing to make sacrifices even to secure a small measure of co-operation. Were the leaders of the Syndicalist movement all like M. Lagardelle, still half Socialists, such an *entente* would be difficult enough ; but when the character of most of them is taken into account, it becomes, for the present at least, unthinkable. It is obvious that M. Lagardelle's denial of the permanent character of the State is capable of being put far more strongly, and that it is only a step from the denial of the State in the future to the denial of it in the present, from the refusal to recognise its theoretical obligation to the practical refusal to have more than a necessary minimum to do with it. Syndicalism of the type favoured by M. Lagardelle passes over naturally into the Syndicalist Anarchism of MM. Pouget and Griffuelhes. We are thus led on inevitably from examining the relation of Syndicalism to the Socialist Party to study its views about the State in general.

It is one of the most frequent causes of quarrel between Revolutionaries and Reformists in the *syndicats* that the Reformists accuse their opponents of introducing anarchist politics under the pretext of taking no part in politics. Niel in his letter resigning the Secretaryship of the C.G.T., speaks of unity as the task " of those *syndicats* which no more want Anarchism than any other form of politics in the *syndicats*"; and the Reformist manifesto, signed among others by Cordier (*Mineurs*), Cleuet (*Employés*), Gervaise (*Travailleurs de l'État*), Guérard (*Chemins de Fer*), Keüfer (*Livre*), Renard (*Textile*), Thil (*Lithographie*), and Niel himself, starts the Reformist *Comité d'Union Syndicaliste* as a protest against " the introduction of anarchist politics into the *syndicats*". Already in Pelloutier the anarchist view is fully developed, and it is largely due to his influence that it still prevails widely in the C.G.T. There is an interesting French Anarchist publication addressed to the Syndicalists under the title *Aux Anarchistes qui s'ignorent*, and the professedly Anarchist section is for ever trying to capture the movement for its own purposes. The C.G.T. in its Statutes (I. 1, 2) professes to "group, outside every political school, all workers who are conscious of the class-war to agitate for the abolition of the Wage-System and the 'master-class'; and this very easily passes over into direct refusal to recognise any obligations other than those which are owed to the working-class itself. The object of Syndicalism is, in the words of M. Berth, " to refer everything to production, to subordinate to production all unproductive social functions". It is not a far cry from this to the 'Don't vote' campaign which has been started within the C.G.T. itself.

Even against those who do not belong to the Anarchist section of the C.G.T. the Reformists have a natural ground of complaint. M. Lagardelle himself is never weary of saying that " direct action is political action". Political neutrality has, he says, two senses: the neutrality the Reformists desire is corporate neutrality, which leaves each *syndicat* to make its own terms, and has no thought of overthrowing capitalist society. This is what M. Guesde calls the *'ornière corporative'* of Trade Unionism. But M. Guesde was wrong in thinking, because at the time of his ascendancy " he saw before him only moderate *syndicats*, that every *syndicat* is fated to be moderate ". The proper political neutrality of the *syndicats* ranges itself with no party in the State, but contents itself with "*sa politique propre*". The general strike is essentially a political act, having for its aim the creation of a new form of political society, answering to the new '*droit ouvrier*', the new ideology of the working-class. M. Lagardelle therefore agrees wholly with the Anarchists where the action of the *syndicats* is concerned : he differs from them when they go on to demand that the acts of individual members shall be interfered with. The '*ne pas voter*' campaign, he points out, places the Anarchists themselves on the political level; in occupying themselves with parliamentary affairs, even by way of opposition, they are neglecting their proper function of organising the class-war within the *syndicats*. The Congress of Amiens in 1906, while declaring that "syndicalism recognises neither the elector of any party nor the believer in any religious or philosophical faith", wisely left the actual members of the *syndicats* free to take what political action they pleased, provided they did not introduce politics into the *syndicats*. In spite of this, Syndicalism has enough natural affinity to Anarchism for directly anti-political tendencies to be continually showing themselves.

This has been especially the case with 'anti-militarism' and 'anti-patriotism'. The assertion of the international solidarity of the working-class passes easily into the denial of its national obligations. "The proletariat", said Marx, "has no country"; and the *Section de Bourses du Travail de la Seine* puts the same point of view more picturesquely. "The country of the workers is their own and their family's belly. . . . *La classe, c'est la patrie*". Here again, the line has been found hard to draw between neutrality and opposition, and refusal on the part of the *syndicats* to concern themselves in their corporate capacity with patriotism and militarism have passed readily into anti-patriotism and violent anti-militarism. "Don't enlist!" has been transformed successively into "Don't shoot!" and "Desert!" and the *Sou du Soldat*, which could be regarded as a harmless expression of a solidarity that cannot be interrupted by conscription, has become the most powerful weapon of direct anti-patriotism. But there seemed to be signs, till the new militaristic policy of M. Poincaré revived it, that the anti-militarist propaganda was slackening its hold, and that the recognition was spreading that such matters are not after all *questions syndicales*.

Paradoxically, the very internationalism of the French movement has sometimes brought with it the penalty of isolation. The French have been too vehemently anti-patriotic and international for the Unions of other countries, and when anti-militarism and the General Strike were definitely refused a place on the agenda of the International Trade Union Conference, the C.G.T. refused to take any part in it, though they have since made up the quarrel. In the minds of French Syndicalists, *patrie* and *propriété* are inseparable ideas: the State and the army are there to protect property, and must be swept out of the way before property can be abolished.

Adopting this attitude towards the State, the C.G.T. is led, naturally, not only to place all its reliance on

Direct Action by the workers themselves in their organisations, but also to attribute to this Direct Action a quite peculiar meaning. Direct Action is for them at once a great educative influence and the actual method of capitalist expropriation. It has therefore taken on an almost religious aspect, and has felt the need of providing itself with a theology. The dogma of the General Strike is the formulation of the philosophy of Direct Action in a popular and compelling manner. The General Strike is presented as historically in the future; but the workers are meant to recognise in it the type of the strikes of the present. " The Revolution ", writes M. Pouget, " is no longer considered as a catastrophe destined to break out some near or distant day; it is conceived as an act realised every day ". And similarly M. Berth says : " The catastrophe, according to the *syndicats*, will not be the mystic Revolution, automatic and idle, but the supreme effort of working-class action coming to crown a long series of patient and toilsome efforts ". Every strike is more or less general, and the same conception embraces all : from the petty strike in a single workshop to the local, regional, national and international general strikes, all are touched with something of the glamour which attaches to the one great ' social general strike ' in which is envisaged the complete overthrow of capitalist society. It is not necessary to go into the complicated theory of social myths and the analogy of the Second Coming which M. Sorel has woven round the conception of the General Strike : we are concerned only to notice how extraordinarily compelling the idea is, how, with al' its catastrophic completeness, it still retains tha ' everydayness ' which is necessary for a good propagandist doctrine.

The General Strike that is realised daily is then one in idea with the Direct Action of the French Labour movement. M. Pouget tells us that " this conception of the strike gives to conflicts a growing bitterness of class-warfare "; that in every strike the workers seem to see the Social Revolution foreshadowed. But this does not prevent them from making on capital temporary and provisional demands. The General Strike, we are told, " has its reformist aspect ". It has the double function of restoring the class-structure of society which democracy obliterates, and of procuring the improvement of the lot of the working-class. From the Syndicalist point of view, failure in either of these respects would destroy the value of this Direct Actionism. Unless the strike has a revolutionary aim extending beyond mere Reformism, it is the end of idealism, and can at any rate be no substitute for Parliamentary Action. If, on the other hand, it is purely revolutionary and secures for the workers no temporary advantages, it is equally useless; for in that case it would be impossible not only to organise a majority of the workers in the *syndicats*, but also ever to persuade the unorganised to go on strike. The C.G.T. depends on winning partial advantages for its power to lead as a conscious minority.

With the advocacy of the General Strike is coupled by many of the leaders that of *Sabotage*. This form of Direct Action is as a rule very ill understood; and in fact the name is used to cover several distinct methods. *Sabotage* in the most general sense means the use of any and every weapon against the master-class. The strike in France not taking the form of a trial of depth between purses, the ' strike with folded arms '[1] is naturally supplemented by other means.

[1] *La grève aux bras croisés.*

Industrial disputes are regarded as definitely acts in an unbroken war with the employers; and it is held that, just as all agreements may be broken, all canons of right and wrong may in such cases be disregarded. Bourgeois morality may proclaim certain acts to be offences against society; but there is no need for the working-class to take any notice of bourgeois ideas. They are, it is said, working out a new morality of their own, a half-Nietzschean, half-Anarchist morality of revolt which throws aside the old 'slave-morality'. Theoretically, all means that are expedient are held to be justified; and, if in practice this does not amount to very much, it is a theory that is at any moment capable of development.[1] The importance of *sabotage* seems even to be declining as the organisations grow older. M. Jouhaux, the present Secretary of the C.G.T., explaining the dangers of using it blindly, says that it is only " incidental " and that it should only be used when circumstances demand it. *Sabotage* may then be regarded as a characteristic, though subordinate, method of the Labour organisations in France and as the outcome of French methods of industrial warfare. But underneath this one name, many things are only superficially unified. *Sabotage* may take a number of forms, varying from the ' Ca' canny ' of Scottish invention to violent destruction of the instruments of production, which is more in harmony with American methods. The motto " a bad day's work for a bad day's pay ",[2] in itself not so revolutionary, may be extended to cover any act from slacking to dynamiting; but in itself it implies no such extension. There is all the difference in the world

---

[1] Just as the militant Suffragists, being wronged by Society, hold themselves free to make war on it.

[2] A mauvaise paye, mauvais travail.

between the 'stop in' strike—the refusal to work more than so many hours unaccompanied by actual stoppage—and such acts as destroying machinery; and again between such an attack on property and the wrecking of trains, which is an attack on life. The herding of all these dissimilar courses of action under a single name is fruitful of misunderstanding. At one extreme, men may, to secure a shorter day, work so slowly as to make long hours unprofitable; they may even, for the same end, follow the classic example of the Paris barbers, who shaved the entire heads of all customers who appeared after what they demanded should be closing time; they may, with a less savage humour, imitate the Italian railwaymen, and hold up all trains by literal obedience to all regulations. All such acts, even those of the second class, which are rare, are a very different matter from the actual destruction of machinery or life. It is quite possible for a worker to put into a machine something that will put it out of action, or to take away a vital piece of it in his pocket; and by this means, it is possible to prevent blacklegs from being used to break a strike. It is even possible to proceed to more wholesale methods of destruction, and all these methods may be used either as alternatives or as helps to a stoppage. But the whole of this last class, besides being usually inexpedient, is either on the border-line of justifiability or entirely outside it. In America, where industrial methods are always brutal, such acts are often justified; but in a civilised country, certain canons of civilised warfare should be observed on both sides.

A particularly interesting form of *sabotage* is that by which work is done slowly, but very well. The journal of the Building trade, *Le Travailleur du Bâtiment*, recommends it to the workers in these words: "*Camarades, sabotons bien les heures du travail, en faisant de l'art dans nos métiers respectifs*". This appeal to commit *sabotage* against the jerry-builder, "by turning out art in their respective trades", is one which, could it be organised, would be open to no complaints on social grounds. It, in fact, meets the complaint made by the theorists of Syndicalism, MM. Sorel and Berth, that most forms of *sabotage* lower the morality of the workers. The essence of Syndicalism, they say, is to be a philosophy of production; it depends on making the *syndicats* fit to control industry, and must, therefore, be imbued with a keen sense of the dignity and sanctity of work: anything which degrades the worker as such is therefore the direct negation of the ideal of self-governing industry. The intellectuals generally condemn 'sabotage', largely on these grounds; but it seems to retain a strong hold, and is indeed bound to do so while the *syndicats* remain poor, and strikes retain their sporadic character. Methods of 'irritation' go naturally along with such movements; but the prevalence of *sabotage* in France has been much exaggerated by the stress generally laid on it in books about Syndicalism.

Two minor methods of Direct Action are worth a short mention. The 'boycott' is used in two ways, both by consumers, abstaining from a particular make of goods, and by producers, refusing to work for a particular firm; the 'label' or *marque syndicale* has also developed considerably in a few trades, and the mark of the *Livre* may be seen on most Syndicalist literature. The label generally signifies work done by *syndiqués*, but sometimes only work done under Trade Union conditions of labour. Neither of these, however, is of great importance.

This philosophy of Direct Action may perhaps be described as the irreducible minimum of Syndicalist thought. That, in acting together, the workers are taking the first step towards constructing a new order of society, is a conception common to all sections of the movement. But in the further development of their views, the Syndicalists stand at many different stages of speculation, and adopt many different lines of thought. On such practical questions as the relation of Syndicalism to the Co-operative movement, or such philosophical questions as the precise theoretical basis of Syndicalism or the need for such a basis, there are wide differences. The movement as a whole is apt to give the impression that it is at the same time feverishly protesting that prediction is useless and impossible, and continually predicting. M. Sorel's later work is a vigorous denunciation of the methods of prediction which he employed in his first book: Pelloutier, writing in 1901, was concerned to predict rather elaborately the future structure of society; MM. Pataud and Pouget more recently have issued a detailed Syndicalist Utopia, while at the same time, M. Pouget himself is fond, in his other works, of insisting on the futility of prediction. It is thus rather difficult to determine how far, in a study of the C.G.T., we ought to take notice of the views its various supporters hold concerning the future of society. We may at least allow ourselves to notice the unanimity of the Syndicalist writers who have actually allowed themselves to be drawn into prediction. As early as 1896, we find in a report on the future function of the *Bourses du Travail*, prepared by the *Bourse* of Nîmes, the idea that the Bourse is the local government unit of the future. Doubtless, this view was due to the influence of

Pelloutier, whose views, as afterwards given in his *Histoire des Bourses du Travail*, published after his death in 1902, definitely set the type for theories of the future structure of society. In the same year, a series of reports on the subject was submitted to the Congress of Montpellier. They revealed entire agreement upon the main points. Property, it was generally agreed, should belong not to the particular *syndicat*, but to the collectivity, and should only be *used* by the *syndicats*. A still more important point of agreement is that, in every case, the reports made the *Bourse du Travail* and not the Industrial Federation, the local and not the national unit, the centre of activity. All the reports insist on the need for decentralisation, and recommend the strengthening of the *Bourses du Travail* and the weakening of the central government into a mere federal committee. The view of Marx that the *syndicats* are to the proletariat what the communes were to the bourgeoisie undergoes an important practical development when the *Bourse du Travail*, rather than the isolated *syndicat*, is considered as the true social individual.

We come now to the close of our general examination into Trade Unionism in France. It is, no doubt, extremely difficult, on the strength of what has been said, to discover how far its theories are carried into practice, and to what extent they really differentiate it from the movement in other countries. It is inevitable, in any discussion of the French movement, that the theory should emerge with far greater distinctness and coherence than the practice ; for the C.G.T. has throughout, in spite of its rejection of theory, been directed in accordance with general views. Its main idea has been throughout that centralisation is fatal, and that the autonomy of the organism must be preserved at every stage. Carrying out this idea, it refrains from becoming, except once in a way, as in the recent strike against war, a directing body. It leaves to the local or national units in each industry the determination of all movements. A further result of this theory is that no adequate statistics are kept, and that it is consequently impossible to present on paper any intelligible account of the actual doings of Labour in France. A few great strikes stand out; but it is very difficult to judge how the advances made correspond with those all the world over. In the next chapter, however, we shall attempt to make some further comments upon the practice, as well as on the theory, of French Syndicalism.

CHAPTER IV

COMMENTS ON THE FRENCH LABOUR MOVEMENT

M. GRIFFUELHES, one of the leaders of the C.G.T., in his *Voyage Révolutionnaire*, from which we have already quoted, surveys the Labour movement with a less partial eye than most leaders are willing to turn upon their own handiwork. He is far from reaching the optimistic conclusions which generally inspire the friends of the C.G.T. : instead, he sees everywhere disorganisation, a floating unrest unaccompanied by any steadfast purpose, and a disposition to be overelated at the least success and disheartened at the slightest reverse. Of such stuff a strong movement is not made, and M. Griffuelhes freely admits that, save in certain districts, the C.G.T. is weak. This weakness, however, is a weakness of solidarity in general : Reformist methods prevail no more than Revolutionary, and the labouring class is scattered, dispirited and hopeless. Sometimes, he tells us, this lack of organisation is due to the slight concentration of industry in certain departments.[1] In these districts, " the conflicts have never extended beyond a single occupation ", and there have been no great and inspiring struggles. In consequence, there is no strong or permanent syndical movement. There are only " passing bursts of anger ",

[1] For instance, Cher, Indre, Haute-Garonne, Pyrénées, Gironde, Charentes, Deux-Sèvres.

such as are congenial to the Latin temperament. In other cases, as in the East, especially in Meurthe-et-Moselle, an organisation has been built up in the past, only to vanish with the first defeat. Where there were 3000 unionists in the district round Nancy in 1905, there were only 100 after the unsuccessful strikes of that year. In Brittany, where Unionism arrived late, it at once made great strides; but there too progress soon ceased, save in the building trade. In Franche Comte there has been no conflict since 1899; yet it is a great industrial district. In yet other districts, political Socialism is strong, and the *syndicats* have been captured for Socialist propaganda, as in the Pas-de-Calais and the North generally, among the miners and weavers. "The North", M. Griffuelhes says, "groans under the burden of domination of concentrated industry"; but "priests and politicians have taken good care not to teach it to reason". In the South, Limoges and Bordeaux are both devoted to politics; and M. Griffuelhes goes so far as to lay down as a general rule that "where electoral life is vigorous, the Union movement is weak". The quarrel between the Socialist Party and the C.G.T. has certainly done the *syndicats* harm in many districts, and, until the quarrel can be patched up and the two go on their way friendly, though independent, there seems little hope of improvement.

For other districts M. Griffuelhes is more hopeful. He does not deal with Paris, which is of course the centre of the activity of the C.G.T., but of Bourges, for instance, he speaks with enthusiasm. Toulon too is well organised, especially the dockyards, though there, as in other maritime towns, there is opposition between the State dockyard workers and unionists in other trades. In Marseilles too he finds Unionism vigorous among the port workers, after a period of decline. In Lyons the *syndicats*, after being weakened by politics, are again growing strong. In Rennes the growth is so rapid as to arouse doubts of its stability.

The impression left by M. Griffuelhes' book, from which these are only a few instances, is that the whole ' syndical ' organisation of France, save in a few industries, is very fluid and unstable. There are constant advances and declines : *syndicats* easily go out of existence after a struggle, and are easily born again a short time after. In certain industries, as in the Textile, Mining and Printing trades, there is greater stability ; but this, as a rule, goes along with the Reformist spirit. The happy-go-lucky methods of the C.G.T. do not suit stable organisations, and in reaction against them, the stronger *syndicats* are often driven too far on the road to ' social peace '. There are undoubtedly many characteristic traits of Syndicalism which persist only through the imperfection of its organisation, though a great parade has been made of them in panegyrics on Direct Action.

But, even if this comparative weakness of Trade Unionism in France is admitted, it will not follow that it is the method which is wrong, or that the C.G.T. has done nothing to benefit the workers. It is at least clear that the weakness is to some extent paralleled and balanced by a similar lack of organisation on the side of the masters. If the small workshop often prevents the men from organising with ease, it has the same effect upon the employers' power of concerted resistance ; and, in judging the C.G.T., we must always bear in mind the large number of small masters who still survive in many trades. The effect of having such a class of employers to deal with is that the conclusion of agreements becomes far more difficult, and this, as well as a deliberate avoidance of 'social peace', may account for much in the methods of the C.G.T. Some of the opposition to conciliation and arbitration is no more than making a virtue of necessity, and, in fact, the latest statement of the policy of the C.G.T. does not pronounce decidedly against all agreements. M. Jouhaux writes in *Le Syndicalisme Français* (1913) :

" Conciliation should be only an incident and not a means of action. When the worker sees that, by this method, advantages can be gained, he should have recourse to it. But never at any moment should he dream that it is the form for the struggle of Labour to assume ".

This is a considerable modification of statements that were freely made a few years back, and it is largely due to the improved facilities for conciliation which recent industrial developments have brought. To arbitration, by which is meant compulsory arbitration, the C.G.T. remains as opposed as ever. National agreements are almost unknown in France; local agreements are in fact very common, and the C.G.T. does not really oppose them.

Opinion then, in the C.G.T. itself, is tending to modify the rigour of revolutionary doctrines which always contained a large element of bluster. The French movement, while retaining its distinguishing features, is being modified by experience, and growing more tolerant of judging particular problems on their merits. It is being realised that revolutionary ardour cannot make up for lack of numbers, and, above all, that it is hard to keep up for long. The need for greater permanence is being admitted, and the disciplinary demands that organisation makes are being met in a more acquiescent spirit. This change is going on gradually and without fuss or noise; but it may well be that there will emerge from it a movement which will be at once strong and revolutionary. The French workers will not throw over their idealism, even if they learn the lessons Germany and England have to teach them in organisation. The C.G.T. will emerge strengthened, but not transformed: it will not abandon its characteristic doctrines, but will mould them to meet practical requirements. And, when they have done this, they may well have the finest Trade Union movement in Europe.

It is a favourite assertion on the part of all sorts of people that the C.G.T. has failed lamentably to ameliorate the position of the workers. Bare juxtaposition of very imperfect statistics of hours worked in certain industries in Germany, France and England is a favourite method of throwing discredit on the French movement. It is no doubt true that in most cases the hours worked in France are much longer than those in vogue in Germany, and even the demands of the French workers often allow a longer day than the German actually works; but such figures by themselves prove nothing. It is indisputable that there has been in France of late years a considerable rise in wages and a considerable fall in the working-day. The *Bûcherons du Cher et du Centre* have reduced their hours from 15 and 16 to 11 and 10, have raised their wages 40 or 50 per cent. and have secured a collective contract. The Postal Workers have secured an eight hours' day and a five-franc minimum. The vineyard strikes in 1904–5 secured an advance of 25 to 30 per cent. in wages, and examples could easily be multiplied.[1] On the side of legislation, the C.G.T. can

[1] See L. Jouhaux, *Le Syndicalisme Français*, pp. 44 ff. E. Pouget, *La C.G.T.*

fairly claim to have brought about not only the closing of the *bureaux de placement* in 1903, but also the legislation of Sunday closing in May 1906, when a few months earlier the Senate had rejected it by a large majority. Not only has the actual number of strikes continually increased, but the percentage of complete successes has also been going up slowly and the percentage of complete failures going down rapidly. How much of this success should be attributed to the C.G.T. and how much to the commercial condition of France can hardly be determined; but we can at any rate see that the mere assertion that the Syndicalist movement has failed finds no support in recent labour statistics.

On its more revolutionary side, the success of the strike policy is more doubtful.[1] Nor do any very tangible advantages seem to have attached to the displays of 'King' Pataud and the Paris electricians; these strikes are to be regarded as dress rehearsals for the supposed coming catastrophe, successful propagandist demonstrations, but no more.

The Reformist argument against the General Strike policy has considerable force. The *Fédération du Livre* balloted against it in 1908 by a majority of six to one, and the Textile Conference rejected it on the ground that in its own industry " such an action might have the effect of annihilating the embryo of organisation (35,000 federated out of 900,000 textile workers) which has so far been realised with infinite pains ". The force of this argument finds support in what

[1] The General Strike called after the successful Postal Strike in 1909 to support a second cessation was very little responded to, and was the immediate cause of the resignation of Niel, the Reformist who had been elected Secretary of the C.G.T. a few months earlier by a majority of one vote. Niel had a very wide following within the C.G.T. in opposing the General Strike.

Griffuelhes tells us of the strikes of the Marseilles dockers in 1902–4.[1] In 1902 and 1903 there were successful movements. In 1904 the men struck again without sufficient consideration, and their organisation was almost swept away in their defeat. Similarly, the organisation of the Nantes dockers disappeared entirely after the unsuccessful strike of 1907. 'Easy go' is so much the rule with French working-class organisations, held together by no ties of vested contributions, that the sympathetic strike may very easily be fatal even to a comparatively strong organisation.

Most nonsense has been talked about French strikes by the theorists, who have pretended to see, in every dispute, the realisation of their pet theories about the class-struggle. It is no doubt possible for a strike in favour of a definite reform to have a 'revolutionary background', more or less consciously realised; but it would be an error to suppose that this background as a rule makes much practical difference. M. Sorel and even the leaders of the C.G.T. may formulate what theories of the 'general strike that is being realised every day' they please; they will not by this means very largely alter the ordinary course of strikes in France. The revolutionary background is at most a fortunate incident; it is not the *raison d'être* of the strike. The strike possesses in France the character it has, not because the C.G.T. says that is what it should be, but because, in the circumstances, it must be such as it is. Isolated local *syndicats*, almost without funds, striking to remedy a definite grievance, are

[1] The parallel with the London Dock Strikes of 1911 and 1912 is close and significant. Such ill-considered movements seem to be characteristic of the rougher and more casual kinds of labour.

bound to pursue the rather violent and disorderly methods associated with Syndicalism. Innumerable parallels could be found for such methods in the early history of English Trade Unionism, and, in that case, we can see that they were the fruits, not of choice, but of necessity. The strikes are what they are because the *syndicats* are jealous of their local autonomy, and above all because they are weak. It may be that strength brings with it dangers, and that the French *syndicats*, with all their weakness, are not inefficient; but there is no reason to credit them with a great refusal on principle to become rich and strong. Theory always distorts the truth by rationalising it; and this has been very much the case with the theory and practice of Direct Action.

A further cause of French strikes preserving their character of violence is to be found in the state of the law. At this time, we find it hard to realise how much disorder we are saved by the legalisation of picketing. The French law on this point is highly unsatisfactory, and it is impossible to have any deterrent effect on blacklegs without resorting to more violent methods. Accordingly, the C.G.T. practises the *chasse aux renards*, and often comes into conflict with the police on account of the measures it adopts to frighten away blacklegs. *Sabotage* of all sorts is largely accounted for by the difficulty French unionists find in preventing 'scabs' from taking their places during a strike. An alteration of the law on this point would certainly produce beneficent results, and would be a great source of strength to the *syndicats* as well.

The views of the Textile Workers concerning the General Strike have already been quoted, and reason has been given for believing that any prolonged attempt at a general strike at present would be very dangerous to the existing *syndicats*. The recent single day's strike against war by no means succeeded as its organisers had hoped; and it is likely to have at least the effect of making clear to the C.G.T. that the day for such a strike is not yet. Even the sympathetic strike, or *grève de solidarité*, when used on a large scale, is dangerous to the weaker *syndicats*, and is not to be undertaken lightly. ' Sympathy ' is as a rule far more useful when it takes the form of voluntary contributions from supporters in other industries and localities.

A further cause of weakness, as M. Lagardelle has said, is to be found in the lack of well-paid permanent officials. French Trade Union officials are not numerous, and are very badly paid. As a result, much necessary work is not done, and men of national experience are few and far between, save in one or two industries. It is true that the extreme democracy of the C.G.T. has so far, in spite of the power of every organisation to recall its delegates at a moment's notice, had the effect of securing the permanence of its officials. " It delegates to its administrators, who are chosen by sure means and under strong control, lasting and uncontested powers ". But these conditions are only imperfectly realised: the local *syndicats* especially, and even the *Bourses*, suffer from the lack of permanent officials well-informed of all the fluctuations of their trades.

" Where ", asks M. Lagardelle, " would the great English Trade Unions be without their specialised governments and body of officials ? Or the English Co-operative Societies without their administrators or directors ? Are not even our French *syndicats*, behindhand as they are, effective in proportion as their committees and secretaries have defined and lasting functions ? " It is interesting to get such a plea for more leadership from a French Syndicalist, when precisely what has attracted many people in Syndicalism is the absence of leadership. Even if leaders sometimes 'lead from behind', the experience of all countries proves that they are absolutely necessary to a healthy movement. M. Lagardelle, however, wants the leaders kept in effective check, and of their not being so he feels little risk where, as in France, the unit of action is nearly always purely local. "The *syndicats*", he says, "can control their secretaries". It is indeed a very different matter to control a local secretary, who is the same as a branch official in England, and to keep watch over a central body of officials, with power over strikes in any and every locality. Such officials the C.G.T. does not want. It wishes to preserve "assured contact" between the official and the rank and file, and this, it holds, can be secured only by the local unit.

A great deal of the misunderstanding of Syndicalism in England is due to the fact that it has an outlandish name, which of itself suggests to most people nothing of its meaning. In France, this is of course not the case; Syndicalism has there too its derivative sense, but it retains as well the ordinary meaning, 'Trade Unionism'. *Syndicat ouvrier* is the French for a Trade Union, and *Le Syndicalisme* literally means neither more nor less than Trade Unionism. Thus the difference between Revolutionaries and Reformists is not a difference between *Le Syndicalisme* and something else, but between *Le Syndicalisme Révolutionnaire* and *Le Syndicalisme Réformiste*. The dominance of the former in the C.G.T. caused their doctrine to become known in France as *Le Syndicalisme* simply, and from that popular usage the name passed into general use in England at the time of the French Railway Strike.

Syndicalism, then, is not an outlandish, newly-manufactured scheme for the organisation of the Labour movement, but the actual form which circumstances and environment, as well as the character of the members, have caused the movement actually to assume in France. This is important not only for our understanding of Syndicalism as a whole, but also for a real appreciation of its position in France. The theory has developed out of the facts, and not the facts out of the theory. The rise of Syndicalism has therefore meant in France no such preoccupation with methods of industrial organisation as we find associated with it in England. Here, the name Syndicalism is being used to cover a campaign for the reorganisation of Trade Unions on industrial, instead of craft, lines; in France, the organisation is indeed mainly of that character, but the question of industrial as against craft organisations has never bulked very largely in the movement. It is, however, so much the question of the moment in this country that we must be quite clear about the position in France.

Before 1906, the C.G.T. had not pronounced officially in favour of either 'industrial' or 'craft' organisation. At the Congress of Amiens, in that year, a resolution was passed that no new 'craft' federations should be admitted into the C.G.T.; but those which already existed were not to be interfered with. The Congress of Marseilles in 1908 confirmed this resolution as it stood. The decision of these congresses was in fact no more than the ratification of a tendency; as the *syndicats* grew stronger, they were tending to fusion, and the C.G.T. naturally welcomed the change. It is much easier to combine many local *syndicats* of different 'crafts', already united by the *Bourses*, into one *Fédération d'Industrie* than to combine two existing

Fédérations de Métier, when once the ' craft ' principle has been given national sanction. Even here, however, M. Jouhaux tells us, progress has been rapid. Not only have local ' craft ' unions (*syndicats de métier*) disappeared to give place to local industrial unions, but also existing national ' craft ' federations " tend more and more to be converted into industrial federations ".[1] It is true that the transformation is as yet by no means complete, especially in the case of weakly organised industries ; but M. Yvetot, another C.G.T. leader, has explained the policy of the Confédération on this question.

" It will easily be understood that the Industrial Federation is gaining ground on the Craft Federation, and will inevitably end by destroying it. . . . In a word, as exploitation in an industry is extended and simplified, ' craft ' categories disappear. . . . But this transformation must be the work of necessity, and must be brought about by its own expediency, without hustle, by mutual understanding between the organisations concerned ".[2]

In adopting this attitude, the C.G.T. has only been adhering to the principle of the autonomy of the individual organisation at every stage. No doubt, interest also prompts it to take up this attitude. It would be as impossible for it to force reluctant federations already within it to adopt any particular form of organisation as it would be for the Trade Union Congress to compel all English Unions to adopt an industrial basis. The only reasonable attitude on the part of a central authority is to give a clear lead and leave the actual organisations to follow it up or not, as they please.

[1] Jouhaux, *Le Syndicalisme Français*, pp. 10, 12.
[2] Georges Yvetot, *ABC Syndicaliste*.

The industrial basis, then, is accepted in France as normal and advantageous. M. Griffuelhes is one of the writers who give their reasons for this attitude. " Industrial federation is the object of the coming together of diverse corporations [*i.e.* ' craft ' *syndicats*]. In a good many cases the opposite course is taken. The material on which the work is done [and not the workshop in which it is done] is made the basis of organisation. Such a basis makes a policy of offensive action absolutely impossible ".[1] M. Lagardelle gives a second reason. " Syndicalism accuses craft Unionism (*corporatisme*) of making ' craft ' selfishness more extreme ", and of creating " a working-class aristocracy ".[2]

The first reason is one of policy. As industry advances and more processes are concentrated in the hands of a single employer, as the parts of a single industry grow more interdependent and industrial conflicts extend over a larger area, it becomes necessary for the workers to organise on a corresponding scale in order to meet the masters in an equality, and, if not to strike all together, at least to give one another support in all strikes within the industry. This is the argument in favour of Industrial Unionism which we shall find to be the commonest in the United States, where industrial concentration has reached the highest point. In its application to France, it is important to clear up a possible misconception. The object of industrial federation is not the calling of a national strike of the whole industry, but the calling of local strikes which shall be effective in a whole factory or district. The problem of industrial organisation has appealed to France as a local problem, and it is im-

---

[1] V. Griffuelhes, *Voyage Révolutionnaire*.
[2] H. Lagardelle, *Le Socialisme Ouvrier*.

portant to realise that Industrial Unionism may make just as much difference to local as to national strikes. It is the disappearance of local *syndicats de métier* that M. Jouhaux regards as a sign of the greatest progress. For French strikes are as a rule small, and the local unit is the main thing.

The second argument in favour of the industrial basis is more general. If the C.G.T. is to be regarded as more than a means of amelioration for the workers —and the above argument need mean no more than that—it must preserve a class-structure. " Class ", M. Lagardelle is always saying, " is a natural division " —it proceeds from the actual condition of Society. If, then, the workers are to strive together for emancipation, skilled and unskilled together, they must be gathered into the same organisations for fear the strong may use their strength at the expense of the weak. The conception of working-class solidarity, which is the basis of the C.G.T., can only be represented by industrial organisation, taking no account of whether a man is skilled or unskilled, but only of his being a worker, and exploited.

Even where the industrial basis is accepted, there may still be considerable differences of organisation. Thus the general principle on which the C.G.T. goes is, we have seen, that at every stage " the autonomy of the organism is complete ".[1] " Within the Federations and the *Bourses du Travail* ", says M. Jouhaux, " the *syndicats* enjoy complete autonomy. We hold that the *syndicat* should be left free within the Federation, in order that, when the moment for a conflict comes, it may be able, without asking anybody's permission, to act freely, profiting by the favourable circumstances and conditions that may

[1] E. Pouget, *La C.G.T.*

arise ".[1] This principle, however, is in practice very elastic. Federations have always a financial basis, but this is not generally intended for the support of strikes; as a rule, they are directly concerned only in national movements, which, in most industries, are rare. But in certain cases, notably in that of the *Fédération du Livre*, which has about 11,000 members divided into 180 *syndicats*, the constitution is highly centralised, and resembles rather one of our own great national Unions. In a few cases, the Federation even gives place to the *Syndicat National*, which is adapted to fight a centralised master-class, in the person either of the State or of the trust. Of this kind may be mentioned the *Syndicat National des Chemins de Fer* (Railwaymen's Union), which has about 270 sections and about 46,000 members. To the same class belongs also the famous P.T.T. (*Postes, Téléphones et Télégraphes*), which conducted the postal strikes of 1908. The *Fédération du Bâtiment*, which is strongly revolutionary, belongs to the same class as the *Livre* in being highly centralised and having high dues, but naturally preserves local initiative in strikes. The recent decrease in the actual number of Federations (sixty-three in 1908, fifty-seven in 1910) is due to amalgamation.[2] Federations vary in membership from 40,000 (Building Trades) down to 100 (Laundry).

There is, then, far less uniformity of organisation within the C.G.T. than most accounts would imply. But, on the whole, local autonomy is fairly strictly preserved, and the right to strike generally remains absolutely with the locality.

This decentralised system naturally gives far more importance to the *Bourses du Travail* than the Trades

[1] L. Jouhaux, *op. cit.* p. 11.   [2] *Ibid.* p. 10.

Councils of this country possess. In the first place, a *Bourse* is something quite different from an English or a German Trades Council. It is not a representative body, though every *syndicat* elects one member to its committee; it is also a meeting-place and a centre of industrial life. It is a Chamber of Labour; it serves as a Labour Exchange, as a club-room, as a library, and as a lecture-hall; it is, above all, not a committee, but a place. In the mind of Pelloutier, to whom their development is largely due, the *Bourses*, and not the Federations, were the centres of working-class life in France. They at least partly succeeded when Federation was failing, and in them a method of organisation suiting French conditions seemed to have been discovered.

It must be remembered that the *Bourses* were founded and kept alive by means of municipal subsidies. These subsidies, which were given them in their capacity of Labour Exchanges, carried along with them no sort of municipal control. It was therefore natural that, when the C.G.T. began to develop its revolutionary policy, the municipal subsidies were in many cases withdrawn, and in some the *Bourses* were expelled from the municipal buildings which had been allotted to them. It had, until the legislation of Waldeck-Rousseau, been illegal for *syndicats* or federations of *syndicats* to possess 'immoveable' property, and they had perforce been content with the use of municipal buildings. When, therefore, the municipal councils showed them the door, they had no funds to buy and support buildings of their own. As a rule, a double system grew up. The *Bourse du Travail* continued to be a labour exchange and a meeting-place, but there grew up besides what are called *Unions de Syndicats* (local or regional), which are more or less Trades Councils, entirely independent of the municipalities. Through these *Unions* there are now being built, in a few centres, *Maisons des Ouvriers*—real Trade Union buildings capable far more efficiently of taking the place of the old *Bourses*.[1]

At the actual time of crisis, when the subsidies were being lost, the *Bourses* greatly declined. At Bordeaux and at Limoges, for instance, M. Griffuelhes says that the *Bourses* were almost extinguished by the withdrawal of subsidies. They had, in fact, been living on a false strength, and when the prop was removed, the structure gave way. M. Louis Barthou, writing in 1904, spoke of their weakness and recommended that attempts at revival should be made.[2] At the same time, the Federations were rapidly growing in power, and in consequence the balance shifted. Then, as the *Bourses*, supplemented by the *Unions de Syndicats*, began to weather the storm, they regained their influence; but so far they have still been suffering under the artificial depression caused by their quarrel with the municipalities. Their growth, however, in spite of amalgamations, has been rapid. From 1900 to 1902 the number grew from 57 to 96,[3] and at the present day it stands at about 160, including about 2600 *syndicats*. The growing numbers of local *Bourses* have led to the foundation of *Unions Départmentales* and *Unions Régionales* to deal with questions covering a wider

[1] In the previous chapter, we for convenience spoke only of *Bourses*, and used the word to include *Unions*. Where there is a *Union*, there is generally also a *Bourse*.

[2] Barthou, *L'Action Syndicale*.

[3] Eighty-three in the F.B.T.

area. These unions are made up of representatives from local *Unions*.

The function of the *Bourses* is, as we have seen, to correct the professional point of view, just as the Federations prevent 'parochialism'. Where Industrial Unionism is the rule, they have therefore more to do with general propaganda than with the actual ordering of strikes. In the first place, they are widely used as methods of preaching the virtues of combination to the unorganised. For instance, they made possible the organisation of the vine-workers of the Midi and the *Bûcherons du Centre*. They also organise the general congresses of the C.G.T. They are, moreover, schools of 'intercorporate solidarity'. "The present function of the *Bourses du Travail* is to secure the disappearance of professional selfishness and thus to make the organisation of the workers more powerful".[1] In strikes, as we have seen, they are the rendezvous for the strikers, and organise *soupes communistes*. In general strikes in a locality, their function is more extensive: they then become the unit, and the charge of the conflict is committed to them. It would be impossible to exaggerate the importance which these duties give them; they are still, in spite of temporary set-backs, the pivot on which the whole movement turns. Failure to understand the peculiar position of the *Bourses* is what has made many English accounts of Syndicalism in France misleading and mistaken.[2]

We have spoken of the Federations and of the *Bourses du Travail* separately: it remains to say something of

[1] Jouhaux, *op. cit.* pp. 17-18.

[2] See, for instance, M. Jouhaux's review, in the *Bataille Syndicaliste*, of Mr. and Mrs. Webb's pamphlet, *What Syndicalism Is*.

the C.G.T. itself, of which they form the two sections. We have seen that the function of the C.G.T. is not, as a rule, to order or institute strikes. It is not, in its own phrase, " an organism of direction ". Just as the *syndicats* are supposed to be autonomous within the Federations and the *Bourses*, these in turn are supposed to enjoy freedom from interference by the C.G.T. " The co-ordination is natural, and begins at the bottom ".[1] Just as the Federations are designed " to co-ordinate, but not to neutralise," the activities of the *syndicats*, the C.G.T. is to interfere only where interference and co-ordination are urgently needed, and is not to take upon itself the normal direction of the movement. "The Confederal Committee gives no orders. Even when immediate measures are called for, it frames, not a command, but an account of the position, and asks the *syndicats* for help. If a *Bourse* or *syndicat* likes, it has a right to postpone action ". . . . " It is false to say that it is the Confederal Committee which arranges strikes ; these are in fact the effect of the will of those directly concerned. Its function should be limited to seconding them, either by organisation, national appeals to solidarity, or by delegating on the fields of action, stalwarts [*militants*] who will not be directors of the strike, but will help by speaking and advising the workers the dispute affects. It is equally wrong to say that it is the C.G.T. which makes strikes violent. Their character is decided by the particular circumstances. It is violent or pacific according to the resistance and the obstacles it has to meet ".[2]

It has been generally remarked that the C.G.T., being centred in Paris, practically consists of a few leaders on the spot. These men have been able to

[1] E. Pouget.   [2] Jouhaux, *op. cit.* p. 19.

convey, abroad and even in France, the impression that the movement is far more directed by constructive revolutionary ideas than is actually the case. The French movement is certainly far more 'class-conscious' than our own; but it is certainly nothing like so much dominated by theories as its literature would make us believe. In this respect, there has been during the last few years a good deal of change. Less has been heard, since the episode of M. Niel's resignation in 1909, of the Anarchism of M. Pouget, and more of the actual reformist work that is being done. The influence of M. Jouhaux, the revolutionary who succeeded M. Niel as secretary, seems to have been cast in this direction, and perhaps certain checks sustained by the more violent policy also tended in that direction. This does not mean in the least that the C.G.T. has abandoned its revolutionary ideas, but only that they are slowly assuming their proper size in proportion to actual ameliorative efforts. Far more is heard now of campaigns in favour of the 'English week' and the eight hours' day, and, apart from the strike against war, the general strike is less talked about. It is still mentioned, but not with the old ring of sincerity and enthusiasm.

This change in policy may seem to have made the function of the C.G.T. much less positive than before. But if it has diminished the noise it makes, it has increased its usefulness. The C.G.T., unless the recrudescence of militarism causes it to be smashed by the Government, will probably settle down into a good administrative and propagandist body. We in England often suffer from the lack of such a co-ordinating force in the Labour Movement. Our General Federation of Trade Unions is too young to have the strength, while the Parliamentary Committee of the

Trade Union Congress, which approaches most nearly what is required, is limited in function and in other ways unsatisfactory. The Labour movement certainly gains by having a single central organisation to represent it, even if it very strictly limits the powers of such a body. The C.G.T. has wholly justified its existence. It alone holds the movement together and secures the harmonious working of the two sections, local and professional. Its existence is, moreover, very important from the point of view of propaganda : it attracts attention, and it sends organisers. It was impossible to create any really strong movement before the C.G.T. existed, and were it removed, much that has been built up would soon fall asunder. That Labour in France is as strong as it is must be reckoned mainly to the credit of the C.G.T.

No judgment on the French movement could be complete without taking account of the question of ' benefits '. When all is said and done, is the comparative lack of benefits [1] in the C.G.T. a source of strength or of weakness ? We saw, in the last chapter, the opposite views of M. Guesde and M. Pouget on this question. M. Pouget, the representative of the extreme revolutionaries, welcomes the ' purely fighting character ' of the *syndicats*, although he believes that it has prevented the membership from increasing as rapidly as it has elsewhere. On the other hand, it is maintained that the whole success of a strike depends on everybody striking, and that this end cannot be secured without organising everybody. It is beyond doubt that the English and German Unions owe a great deal of their membership to the desire for benefits, and equally so that the raising of contributions and

[1] It should be noted that this lack extends to ' dispute ' as well as ' friendly ' benefits.

benefits in Belgium actually caused a big increase in the number of unionists. If, then, the *syndicats* could, by increasing their benefits, send up their membership, are they right not to do so?

This is how the question is often put; but in this form it is misleading. If, in any *syndicat*, a majority of workers desires high benefits, there is absolutely nothing to prevent them from having them. The C.G.T. exercises no compulsion in such questions, which depend solely on the will of the members. The low average of benefits may therefore be taken as a sign that the workers as a whole do not want them any higher. The tendency is no doubt towards the raising of the contributions; but this tendency is slow, and any rapid increase, however desirable from some points of view, is out of the question. In fact, the 'friendly' movement reached maturity in France before Trade Unionism, and the tendency to keep the two separate is still marked. "We are not opposed to mutuality", says M. Pouget; "but we keep it out of the *syndicats*".

In fact, the whole tendency in France is towards the separation of each part of the Labour movement. Politics and industrial action after long disputes have become wholly separate, and are beginning, under these conditions, to lose their antagonism. Socialistic Co-operation has been tried; but the recent coalition of the Socialist Co-operative Societies with the *Union Co-operative* seems to mark the victory of neutrality here too. Syndicalist Co-operative Societies have never taken root. Similarly, it seems to suit the French to keep 'mutual insurance' apart from the 'class-struggle'. This extreme case of separation will no doubt in time be modified; but it is easier to understand its persistence when we look at it alongside the other branches of the movement. A catastrophic change in such a matter is not practical Syndicalism; but the constitution of the C.G.T. leaves the way always open for a gradual modification of programme.[1]

We should not, therefore, be too ready to censure the C.G.T. for not doing what would not suit it, and what it could not do if it tried. It is indeed likely that the C.G.T. has united as many workers as could be got together anywhere except in Germany on a purely 'fighting' basis, and that it will find rapid progress difficult : but this by no means shows that more attention to ' benefits ' would make a difference ; it merely shows that movements in other countries are not so strong as they look. The ' benefit ' question is not one to be settled at will by the leaders ; it settles itself according to the situation of the movement.

In this examination of the practical working and the prospects of the C.G.T., there has been throughout an undercurrent of criticism on the manner in which the movement is generally regarded, both here and in France. It has been judged far too much by its theorists, and far too little by itself. In a theory which does not make, but arises out of, action, it is inevitable that much should be rationalised and tabulated that ought to be left to the decisions of the moment. It is further natural that, in passing judgment, men should be influenced more by the literature, which is accessible, than by the facts, which are often unchronicled. In discussions of Syndicalism, far too much has been heard of M. Sorel and the ' Social Myth ', and far too little of the C.G.T. Syndicalism has appeared too much as a

[1] Of course, in not a few cases high benefits are already paid, as in the *Fédération du Livre* and the *Fédération du Bâtiment*.

theory of society, where it is weak, and too little as a gospel of industrial action, where it is strong. Critics have busied themselves with the absurdities of the doctrine of the 'Mines for the Miners' and the 'patients for the doctors', and have forgotten that Syndicalism is far more concerned with progressive demands for better workshop conditions. The doctrine of '*la Mine aux Mineurs*' does indeed appear in Syndicalist writings, especially in Pelloutier's *Histoire des Bourses du Travail* and in MM. Pataud and Pouget's Syndicalist romance, *Comment nous ferons la Révolution*; but in the actual life of the C.G.T., and at its Congresses, it takes a very small place. It is mainly an Anarchist importation, a revival in another form of the old advocacy of the 'self-governing workshop'. Its validity we shall have to examine later; here we are only concerned to state its importance in the action of the C.G.T. A much more reasonable point of view is to be found in M. Gabriel Beaubois' book, *La Crise Postale et les Monopoles d'État*, published at the time of the postal strikes, where the demand is not for absolute control, but for a more effective share in the management. It is in the minds of theorists and Anarchists that '*la Mine aux Mineurs*' becomes an important doctrine.

It is, however, true that, in the domain of theory, the transference to this form of Anarchist Communism is easy. Syndicalism, in contrast to Collectivism, does lay all the stress on the producer and none on the consumer. It does refuse to recognise the function of the great league of consumers we call the State. But this refusal, where it is not an unjustifiable theoretical development, is an unreflective antipathy to the bourgeois State of the present.

Syndicalism is an organisation of producers, and, until it reflects, naturally considers the producer rather than the consumer. Were it face to face with a State and municipalities equally democratic, it would not be led to draw the same conclusions, or to insist on " sweeping from the workshop, the factory, and the administration every authority external to the world of Labour ".[1] The opposition to the State is fundamental as long as the State remains irretrievably bourgeois ; but the opposition to all authority is not a necessary consequence of Syndicalism. In fact, as M. Lagardelle on one side and the Reformists on the other maintain, Syndicalism has nothing to do with Anarchism.

What then, when we have made away with these pretenders, is left as the real basis on which Syndicalism rests. M. Lagardelle has put it very neatly in a phrase which we have used already. ' Socialism of Institutions', the name which he gives to Syndicalism, expresses its fundamental character. Its essence is the ' class-struggle ', the war of the exploited against the exploiters, the denial that ' social peace ' is possible under Capitalism. Along with this characteristic conception goes a method. Marx's phrase, " the emancipation of Labour must be the work of Labour itself ", is the watchword of the movement, which aims at creating its own organs of revolution. Bourgeois society can only be supplanted as the workers develop ' social tissue ' of their own, as they create new organisms capable of expressing their point of view. " Within its *syndicats* and Co-operative Societies, the working-class hands down its ways of thinking, and elaborates new rules of life, morality, and right ". The ' class ', if it is not to be a mob,

[1] H. Lagardelle, *Le Socialisme Ouvrier*.

must find for its ideas ordered and permanent expression. The *syndicat* must be recognised as the representative of Labour, as the voice of the whole working-class, which is inarticulate without it. It is the new social individual, a force to be reckoned with in every sphere of the State's activity.

Such a definition of the *syndicat* would be accepted not only by M. Lagardelle and the Syndicalists, but also by many Radicals, whose first desire is to secure the orderly settlement of industrial disputes. We should therefore hesitate to draw from it the conclusions which are often drawn. It does not follow, because the *syndicats* are the new individuals created by the workers, that they are the only individuals possible in a modern State. The industrial conflict has indeed so overshadowed all other questions that those especially who are themselves the victims of industrial tyranny can hardly be expected to perceive that the wood contains any other trees. But, however important a part the workers may be, they are not, even numerically, the whole State, and a theory that takes account only of them must inevitably have limitations. Syndicalism, in fact, like most practical doctrines, is strong where it affirms and weak where it denies. In affirming the value of industrial action and of the workers' natural organisations, it lays down the true principle of a philosophy of Labour; but in taking this doctrine to imply the denial of the State, it goes too far, and is led into extravagance and perversity. That way lie 'the impossibilities of Anarchism'.

On the whole, then, what have we learnt from the French movement? If we have learnt to be guarded in applying its theories or its practice outside France, we shall have done much. If we have learnt to regard it, in anything that goes beyond the fundamental principle we have just been discussing, as a national movement to be studied as such, rather than as a gospel to be taken or left whole and undiluted, we shall have done more. The Syndicalism of which we have been speaking is in fact simply French Trade Unionism or rather that form of French Trade Unionism which has dominated the movement. Put that way, it is less likely to become a theme for ill-informed execration or undiscriminating idolatry. We must pick and choose, and, where Trade Unionism in this country presents particular problems for solution, we must see if the actual experience of the French *syndicats* can help us. National movements, studied in that way, may be helpful to other countries; but as it happens to be easier to copy M. Sorel's opinions out of one book into another, that method is more generally adopted. That, however, does not tell us what the C.G.T. is really doing; or, above all, what we ought to do.

CHAPTER V

LABOUR IN AMERICA

FROM France to America seems a step into a new world—into an economic system so different from any we know in Europe that all discussion of it may at first sight appear utterly irrelevant here. Conditions seem so dissimilar that the learning of any lessons from them looks like an impossibility. Yet we are compelled to deal with the American Labour movement because it has, in fact, exercised a considerable influence in Great Britain. It was in America that the question of Industrial Unionism first came to the front, and it was from America that the earlier advocates of it in this country borrowed their ideas and arguments. We must not therefore shirk the trouble of a thorough examination.

M. Jouhaux[1] has himself recognised the wide difference between the French and the American situations. "Where we French Trade Unionists", he writes, "are stronger than the English is in having the Syndicalist idea of the association of members of different Trade Unions, so that they may understand and sympathise with one another". "But", said the interviewer, "that was the origin of the Industrial Workers of the World in the United States". "Precisely", M. Jouhaux replied, "but the I.W.W. preach

[1] In an interview published in the *Daily Citizen*.

a policy of militant action, very necessary in parts of America, which would not do in France ". The C.G.T. has often been denounced for violence; but, on the authority of its secretary, we may expect to find it mild in comparison with the workers of America.

In what, then, does this difference actually consist ? In the first place, the difference is one of industrial structure. We have seen reason to believe that many of the peculiar characteristics of the C.G.T. are due to, and are passing away with, *la petite industrie*—the survival of the small master and the backwardness of industrial development. But if France stands at one end of the scale, America clearly stands at the other. Nowhere is capital so concentrated, industrial method so advanced, industry itself so ' trustified '. If in France the difficulty was to organise in face of the small master, in America it is to do so in face of the great impersonal force of the trusts. ' Trustified ' industry appears to the American worker as the inevitable development of the national life. He has no confidence in the professions of politicians about ' trust-smashing '. " It is just as foolish to try to smash the trusts as it would be to smash corporations and partnerships. The bigger the machines and the larger the market, the greater must be the organisation of industry ".[1] Face to face with organisations like the Steel Trust, which, working fully, employs 200,000 persons and has a capital of $1,400,000,000, the workers must organise on a similar scale, and must adopt every method that comes handy. The organisation of the capitalists is " a centralised Empire ", and the workers can only make headway by building up such another Empire of their own.

Secondly, in industry as in public life, America is

[1] W. D. Haywood and Frank Bohn, *Industrial Socialism*.

still fiercely individualistic. With all its centralised capital and organisation on a huge scale, no spirit of solidarity has sprung up. Within the trusts, and within the Labour Unions, there reign still rampant egoism and fierce competition. Among English-speaking workers, the path of personal advancement is still so far open that this spirit has hardly begun to break down. There is indeed, as such paths are closed, and as a Social Reform movement arises, a tendency to mitigate its intensity; but it will be long before it ceases to be a barrier both to organisation of any sort and to effective co-operation between those who are a ready organised. At the same time, it sometimes stands in the way of a complete development of organisation on the side of the employers.

Thirdly—and for our present purpose this is the most important differentiation—immigration makes the industrial problem in America wholly different from any that has to be faced in Western Europe. The tide of immigration never ceases to flow to the United States more and more rapidly. Formerly, the immigrants were mostly of races not very unlike those actually settled in America, and possessed, at least approximately, the same standards of life; in spite therefore of their numbers, there was no great difficulty in absorbing them in the huge and half-populated continent on which they sought their fortune. But in the last few years a great change has come over American immigration: there is pouring into the industrial districts a mass of East European immigrants, who bring with them their own outlook and standards of life. They come to find fortune; they live as sojourners in a strange land; and, when they have worked their time in the factories, many of them go back to Europe. The change that this new stream of emigration and return is bringing upon Eastern Europe and Italy cannot possibly be overestimated; but the change in America is no less tremendous. These Poles, Slavs, Southern Italians and even Syrians, who are pouring into the States at the rate of nearly a million a year and will soon be coming very much faster, cannot, like the old class of immigrants, easily be assimilated. They do not, when they have been a few years in the States, become 'Americans' either by naturalisation or by culture: they keep their own languages, ways of living and standards of comfort. For the capitalist, they are merely cheap labour, a commodity to be used for its full commercial value. They are unskilled, and they become machine-minders, intent only on making a bare living and enough over and above to send something back to their homes in Europe, and to lay up a nest-egg for themselves. They are a class apart, housed in mushroom cities of shanties which the civilised American never sees, carrying on, in the midst of the most prodigious industrial development that has ever been, the simple ways of life of the most backward parts of Europe. If we compare the description of this class as it lives at home—say in Mr. Booker Washington's *The Man Farthest Down in Europe*—with a parallel description of their coming to America—say in Mr. A. E. Zimmern's admirable *American Impressions* in the *Sociological Review* of July 1912—we shall realise how little they are changed by the change of environment. Not merely are they not being assimilated; they cannot be, and do not want to be, assimilated. As they are mere commodities in the eyes of the American capitalist, so all America is in their eyes merely a hell that is not eternal, a very unpleasant place where money is to be made. When they have done their part, home they go, and a new and larger batch of their countrymen takes their place.

America, in fact, is drawing on the world-market of unskilled labour. That these immigrants have a standard of life wholly different from that of the American or West European worker is not a mere accident; it is the whole reason for their being in the States at all. American industry has, during the last decade, been undergoing a great transformation. The advance from hand to machine labour has been there very largely a movement to substitute unskilled for skilled labour. In industry, as a recent editorial in the *New Age* [1] pointed out, it is possible to pursue either of two ideals in production—quantity or quality. It is possible to devote attention to turning out work of a really high order, to specialise in skill, as England has done, for instance, in the case of shipbuilding. This method demands high wages, short hours and the development of skill and intelligence among the workers. Or a nation may set before itself the purely quantitative ideal and aim at turning out the greatest possible amount of goods irrespective of quality; and in this case it will develop its machinery to the highest point of mechanical perfection—and underpay its labour. It will secure machines so simple that a child can work them; and, when the supply of children gives out, or the law steps in, as it has begun to do in the States, some means will be found of getting labour inefficient and nasty, but at the same time cheap. All the circumstances combined to drive America along the road of quantitative production. Competition was severe, individualism strong, and the new labour power, once discovered, inexhaustible.

[1] April 16, 1913. The whole article is admirable, and to the point.

So we have now the spectacle of Europe providing America with its unskilled labour and making the United States a competitor soon to be reckoned with by England, and Europe generally, in the world-market.

It is more to the point for us to notice that these new methods of production have divided the working-classes of America sharply into two sections. The old skilled labour often felt its separateness from the old unskilled; sectionalism was rife long before the new wave of immigration began. But the old labouring class as a whole has nothing whatever in common with the new unskilled. The immigrants are to them merely competitors, cheapeners of wages, rivals for employment, natural enemies. They cannot unite in the same movement; they cannot even stand shoulder to shoulder in a conflict with the employer who exploits both alike. The old working-class can only stand aghast and impotent in face of these new rivals, whose ways of life are not its ways, and whose gods are not its gods.

Indeed, the whole body of immigrant labour cannot help being, in the eyes of the old American workmen, a 'blackleg' class. Their acceptance of a lower standard of life has depressed wages in every grade of industry; and their abundance, going along with the improvement in machinery, has decreased the demand for skilled labour. The machine and the unskilled between them are driving the members of the old 'skilled' unions from their cherished monopoly, and are making them fear even for their livelihood; and every step that America takes in the direction of quantitative production is a nail more in the coffin of the old labour aristocracy. Along with these causes goes another, which it is best to give in the actual words of those who have seen it at work :

" The unemployed army and the new machines are constantly forcing wages in many industries down to a point below what is absolutely necessary to support a wife alone, not to mention children. Also, until about twenty years ago, there was another factor in American life that tended to keep wages up. There was plenty of free land in the West. The strongest, boldest workers, especially those who had a little money in the bank, could always go West and take up free land or get a good job. In the West there was much work to be done and workers were scarce. As some left the East, the wages of others went up or were prevented from going down. So there developed among the working people in America what has been known as ' the American standard of living '. But during the last twenty years American workers have been constantly getting less and less for their work. In dollars and cents the average wages have probably not gone down at all during the past fifteen years. In many cases, they have actually risen. But measured by the food, clothing and shelter the worker can buy with his wages, which is the only true way to measure an income, wages have gone down at least 50 per cent. in this time. . . . It takes three dollars to buy as much as two would buy formerly. . . . Nothing but Socialism can prevent the condition of the American workers from becoming just as bad as that of the working people of Europe, or even worse. . . . Finally, wages go down because it takes less food, clothing and shelter to keep a worker alive to-day than his father required, demanded and received fifty years ago ".[1]

[1] Haywood and Bohn, *op. cit.*

LABOUR IN AMERICA 135

The lot of Labour in America, then, as the statistics would by themselves show, is getting worse rather than better. According to the figures published by the Bureau of Labour, if the average of the wages paid from 1890 to 1900 is taken as 100, nominal wages stood, in 1912, at 129, and real wages, allowing for the rise in prices, at 98. But these figures, being taken only from a few industries, very greatly minimise the decline, which affects old skilled industries more slowly than the newer ' trustified ' machine industries. There can be no doubt that, on the whole, the lot of Labour is getting worse, and that old methods of organisation can do nothing to arrest the decline.

There are, then, now in America two working-classes, with different standards of life, and both are at present almost impotent in face of the employers. Nor is it possible for these two classes to unite, or put forward common demands. Not only are their interests in many respects conflicting; but there is an entire lack of that spiritual unity which alone can form a basis for permanent common action. The old methods of organisation do not suit the new personnel, and there is no possible basis for a new common method. It is therefore not merely a passing accident that there are two forms of labour organisation standing in direct opposition one to the other, and yet in an opposition that is more apparent than real; for they are really trying to do two different and quite reconcilable things. The American Federation of Labour and the Industrial Workers of the World represent two different principles of combination; but they also represent two different classes of Labour.

These two forms of combination may be described roughly as ' Craft ' and ' Industrial ' Unionism. It must not, however, be assumed that these words have here the same sense as we attributed to them in dealing with the French movement. The opposition is here much more defined, and the working compromise between the two principles, which has acted quite smoothly in France, would be unthinkable in America. 'Industrial Unionism', as we shall see, really bears, when used by the Industrial Workers of the World, far more than its surface meaning.

The American Federation of Labour, formed in 1886, which caters for the skilled and 'American' workers, is by far the older, larger and stronger body of the two. Embracing nearly two millions of workers,[1] it claims to stand for the Labour movement in America, and is accepted as doing so in international Labour congresses. By the Industrial Workers of the World, and by nearly all sections of the American public, it is freely denounced as "fostering demarcation disputes and aristocratic spirit", as "inapplicable to modern conditions", and as "preventing concerted action".[2] The *principle*[3] of the American Federation of Labour is a strict 'craft' unionism. It is rigidly organised from the centre by Mr. Samuel Gompers and a few other leaders, who keep a tight hold over all questions of discipline. In spite, however, of this strong centralisation in some respects, it is in others very deficient. Its strict adherence to the 'craft' principle has raised sectionalism to the highest pitch, and there is no security that any one section will support another in disputes. The unity is strong where it should be

---

[1] The A. F. of L. now has 1,770,145 members. There are also many independent craft unions similar to those it contains.

[2] Miss A. E. Hughan, *American Socialism at the Present Time*.

[3] See, however, later on.

weak, and weak where it should be strong. These "corrupt and aristocratic craft unions" can be charged with even graver faults. Their government is highly undemocratic, and some of the officials are suspected of being secretly in league with the employers. It is said, for instance, that the Boot and Shoe Workers, the United Textile Workers, and the International Association of Machinists are notorious instances of undemocratic practices, and that some Unions only hold their membership by terrorism. It is further complained that the A. F. of L. makes no attempt to organise the mass of the workers. It consists of Unions intended to benefit the skilled at the expense of the unskilled, to force up the price of certain classes of labour, and not to raise the general standard among the working population. With this end in view, it tries to secure monopolies, not merely as against non-union labour, but against all labour that does not belong to it, and follow the lead it gives. Even internecine conflicts between two of the Unions composing it are not uncommon, and everything is done to secure for the craft-members a peculiar position. Apprenticeship is severely limited, and the Unions aim, as a rule, at creating a barrier against the entrance of new labour by the imposition of very high entrance fees. These often range from $50 to $200, and in the case of the National Association of Green Bottle Blowers, which is not an isolated instance, they rise to $500. Their central unity is largely used as a means of preserving their sectional autonomy, with the result that they are merely pitted one against another. "The A. F. of L. furnishes one craft union with no protection against another. The plan of Federation with local and international autonomy furnishes a weapon that is as ineffective as independent craft unionism ".[1] In fact, the charge against the Craft Unions is that they are obsolete. "The trusts are rapidly organising into one great system ",[2] and such organisation on the one side means a corresponding development on the other. Antagonism, which was not bitter while small capitalists survived, or were not forced by the opposition of the trusts to pay even worse wages than they, "increases with the concentration of industry". Take an instance from the steel industry. "In the old days of small production the workers were protected by the Amalgamated Association of Iron and Steel Workers. This Union secured the eight hours' day for many of its members. To-day, many of the slaves of the Steel Trust toil twelve hours a day on seven days a week."[2] The trusts can smash the old Unions. "These Unions were composed of skilled workers. The progress of machine industry, making their skill unnecessary, destroyed their effectiveness, as it did that of the small corporation."[2] It is easy for employers now to evade the power of craft Unionism by importing workers, whom it makes no attempt to organise. "It [the A. F. of L.] does not exist for the purpose of organising the working-class. It is a loose association of craft Unions, each of which merely desires to keep up the standard of wages and hours in its own trade. It has no message for the working-class. It does not seek to make an

[1] From *On the Firing Line* (1912), published by the *Industrial Worker*, Spokane, Washington. 'International' in this passage needs explaining. Federations often include workers from Canada and other parts outside the U.S.A. In such cases they may be called either 'National' or 'International' Federations indifferently. In practice, 'international' means 'national.'

[2] Haywood and Bohn, *op. cit.*

end of unemployment, of child labour, and of all the other frightful conditions of labour ".[1]

This is the portrait of the American Federation of Labour, as it is painted by its enemies. We shall have, later in this chapter, to modify the indictment; but it is best here to state it in its broadly correct outline. "Craft Unions will exist as long as they are successful"[1] even for the restricted class for which they cater; but we have said enough to show at least that the Federation has indeed 'no message' for the millions of unskilled labourers who form the real industrial proletariat of the United States. Messrs. Haywood and Bohn estimate that there are in the States thirty million persons working for others, that is, subject to the wage system. The actual manual wage-earners include no less than seven million women and four million children. Of all this vast industrial population, the craft Unions of all sorts have not gathered in more than three millions, and there has been practically no attempt to organise the unskilled. The membership of the Federation only increased by eight thousand last year, in a period of considerable unrest following upon the Lawrence strike. In face of such a situation, new forms of action are clearly necessary.

This brings us to the Industrial Workers of the World. The failure of craft Unionism to meet the position demanded that a trial should be given to the rival principle of 'class' Unionism. The great unskilled must somehow be put in a position to take common action, and all attempts to do this demanded the complete abandonment of craft autonomy. In the new 'machine' industry, crafts do not exist, or at least do not touch the greater part of the workers.

[1] Haywood and Bohn, *op. cit.*

A long time ago, the ' class ' principle in organisation was given its first trial. The Knights of Labour, organised in 1869, were, in fact, the ' One Big Union ' of the Industrial Workers' dream. But after a period of great strength between 1880 and 1890, the Knights gradually lost their hold, and in 1895 were already practically extinct. They conformed, in their organisation, to the extreme principle of ' class ' Unionism; no industrial sections or ' craft locals ' were allowed, and they constituted, in fact, rather a society of practical social theorists than a Labour Union. Their chief campaigns were fought in favour of the eight hour day. But the Knights of Labour were not an instance of ' class ' Unionism following upon the failure of strong ' craft ' Unions. They were, in fact, an embryonic organisation which included highly skilled workers, and therefore they soon began to disintegrate into special craft Unions. The ' class ' structure was not suited to the conditions of American industry at the time of their power.

The second assertion of the ' class,' or rather, this time, of the ' Industrial ' principle was in the case of the Western Federation of Miners, who were first organised in 1892. In this organisation were gathered together all classes of workers in the metal mines to the West, including engineers and mill-men as well as the actual getters of the metal. Their period of success was about 1903–4; and in many cases they won a minimum of $3 a day, and a general eight hours' day.[1] But continual militancy finally brought exhaustion; in 1905 the W.F.M. suffered

[1] These agreements have been, we are told, a dead letter except where the Unions are strong enough to enforce them. See *Eleven Blind Leaders*, by B. H. Williams, published by the I.W.W

a great defeat, and though in that year they joined in forming the Industrial Workers of the World, they withdrew in 1906, and from that time onwards have become steadily less militant. Even in what is known to American Syndicalists as "their best period", it is said that "they were dominated by a militant minority of 10 per cent.".[1]

The Western Federation of Miners showed the way and were indeed the chief organisation among those which formed the Industrial Workers of the World in 1905. From 1901 to 1905 there had been a great period of industrial unrest. Workers had 'flocked into the Unions'; times had been good for American trade, and there was a scarcity of workers.[2] In 1900 the membership of the American Federation of Labour was 548,321 : in 1906 it had risen to over two millions. This labour unrest is attributable to several causes, of which the most important was the closing of the West, where free land had been exhausted in the 'nineties. The continual weakening of the Labour movement by the buying of its leaders for Tammany Hall purposes seems also at this time to have slackened ; and, with trade booming, a good deal of progress was made. The foundation of the Industrial Workers thus came at the end of a great advance, and was the expression of a dissatisfaction with the methods of the Federation of Labour. The conference, held at Chicago, where it was definitely constituted, claimed to represent 90,000 workers ; but only in the case of 40,000 were the delegates authorised by their associations, and of these 27,000 were the Western Federation

[1] *Syndicalism*, by E. C. Ford and W. Z. Foster.

[2] *Why Strikes are Lost*, by W. E. Trautmann, published by the I.W.W.

of Miners.[1] It is not worth while to follow the I.W.W. through all its subsequent difficulties and conflicts. Those who first set it up included three sections at least—opponents of all political action, opponents of all actual parties, and advocates of a combination of industrial and political action alongside the Socialist Party. The differences were strong from the first, and it was not long before the orthodox Socialist section left. Then the personal followers of Daniel Deleon, one of the founders, who had had, long before the I.W.W. came into existence, a Socialist-Labour Party all of his own, also broke away, and founded a second I.W.W. with its headquarters at Detroit. The Deleonites, who are extremists of the most curious sort, are at the same time strong advocates of political action and strenuous opponents of every actual party. Their method of political activity is the ' Don't Vote ' campaign. They are known in England through their attempts to spread Industrial Unionism here, and through their paper, *The Socialist*, which is published in Glasgow,[2] as the official organ of the Socialist-Labour Party. In America, they have remained insignificant ; their leaders are mostly not of the working-class, and their attempts at organisation in the towns of New Jersey have not met with much response. They got a good deal of credit for the first strike of weavers at Paterson, but this movement was a direct result of the more important strike at Lawrence, and it is unlikely that the workers of Paterson knew that the Detroit I.W.W.

[1] See throughout, for the history of the I.W.W., *The Industrial Workers of the World*, by Vincent St. John, published by the I.W.W. Some facts in the text, however, are from unpublished sources.

[2] Formerly at Edinburgh.

was a different organisation from that which had conducted the Lawrence movement. Moreover, the Paterson strike was in its settlement by no means so satisfactory as the Lawrence strike, and after the second stoppage was over the organisation soon began to filter away. The Chicago I.W.W. has now come on the scene and gathered up what remains of the work done by its rival. The Paterson strike of 1913 was actually conducted by the Chicago I.W.W.

The real Industrial Workers of the World are then the body which has its centre at Chicago, and to which all the leaders, Messrs. Haywood, Trautmann, St. John and others, belong. It is therefore the body which we shall hereafter mean when we use the name by itself. At its first congress, the I.W.W. adopted a ' Preamble ' or declaration of objects, which allowed a place to political as well as to industrial action. As successive elements left, the Preamble was modified, and political action was dropped. In its present form it is worth giving in full :

" The working class and the employing class have nothing in common. There can be no peace so long as hunger and want are found among millions of working people, and the few, who make up the employing class, have all the good things of life.

" Between these two classes a struggle must go on until all the toilers come together on the industrial field, and take and hold that which they produce by their labor, through an economic organisation of the working class without affiliation to any political party.

" The rapid gathering of wealth and the centering of the management of industries into fewer and fewer hands make the trades union unable to cope with the ever-growing power of the employing class, because the trades unions foster a state of things which allows one set of workers to be pitted against another set of workers in the same industry, thereby helping defeat one another in wage-wars. The trades unions aid the employing class to mislead the workers into the belief that the working class have interests in common with their employers.

"These sad conditions can be changed and the interests of the working class upheld only by an organisation formed in such a way that all its members in any one industry, or in all industries, if necessary, cease work whenever a strike or lock-out is on in any department thereof, thus making an injury to one an injury to all".

The best idea of the characteristic work of the I.W.W. will probably be conveyed by giving a description of its greatest achievement, the Lawrence strike. With that in mind, we shall be better able to form an estimate of its function and importance. Fortunately, we are in a good position to do this. The Bureau of Labour has published an admirable account of the whole movement, and there are also the accounts of the I.W.W. itself to corroborate the Government's testimony.[1] This strike has been recognised all the world over as an event of the greatest significance, as the first big uprising of the new American proletariat, and as necessarily the precursor of many such strikes in the future. Lawrence is an average New England industrial town, with labour conditions just like those in other textile towns. "The strike might have occurred anywhere". The conditions then that made for the success of this strike must often recur, and the problem is to find a method of organisation to suit this class of labour.

[1] See *A Report on the Strike of Textile Workers in Lawrence, Mass., in 1912*, Washington, Government Printing Office, and see also *On the Firing Line*, already quoted.

The population of Lawrence in 1910 was 85,892, of whom about 60,000 were dependent on the textile mills for a living. Of the population over fourteen, half actually worked in the mills, 73,928 were of foreign birth or parentage, 41,375 actually foreign born, and the 11,964 of native parentage included negroes. Of those born out of the States, 7696 were French Canadians, 6693 Italians, 5943 Irish, 5659 English, 4352 Russian, etc. Before the strike very few of the workers were organised. The Government Report says that there were 2500 skilled members of 'craft' unions, some affiliated to the United Textile Workers of America, who form part of the American Federation of Labour, but others, such as the wood-sorters and loom-fixers, in independent unions. On paper, there were over 1000 members of the I.W.W., but the Report estimates their real strength as 300, mostly in the Belgo-French branch, organised in 1905, which included over 200. There were also English members, who opposed any strike till organisation was better, and there had been Polish and Portuguese branches, which were dead or moribund. A small Italian branch had been newly started in 1911. The figures given by the I.W.W. differ from these. They state that only 1500 were organised at all: 1200 in the Textile Workers' Industrial Union, belonging to the I.W.W., and 300 in the United Textile Workers' Association, a part of the A. F. of L., or in independent 'craft' Unions. But these figures refer to actual strikers: the skilled workers, even when they were forced to come out owing to lack of work, mostly had nothing to do with the Strike Committee.

The strike was then almost purely a revolt of unskilled and unorganised workers. During the two months it lasted, the number of strikers varied. It began in January at 14,000, went up steadily to 23,000 in February, and came down, as certain classes of workers began to go back, to 17,000 at the end of the strike. The immediate cause was simple. A State law had just been passed reducing the hours to be worked by women and by children under eighteen from 56 to 54. On the occasion of a like reduction from 58 to 56 in 1910, the rates of wages had been put up to cover the loss to the employees; but on this occasion no notices of a coming rise were posted at the works. The management merely remained silent. In December a deputation of skilled English-speaking workers called on the management, and was informed that there would be no rise. Early in January the I.W.W. also sent a deputation to the American Woollen Company, but the management referred them to the head office at Boston, and nothing was done. It is clear, however, that trouble was anticipated in some quarters; for a leading official of the Company wrote from Boston to ask the management if there was not danger of a strike, and the management confidently replied that there was not.

At this stage, the dominant factor was the nationality of the employees. It is clear that they did not understand in advance that a reduction in their pay would be made. Communication between different sections was very difficult, and, at that point, concerted negotiation was impossible. But meetings of single nationalities began to be held, especially among the Italians; and both Italians and Poles voted in favour of a strike should the reduction occur. The employees could not negotiate, and, naturally enough, the employers made no move. On the first reduction actually being made, the cessation of work was largely automatic, and in a day or two 14,000 workers were out. At first, no further demands were made than the same pay for 54 as had been given for 56 hours; but soon after the strike began, the Strike Committee, representing the I.W.W., a few 'craft' Unionists, and the great mass of unorganised labour, formulated demands for a 15 per cent. increase in time and piece rates, double time for overtime and no discrimination against strikers. In February the skilled Unions, which were idle, but not in the strike, first formulated specific demands of their own. In the end the settlements generally granted a 5 per cent. increase on piece work, rises of from one to two cents an hour on time work, and time and a quarter for overtime, and there was to be no favouring of non-strikers. The net result was that 30,000 workers got increases of from 5 to 20 per cent. in wages, as well as certain minor advantages.

The whole conduct of the strike was an extraordinary instance of mass-action. The enormous barriers set in the way by difference of language were overcome in the main, not by artificial devices, but naturally. There was nothing to do but wait; and what had to be done could be carried out, it was found, largely without the need for words. Nationalities were organised separately; but little intercommunication was required. Many of the Strike Committee understood one another, and that was enough. Mr. Haywood could make himself understood by a crowd that did not know a word he said, merely by waving his arms and shouting. The workers wanted something so essentially simple that this was enough, and it was mainly because their demands were simple that they got what they asked.

The great problem for the Strike Committee was, of course, the feeding of this great resourceless mass.

At the height of the strike, 50,000 persons were without means of support, and the ' craft Unions,' while they were easily able to provide for their own members, did nothing to help the others. Relief was accordingly organised; appeals were sent out and subscriptions received from Trade Unions, Socialist bodies and private individuals. Over the whole two months the average receipts from these sources reached $1000 a day, and sometimes $3000 were received in a single day. With this money national soup-kitchens were organised and relief distributed. The strikers took another leaf out of the book of the C.G.T. Strikers' children were sent off to sympathisers in New York, Philadelphia and elsewhere, until on February 17 the colonel of the troops stationed at Lawrence refused to allow further departures save under regulations so strict as to make them impossible. The departures were made in large groups and everything was done to attract, by this means, public attention and sympathy. In spite of the prohibitions, forty more children were sent off on March 8 to Philadelphia without interference from the authorities.

When the strike broke out, considerable violence was naturally expected from so unorganised a mass. In fact, the Government Report admits that after the first few days there was little serious trouble, though it states that " there was always danger " of it. During the whole strike, 296 arrests were made, 220 ending in fines, and 54 in imprisonment. To anyone who knows American police methods, these figures themselves proclaim the absolutely peaceful nature of the strike. Two persons were killed, a boy and a woman, both shot by the police. The death of the woman provoked the police prosecution of Joseph Ettor, Chairman of the Strike Committee, for having caused her death by inciting to violence. Long after the strike was over, he and his comrade, Giovanitti, were triumphantly acquitted. The prosecution succeeded, however, in removing him from the leadership of the strike at its most critical point, and this was probably all it aimed at. The death of the boy was never even made the subject of inquiry. Mr. Ettor was arrested on January 29, and his place at the head of the Committee was taken by Mr. Haywood. Perhaps the most curious comment on the accusations of violence made against the strikers was the condemnation in May of a Lawrence man of business, not connected with the strike, for placing dynamite in a striker's house and then declaring its presence to the police. Such are American business methods. He was fined $500. Such is the rigour of American justice—for the rich.

Throughout the strike there was deepening hostility between skilled and unskilled. A fortnight before the strike ended, the craft Unions were already making their own agreements with the employers and returning to work without regard for the rest. The Government Report sums up the position in these words:

"While there was opposition on the part of the employers to the organisation of this great mass of unskilled, non-English-speaking employees, it is equally true that the existing forms of Unions built up on trade lines do not really make provision for the organisation of this class of employees. The net result was that such employees were left unorganised, with no ready means of formulating any protest against the conditions under which they felt themselves to be suffering."

Hence, the Report concludes, they were led readily to accept the revolutionary doctrines of the Industrial Workers of the World.

"It is obvious from the figures of earnings [given in the Report] that the full-time earnings of a large number of adult employees are entirely inadequate to maintain a family. . . . These wages are not peculiar to Lawrence, . . . and are not lower than elsewhere. . . . The plain fact is that the textile industry, as far as earnings are concerned, is in large part a family industry. . . . The normal family of five is compelled to supply two wage-earners in order to secure the necessaries of life ".

We have dwelt at such length upon the Lawrence strike because it is the typical conflict in which the forces the American movement has to reckon with can be seen in play. First come the 'craft Unions', corporations of skilled workers cold-shouldering the rest. After them, led indeed by English-speaking and Franco-Belgian workers, comes the vast horde of immigrants of every conceivable race and language whom it is impossible to assimilate and seems nearly hopeless to attempt to organise. The importance of the Lawrence strike is that it has shown such organisation to be possible. It is the beginning of a tremendous new industrial movement.

We have dwelt upon it also because it represents the transformation of the I.W.W. At its foundation in 1905, that organisation was not at all meant merely to provide a means of expression for the lower races of America. The stream of East European immigration had hardly begun, and the dimensions of the problem were not at all realised. The I.W.W. grew out of the example set by the Western Federation of Miners, and was intended not to supplement, but to take the place of the American Federation of Labour. It was in its origin 'Industrial Unionism' in the proper sense of the word. It looked forward to organising in single great Unions, linked up in a single greater central body, all the various crafts and processes of a single industry. It was to be not merely an organisation of the unskilled, but of skilled and unskilled together. It was to embrace in its scope not one 'class', but the whole of Labour. It was indeed ' class ' Unionism, but it was class Unionism on an industrial basis. This aim will be quite clear to anyone who reads the published Report of the first congress, held at Chicago in 1905, or who looks, say, at Mr. Eugene Debs' pamphlet on *Industrial Unionism*.

In fact, what has happened ? In the first place, the American Federation of Labour has not perished. Its membership is, as we have seen, one million and three-quarters, while that of the I.W.W. was reckoned in 1911 at 60,000, of whom only 10,437 actually paid their dues.[1] The Western Federation of Miners has left the I.W.W., and now forms part of the American Federation of Labour. If it is to be judged by its aims, the I.W.W. has been a lamentable failure. But in reality this is not how it should be judged. It has sought one thing, and found another : in seeking to unite skilled and unskilled, it has found out how to organise the great mass of the unskilled. Little by little, it is recognising this transformation, and accepting its new function. But, naturally, the old phrases die hard, and old oppositions outlast their meaning. The I.W.W. has been so long the enemy of the A. F. of L. that it will take it long to realise that there has ceased to be any real reason for enmity. It has so long been proclaiming a social theory that it finds it hard to haul down its flag, and hoist new colours.

[1] Since the Lawrence and Paterson strikes, the membership has greatly increased. In 1913, the paying membership was estimated at between 30,000 and 40,000.

It is, however, undeniable that this change of function, this lucky accident by which the I.W.W. has stumbled upon its real work, involves a great transformation of idea and aim. The I.W.W. began with a revolutionary theory of society; it was intended to subvert the existing order, and to bring in the Workers' Commonwealth. Its early history was full of disputes between Socialists and Anarchists, and, still more, between Socialists and Socialists. But all this is already changing; considerations about the future state of Society have become, for the I.W.W., broadly speaking irrelevant. Its task is at present not revolution, but reform: it must, with the materials it has to work upon, aim, not at reconstructing society, but at getting better wages. It is true that there is, in the pamphlets and journals it publishes, a great deal about 'The Abolition of the Wage System'; but this is mainly because the old ideas and the old leaders are still uppermost. What the proletariat of Eastern Europe comes to America for is wages, and for them any suggestion of social revolution is meaningless. They are not American citizens enslaved by capital; they are, by their own will, hireling sojourners, who have sold themselves for gain to the devil of American Capitalism.

The first modification, then, is one of ends. In spite of all its protestations, the I.W.W., to be effective, will have to accept the wage system, in the sense in which all meliorative organisations accept it. The second change is one of method. From the days of the strikes conducted by the Western Federation of Miners in 1901–5, the new movement has been associated with methods of violence. These methods will, no doubt, still persist among the roving bands of adventurous and disappointed labourers in the Far West;

but the Lawrence strike has taught the I.W.W. that successful strikes can be conducted without violence, even by the unskilled. Far less will consequently be heard of 'sabotage' and similar devices, save in the West, where every difference of opinion is an act of war, and heads are always broken to save the trouble of convincing them. This state of violence will become far less the normal situation in Labour disputes, and, especially in the industrial towns of New England, there will be, in the near future, many mass movements conducted without more violence than there was at Lawrence.

With regard to conciliation and agreements, the policy will change very little. Agreements tie the workers' hands, without preventing the employer from discharging whom he pleases; they may do for a well-informed and well-drilled body of men like a skilled craft Union; but they are merely fatal in the case of unorganised workers like the Lawrence strikers. With such labour there are only two ways of dealing—legislation or war. Both of these were seen at work in the Lawrence strike, and both together produced an effect which legislation at any rate could not have had singly. But all attempts at conciliation—at Lawrence there were three— failed hopelessly. Time contracts and conciliatory methods are out of place where the sole value of labour is its cheapness, and no importance at all is attached to raising its standard of efficiency.

It has been seen that the I.W.W., beginning with Industrial Unionism', has now changed its function to a 'class' Unionism, which cannot properly be described as industrial. It is, in fact, an impossibility, in America, to unite in one organisation all the classes of labour engaged in an industry. It may be possible some day to secure co-operation between all sections in case of need; but there must be at least two different forms of combination, following the line of the broad cleavage in standard of living and class of work. The function of the Industrial Workers of the World is the organisation of the unskilled upon the broadest possible basis. That this basis will be, for some time at least, broader than the Industrial can be seen easily from the actual structure of the I.W.W. Mr. St. John, in his pamphlet,[1] begins by laying down the theoretical structure. At the base, there is to be in every industry a series of Local Industrial Unions, which are always to be the units of negotiation with the employers. These Local Unions are to be divided into shop, district, departmental and language[2] branches, but never into 'craft' locals. These Local Industrial Unions are to be combined in National Industrial Unions and also in District Industrial Councils.[3] National Unions, in turn, are to be combined in Industrial Departments representing allied industries, and these finally are to be united in the central organisation, over which there is in time to be one great world-wide Union.

Such is the ideal organisation; but the actuality is different. There is no trace of the functioning of Industrial Councils, and there is only one National Industrial Union, that of the Textile Workers, which we have already seen at work in Lawrence. In everything save theory, the I.W.W. is the 'One Big Union' which is a denial of the 'Industrial' basis,

---

[1] *The I.W.W.*, by V. St. John.

[2] Here the difficulty of organising workers of many nationalities is to some extent met.

[3] Here the French influence intervenes and causes imitation of the *Bourses*.

a pure 'class' Unionism. But this makes less difference than might be expected. American towns tend very much to be devoted solely or mainly to a single industry, and in such cases the complicated structure which the I.W.W. favours in theory becomes unnecessary. In France, we found that industry was organised far more locally than in England; but America, especially where the unskilled workers are concerned, is infinitely more local still. Here, however, the localism arises not from the backwardness, but from the prodigious development, of industrial life. These mushroom cities of one industry are the latest product of American 'hustle', and result from an unparalleled concentration of industrial processes. The trust creates a higher 'localism'; organisation is so huge and so concentrated that it splits up by localities, where before it could be dealt with nationally. The 'locals' of the I.W.W. are then the storm-centre of its being; it is organised against the employer, and as he concentrates his business in one place, so they must make their Unions strong locally. The aim is to call out the whole personnel of the factory, at any rate with the exception of a few skilled workers, and accordingly the organisation must follow local lines. The same cause leads to subdivision along 'shop' lines; all the workers in a locality form the higher unit, all those in a single shop the lower. Thus either a 'shop' or a locality can be stopped, and the workers are organised as strongly as they can possibly be. Mr. W. E. Trautmann, in a pamphlet entitled *Why Strikes are Lost*, has clearly shown the necessity for both these forms of organisation; and the Lawrence strike is indeed the clearest testimony. For effective action, the workers must have, within their local Union, not merely language branches for those of different nationalities, but also 'shop' organisations, each covering the business of a single employer. Nearly all the strikes from 1905 to 1912 were failures, and Mr. Trautmann goes through the melancholy catalogue and traces the failure to sectionalism. He is indeed dealing mainly with the sins of the 'craft' Unions; but all the arguments hold in favour of the 'shop' and local industrial forms of organisation.

All through this inquiry, though we have often seemed to be near the border of it, we have said nothing of Syndicalism. Yet it will certainly be asked if there is no Syndicalism in the United States. As in England, there is and there is not: the theorists of Industrial Unionism, Mr. English Walling, for instance, have been a good deal influenced by French writers and ideas; but these have not sunk at all deep, and on the rank and file they have made no impression whatsoever. The I.W.W. at any rate should not be much occupied with theories; it has a work to do, but that work will not admit of being expressed as a social theory. It is a practical task of limited extent; it is not a new construction of Society, or indeed an ' -ism ' of any kind.

Outside the I.W.W., however, there is Syndicalism of a sort. There is a body called The Syndicalist League of North America[1] which "is not a labor Union, and allows no affiliation with labor Unionism", though it has local and industrial branches. It is, in fact, like our own Industrial Syndicalist Education League, a propagandist body, which "works for education in revolutionism". It accuses the I.W.W. of being "democratic and statist", and of having "a Socialist origin and taint", and stands

[1] There are also other similar bodies about which little information is to be got.

itself for the negation of all Government.[1] It looks to the taking over of industry by the workers, and, with this end in view, in theory supports the 'shop' against the 'Trade Union' as the unit of organisation. That is to say, it still believes in Co-operation of Producers, and hardly improves on the old ideal of the 'self-governing workshop' by turning it into that of the "autonomous shop". Like our Industrial Syndicalist Education League, it is very apt to talk nonsense when it theorises; but it also resembles that body in combining with airy theory a certain amount of practical work. Its real importance lies in the recognition that the I.W.W. has failed to solve the problem of industrial organisation. If the American Federation of Labour "has no message" for the unskilled, neither have the Workers of the World any for the skilled. The Syndicalist League of North America and similar bodies, perceiving this, have turned back to the American Federation of Labour and are seeing again what can be done with it. The recent history of the Labour movement in America is the history of a renewed attempt to reform the A. F. of L. from within.

This, then, is what Syndicalism means in America. Syndicalists are urged to join the craft Unions and turn them into industrial Unions from within. The moral of the failure of craft Unionism is taken as being not that the workers should form a new association outside the old bodies, but that old Unions should be amalgamated on an industrial basis. Mr. W. Z. Foster, writing in the English *Syndicalist*,[2] says:

"Amongst many of the Syndicalists, the sentiment is strong and growing ceaselessly that the tactics

[1] Quotations from E. C. Ford and W. Z. Foster's *Syndicalism*.
[2] March 1913.

followed by the I.W.W. are bad, and that endeavours should be made inside the A. F. of L.; that it is in the existing Unions that the Syndicalists must struggle without ceasing to accomplish the triumph of their methods."

This change of front—for the present Syndicalists have, as a rule, been Industrial Workers first—is due mainly to the change in the I.W.W., but also largely to a change within the American Federation of Labour. In the previous discussion of the A. F. of L., the criticism was put strongly, from the I.W.W. point of view, and it was suggested that there might be qualifications to make later on. It is not necessary to withdraw any of the charges that were then made, but only in one respect to modify them. The A. F. of L. is not so purely or irrevocably a federation of craft Unions as might be believed. It has long included certain Unions which have an industrial basis, and approximate more or less nearly to being real industrial Unions. Such, for example, are the United Brewery Workers' Union and the United Mine Workers' Association.[1] A further breach was made in the old system when the Western Federation of Miners, who, in spite of their name, are a Union and not a Federation, demanded a charter from the A. F. of L. There was a heated debate at the Annual Conference, in which the forces of reaction took the field against the Western Federation; but the recruit was too valuable to be lost, and in the end it was admitted. The principle of craft Unionism was already showing signs of collapse, and the Industrial Workers had been forced to start a campaign against "fake

[1] Moreover, the craft Unions are linked up in strong central and local industrial Federations, on which the success of the A. F. of L. largely depends.

Industrial Unionism in the A. F. of L ".[1] Difficulties had long arisen in connection with strikes, when newly organised strikers demanded admission into the A. F. of L. For instance, in the 1910 Car Strike at Philadelphia—when, incidentally, the unorganised workers struck, while the organised workers, as often, stayed at work and ' blacklegged '—the unorganised workers demanded a collective charter and refused to be sorted out into craft Unions. The A. F. of L. was forced to grant their demand, but the President of the American Association of Street and Electric Car Employees is known to have said at the time that they could " easily be allotted to their respective craft Unions when the strike was over ".[2] Other cases are quoted in which men who had won advantages by striking together were then, through the A. F. of L., tied down by sectional contracts which made such a strike impossible for the future. At Chicago, for instance, the packing-house workers are divided up among fourteen National Trade Unions belonging to the American Federation.

Such tyranny on the part of Mr. Samuel Gompers and the ' Old Gang ' gets every day more difficult. The situation is still further complicated by the determined efforts that are now being made by the orthodox Socialist Party to capture the Federation. Once described by the *Wall Street Journal* as " the strongest bulwark against Socialism in America ", the A. F. of L., Mr. A. M. Simons holds, is turning to Socialism, " modifying its form and changing its tactics ". Of the members of the Socialist Party who are engaged in production and distribution,

[1] *In the Firing Line.*
[2] Trautmann, in *Why Strikes are Lost*, quoting the *Tageblatt* of Philadelphia, a German Trades Council journal.

66 per cent. are Unionists, and of these 44 per cent. are in the American Federation of Labour, 5 per cent. in the I.W.W., and 13 per cent. in other Unions. The Socialist Party has thus a strong nucleus of support within the A. F. of L., and every year at the Trade Union Congress there is a trial of strength. The Socialists have flung themselves in on the side of Industrial Unionism, though officially they refuse to commit themselves to any policy. In January 1910, their official *Bulletin* declared that " the Socialist Party does not seek to dictate to organised labour in matters of internal organisation and Union policy. It recognises the necessary autonomy of the Union movement in the economic field, as it insists on maintaining its own autonomy in the political field. It is confident that in the school of experience organised labour will as rapidly as possible develop the most effective forms of organisation and methods of action." But in practice, the younger members of the Party are all in favour of Industrial Unionism. It was at their instance that the following motion was laid before the 1913 Congress of the A. F. of L.

" That, wherever practical, one organisation should have jurisdiction over an industry, and where, in the judgment of the men actually involved, it is not practical, then the committee recommends that they organise and federate in a department and work together in such a manner as to protect, as far as possible, the interests of all connecting branches."

This resolution, strongly opposed by the ' Old Gang ', was defeated by 10,934 votes to 5929, which were the Congress's usual figures for measures against Mr. Gompers' policy. However, it is contended that the defeat was largely due to the method of voting, which favours small, at the expense of large, Unions.

The large Unions are now mostly in favour of the industrial basis.[1] It is coming to be regarded as inevitable that the Socialists should shortly gain control of the A. F. of L., and oust the 'Old Gang'. When they have done this, Industrial Unionism will be merely a matter of time.

This Industrial Unionism, it should be remarked, differs from that of the Chicago I.W.W. and still more from that of the Deleonite I.W.W., which has been chiefly in evidence in this country. From the point of view of the I.W.W., all 'Industrial Unionism' within the American Federation of Labour must be 'fake' Industrial Unionism. It is, in fact, the Union of all the skilled crafts of a single industry in one organisation, and not, except in rare cases, of all the workers in an industry. In the textile trades, for example, there will be no attempt to get in the whole mass of immigrant labour, which will be left to the I.W.W. The American Federation will organise the skilled, and perhaps also the unskilled so far as they are of like nationality and standards of life ; it will not attempt to realise the I.W.W. motto, ' One Union for all—and once a Union man, always a Union man '. Nor will it aim at the universal transfer card and initiation fee which the I.W.W. advocates.[2] The Industrial Unionism which is gradually conquering the English-speaking world of Labour in America is exactly similar to the amalgamation movement in England, and has many of the same difficulties to contend with.

All the difficulties it has not, though it has others

[1] W. Z. Foster in the *Syndicalist*, March 1913.

[2] Tom Mann, who toured the U.S.A. in 1913, strongly urged the need for co-operation on these lines between the A.F. of L. and the I.W.W.

as serious—for the American Unions, even among the
skilled workers, have not dealt much in ' benefits '.[1]
They are fighting organisations, and their benefits
take the form of high wages, monopolies of labour
and security of employment. There are therefore
less problems arising out of different scales of contributions and benefits than in this country ; but this
is counterbalanced by the extraordinary spirit of
sectionalism that prevails. Still, there seems little
doubt that in the most important industries the
industrial form of organisation will soon carry the
day, and the Socialists triumph over Mr. Gompers
and his friends. There will then be two separate
Industrial Unionisms in America ; but neither will
be what is generally meant by Industrial Unionism,
and still more, neither will be that pure Class Unionism
which unites all the working-classes, irrespective of
industry, in one big organisation. There are thus
four different brands of Industrial Unionism, even
without taking into account rival methods of defining
the limits of industries. In America, two at least of
these are prevailing ; but neither the doctrines of the
old Chicago I.W.W. leaders nor Deleonite Class
Unionism is any longer likely to make headway. The
two forms that survive are the creation of new Unions
solely for the unskilled, and the amalgamation of
existing Unions mainly for the skilled. In the latter
process at least we in England may take an interest ;
for, though industrial concentration has gone even

[1] The I.W.W. of course does not deal in benefits at all.
For the A. F. of L. see on this point Werner Sombart's *Socialism
and the Social Movement* (English translation). The figures
published by the A. F. of L. are, however, misleading, as they
leave out of account large sums expended by the local branches
of the various Associations.

farther in America than here, the tendencies that are to be found in the A. F. of L. are in many respects equally applicable to our own Trade Union difficulties. Sectionalism is out of date here as well as in America, and, as we have no completely distinct class of unskilled labour in this country, we may well hope that Industrial Unionism, if it be practicable, may afford a more perfect solution of our problems than we have found that it can provide in America. The existence of a strong tendency in America to organise industrially is an additional incitement to us not to leave proposals for Industrial Unionism at home unwelcomed and unexamined. So long as fusion and not destruction be the method adopted, we may reasonably hope from that source for a great accession of strength. The difficulties in the way may of course be in some cases insuperable ; and it will be our task later on to examine them. But the American movement is at least a hint of the direction in which we should look for a solution of the problems that are constantly perplexing us at home.

It will be well in this place to clear up a very general misconception, because here its absurdity is most easily seen. It is often assumed without examination that the object of the industrial form of organisation is to allow national strikes in any industry to be called whenever a dispute arises. To an American, as to a German, such a suggestion would at once appear in all its absurdity ; to an Englishman, fresh from the Coal Strike and the Railway Strike, it is not at first sight so unnatural. It will therefore be well to see what Americans have to say of the conduct of strikes. We must take our examples mainly from the I.W.W., and first from Mr. Vincent St. John.

" The I.W.W. recognise that the day of successful

long strikes is past. Under all ordinary circumstances, a strike that is not won in four to six weeks cannot be won by remaining out longer. In trustified industry the employer can better afford to fight one strike that lasts six months than he can six strikes that take place in that period."

Whatever may be thought of the last part of this statement, the first is very largely true. It is the employers' interest to keep on a strike till the men are utterly exhausted and their organisation falls to pieces : and, to defeat this, the men must learn to return to work when they feel they cannot win, without waiting to be starved into submission. It must be realised that the strikes in question are not national, but local. Except in a very few small industries, a national strike in America is unthinkable. The locality is self-contained, and the strike is effective if it completely covers the locality. But even there, the workers cannot hope to be able to outlast the capitalist. They can only get concessions by striking suddenly when it will be most inconvenient for him, and so cutting off work at the time when profits are greatest. Only by such methods can highly concentrated capital be met and defeated.

On the whole then, unlike our own as the American movement appears at first sight, there are lessons to be learnt from it and resemblances to be noticed on a closer scrutiny. It is, however, least important for us where it is most interesting in itself. We have no class of workers in any degree comparable with the great new proletarian army of the United States, and adjurations addressed to our Unions, in the hope of making them mould themselves after such a pattern, are bound to be useless and ill-conceived. It is not until the cleavage in the American   ld of Labour, the absolute division between skilled and unskilled, is properly realised, that we are in a position to tell what may be of use to us and guide us in solving our own problems. For the American movement is as characteristically American as ours is characteristically English, and it is a truth to be remembered that institutions are born and not made. American 'Syndicalism', if we choose to call it so, is for America, as French Syndicalism is for France. The greatest service that can be done us by the intelligent study of foreign Labour movements is to save us at least from becoming cosmopolitans.

CHAPTER VI

FURTHER LESSONS FROM ABROAD—THE GENERAL STRIKE

FRANCE and America have been dealt with in such detail because they are new and wide movements, of just the sort that most readily exercises a widespread influence. They were further pointed out to us as worthy of investigation because they were the begetters respectively of the Syndicalist and of the Industrial Unionist movements, whose absorption and reconciliation we are now actually witnessing. There is no need for our present purpose to treat of any other foreign Labour movement with equal detail; for neither have the rest so much that is fresh and distinctive, nor is there any question of the importation, at present, of any new gospel from abroad. Neither Germany, with its elaborate and efficient Trade Unionism, nor Italy, with a growing force of revolt behind it, is likely to convey to any body of men in this country the idea of a new gospel. The problem for Trade Unionists in Great Britain is now, not the discovery of new sources of inspiration, but the utilisation of the sources it has already recognised.

While, however, it is unnecessary to go into detail concerning these other movements, it is worth while to pick out a few points in which we may learn from them useful lessons, and discover either what to seek or what to avoid. Of Italy, interesting in itself though the Italian movement undoubtedly is, we shall say little. Italy is above all a Latin country, and, in the realm of ideas, its kinship with France is remarkable. On the theoretical side, Italy has accepted and developed the gospel of Syndicalism almost in the French form. M. Sorel's influence has been there also very great, and, as Italian Socialism has always been much devoted to the criticism and interpretation of Marxian doctrine, his neo-Marxism has probably had even more effect on theory there than in France. In spite, however, of these theoretical impulses, the actual Labour movement in Italy seems to be going its own way. In industry, it is, in the main, a new country; conditions of labour are, in most parts, shockingly bad, and organisation among the workers, though not a new thing, is only beginning to be really important. The Italian movement is still mainly in the experimental stage; the circumstances of industry allow of no co-operation between the workers of the South, where modern methods have not greatly developed, and the factory-workers of the North; and differences of theory arise about labour organisation where differences are really only of circumstance and stage of development. Italy is not, industrially speaking, a unity; and, until it becomes one, it cannot have a strong national Labour movement, possessed of a defined character and a common ideal.

The first lesson, therefore, we should learn about Italy is not to take much notice when Syndicalists, or any other class of persons, call our attention to the wonders that are being accomplished there. It would be possible to dismiss the whole Italian movement without more said, had not an article in the *English Review* for June 1912 caused widespread misunderstanding and raised many false hopes. In that number appeared an article entitled 'Syndicalism', by Odon Por and F. M. Atkinson. It dealt mainly, though not exclusively, with the supposed 'syndicalisation' of the industry of Bottle-Blowing in Italy. The workers, it appeared, had struck for better wages, and then, as the 'trust' which employed them would not yield, had succeeded in starting factories of their own, owned and controlled by the workers. This, it was announced, was the first great triumph of Syndicalism, a foretaste of the coming order. Soon all the workers would be owning their own factories, the capitalist would have been expropriated, and the Syndicalist State would be in full blast. In point of fact, the Co-operative (not Syndicalist) Glass-blowers have no connection with Syndicalism, and Italy still goes on in the good old capitalist way.

All questions of the success or failure of such enterprises apart, there is here nothing that can reasonably be called Syndicalism. We in England are familiar enough with the sporadic appearances and nearly invariable failures of the 'self-governing workshop', and the experience of Continental countries is almost exactly the same. Why these experiments fail we may see better hereafter; it is enough for the moment that they have behind them a long record of failures, and hardly any successes. The Bottle-blowers, in the course of a strike, founded such a factory, the only distinctive feature being that it was founded by the Union itself, though it was a separate organisation from the Union. The new factory enjoyed, for a time, considerable success, and further factories were started in connection with it. But from the first it was Co-operative and not Syndicalist, and even its co-operation was not of the purest sort. Many of the workers were indeed shareholders, but their share depended on their investment, and did not go necessarily along with the work they did. In the Syndicalist idea, the Union would control the industry, and the worker would be, merely because he worked in it, a part *controller* of it ; here the worker, because he had invested money, was a part *proprietor* of the factory. He was a worker, and a shareholder ; but the two facts were not essentially connected. The concern was then merely an instance of Co-operation of Producers, and even as such it was by no means a pure instance. All along, the workers who were shareholders employed others who were not ; they were, in fact, an aristocracy of working-proprietors, and sometimes even, as time went on, of non-working proprietors. Such concerns have no more to do with Syndicalism than Sir William Lever's famous ' advertisement ' village, Port Sunlight. They may, or may not, be successful commercial experiments ; but the less notice that is taken of them by revolutionaries the better for clear thinking, and the worse for friends of ' things as they are '.

With that, we may leave Italy with a clear conscience. Its Labour movement is in itself deeply interesting, but it throws no light on the situation in this country, and its interest is that of rudimentary rather than developed organisation.

Germany stands quite at the other end of the line of advance. Its Trade Unions are as firmly established as our own, and far better organised against the employer. Modelled in the first instance mainly on the English Unions, the German ' *Gewerkschaften* ' have grown so fast that they now equal them in effective membership, without losing strength from the subdivision of their forces into a very great number of small and inefficient 'local' or 'sectional' Unions. They have secured this comprehensive and simple organisation largely through starting late, with the initial backing of a strong political Labour movement; but, whatever their origin, it is indisputable that their complete solidarity makes them much more formidable than they could possibly be without it. In spite of all the difficulties monarchical Germany throws in the way of effective industrial action, the German Unions have been powerful instruments for the raising of wages and for the education in class-consciousness of the industrial proletariat.

It is, of course, true that German Trade Unionism has had to face difficulties that have not appeared in England. There are in Germany three different and opposing forms of trade combination, each with its central commission or Federation, without counting minor varieties. But, in reality, the history of industrial organisation in Germany is the history of the 'Free' or 'Social-Democratic' Unions. Neither the 'Christian' Unions nor the 'Hirsch-Duncker' or 'Liberal' Unions are really of any great importance in comparison. The 'Christian' Unions are indeed growing rapidly; but the 'Hirsch-Duncker' *Gewerkvereine* are stationary, and will probably gradually disappear.

There is no need to recapitulate the early struggles of Trade Unionism in Germany. The movement first arose in the 'sixties, but in 1874, owing partly to official repression, and partly to the quarrels of the followers of Marx and Lassalle, the first Trade Union Federation perished. Attempts to revive the Unions after the realisation of Socialist unity in 1875 were easily repressed by the Government, and in 1879 the Anti-Socialist Law made effective trade combina-

LABOUR IN GERMANY

tion, as well as political action, impossible. It was not till 1890, the year in which the General Commission of Trade Unions was founded, that German Unionism had any chance of becoming imporant. From 1894 to the present time, the growth of the 'Social-Democratic' Unions has been continuous; from having a quarter of a million members they had come to include two and a half millions in 1911.

The 'Christian' Unions were established in 1893, in opposition to the new 'Socialist' Unions. They include both Catholics and Protestants, but have been from the first mainly Catholic. One of their great sources of weakness, which grows worse rather than better, is internal religious bickering. The last report of the Social-Democratic Unions is highly jubilant over the quarrel between the Christian Unions and the Catholic Church. These Unions were originally intended to be peaceful, and were founded by agreement with the employers; but with time they are being driven by force of circumstances to take action in the same manner as the 'free' Unions. In fact, the Catholics and reactionaries who founded them have often got more than they bargained for. These Unions have the less effect in weakening the hold of the Social-Democrats, because their membership, which is in all under 350,000, comes mainly from districts in which the Socialists cannot hope at present to make much headway. By far the largest body within the Christian Unions is that of the Miners, who numbered 78,000 in 1909, since when there has been a great increase. These Miners come mostly from coalfields the Social-Democrats, who had organised 113,000 Miners in 1909,[1] could not possibly affect.

[1] 120,000 in 1911.

The existence of the 'Christian' and 'Hirsch-Duncker' Unions, together with such minor bodies as the 'Syndicalist' (formerly 'Anarchist') and the many independent Unions, does not then make much difference to the Social-Democrats in their task of organisation. The membership of the three chief organisations in 1911 speaks for itself.

 Free ('Social-Democratic') Unions, . . 2,320,986
 Christian Unions, ... 340,937
 'Hirsch-Duncker' Unions, . . . 107,743

With that much history, we can proceed at once to review the chief points in the German organisation which are of interest to us. It is often urged that the 'Social-Democratic' Unions are not really 'free', but mere tools in the hands of the political party. Such an accusation could only be made in complete ignorance of their structure and history. It is, indeed, true that the German Unions were enabled to reach an almost perfect form of organisation so rapidly mainly because they had the immense influence of the Socialists behind them. English Trade Unionism, wonderful as its growth was, grew up spasmodically and almost at haphazard, without guidance from a centre. Its central links are indeed still very weak, and the independence of each Union is not mere self-government, but vicious individualism. In Germany the historical evolution has been completely different. There were indeed Unions before the foundation of the Central Commission in 1890; but, broadly speaking, the Trade Union movement owes its whole growth, and still more the whole form of its organisation, to ideas fostered at the centre. It is not so much a federation, constituted by the coming together of independent units, as a devolution from a centre, a ' class ' organisation broken up into separate branches for convenience and utility. It can be said, far more than British, or even than French, Unionism, to have a concerted policy directed from the centre, and conscious of the aims and methods to be pursued.

This centralised control of policy, however, is far from implying political subservience on the part of the Unions. It has been seen throughout that either the capture of the Unions for politics, or the capture of the Socialistic Party for Trade Unionism, would be fatal to both. The Socialists saw that it would be to their advantage, and to the good of Labour as a whole, that there should be a strong Trade Union movement. They saw, no doubt, also that such a movement would be electorally of the greatest help to them. But they did not make the mistake of the followers of M. Jules Guesde in France, and try to collar the movement wholly for politics. They realised that the best chance of harmonious working lay in a clear separation of function, within a recognised unity of purpose. They made no conditions that members of the Free Unions must be Social-Democrats, nor did they attempt to give the Socialist Party a false appearance of strength by tacking the Trade Unions forcibly on to its tail. As a result, they have at once the strongest Socialist Party and the strongest Trade Union movement in the world.

No doubt, this was made very much easier for them by the political condition of the German Empire. In an industrial country that makes no pretence of being a democracy it is far easier to build up democratic movements and rouse strong democratic feeling. There is less, on the side of his opponents, to deceive the German worker into siding with his enemies.

The German is, moreover, at all times a very easy person to organise. There was therefore the less trouble in getting men to join two separate organisations, and play their part in both sections of the Labour movement, working independently. The Socialist Party had, in fact, no reason for hesitating to give the Trade Unions full autonomy at the outset, and leave them to take care of their own prospects and organisation.

This in no way invalidates the conclusion that the influence of the Socialist Party in German Trade Unionism has been enormous, and all to the good. Germany is indeed the only country that has in effect realised the Greater Unionism. In Great Britain there are now about three and a quarter million Trade Unionists and about eleven hundred Unions, and, whereas the membership is increasing rapidly, the number of Unions is decreasing only very slowly. In Germany, the two and a half millions of the Free Unions were divided into only 51 Unions in 1911, and, while the number of members was growing fast, the number of Unions was as sensibly diminishing.[1] Since 1906 the number of Unions has dropped from 66 to 51, and further amalgamations may be expected. This process is largely due to Social-Democratic influence, which enables ideal pressure to be put on German Unionists in a manner that is not conceivable here.

When the list of the German Unions is compared

[1] The official figures for 1909 gave the number of 'Social-Democratic' Unions as 57, and the number of 'Hirsch-Duncker' *Gewerkvereine* as 2102. The Social-Democratic figures are for close national amalgamations (11,725 branches); the others for Unions more loosely *federated*. This close amalgamation, we shall see, is the strength of the Free Unions.

with any list of the great British Trade Unions, several important differences at once appear. The first, and the most significant, is, of course, the great disparity in numbers. In nearly every case, except those of the Miners and the Railwaymen, we have at least several Unions trying to do exactly the same things. Within the German organisation, there is no single instance of such overlapping. Sectionalism there is, as in the case of the three or four Printers' Unions that still exist; but the cases that call for further amalgamation are always those in which two different branches of a single industry are catered for by different organisations. The process of fusion among such Unions is going on steadily, and though difficult marginal cases must arise—that of the Ships' Carpenters, for instance—it may be regarded as certain that the process will, at no very remote date, be practically completed. This does not, of course, mean that the total number of Unions in Germany is 51, and the total number in England 1168. The figures are not in any sense comparable. We have here no ready method of distinguishing between real national Unions and little local Unions, which figure side by side without distinction in the Board of Trade and Registrars' Reports. As an additional complication, many local Unions have grandiloquent national names, and their real condition is only betrayed by their membership. No doubt a complete return of all the Trade Unions in Germany would present an appearance even more absurd than the long list of our Unions. This, however, does not at all invalidate what we have said. In the 'Social-Democratic' Unions, nearly three million workers really work together in 51 National Unions; according to the figures for 1910, our 51 biggest Unions had only just over 1,500,000 members, and these neither covered the same range of trades, nor worked together with any cohesion like that of the German Unions.

In form, then, the German Unions are almost perfectly co-ordinated amalgamations, sometimes on 'Industrial', and sometimes on 'occupational' lines. But, in saying this, we have not said all. It has been the weakness of many Syndicalists and Industrial Unionists that, in urging the 'industrial' or 'greater' as opposed to the 'craft' structure, they have set their thoughts so much upon the object of organising all the workers as a 'class' that they have quite forgotten to provide for the representation of sectional and 'trade' or 'craft' interests within the Greater Union. In the case of the Industrial Workers of the World, as we saw, such an omission did not matter, because none of the workers concerned were more than half-skilled; but as soon as highly skilled workers have to be organised, sectional problems become very important. The German workers, while securing united action, have therefore taken great care to get sectional interests well looked after. This has been done, not by means of 'craft' autonomy, which cannot but make concerted action impossible, but by giving adequate representation to sectional interests. It is simplest to take an actual example, though the precise formation, of course, differs very greatly according to the circumstances of each industry. The Metal Workers' Union, with 515,145 members, is divided into 451 branches, 11 districts, and 26 'craft' sections. The District Council, to which all disputes are referred in the first instance, is elected on a 'sectional' basis, so that all branches of the occupation are represented. In the National

Executive, districts, and not 'crafts', are the units of representation.[1]

By this means the difficulty of reconciling sectional interests has been overcome, and a ready means of settling disputes within the industry devised. At the same time, sectional interests have not been given too much power, and concerted action has not been impaired. The District Council represents all sections of the industry; but its sectional basis is found to be enough to give the sections proper representation. The main need of a section in a big industrial Union is to secure a proper understanding, on the part of the authorities, of its peculiar requirements; and this is done within the whole Union by the District Council. It is the task which the Trades Councils in England, in spite of all endeavours, continually fail to accomplish. In the Trades Council, the sections are represented, but there is nothing to reconcile them; in the German District Council (of one *industry* or group of occupations only, it is true) interests are at once represented and reconciled.

This machinery alone would not be enough to secure smooth working. Two important points remain to be dealt with. These are, first, the position of the officials, and secondly, the question of local and central control of strikes. A great deal of the discontent in our Trade Unions has been directed against the officials, who are said to have hung back, and aimed at peace at any price. There will be more to say of this when we come to speak of England directly; it is here enough to declare that, roughly

[1] W. Stephen Sanders, *Industrial Organisation in Germany*— a pamphlet of which the author has very kindly allowed me to make use throughout this chapter.

speaking, every movement gets the leaders it deserves. If the rank and file really and consistently wanted a fighting policy, they could soon force their leaders to give it them. This attitude, however, is important for our present purpose only because German Unionism is often distrusted on account of the enormous power that rests in the hands of officials. The governing body of the Union is the paid Executive Committee representing the districts. This Executive has the last word in all questions of policy. If a District Council wishes to call a strike, it has to submit its proposals to the Executive Committee, which has full power to decide for or against. Moreover, it seems that, in the districts also, the power of the paid officials is immense. When a question comes before the District Committee, before a decision is reached, the officials are asked to report upon it, and their report seems generally to be adopted. There is no question of a ballot of all the members before a strike is called in some section or other. As in the case of our new National Union of Railwaymen, the Executive Committee decides.

Before our 'advanced' Trade Unionists condemn this method, there are further considerations to put before them. First, the machinery for enabling districts to make their representations to headquarters is far better conceived than any our Unions possess. The Executive Committee is only called upon to decide with full knowledge of the case, and of the feeling of the district. The whole matter has already been argued out thoroughly in the District Council, and the Executive Committee seldom goes directly against local opinion. The control is, in fact, far less oppressive than it looks, and everything is done, by the provision of ample opportunity for discussion, to make the chances of friction as slight as possible.

Secondly, it should be borne in mind that the men make the movement. Every developed movement is bound to require strong officials, and to give them a great deal of power. We have seen that it is for the want of such a body of officials that the French movement is weak and ill-directed. The question for Trade Unionists is not how to get rid of their officials, but how best to control them; and it is quite false logic to argue, because our officials have disappointed us, that we have to make short work of officialism. The German movement has, in great measure, both strong officials and effective control. It has shown that in the Greater Unionism, it is, in the end, far easier to combine the two than in sectional Unionism. But our common sense should tell us that there can be no popular control without popular will to control, and it is this that is lacking in England, and, to a great extent, present in Germany.

In close connection with the position of the officials is the 'strike policy' of the German Unions. Here, too, we find that the Greater Unionism in practice comes into direct conflict with the theoretical Industrial Unionism that is commonly preached in this country. We are often told that the Greater Unionism alone makes the 'general strike' possible, and even the practice of the Unions that are organised on the widest basis lends colour to the view that the object of such a method of organisation is to make the 'national' or 'general' strike within the industry or occupational group easy to accomplish. Railwaymen and Miners in this country seem to regard the national strike as their most powerful weapon.

In Germany, on the other hand, the General Strike

has found practically no supporters. The theoretical General Strike that is to revolutionise society has been received there even more coldly than in England; and even the national strike of a single industry or occupation is directly contrary to the German practice. The policy of the German Unions is, on the whole, peaceful; they prefer getting their advantages by means of conciliation to fighting for them; and, while their declared policy is to reject national agreements extending over the whole country, they encourage the conclusion of district agreements. This is, of course, very much easier for them because there is less risk of one 'craft' being bound by an agreement when it wishes to act with another within one great Union; the broad basis makes possible regional and local agreements covering a whole industry or group of occupations. The effect of this normal method of conciliation is to make the district the natural unit of negotiation, and therefore the area over which disputes most easily arise. We have seen that the first reference in case of a dispute is to the District Council, and indeed, in all things, the district is the centre of action. Strikes, too, consequently extend only over a single district, and the national strike is almost unknown. It is from the employers, rather than from the workers, that attempts to extend the area of disputes habitually come.

Essential to this policy of the German Unions is the strong central control of funds, which is a feature of the Social-Democratic Unions. All the normal levies are paid to the Central office, which administers benefits and controls strike-funds. The branches have only the power, which they exercise to a considerable extent, to make supplementary levies for their own purposes. When a strike breaks out in

LABOUR IN GERMANY

one district, there is at once behind it the whole financial force of all the districts combined in the National Union, which, over a restricted area, can meet the employers on equal terms. A national strike, in these circumstances, is regarded as a calamity threatening the Union with severe financial loss. It is held to be far better to support the district in which a strike has been sanctioned with the whole force of the Union than to fight at once over the whole area of the industry or group of occupations, and so enable the employer to resist successfully until the Union funds are exhausted. Such a policy, of course, necessitates strong central control of strikes; sporadic strikes on the unsupported initiative of a single district are not allowed; but, when once the district has got the backing of the central Executive Committee of the Union, the whole force of the organised industry is behind it, and, if its demands are reasonable, the employer is unlikely to be able to resist them. No doubt this policy of centralisation can be, and in some cases is, carried too far; but it is an integral part of German industrial policy, and cannot be separated from the other leading features of which we have already spoken.

On the whole, then, we may learn from German Trade Unionism a good deal to hope for, and some things to fear. There can be no doubt at all that its organisation is altogether very efficient, and the practical advantages it secures considerable. It is indeed essentially reformist and ameliorative rather than revolutionary and catastrophic. It leaves the Social Revolution to the Socialist Party and is content to build up the working-class of Germany into a strong class-conscious organisation, which, even if it does not introduce the bitterness of the class-war into its industrial tactics, passes over continually, with an enlarged conception of its meaning, into the ranks of the Social-Democratic Party. The inevitable result of having a reformist Labour Party is the uprising of a revolutionary Trade Union movement; the presence of a more or less revolutionary Socialist Party in Germany does much to keep the Trade Union movement reformist. But its moderation is far less that of stagnation than its enemies would have us believe; it is keenly alive to the limited problems it consents to confront, and, in its own sphere, it has shown itself very difficult to defeat and still harder to deceive. In this sense, the best rebels and revolutionaries have a full right to be reformists.

In the end, everything depends on the rank and file. The German Trade Unions can without danger be ameliorative rather than revolutionary largely because their members are to a great extent conscious of broad issues behind Trade Unionism in a manner that is quite beyond the range of the rank and file in England. The German Trade Unionist is strong enough to control strong officials; our officials are no sooner allowed to become strong than they make themselves autocrats. We must therefore be chary of regarding all the good points of the German organisation as readily transferable to England. Our problem is different, because our rank and file are not the same.

The German view of the general strike is, however, of sufficient importance to deserve further discussion. It is worth while for a moment to set beside it the experience of yet another foreign Labour movement. We all remember the disastrous failure of the Swedish General Strike of 1909; but at the time, it was almost impossible to understand any of the deeper issues involved in that conflict. The Swedish Labour movement is practically unknown in the country, and without a knowledge of its history, it is impossible to understand the situation which faced the Swedish workers at that time.

The chief importance of the Swedish Labour movement is that there, on the small scale of Swedish industry, many of the problems that face Trade Unionism in other countries have reached the stage of actual experiment. A country which employs altogether only about 400,000 persons in industry may seem at first sight too unimportant to deserve attention : its importance arises from the fact that well over 200,000 persons, or 50 per cent. of the whole, are organised in real Unions. Industrial organisation began about 1880, in the form of local Unions at Scanie, founded under the influence of German and Danish Social-Democracy. At first the development was slow, but as the rigid pattern of German Unionism was adapted to Swedish conditions, the rate of advance gradually increased. The first local craft Unions were easily beaten by temporary combinations of masters. From 1886 national ' craft ' Federations began to spring up.

From the first, there was a close alliance between the Socialist Party and the Unions, and there can be no doubt that, in the words of the Government Report,[1] " this intimate union favoured—at least at the outset—the development of both ". It is, however, becoming harder to maintain as the organisation progresses, and it is not improbable that the two bodies will ultimately become independent.

[1] *Les Lock-out et la Grève Générale en Suede en 1909* (Stockholm, 1912).

In spite of the growth of the Unions from 1886 onwards, they still met mainly with reverses at the hands of the masters. As the Report says, " the greater part of the Federations being strictly specialised according to the particular profession of the workers, and not according to the industry or general class of production of the places in which they worked, it necessarily happened that under the same master there were workers belonging to different Federations. Where negotiations, agreements, or disputes occurred between the master and a special group, the other groups could have nothing to do with them, although every modification in the conditions of work of one group necessarily reacted more or less directly on those of others. For these reasons, as well as for the uniform defence of their common interests against the masters, it soon became necessary to form a general organisation, including the different Federations." Accordingly, after several abortive efforts, the *Sveriges Landsorganisation* came into being in 1898. In April 1899 this General Confederation had 27,000 members. Its growth from 1900 to 1909 was continuous and rapid. At the end of 1900 it already had 44,000 members; and in 1909 it included 27 Federations with 162,000 members, nearly all engaged in industry and land transport.[1] Outside the General Confederation, but in close co-operation with it, were 25,000 Railwaymen and about 6000 members of the Typographical Federation. All these Unions are affiliated to the Socialist Party. There were various minor Unions of a non-political character; but these are unimportant, and play no independent part in the events of 1909.

[1] The Agricultural Federation had only 7000 members, and these were mainly engaged in forest work.

In 1898, when the General Confederation came into being, the masters were practically unorganised. Consequently, the period was marked by a long series of successful strikes. Between 1895 and 1902, out of 490 strikes, the men won in 240, the masters only in 63, and there were 184 compromises, mostly rather in the men's favour. Wages rose, hours fell, contracts had to be kept faithfully by the masters, and priority of work for Unionists was often secured. The new organisation seemed to be justifying its existence most manfully. Then, in 1902, the Socialist Party called a general strike to demand universal suffrage. This at last roused the masters to organise. Professional Federations of employers were formed, and these were linked up into national organisations. The Syndicate of Swedish Employers, which, one or two trades apart, includes almost all the masters in ' great industry', covered 101 masters employing 29,000 men in 1903, and 1423 masters employing 160,000 men in 1909. Its professed objects were " to facilitate understanding between employers, to encourage the foundation of professional and local (masters') federations, to help these and individual employers to settle labour disputes, and to indemnify employers for losses occasioned by strikes and lockouts." For this purpose, it has built up enormous funds out of which indemnities are paid, and has grown in its organisation continually more centralised and powerful. Beginning as a sort of employers' insurance company, it has gradually extended its operations, till now it is the chief force to be reckoned with in labour disputes. The Syndicate of Employers and the General Confederation tend more and more to meet as the representatives of the two conflicting parties in all great disputes. In the Syndicate of

Employers there are 27 Federations, corresponding to the 27 in the Confederation.

In addition to the Syndicate of Swedish Employers, the masters formed in 1902, on the basis of an older organisation, the Syndicate of Swedish Workshops, which covers mainly engineering, shipbuilding, coach-building and the electrical industry. In 1908 it included 162 masters employing 25,000 men. In 1905 it obtained a national agreement covering the whole country; this was renewed in 1908, and is still in force. It has established conciliation boards, and disputes in its province are as a rule arranged without strikes.

Thirdly, the Central Employers' Federation, founded in 1903, grouped in 1909 about 2000 masters employing about 40,000 men in the building and allied trades. There are also independent employers' associations in certain industries, the most important being those covering the Railways, the Printing industry, and agriculture.

By far the most important, however, of all the organisations is the Syndicate of Swedish Employers, of which we shall in future speak. The others attain to national importance only when, as in 1909, they are working in co-operation with it. The situation before the employers in 1903 was this. The Trade Unions, by organising on a large scale, had easily succeeded in putting pressure on the isolated masters who resisted their demands. The condition of the workers had greatly improved, and the masters saw no possibility of resistance on the old lines. By means of the new central organisations they saw that they would be able to meet the Confederation on an equal footing. The old policy of the federated Trade Unions had been to secure *local* agreements on every possible occasion. These local agreements they had been strong enough to enforce, and the fairly frequent revisions had gone for the most part in their favour. About 1905 the Syndicate of Employers was already strong enough to move. It aimed at replacing local agreements by national agreements covering the whole of an industry. By this means they were enabled to unite their whole forces against the Confederation. The early agreements contained, at the instance of the masters, clauses forbidding any stoppage during their currency, and set up machinery for dealing with disputes that might arise ; but when the employers had reached solidarity, they found this no longer suit them. Though they supported one another during strikes, and indemnified one another for losses incurred, they found that the workers also did this, and that the strikers could be maintained indefinitely on the wages of those at work. They therefore accepted amendments making the sympathetic strike and lock-out possible, and aimed, as far as possible, at making every dispute national, and every strike general. To every demand of a particular class of workers, they replied with the threat of a general lock-out, and so well were they organised that the Confederation dared not force such an event. Agreements became national instead of local, and every dispute became at once a trial of strength between the two great central organisations.

This is what happened in the general strike of 1909. Already in 1906 the employers, conscious of their strength, had used their whole force against the Confederation and won merely by the threat of action. They had demanded that there should be no clause in any agreement forbidding the employment of non-

Unionists, and, as every employer in the Syndicate had to get his agreement ratified by it, this meant a general abandonment of the campaign against non-Unionists. The Confederation tried to show fight, but dared not face a struggle, and finally accepted the compromise that there should be no discrimination against Trade Unionists. Then a dispute arose in the transport industry; again the Syndicate threatened a lock-out, and again the Confederation gave way. In 1908 came a trade depression; and reductions in wages were generally demanded by the masters. The Confederation knew that it was not in a position to fight, and that the moment was very favourable to the masters. It would have given way; but at this point it found its action forced by the workers themselves. In the few years since 1902 the Syndicate had become a highly centralised body, with a uniform policy and under uniform control. It could rely on being followed by the employers it included, and further controlled the policy of the other organisations of masters. The Confederation, on the other hand, was a loose, federal organisation; the Unions at the base had indeed been forced to surrender some of their powers to the Federations and to the Confederation itself; but, although normally the Confederation could claim to represent the organised workers, it had no power to control their actions. Worse still, by its constitution it was responsible for the support of any strike that might be declared by one of the constituent Unions, even when it had refused its sanction. The Confederation, therefore, found itself powerless to resist the resentment which followed the threats of reductions in wages. It became plain that, whatever attitude it chose to adopt, it was in for a fight, and, that being so, its best chance lay in declaring war instantly. Out of two or three small disputes arose the general strike of 1909. The Confederation went into the dispute knowing that it was bound to be defeated, and the strike was lost. The masters had beaten the workers at their own game of Trade Unionism.

We have seen with what astonishing rapidity the Swedish employers, as soon as they became conscious that they were face to face with the united forces of Labour, were able to organise themselves into bodies possessing far greater coherence and power of concerted action than the older Confederation of Labour had been able to approach. It is far easier for masters than for slaves to organise; the Trade Unionism of the workers has been won in the past by infinite labour and in the teeth of infinite difficulties. The masters, when they choose to organise, will find themselves confronted by no such terrors; as soon as organisation suits their purposes, they can accomplish it rapidly, painlessly and thoroughly. The lesson we may learn from the Swedish Labour movement is that it is of no manner of use for the workers to rely permanently on the mere size of their organisations: at that game they will be beaten by the employer, whenever he chooses to exert himself. The master-class is, by its nature, capable of far greater cohesion and far prompter joint action than working-class bodies seem likely to attain. In the contest of organisation, the workers seem certain to be outwitted by their more subtle opponents. Plutocracy will beat democracy, as long as the democrats leave the plutocrats the choice of weapons.

On the other hand, it seems difficult for democracy to get the chance of using its own weapon. For if the great strike must in the end be beaten by the great lock-out, it is equally certain that, in face of a capitalist class organised on the grand scale, the sporadic strike and the small organisation are equally helpless. Here again the case of Sweden shows what to expect. The workers were the first to organise; but they aimed, not at putting direct pressure on the whole employing class to grant definite and uniform terms, but at exercising sporadic pressure in every individual case upon the isolated capitalist. Labour's game was to get as much as possible out of the individual master, and not to come to a general agreement which must to some extent be based on the resources of the weaker capitalists. The masters, on the other hand, were no sooner organised than they demanded this very thing: their interests were best suited by national agreements covering the whole of an industry. Nay more, they soon found that it paid them to use, at every point, the threat of a general lock-out, even at the cost of a general strike. The workers then seemed to be altogether beaten; the general strike would fail because of the superior resources at the back of the employers, and the sectional or local strike merely brought on a general lock-out. This was the more disastrous because the Confederation of Labour, without controlling the acts of its constituent Unions and Federations, was financially responsible for their mistakes. Such a position would be intolerable anywhere: where the workers are confronted with a centralised organisation of masters, they must either surrender some measure of control over their acts to the central organisation of Labour, or else they must stand alone, and look for no financial assistance from headquarters. If they do the latter, the master will be fully insured against damage by his organisation, and they are bound to be defeated.

LESSONS FROM ABROAD

The central organisation must therefore inevitably take on new powers and functions as the struggle between Capital and Labour becomes more centralised. But if, as we have argued, the general strike is equally easily defeated by a class of well-organised masters, of what use is this centralisation? It is here that the example of Germany is again valuable. Where a general strike will fail for lack of funds, a local strike well supported by the wages of those at work may succeed; but in order that such successes shall be permanent, strikes must require the sanction of the central body. It is still, of course, quite possible for the masters to retaliate with the general lock-out; but, in the first place, this in itself prejudices their case in the eyes of the public, and, in the second, they may not always be ready to do so. The Swedish General Strike followed upon the beginning of a trade depression; at such a time, a general lock-out is most likely to suit the master-class. But it is just at such times, when reductions are threatened, that sporadic strikes are sure to break out, unless the central authority has the power to control them. The local strike at the beginning of a boom will seldom be answered by a general lock-out, just because each individual master wants to make hay while the sun shines. A local strike at such a moment may be the best method of breaking up the solidarity of the master-class, and obtaining the concessions demanded one by one, in locality after locality. But, for the successful pursuit of such tactics, a great deal of centralisation is necessary, and to centralisation there is, at the present time, a great and growing opposition among those of the rank and file who, because they are rebels, really matter.

The fact that the leaders of Trade Unionism in England have, for the most part, singularly thick heads is naturally responsible for this attitude. Men do not want to entrust their liberty of action to those by whom they have no confidence of its being safeguarded. There is abroad a legitimate spirit of resentment at the inaction and stupidity of many of the leaders, and, until the leaders have shown themselves more worthy of receiving authority, it is unlikely that the people will consent to confer any more on them. Here, however, we are dealing in generalisations; we are now to think, not of the personality of the leaders of English Trade Unionism, but of the general lessons about Trade Union policy we can get from abroad. And, personalities apart, everything points to the conclusion that, in the great industries at least, the only kind of strike that has much chance of success is the strike that is backed by the whole industry, and perhaps by the whole Trade Union movement. And, if local strikes are to be successful, they must be under firm central control. The local organisation cannot claim to draw on central funds without coming under central control, and without central funds the local unit will, in the end, when capital is fully organised, be wholly impotent.

When we come to deal more at length with the strike policy that is possible and desirable for this country, we shall doubtless have many reservations and modifications to make in respect of these conclusions. In particular, we shall have to make an exception in the case of small strikes of underpaid workers. At present, the attempt is only to lay down the general lines, and to inquire what, in the most general terms, is the secret of German success and of Swedish failure in Trade Unionism. It is, of course, true that the situation in Sweden has been profoundly modified by the smallness of the country, as well as by the comparative insignificance of its industry. It has been far easier there for both workers and masters, once a start was made, to organise into opposing compact central bodies. What is contended is that Sweden presents in miniature the inevitable future of industry in greater countries. There are, of course, infinitely more difficulties in the way of absolute solidarity in countries where industry is more complicated. At present, we in England have not reached the stage of complete solidarity even of the masters in each industry by itself; but towards this we are visibly and increasingly tending.

Whatever the degree of industrial concentration, the comparative desirability of national and local strikes varies widely with the industry concerned, and it is dangerous to generalise in favour of either. What the example of Sweden teaches is not so much the failure of either, as the impossibility of combining centralised finance with absolute local autonomy in the declaration of strikes. This at once gives the employer the chance to suck the life-blood from an organisation by provoking a local dispute, and causing the Union to spend its funds, and then to follow this manœuvre up by declaring a national lock-out. As we shall see, the experience of the South Wales Miners goes to prove this. The case for and against local autonomy will be examined in a later chapter, when we come to speak of Trade Union government. Whatever the uses of the local strike, the national strike is increasingly the weapon for great national issues.

It may seem that the General Strike, of which we have recently been hearing so much, has been far too brusquely and summarily dismissed. It is such a vague name that, if we are to understand it, we must now examine it in some detail. It is possible to divide the phenomena, actual or conceivable, which are called 'general strikes' in many ways. We will attempt a rough classification, and deal with each form in turn. According to their aims, we may divide general strikes into four classes, political, anti-militaristic, economic and social. According to the enemy at which they are directed, we might divide them into three classes, strikes against the Government, strikes against employers, and strikes against Society. Neither classification is satisfactory; but the first will serve. All these forms have their advocates, and two of them at least have been tried.

I. A *political* general strike aims at a specific reform, which it calls on the legislature to pass into law. It uses the industrial weapon for a specific political object, and therefore comes into conflict with the General Strike of the Syndicalists, and with syndicalist theory generally. It accepts the State, and acknowledges that the worker is concerned with politics. The object of this form of strike has, as a rule, been the extension of the suffrage; but there is no reason why it should not be applied to any political object. In some cases, it may approach in character either the 'economic' or the 'social' form. When M. Sorel says that "useful laws may be won by direct action", he is at least departing from the extreme doctrine that the State is nothing to the workers. A strike for or against a law may have either a political or an economic object, and it is doubtful whether strikes against the Government for an economic end should be called 'political' or 'economic'. To which class, for instance, would a strike against the Insurance Act belong?

For our present purpose, it is best to confine ourselves to the chief class of 'political' general strikes,

THE GENERAL STRIKE

those in favour of franchise reform, generally of universal suffrage. Very recently, we have had an instance of such a strike in Belgium, where, in addition, there had been two earlier attempts. We have already mentioned the 'political' general strike of 1902 in Sweden. The Belgian strike of 1893 was the first, and though it was by no means complete or well organised, it succeeded in some measure, because of the fear it struck to the heart of the middle classes. It secured not 'one man, one vote', but universal suffrage combined with plural voting. The second strike, in 1902, though more general and better organised, failed. The country was no longer frightened of it; its terrors were known, and it was seen not to be irresistible. The third strike, in 1913, though it afforded a fine display of solidarity, made it clear from the attitude the Government took up that the general strike has lost its terrors. There was never any risk that it would develop into a revolution; it was an organised and powerful protest, and no more. The weight it carried was merely that of an exceptionally great demonstration. The force behind it was the force of public opinion, and not the threat of revolution.

The Swedish strike of 1902 professedly accepted these limitations. It was fixed definitely for the days during which Parliament was to debate the question of electoral reform, and was never intended to go on beyond that period. It was merely an organised protest, successful in that it secured the withdrawal of the Government Bill.

These examples seem to prove that the political general strike can be used with effect as a means of demonstrating on a large scale, but that it cannot hope to conquer by mere force. The strikers can succeed only by influencing public opinion, and so acting on the fears of the Government. If the Government is sure of its electorate, there is no chance of the strikers outlasting it. Nor, in the present state of Labour, is there more chance of the political strike developing into a revolution. Naturally, this kind of strike has arisen where, as in Belgium and Sweden, the Trade Unions act in close co-operation with the Socialist Party. This has certainly tended to make them more pacific than they would otherwise have been ; but in any case there is little prospect of a strike directed to the gaining of a definite reform, and necessarily limited in duration, developing into a real manifestation of the revolutionary spirit. It is as an organised demonstration that the political general strike is acceptable ; it is a weapon of some importance where the Government tries to force through a bad and unpopular Bill. It might well have been used in the case of the Insurance Act.

II. Second comes the *anti-militaristic* general strike. Of this there is no actual case, though France has several times come near furnishing one. Its most popular form is that generally preached by Mr. Keir Hardie, the ' strike against war '. When two powers declare war on each other, it is urged, let the workers of both countries go on strike, and refuse to play the capitalists' game. This looks very well on paper, and it is possible, in times of peace, to get up, among a limited class, quite a lot of enthusiasm for such a proposal. But there is nothing so certain as that, at the first breath of a war-scare, all the peaceable professions of the workers will be forgotten, and jingoism will sweep like a scourge over the country. However true it may be that the interests of the working-class are in all countries identical, there is assuredly no working-class educated enough or sober enough to recognise the identity in the midst of a war-scare. A strike against war on a large scale is, in this country at any rate, absolutely inconceivable; in Germany the attempt is more possible, but its failure is equally sure. The strike against war may be ruled out at once as a sheer impossibility.[1]

III. The *economic* general strike is devoted to gaining some definite concession from the employer, and differs from the ordinary partial strike only in extent. The classical instance is, of course, the Swedish strike of 1909, with which we have already dealt. The Dutch General Strike of 1903, which was directed against the State, was economic in aim, as it was declared to resist legislation against strikes in public services. It was an utter failure; but too much importance should not be attached to it, as want of organisation was the chief cause of its ill-success: it was general in little more than name.

The name 'general strike' is sometimes used loosely to cover national strikes in a particular industry. We have seen, in speaking of Sweden, to what extent the two cases are similar; but the confusion of them, in a discussion of the general strike as a whole, merely leads to difficulties. It is quite possible to approve of the national industrial strike, a railway or a coal strike for instance, without expressing approval of the economic general strike, properly so called.

It is clear from the beginning that such a strike demands a degree of solidarity among the workers which they are far from having attained, or else an extraordinarily broad issue. In Sweden, the element of solidarity was present, the broad issue mainly lacking. In this country, it is clear that, for a long

[1] Written in 1913.

time at any rate, we shall not have a Labour movement prepared to call a general strike in support of any one section, nor would such a strike as a rule make it any the easier for the section to gain its demands. The case only arises, the general strike only becomes possible on such issues, when both workers and employers are organised into single confederacies capable, in a high degree, of concerted action. When there is a General Federation of Trade Unions including nearly all the working-class organisations, confronted by a body representing nearly all employers, it will be time to face the possibility of the smallest dispute becoming general, as a quarrel about a single employee may now lead to a national strike of railwaymen, or a national lock-out of textile workers.

The second class of economic general strikes is hard to distinguish from some kinds of 'political' strikes. An issue sufficiently broad to bring out all the workers, even if it is economic rather than political, will inevitably involve the State. If a general strike in favour of an eight hours' day were to be declared, it is quite certain that, in case of its success, it would be necessary for the State to step in and legalise what the workers had won. The same would be the case with general strikes against non-unionists, against a Government Bill regulating Trade Unions, in favour of a Minimum Wage, or the like. In every case the State, as well as the employer, would be more or less directly involved, and the strike would be political as well as economic.

That such general strikes are a possibility it would be folly to deny; that they would have, at present, much chance of success appears to be very improbable. It is hardly to be inferred from the phenomena of the Labour unrest that the feeling of solidarity is strong enough to bring about action on so great a scale even on the broadest and most universal issues. But, if the necessary solidarity could be attained, there seems no reason why such strikes should not have their use. It is necessary here again to distinguish between their possible uses. Some advocates hold that direct action would itself win the eight hours' day, and that the State Bill legalising it would come as a mere ratification of what the workers had won. This conclusion is optimistic, and seems hardly justified. It is perfectly true that nobody could make the worker labour for more than eight hours if he did not want to; but it is equally clear that there would be a good many 'blacklegs' ready to work a long time, and, further, that no power on earth could prevent the employers from docking wages to meet the loss of time. But the eight hours' day is no use if wages go down; the general strike on behalf of it would merely commit the Trade Unions to a far longer and fiercer battle of hopeless resistance to a general fall in wages.

The economic general strike, therefore, though it may in certain extreme cases be justifiable, is not a weapon for everyday use, and not one that should be carelessly applied. It would be too much to say that it is always a mistake; but we can at least say that in no great country has it, at present, the slightest chance of succeeding. For the distant future, it is easier to find inspiration, if we like 'vital lies' and 'social myths', and similar tomfoolery, in the social general strike of the Syndicalists and the Anarchists.

IV. The *social* general strike aims at the complete overthrow of capitalist society, and the substitution of a new order. We have already had something to say of it in dealing with the doctrines of French

Syndicalism, in the rhetorical expositions of MM. Sorel, Berth and Lagardelle. Here we have to do with only a part of what was there included under the head of the General Strike. We are no longer concerned with the " general strike that is realised daily ", with the revolutionary aspiration that should be present in every movement of the working-class ; we are concerned solely with the historical dogma of the General Strike that is some day to burst out and overwhelm capitalist society. For it is certain that, although some writers regard the general strike merely as a ' vital lie ', a necessary falsehood designed to instil courage into the workers, there are others who take the idea seriously, and in all honesty propose to consummate the overthrow of bourgeois society by means of the social general strike—no longer with folded arms, with the peace that characterised the political strike, but, as the French say, *perlée*, and scorning no weapons, however savage and lawless, that may contribute to the destruction of Capitalism.

It is therefore necessary to take the idea of the social general strike seriously, and to escape from the region of ' myth ' into that of prophecy. The General Strike is by no means a new idea ; its antiquity has been sufficiently insisted on by every writer who has advocated its use. For us, it is most important to remark that it found its way into Syndicalism straight out of Anarchist Communism. William Morris made it the method of the social revolution in *News from Nowhere*, and it has long been a leading feature of Communist propaganda. MM. Pataud and Pouget, in their Syndicalist Utopia *Comment nous ferons la Révolution*,[1] by no means hit on a new idea in ushering

[1] *Syndicalism and the Co-operative Commonwealth*, Oxford, 1913.

THE GENERAL STRIKE

in their 'great change' by means of a half-conscious strike gradually extending over the whole working-class. The idea is old, and has always exercised a powerful fascination over young rebels of every school. M. Briand, the most notorious strike-breaker of all French Premiers, was in earlier days a notable advocate of it, and it has always been over the idealist and the middle-class Socialist that it has cast the strongest spell.

The idea is presented in two different forms. Either the General Strike is to come like a thief in the night, arising out of some small and unimportant dispute and spreading like wild-fire through the whole country, or it is to be a carefully calculated outbreak, arranged in advance and prepared for by all the Trade Unions and Co-operative Societies in the country. In discussing these two forms, we must remember that the object of the strike is the entire overthrow of the present social system, and the substitution for it of a new society, based wholly on production. The common answer to advocates of such a strike is to say that if the workers were educated up to such a point as to be capable of declaring it, it would be already unnecessary, and they would find it far easier to substitute the new for the old order by more peaceful methods, industrial and political. If we regard the General Strike as taking the second form, as carefully prepared in advance, this argument seems to have force. Syndicalists generally answer it by repudiating the preconceived strike, and arguing that the General Strike will come on us when we least expect it, by a sudden uprising of the great mass of the workers and a sudden realisation of their position in the world of Capitalism. The answer to this is that the workers will do nothing of the sort. It is possible that such an upheaval may occur in France or Italy or Spain, where it will certainly fail if it does occur; but in England or Germany or America it is quite inconceivable. The English worker is far too stably organised, and far too conservative in nature, to take any such leap in the dark; for him, as for the German, the General Strike is an idea that is at once grotesquely unpractical and even without instinctive appeal. Even in France, it is clear that the leaders are well aware that the Social General Strike and the 'Great Change' are only a 'myth'; but in countries that are used to revolutions such an idea has its appeal, and serves as a good propagandist notion. Its importation into England is a mistaken policy. We want more revolutionary feeling in this country; but we must make our own revolutionary conceptions, and not import the less successful of French ideas. For this country, the Social General Strike is irrelevant. Mr. Tom Mann may preach it; but he will not get anybody to take it seriously. And, to judge from his recent book,[1] he has realised this and practically dropped it.

The nearest approach to a Social General Strike that has actually occurred is the general and instinctive movement in Italy in 1904. The Government had been using troops against strikers, and certain workers had been killed. In answer, there broke out, in a hundred towns all over Italy, an instinctive strike which lasted for five days. The revolutionaries claim that it was victorious; the reformists, headed by Turati, assert that the sole effect was to strengthen the hands of the reactionaries. In any case, the movement had only the value of an instinctive protest, and is quite without further significance. The success

[1] *From Single Tax to Syndicalism.*

of such a strike would not prove at all the possibility of success in a great outbreak aiming at the overthrow of Society generally.

Spanish General Strikes are merely revolutions on a small scale, and are not really economic in character. They break out whenever revolutionary feeling runs high, and are purely political movements which do not concern us here.

On the whole the social General Strike may be dismissed as a rather barren contribution of the theorists to economic propaganda. It is Anarchist in its origin, and has throughout the unpractical and Utopian character of Anarchistic ideas in a very marked degree. To that small minority which is always dreaming of the great to-morrow that never comes it will continue to appeal as a dramatic representation of the recovery by the disinherited of the birthright they have lost ; in revolutionary countries, it may even, in combination with political causes and forces, play a part in actual revolutions ; but in countries like England, painfully afflicted with the art of compromise and ' muddling through ', ideas gain more by being turned into ' business propositions ' than by being artistically and dramatically expressed. The idea behind the General Strike is sound enough, and in a romance like *News from Nowhere* there is no reason for objecting to its use ; but the main business of the friends of Labour to-day is to convince the workers, and that, in Great Britain at any rate, they will never succeed in doing by means of such imaginative conceptions as the General Strike. For the unimaginative, mysticism is merely mystification ; the General Strike is the General Strike and nothing more. It does not, for the average worker, symbolise the class-struggle and the final triumph of democracy ;

it is merely 'a fool's idea of running a revolution'. If it is to be received in that spirit, the less we hear of it on this side of the Channel the better England will never breed the wilder revolutionaries in any numbers, just as it has never bred Anarchists. It may import them ; but, on the whole, imported ideas do not pay. If we are to have a gospel of revolt, we must create it for ourselves, out of the materials in our hands. Neither pure Marxism nor pure Syndicalism will suit us ; and it is as a sign that we are beginning to struggle for ideas of our own that the recent intellectual unrest is hopeful. But the finding of a new theory is a long business ; and revolutionaries are too often half-educated.

CHAPTER VII

TRADE UNION STRUCTURE—INDUSTRIAL UNIONISM AND AMALGAMATION

FROM these long preliminary studies, we return at last to face the problem as it exists in our own country. Some of the more interesting of the world's Labour movements have passed before us in rapid review, and the attempt has been made to single out in each the features which are likely to be most helpful for the strengthening of our own. But perhaps at this stage we may still be met with a douche of cold water. The Trade Union movement, we shall be told, knows its own business best : through its long and troublous history it has continually been finding out what is good for it ; experience is the best teacher, and in experience our Trade Unions are rich indeed. Trade Unionists and, still more, Trade Union officials, know best what is good for them ; it is no outsider's business to teach them what he cannot know, while they must understand very well what is best. It is in the conviction that this attitude is wrong, and that the last word in all matters does not rest with the official expert, that this book has been written.

The long continuous history of the Trade Union movement in this country, while it is undoubtedly a great element of strength, has its dangers also. During the last few years, it has begun to dawn on us that the Labour movement is no more immune than any other from the official type of mind. One of the most striking facts about our Unions is the slight change which their methods have undergone through long stretches of years. Union officials are not, as a rule, persons of great original capacity; they are content to do their work efficiently in the old way, without striking out new lines or attempting to experiment till they are quite sure. They are largely of the type that makes good head clerks, but is incapable of the onerous tasks of management and initiation. They generally possess administrative ability; but they very seldom even attempt to get any general view of the problems they have to face. Such men make good officials, when there is a strong body of the rank and file to stir them up and tell them what to do. When the rank and file is itself unenlightened, they are not the sort of leaders to enable a movement to adapt itself readily to changing conditions.

If the leaders are dull and unimaginative, the followers are little better. The Trade Union movement, after the great unrest of 1889-90, sank into a deep slumber. Problems in which the rank and file had then been keenly interested were forgotten, and most of the leaders were only too glad to be allowed to let them rest. Our Trade Unions, growing continually in numbers, lost really more than they gained. The community represented by Union membership grew slacker; the Union tended to become a mere benefit society, and to forget that its sole *raison d'être* was the ceaseless war against Capitalism and exploitation. The fighting spirit slumbered: as, in the Co-operative Societies, dividends became of more account than Co-operation, so, in the Trade Unions, benefits were more than the class-struggle. In a word, Trade Unionism became respectable.

Respectability is the death of all working-class movements. With the change in the public attitude towards Trade Unionism came a change in the social standing of its officials. They too became respectable, and with their new position came their divorce from the working-class point of view, the growing breach between the official caste and the rank and file. Divorced from manual labour, the leaders ceased to understand the needs of the wage-earner, and with the crowning *camaraderie* of the House of Commons died the last semblance of the old unity. The Labour leaders entered the governing classes, and Labour was left, perplexed and unmanned, to find new leaders in its own ranks, without any assurance that it would not be merely making more recruits for the Liberal party. The worker, given a little lead, climbs so easily into the middle class, and, in the modern world, origin and original sympathy are so easily forgotten.

No wonder, then, that our Labour movement has suffered. Unfortunately, there seems no remedy. The rank and file can at most only learn to keep more control over their leaders, and to make it harder for them to get out of touch. It is easy for them to do so now just because the workers themselves have no decided point of view, and are easily led away by the first clap-trap of an election-agent. It is at least time that all the forces of Labour in this country learnt to forsake the old superstitions that our Trade Unionists are class-conscious proletarians, that the Labour Party is a Socialist Party, and that Trade Union officials know best what is good for Trade Unionism. The recent history of the Unions in this country is a history of muddle and mismanagement ; there has been no attempt to face actual problems in a statesmanlike manner, still less to anticipate difficulties before they arise. The officials have muddled through, and the rank and file have let them do it almost without protest. Meanwhile, Capital has been equipping itself to fight Labour when it wakes, and in the preliminary rounds that have been fought, the Unions, disorganised as ever, have found themselves faced by an organised opposition. We have seen, in the case of Sweden, to what perfection capitalist organisation may be brought; but, apparently, our Unions refuse to heed the warning. The strivings of a few restless spirits have made little impression on the mass of Trade Unionists. The apathy is still profound, the stupidity incredible. Even those who see what is wrong have been so long without leaders that they know not how to mend matters. They are forced to make bricks without straw, amid the contemptuous amusement of Labour leaders who will not stir a finger to help in the struggle.

Trade Union affairs are naturally first of all the affair of Trade Unionists. An outsider who dares to discuss the matter is certain to be met with a good deal of hostility, and to be told that such things are none of his business. The answer to this objection must be that Trade Unionism is far too important to be left for Trade Unionists alone to control. Whether they like it or not, Trade Unions are national institutions, and every man who interests himself at all in the condition of the workers is bound to face and think out for himself all the problems with which they are confronted. Largely against the will of their members, the Unions are gradually becoming connected in many different ways with the whole system of associations, governmental and voluntary, which makes up the modern State. Their private affairs have become

TRADE UNION STRUCTURE

matters of public interest, and as soon as it is even suggested that their competence may extend beyond the sphere of collective bargaining into other spheres as yet undefined, their internal system comes to be of direct interest to every politician and to every revolutionary.

No doubt there are certain problems which are, more intimately than others, the primary concern of Trade Unionists themselves. These are problems relating to the internal organisation, rather than to the functions, of the Unions. When, however, it is widely suggested that the Unions may themselves furnish the instruments for the overthrow of Capitalism, and that their adaptability to this end depends directly upon the way in which they are organised, even such internal problems become at once of general interest, and have to be faced by every one. In this chapter, we shall turn our attention to Trade Union structure ; in the next, we shall deal with the internal affairs of the Unions, and attempt, in the broadest outline, to describe the chief problems now awaiting solution in Trade Union government and control.

Until very recently, most people were ready to accept Trade Union structure as something settled, natural and unalterable. They knew that there were a certain number of Unions, which occasionally organised strikes, and the problem seemed to be merely one of endurance on both sides. They were perhaps vaguely aware of the existence of Federations, both of masters and of men, in certain industries ; they had heard of the Miners' Federation of Great Britain, and knew that the cotton industry had a peculiar system of organisation which they connected vaguely with the Brooklands Agreement. But they did not regard Trade Union structure as a problem calling for discussion or solution : it was supposed to be inevitable and to follow naturally the divisions of occupation and the needs of the particular industries concerned.

No doubt some Trade Unionists were aware all along of problems to be faced. Disputes about amalgamation of Unions in particular industries are not new, and the Amalgamated Society of Engineers, in particular, has always been a storm-centre. But Trade Union officials—who naturally tend to uphold the *status quo*—and even the rank and file of Trade Unionists—had not till quite recently perceived that there was a problem which, although it would have to be solved differently in every particular case, could still be faced generally and on a broad issue. To-day, the question of Trade Union structure is the central problem before the Labour movement.

It is important that we should emphasise at the outset the extraordinary complication and lack of uniformity which Union organisation now presents. As we took the lead in time, and as the growth of our Trade Unions was not inspired from any centre, but was in essence local and voluntary, it was inevitable, in the absence of any guiding principle of uniformity such as the Rochdale system imposed on local Co-operative effort, that the forms taken by the new organisations should be conflicting and various. Moreover, the Co-operative movement was able to secure a natural uniformity because the problems its different societies had to face were in all cases nearly identical ; but the Trade Unions were faced with such a diversity of complex situations that they could not possibly have more than the broadest traits in common. England then, largely because it was the first country to develop Trade Unionism, as well as because it is industrially still the most complicated, has evolved a

TRADE UNION STRUCTURE

Trade Union structure that is the merest chaos. It is in England that the organisation of the Labour movement on a 'class' basis presents the greatest difficulties and dangers. Another country may perhaps almost solve the question for itself by the talismanic phrase 'Industrial Unionism'; but it is clear that such easy solutions are not for us.

The movement known in this country as 'Industrial Syndicalism' is a combination of two streams of influence: it comes half from France and half from America. In essence, it is throughout far more English than either French or American; it has taken over foreign names and ideas, and adapted them to an English situation. As a result, it has been often vague and indefinite; it has devoted much of its attention to the gentle art of reconciling contraries, and it has ended by becoming not so much a dogma as a point of view. Its practical policy has been reduced almost to proposals for the amalgamation of existing Trade Unions, seasoned with advocacy of strikes and abuse of the Labour Party.

The movement towards what is vaguely called 'Industrial Unionism' is, as a rule, very imperfectly understood. The old Industrial Unionists, who were the English adherents of the Industrial Workers of the World, called upon the working-classes to leave the existing Unions, which they held to be corrupt 'craft' organisations fatal to working-class solidarity, and to form entirely new Unions on an industrial basis, linked up in a national branch of the Industrial Workers of the World, and professedly international and revolutionary in aim. Naturally enough, this movement made little headway among the Trade Unionists of this country; they had, with enormous pains, built up their organisations and set them on a firm financial basis; and now they were asked to put all this behind them, to 'scrap' all the work of the last century, and to begin afresh in a new way. The first step towards practicable Industrial Unionism was the abandonment of this attitude: and it was not until the advocates of 'Revolutionary Unionism' accepted the situation and declared their readiness to work through the existing Unions that their movement became important. As soon, however, as they passed from academic 'Industrial Unionism' to practicable proposals for amalgamation of rival and overlapping Unions, an entirely new phase set in. Every one agreed that closer unity is essential to effective industrial action; but there were wide differences as to method and object.

Broadly speaking, there are three possible methods of organisation for the workers. The first is pure 'craft' Unionism, which unites in a single association those workers who are engaged on a single industrial process, or on processes so nearly akin that anyone can do another's work. This is the bond of association in most of the smaller Trade Unions, as for instance in the Ironfounders or the Bricklayers. The second form is that which unites all the workers engaged upon a larger group of kindred processes, still following the lines of the type of work done. Under this system, all Engineers (perhaps all Metal Workers) would be in one Union, all Wood Workers in a second, all Leather Workers in a third, and all underground Miners in a fourth. This type of organisation we shall in future call simply *occupational* Unionism. There is, however, a third possibility. Organisation may follow the lines, not of the work done, but of the actual structure of industry. All workers working at producing a particular kind of commodity may be organised in a single Union. This would place some Metal Workers in the Miners' Union, some in the Railway Union, some in the Shipbuilding Union, and some in almost every important industrial group. Again, it would put some Carters in the Union of Transport Workers and some in the Railway Union. It would place some Carpenters and Joiners among Shipbuilders and others in the Building Union. The basis of organisation would be neither the craft to which a man belonged nor the employer under whom he worked, but the service on which he was engaged. This is *Industrial Unionism* properly so called.

When, therefore, ' Industrial Unionism ' is contrasted broadly with ' craft ' Unionism, it is well to understand exactly what is meant. The use of the phrase to cover ' occupational ' or real ' industrial ' Unionism indifferently is productive of much confused thinking, and, still worse, of much contradictory endeavour. It will be our buisiness in this chapter to see how far either form of organisation is applicable to the needs of Trade Unionism in this country.

I. Advocates of ' craft ' Unionism maintain that, by associating only those persons whose interests are throughout uniform, it secures at once the closest possible unity and the most intelligent collective bargaining. Having but a single interest, the ' craft ' Union, we are told, is protected from dissension within, and, perfectly understanding its own interest, it is in the best possible position for getting good terms from the employer. There is, in these arguments, an element of truth. Members of the Ironfounders' Union quote the terms they have secured as a justification for remaining outside the Aamlgamated Society of Engineers. A small Union of highly skilled workers, exercising a practical monopoly of its craft, has probably little or nothing to gain from association with other crafts, as long as it remains on good terms with the employers, and as long as a semi-skilled class does not spring up capable of doing its work at a pinch. There are undoubtedly craft interests which require that the craft should not wholly merge its individuality in any larger body; it has separate concerns which its members alone can understand, and which it cannot leave to be settled by a general vote of members of other crafts besides. A small craft, unless care is taken to secure its representation in a larger association, may easily be swamped, and actually lose by association with others. The Amalgamated Society of Engineers has never succeeded in absorbing the smaller 'craft' Unions dealing with Engineering just because it has made no provision for the representation of crafts within the great association. The German Metal Workers' Union, far larger and more inclusive, succeeds just because such representation is secured. The argument for independent 'craft' Unionism rests, in fact, on the fallacy that in the 'greater' Unionism the smaller 'crafts' must necessarily lose their identity. If a system can be devised to secure unity and preserve difference, the main argument in favour of the small Union will have disappeared.

So far, however, the case against 'craft' Unionism has not been clearly stated. It pursues broadly two lines of argument. First, the larger Union scores financially. The example of the private Insurance Companies is enough to prove that it pays to have as many members as possible. In its friendly activities, the Union that does a lot of business, *i.e.* has many members, is, on the whole, in a better financial position than the small Union. Again, the larger Union is, as a rule, in a better position for building up a strike fund than any small Union can be. Of course, a small skilled 'craft' Union that pursues peaceful methods and has few strikes may actually lose in this respect by association with other less peaceful 'crafts'; but, on the whole, here too, 'big' organisations pay best. All these questions are, however, secondary. The real point in which the 'greater' Unionism is superior is in its better adaptation to the needs of industrial warfare. It is becoming continually easier for the employers to beat any craft Union that stands alone. The separateness of crafts is being broken down by the improvement of machinery, and it is becoming more possible for the work of the skilled to be done by the semi-skilled. A strike of a single craft thus becomes less and less likely to succeed. The skilled are forced to stand together, and to make common cause with the unskilled. Craft Unionism is out of date because the isolation of the craft is itself becoming a thing of the past. The small Unions have to act together, and, in order to do this at all, they must at least federate.[1] There are still cases in which the separateness of a craft remains so sharp that, from the point of view of pure self-interest, it is justified in standing out of all larger associations; but such cases are already few, and their number is rapidly diminishing. The need for closer co-operation is almost universally recognised, and friends of craft Unionism are driven back upon their second line of defence.

II. Cannot all the co-operation that is necessary, they ask, be secured by the *Federation* of Unions? Is actual *Amalgamation* necessary? Federation enables all to act together, without robbing each craft of its autonomy or its individuality. Instead of

[1] Only complete amalgamation can make this co-operation really effective.

being crushed and overwhelmed in a great association of which it is only an insignificant part, the craft can retain its freedom of action and judgment, and at the same time receive the help of its fellows when it needs it. This idyllic picture of the perfect Federation is, unfortunately, far from the originals. The desire to get everything and give nothing is the most prevalent characteristic of federated Unions.

The independent craft Union of skilled workers is almost always peaceful in character. It works by means of conciliation and agreements. As long as it is able to go on in absolute isolation, this method has no obvious disadvantages; but as soon as it becomes necessary to co-operate with other Unions, difficulties begin. Agreements have generally been made by the different crafts for varying periods. When, therefore, they desire to take common action, some of them are always bound down by agreements and cannot join in. At last, they may perhaps combine into a Federation, and attempt by this means to secure better concerted action. This is the stage which has already been reached in the more important British industries.

Advocates of Federation, however, are not always very careful to explain what they mean by it. They point to all the masses of organisations which are classified by the Board of Trade under that head, and are at no pains to point out that the name means very different things in different cases. The typical example of Federation as opposed to Amalgamation is generally supposed to be the Cotton Industry of Lancashire; but those who quote the instance usually omit to point out even the elementary difference between *local* and *national* Federation. In any industry which is not purely localised in character, or producing for a purely local market, the object which either Federation or Amalgamation aims at securing is the cohesion of the whole of the workers in that industry, on a national and not on a local basis. There is no reason for supposing that this demand will be met by local Federation, even if local Federation is a good thing. Local Federation is entirely compatible with national Amalgamation, as we shall see later on.

What the supporters of Federation really mean is that strong *national* ' craft ' or ' sectional ' Unions should be built up and federated *nationally*. They aim in fact at organisation of the type of the Engineering and Shipbuilding Federation, The Iron and Steel Trades Federation, or the Transport Workers' Federation. The difficulty here too is that Federation may mean so many different things. It implies, as we have seen, merely the retention of their individuality by the Unions concerned, without specifying the degree of power which is conceded to the body in which they are united. It may therefore possess almost any degree of strength or weakness, and mean anything from a pious expression of sympathy and brotherhood to the practical equivalent of a real Amalgamation. In fact, Federations of almost every degree of intensity exist : and it is never possible, without particular study of each case, to discover what the mere fact of Federation implies. Some Federations are merely political, some in practice concern themselves almost solely with demarcation disputes ; others are regarded by their promoters merely as steps to Amalgamation, and yet others are the real centres of industrial action. Their efficiency depends partly on their constitution and powers, and partly on the nature of the industry which they cover.

Apart from the perpetual problem of surfacemen and mine engine-men, the Miners possess industrial Unionism, as far as membership is concerned. The Miners' Federation of Great Britain consists, not of local 'sectional' Unions, but of county or district Industrial Unions. Sometimes the county unit is itself in name a Federation, as in South Wales; but Federation in this case merely means a Union in which the local lodges have preserved a good deal of power. The question of organisation in the Mining Industry is never one of ' section ' against ' section,' but always of the balance of local and central control. It cannot therefore be in any way compared with the problem to be faced, for instance, by the Engineering Unions.

The Engineering and Shipbuilding Trades Federation is in practice concerned largely with questions of demarcation. It makes no pretence of being an effective fighting force in trade disputes. It leaves the support of members during strikes to the individual Unions concerned, and the separate Unions, and not the Federation, are the signatories to the Shipyard and Engineering Agreements. Such a Federation may do excellent work in setting up machinery for the settlement of demarcation disputes,—though even in this respect the present Federation is not very successful,—but it will not add appreciably to the fighting force of the Unions concerned. Thus we have recently seen the Boilermakers severing themselves from the rest of the Unions and deciding to do their bargaining on their own in future.

It may be said generally that, except in very peculiar circumstances, as, for instance, in the Cotton Trade, no Federation which has not a financial basis of permanent contributions per member of all affiliated Unions will add appreciably to the collective bargaining power of the workers. This is the real test of the validity of a Federation, and, under it, most of the existing Federations fail. Some have not even the power of levying their affiliated societies in support of disputes; others have the power of levy, but exact no regular contributions. In practice, neither of these provisions really secures concerted action. There is no security that a particular section will not break away from the rest as soon as independent action suits it best. To be effective, the Federation must have, in most industries, a basis of permanent contributions; but this at once raises difficulties. The Unions in many cases join Federations in the hope of getting something for nothing; each has its own business basis, and is probably liable to strikes in a degree different from the rest. Each section is therefore unwilling to merge its individuality unless it is sure of getting as much as it gives, and a Federation is seldom in a position to ensure this. It is too liable to have its whole resources drained in support of one section, so that the rest pay in, and when their turn comes to draw out, find that there is no money left. It has been found impossible for a Federation to keep a real check over the sections composing it; their freedom of action is too often financially disastrous.

It is sometimes argued that these difficulties may be met by the delegation of greater powers to the Federation by the various Unions. Where this is done, the Federation tends to pass over into an Amalgamation purely for fighting purposes. But if it is necessary to amalgamate for one purpose, will not Amalgamation prove an advantage for all? Federation, conceived in this manner, turns out to be a half-way house to complete Amalgamation.

No doubt, the difficulties in the way of complete

Amalgamation on anything like an industrial basis are far too great to be overcome in a few years. Federation, therefore, even in those industries in which it cannot possibly be regarded as a final solution of the problem, may sometimes be a first step. If a Federation is formed, its inadequacy may gradually be seen; greater and greater powers may be delegated to it, and the Unions composing it may tend finally to coalesce.[1]

Take, for example, the schemes for closer union now being discussed by ten General Labour societies. Two sets of proposals have been prepared: one set provides for complete amalgamation of all the Unions concerned; the other for what is in effect an amalgamation for fighting purposes. This second scheme, however, is regarded as being only temporary, and the Unions joining together on that basis have in view a complete amalgamation at some future time.

Federation, then, in the sense of amalgamation for purely industrial purposes, it may be necessary to accept in a few industries as a first step in the direction of the complete fusion that is bound to come in the end. We shall be in a better position to apply this view to particular industries when we have seen what are the difficulties that stand, in the various cases, in the way of fusion.

Amalgamation, we have seen, may proceed along the lines of either 'occupational' or 'industrial' Unionism. The attempt to apply these two methods at once over the whole of industry can only end in bickering and disunion. The great new organisations thus created will at once become involved in squabbles and recriminations that may well prove a greater danger to Trade Unionism than the whole demarcation

[1] On the other hand, some Federations have only been created for the purpose of staving off amalgamation.

problem has ever been. Knowing how employers have used the question of demarcation to sow dissension among the workers, we have every reason to fear that they will not be slow in grasping their new advantage, and turning the weapon of solidarity against the workers themselves. An instance will make the danger plainer. The General Railway Workers' Union, now fused in the National Union of Railwaymen, catered for all classes of workers employed by Railway Companies. The Amalgamated Society of Railway Servants, on the other hand, made no attempt to organise workers employed in Railway construction shops ! When fusion was proposed, the General Railway Workers' Union refused [1] to come into any scheme which did not provide for complete ' Industrial ' Unionism. They carried their point, and membership of the N.U.R. was made open to all employees of Railway Companies. There was, at the time, a great deal of ill feeling on the question, and Mr. J. H. Thomas, M.P., of the A.S.R.S., definitely declared that no attempt would actually be made to organise workers in the sheds. This remark, on representation from the G.R.W.U., he was at once compelled to withdraw. However, pressure from Industrial Unionists and the views of individual organisers have forced the hand of the N.U.R., and in some centres a campaign is being waged to enrol all Railway workers in the one organisation. This at once gives rise to a difficult problem. The skilled mechanics of all crafts employed in the Railway sheds have long been organised, for the most part, in the Amalgamated Society of Engineers, the Boilermakers,

[1] See the interesting and angry series of articles published at the time of the fusion in the *Daily Herald* and the *Daily Citizen.*

the Steam Engine Makers, the United Machine Workers, and certain 'craft' Unions of a similar type. As soon, therefore, as the N.U.R. attempts to touch the skilled workers in the 'shops' it will come into direct conflict with the A.S.E. and other craft Unions. Such a conflict between Unions can end only in disaster. This, however, is not the only difficulty. The A.S.E. has been, up to the present, mainly an amalgamated society of *skilled* crafts. It has done very little to organise the unskilled or even the semi-skilled workers in the engineering trades. Now, however, a new situation is arising, and it is broadening its basis of membership. The great barrier to the organisation of the unskilled in the A.S.E. has been, in the past, the comparatively shifting and temporary character of unskilled work. If the unskilled worker had joined the A.S.E., he might have left the day after for some quite different occupation. But of late years, beside the skilled mechanic, there has been growing up a new class of workers; at first unskilled, they gradually develop into machine-minders capable of doing, with the best modern machinery, a great deal of work that formerly went exclusively to the skilled mechanic. These men are at present, for the most part, either unorganised, or members of General Labour Unions, and it is among them that the propaganda of the N.U.R. may be expected to make headway. But once many of these workers are organised in the N.U.R., there is bound to be a conflict with the A.S.E. Already the barrier between skilled and unskilled is breaking down; the A.S.E. is beginning to realise that it must broaden its basis to include the semi-skilled, who have already ceased to be casual or 'general' labourers, and we may expect, unless a compromise is reached, a struggle, in the near future, between the A.S.E., the N.U.R., and the General Labour Unions.

This is only a typical instance of the problems to which conflicting attempts at closer unity are now giving rise. The number of such cases could easily be multiplied, and more will become apparent as we proceed to deal with the problem of organisation in several of our great industries and occupational groupings.

The Mining Industry is, as we have seen, the simplest, because it already possesses what is, in effect, an approximation to Industrial Unionism. The chief problem with which it is now faced is not that of membership, but that of internal structure, with which we shall deal later on. There are, however, certain great questions relating to the membership of Miners' Unions which must be discussed here. To what extent should surface-workers be enrolled in the Miners' Union? Before attempting to answer this question, we had better get clear as to what we meant by saying that the Miners have already got something like 'Industrial' Unionism. That statement was, in fact, misleading; the Miners' Unions are only 'Industrial', in so far as they are at the same time 'occupational'. That is to say, the Mining Industry differs from most others in being essentially simple; it is not a group of trades, but a single great industry; and the main point is that, in consequence, the organisation of the employers follows, on the whole, the lines of the workers' occupation. The greater 'occupational' Unionism which the Miners possess, is itself in this instance an approximation to 'Industrial' Unionism.

It is, however, an interesting feature in the Mining world just now that the attention of the Miners'

Federation is gradually turning in the direction of the Surfacemen, who were excluded from the Eight Hours Act and the Minimum Wage Act. These surface-workers are, as a whole, a lowly paid class, and in turning its attention to them, the Miners' Federation is practically declaring in favour of real and effective 'Industrial' Unionism. It does seem to be true that the success of mine workers in securing decent conditions of life and labour depends solely on their power to paralyse the industry. This should apply no less to surface-workers, who number in all about 100,000, than to actual coal-getters, and therefore the interests of the surfacemen seem to lie on the side of throwing in their lot with the underground workers. As far as the 'unskilled' surface-worker is concerned, there seems to be clearly this identity of interest; but what of the skilled machine-worker employed about a mine? The engineer may pass from one industry to another in pursuit of his calling; he may be one year in a railway shed, the next in a mine, and the next again in a textile factory. This transference, however, is becoming more rare; engineers pass into Mining from other industries; but they tend less and less to pass out again. To some extent, therefore, there are no longer the old difficulties in the way of organising surface workers in an Industrial Union. The miner's object is to paralyse the mine when and as he pleases; any worker, therefore, who can aid in this process he feels the importance of organising. Now, the handful of mining enginemen, by concerted action, could absolutely paralyse the whole industry. A strike of a few enginemen in a mine is, by itself, enough to stop the mine, whatever attitude the underground workers may adopt. The Miners have realised this, and consequently, in South Wales especially, there is

TRADE UNION STRUCTURE

a vigorous movement in favour of complete Industrial Unionism. Where, as in South Wales, the workers pursue a militant policy, it becomes important to secure complete cohesion against the employer; in other counties, where the policy of the Union is less militant, the position of the surfaceman has not led to trouble. It seems, however, quite clear that the problem of Industrial Unionism will first become really acute in the Mining Industry, and it is essential to define our attitude towards it.

The unskilled worker on the surface is, of course, in a different position from the craftsman. It does seem desirable, and, as the Miners' Federation turns its attention more to the surfacemen, inevitable, that all such workers should gradually be absorbed by it. Probably this transference will be accomplished without very disastrous friction,[1] but the problem of the craftsman is far more serious. In the absence of any scheme for transferring mechanics from one Union to another as they shift from industry to industry, it does seem that we have to choose between abandoning all hope of industrial solidarity and accepting the inconvenience of making a mechanic shift his Union with his employment. In fact, however, mine craftsmen are usually permanently attached to the industry and are organised in separate small Unions of their own. The real problem is that of absorbing these Unions, which show no desire for fusion. The problem does not seem to admit of immediate solution, but on the whole it must be recognised that craftsmen will not be prepared to come into the Miners' Unions unless the miners are ready to make them some return. The craftsmen, if they are

[1] Though it is already the cause of serious trouble with the general labour Unions.

to secure their interests, must have special representation as a section. If their sectional interests are properly safeguarded, there seems no final reason why they should not come into the Miners' Union. The miners rightly aim at complete Industrial Unionism.

In the Railway world, also, something resembling an Industrial Union is an actual fact.[1] The N.U.R., with roughly 300,000 members, admits any worker employed by a Railway Company, though its policy in relation to 'shop' workers is not yet well defined. We took this particular case as an illustration of the difficulties of 'Industrial' Unionism, and pointed out the pitfalls ahead of the N.U.R. Briefly, the situation is this. Any attempt, on the part of the N.U.R., to destroy the hold of the craft Unions over railway mechanics must fail. The A.S.E. is too strong to be driven off the field, and if the rivals merely divide up the members between them, the last state will be worse than the first. The N.U.R., it is true, is to some extent justified in its attitude by the past policy of the craft Unions, which, with a very large membership in railway shops, have done little to secure the interests of those members. This may lend colour to the view that even skilled railway mechanics should leave the A.S.E. and pass into the N.U.R. But if the A.S.E. has done little for its railway members, the mechanic needs assurance that the N.U.R. will do more. He is always chary of merging his individuality in a great whole of all sorts of workers, and he is not likely to succumb to the blandishments of N.U.R. organisers. This, however, is only half the difficulty. The unskilled and semi-skilled workers in railway shops are now

[1] The Locomotive Engineers and Firemen and the Railway Clerks remain outside.

TRADE UNION STRUCTURE

divided between the General Labour Unions, the actual Engineering Unions, and the N.U.R. These workers range from the quite unskilled and semi-casual labourer to the almost skilled machine-tender who began as a labourer. Clearly their organisation presents considerable difficulty. If they get into the N.U.R., while the skilled workers remain in the A.S.E. and the craft Unions, demarcation disputes of the most virulent type may be expected.

For the present, then, any attempt on the part of the N.U.R. to get all railway mechanics into its ranks is likely to be disastrous; but this should not blind us to the fact that in the N.U.R., ultimately, they ought to be. The only hope is that it will be possible to avert a contest of national scope until there is more hope of an amicable settlement. When the Industrial Unionist principle has found general acceptance, there will be a good deal of shifting of workers from one Union to another. If the craft Unions are called upon to give up their railway mechanics, they will gain from other sources as many members as they will lose. The duty of all who have the interests of Trade Unionism at heart is to try to avert a conflict at a time so inopportune as the present. The attempts of the N.U.R. to enrol craftsmen have already, by the success they have had, caused the A.S.E., the Boilermakers, and other Unions to pay more attention to the position of their railway members, and the retention of these members by the craft Unions seems, for the moment, the only possible solution.[1]

The organisation of the engineering trades and the

[1] As I write, a deadlock seems to have been reached. Joint negotiations between the N.U.R. and the craft Unions have broken down, and a fight seems imminent.

Shipbuilding industry raises many of the most perplexing questions of modern Trade Unionism. The two are very closely connected, and many of the same Unions are engaged in both; but, broadly speaking, Shipbuilding is an industry, while Engineering is, at most, only a group of trades. It will therefore be most convenient to begin with Shipbuilding, which possesses, at any rate, more superficial unity. Here, however, the problem is highly complex. It is of the first importance to secure really concerted action in the shipyards; but unfortunately the workers are not merely divided into a number of craft Unions, but into Unions which cut across several industries. The Boilermakers are pre-eminently a shipbuilding Union, but they are employed also in the railway shops; Carpenters and Joiners are equally occupied in Shipbuilding and in the Building industry, while Engineers are found in large numbers and are organised largely in the A.S.E. There are, further, among shipbuilders themselves, sharp barriers of class and prejudice. The Shipwright is clearly differentiated, in most places, from the Boilermaker on one side, and from the Carpenter and Joiner on the other. The Shipbuilding industry is a great complex of craft Unions; and as soon as effective union is preached in the shipyards, trouble may be expected. The A.S.E. and the Carpenters and Joiners are too strong to be broken, and fusion into a single organisation is, among such partners, inconceivable. There are few signs at present that the workers are alive to a need for closer unity; indeed, the most recent event is the actual secession of the Boilermakers, by far the most important Union, from the Shipyard Agreement. The Boilermakers now believe that they can make better terms on their own account, and, in face of such an attitude, nothing can be effected. Shipyard organisation still bears about it the traces of the time when wood was the material mainly used; as iron and, later on, steel took its place, new classes of workers took the place of the old, and sometimes old classes changed their occupation. Thus Shipwrights are no longer exclusively wood-workers, though they still monopolise the heavy wood work, while the lighter is done by Carpenters and Joiners. Metal Work is done partly by Boilermakers, but also to some extent by Unions of Smiths and Strikers, Blacksmiths, etc., who had originally no connection with Shipbuilding. The general result is a hopeless disorganisation; there is no prospect, even were it desirable, of a separate Industrial Union in the Shipyards. The existing method of a national agreement between distinct Unions on the one side and a strong Employers' Federation on the other seems inevitable, and even this amount of concerted action has become extremely difficult in face of the attitude of the Boilermakers. It may be, however, that this is only a passing phase; it is certain that no separate reorganisation of the Shipbuilding Unions on ' Industrial' lines is anything like a possibility at present. How the situation may be modified by developments in other industries it is hard to say; but it is clear that a further complication would be created by the absorption of the Carpenters and Joiners into a Building Industrial Union. This, however, the present position in the building industry makes very improbable.

The Amalgamated Society of Engineers, founded in 1851, was the earliest of the great amalgamated craft Unions which we have decided to call ' occupational.' We might therefore expect to find in this case at least a really developed form of organisation. Nevertheless, although there have been constant disputes and keen interest taken within the Union in theoretical questions of function and membership, the Engineering trades afford at present the worst examples in the country of contending and overlapping Unions. This is no doubt to some extent the result of changes in methods of manufacture; but it is also very largely the fault of the A.S.E. itself. In general, two difficulties have presented themselves. First, the A.S.E. has never succeeded in suppressing craft Unionism among the skilled workers. Not only have some of the smaller Unions refused to come in, but sections that once formed part of the A.S.E. have split off and proclaimed themselves independent. In fact, the A.S.E. has to a great extent failed even in the limited task which it set before itself. The causes of this failure are not far to seek; the A.S.E. has ignored the differences of section and occupation among its members, and, by its refusal to provide for sectional interests, has made it impossible for particular crafts and occupations to back up their grievances with the united force of the Union. What is said of the A.S.E. applies with equal force to the other general engineering Unions, which persist in spite of all attempts at amalgamation. The Steam Engine Makers and the Toolmakers, for instance, serve no useful purpose by continuing to exist separately. They have not even the excuse of the pure craft Unions—Patternmakers and Ironfounders. A vast amount of more or less articulate discontent exists even among those who are in the A.S.E.

The second difficulty cannot be laid equally to the charge of the Union officials. In recent years, Engineering, more than any other group of trades, has been affected by the change in industrial processes.

In the early days of the Society, the gulf between skilled and unskilled was so wide, and the unskilled worker so shifting in his occupation, that naturally the A.S.E. even attempted to organise only the skilled. The result was a strong Union of skilled workers entirely separate from, and seldom even acting in concert with, the unskilled. We have seen already how profoundly the recent rise of a semi-skilled class has modified this situation: the skilled worker can no longer stand in isolation and neglect the less skilled. The interests of the two classes are becoming identical; and a beginning of the recognition of this change may be seen in the dawning of almost unorganised co-operation between them in the largest centres. The Workers' Union and the A.S.E. are at last beginning to feel the need for combined action.

It is not, however, easy to see what will immediately follow from this tendency. It is clear that a levelling-up of the standard of life between skilled and semi-skilled is coming about; but their standards are still different enough to make unity hard to bring about. The less skilled workers in the engineering trades, where they are organised at all, belong largely to General Labour Unions, in which the standards of benefits and the expenses of organisation are both lower than in the A.S.E. These Unions are sometimes financially unsound, and are nearly always spending all they receive; the workers who belong to them are therefore getting benefits almost without paying for organisation. But it is probable that a bad time is ahead for some of the General Labour Unions, and when that bad time comes, the chance of the A.S.E. will come with it.[1] There are plenty

[1] It may come, under happier auspices, when the real functions of the General Labour Unions are recognised.

of signs that the members of the A.S.E. now realise that the reform of their organisation is essential; they have already thrown open their Union to a good many of the semi-skilled, but at present they have not made for them all the separate provision that is necessary. It seems clear, however, that as the semi-skilled mechanic becomes everywhere a permanent and integral member of the engineering group of trades, he must either form yet more Unions of his own, or else come into the A.S.E. Let the A.S.E. but remodel itself more or less on the lines of the German Metal Workers' Union, which we have already described,[1] and there will be a possibility of real unity in the engineering trades. Such unity must carry with it the almost complete inclusion of the shipbuilding industry. Shipbuilding and engineering are so closely connected; workers shift so easily from one class of shop to another; and the same problems occur to such an extent in all branches of these metal industries that complete fusion is essential. Already both are linked up in the Engineering and Shipbuilding Trades Federation, which, as we saw, is ineffective for fighting purposes. Scheme after scheme of amalgamation and closer unity has been put forward; perhaps some day the workers or the officials will decide to act. Then the main problem for both engineering and shipbuilding would have been solved by the creation of a metal workers' Union, and there would only remain the very difficult problem of bringing in the major part of the woodworkers in the shipyards.

The foregoing account may seem to make the problem too simple, by leaving the really unskilled worker out of the reckoning. It is true that a semi-

[1] In Chapter VI.

skilled class has, of late years, risen to importance out of the ranks of the unskilled; but this class by no means covers the whole field of general labour. There would remain, outside any such Metal Workers' Union as we have suggested, a large number of general labourers attached to the Metal trades. The question therefore arises whether these too should be absorbed. The problem is, in this case, altogether different. The semi-skilled machine-minder has become, broadly speaking, permanently a member of the engineering group of trades; his acquired knack represents his industrial value, and he is unlikely to sacrifice it by departing to an industry in which he will merely revert to the ranks of the unskilled. He may of course be discharged in times of trade depression, and this gives rise to one of the most difficult problems a skilled Union has to face when it admits the unskilled; but, broadly and in the majority of cases, he may be regarded as a permanent member of his trade. Even where he shifts from industry to industry, he is no less dangerous a potential blackleg, and should therefore be in the Industrial Union of his work for the time being. What is needed is a transfer system from Union to Union.

The way in which this change will be accomplished cannot, as yet, be foreseen. The method most usually advocated is a gradual strengthening of the Engineering Trades' Federation; but there seems to be little hope that the Unions will be prepared to surrender to such a body the necessary powers. Could the A.S.E. only remodel itself from within, so as to allow adequate representation of sectional interests, there is little doubt that it would soon tend to absorb its rivals in the Engineering trades. By loss of membership or by actual amalgamation, all these rival Unions might be fused into a single compact body, which would soon become a general Metal Workers' Union. This is, doubtless, looking far ahead; but, until the A.S.E. gives such a lead, there will be no great change in the present forms of organisation. The Engineering Federation is deplorably weak, and there seems to be no general wish to strengthen it. The A.S.E. alone is in a position to give a lead; where it goes, the Steam Engine Makers, the United Machine Workers and the rest will follow. The sole hope of effective organisation in this group of trades rests on the A.S.E.

It will have been noticed that, whatever the industry in question, proposals for Industrial Unionism almost always came up against the same two problems—that of the mechanic and that of the general labourer. So far, we have been dealing mainly with the former; but we now come to an industry in which the really acute problem is that of the general labourer. Certainly the best known of the 'Industrial' Federations at present in existence is that of the Transport Workers, created in March 1911, on the motion of Ben Tillett, the Secretary of the Dock, Wharf, Riverside and General Workers' Union. The Federation now embraces twenty-eight Unions concerned in Transport, six of these being General Labour Unions, paying affiliation fees on behalf of only a part of their membership. The Federation was highly successful in 1911; but its weakness was demonstrated in the strike of 1912, which proved conclusively that, for the Transport Industry, mere Federation, without a strong financial basis, is totally inadequate. All through the 1912 strike, which, mistaken though it was, should have been supported when once it had begun, the Unions affiliated showed a lamentable lack of cohesion, and the Federation found itself powerless to secure really effective action. This is to be accounted for mainly by the nature of the industry. A Federation of highly skilled workers in a localised industry such as those engaged in the textile industry, can often without difficulty take united action. Between highly skilled trades, 'blacklegging' on a large scale is impossible, and no Union has anything to gain, even for the moment, by breaking away from the rest. But with comparatively unskilled work, such as a good deal of the work done at the docks, it is fatally easy for one Union to blackleg another, and, except by united action of the whole industry, any effective revolt is impossible. This was demonstrated very clearly in 1912, when the refusal of the Seamen and Firemen's Union to co-operate contributed largely to wreck the Transport strike. The 1912 failure was not the fault of the Federation, but it has shown once for all the need for much closer unity. The present Federation has done its best, but it has too little power, and it is therefore necessary to investigate the possibilities of either strengthening it or securing complete amalgamation.

Fusion long presented grave difficulties, arising largely from the presence in the field of two alternative methods. Long before the Federation of Transport Workers was even suggested, attempts had been made to unite in a single union all general labourers. At the very time when Ben Tillett succeeded in founding the Transport Workers' Federation, a council representing Labourers' Unions was engaged in drawing up a scheme of amalgamation, and in August 1912 Mr. J. R. Clynes published a scheme he had been asked to prepare for the Gasworkers' and General Labourers' Union. It is well known that many of the workers at the Docks are members of the Gasworkers' and other Labourers' Unions. There was thus a direct conflict between the two schemes, and a situation only tolerable with the Transport Workers federated would become impossible if federation gave place to amalgamation. " The forces," writes Mr. Clynes, " that are making for the amalgamation of labourers in all classes of work can be disturbed by the appeals, for instance, to amalgamate the Unions which cover labouring men in the Transport trades. There are Unions which include thousands of transport workers, but at the same time cover thousands of other men not engaged in transport work at all. It is surely better to build on lines that will cover all the conditions of a man's varying chances of employment than to limit an amalgamated body to just the one class of work that for the time being a man may be allowed to follow."

This raised an awkward problem. On the one hand, it was clear that the Transport Workers' Federation, or better Union, would be by far the most efficient unit in trade disputes, and on the other hand, while waterside work retains the characteristics of casual labour, it is impossible to secure that a man's membership of such a Union shall cover the whole of his activities. Though, with the gradual decasualisation of waterside labour, such as is being brought about at some of the docks, it seems that the latter disadvantage will partially disappear, yet, when the permanent nature of labour organisation is taken into account, it seems essential, even at the cost of some difficulties in the present, to preserve to some extent the separateness of the transport workers. What is needed is co-operation between the united transport workers and the united general labourers, including effective arrangements for regulating the influx of general labourers to the docks. In any case, closer union in the transport trade is so urgently needed that the considerations brought forward by Mr. Clynes cannot be allowed to outweigh that necessity. Still, there is something in his protest that " it is futile on one day to recommend amalgamation on the basis of trades, on the next day on the basis of class, and on the third day on the basis of the industry in which a man may be employed ". But on the whole, this is not so foolish and futile as he seems to think. The different plans proposed arose from the different circumstances of various industries, and the foolishness arises only when it is attempted to make each particular principle hold generally, over every industry, no matter how different the conditions may be.[1]

It is clear that, while so many Transport workers remain organised in General Labour Unions, and while, on the other side, so many Transport Unions contain a large percentage of General Labourers, all attempts at amalgamating the Transport industry separately are bound to fail. It is necessary to make the best of a bad job, and to set about the task of strengthening the Federation. Unless the Federation can be provided with a big enough centralised fighting fund to enable it to take the conduct of disputes into its own

[1] In the event, the two parties took the only course that seemed open to them. The two amalgamation schemes were fused into one, and proposals were laid before a joint meeting. Just as it seemed possible that something might be done, the European War broke out. Very unwisely, it seems to have been decided to shelve the scheme. It seems probable that the desire of certain officials to scotch it was largely responsible for this decision. It is essential, as the Secretary of the Transport Workers' Federation maintained, that fusion of the composite body shall be accompanied by sectional organisation.

hands, the successes of 1911 will not be repeated. The Transport Workers succeeded in 1911 mainly because their revolt was unexpected: the strength of their organisation was not, by itself, enough to account for their victory. The failure of 1912 proved the inadequacy of their organisation to explain their success. A strong fighting fund is absolutely essential: not only does it enable a Federation to carry on a strike with confidence in its own powers; it also gives the individual Unions a motive for loyalty. A Federation without a strong financial basis fails not merely from financial exhaustion, but because it has no hold over the Unions composing it. Give the Transport industry a really strong Federation, in which adequate fees are paid by the Unions for all their members engaged in Transport, and the organisation of the workers will have been given an enormous impetus. Complete amalgamation will follow in time; but any attempt to hasten it just now will merely cause the withdrawal of the General Labour Unions from the Federation, and instead of securing solidarity, will prevent even the present amount of concerted action.

Germany, we have seen, differs from Great Britain in having no General Labour Unions. The labourer is, in nearly all cases, organised there in the same Union as the skilled worker. In England, we find exactly the opposite tendency. Not merely the unskilled labourers, but even a good many workers possessed of considerable skill, are organised in great rival General Labour Unions. It is impossible to discover at all accurately to what industries the members of these Unions belong; but it is clear that they have a considerable membership in nearly all the staple industries, except Cotton and Railway Transport. They are particularly important in the underpaid trades of the Black Country, in Engineering and Shipbuilding, and, above all, in the docks. It has for some time been realised that the competition between the existing General Labour Unions is mere waste of energy, and, as we have seen, plans for their amalgamation have been presented in full draft to the Unions concerned. It is very improbable that complete amalgamation will follow immediately, but it is quite clear that the step already taken will make such amalgamation merely a matter of time. Now, only a madman would dream of attempting directly to split up and destroy the General Labour Unions as they exist to-day; and it is clear that fusion will make their position even more unassailable. The General Labour Unions cannot be smashed in a day, and any plans for Industrial Unionism that rest on the hope of smashing them are bound to fail. What then should be the attitude towards General Labour amalgamation of those who regard the present position of these Unions as, at best, a necessary evil ? It is sometimes urged that one great Union will be stronger than several smaller ones, and that it is therefore best to hope for the failure of the fusion scheme. It is no doubt true that the one great Union will be stronger ; but, the existence of these Unions being inevitable, may it not be better to have them strong ? It will be easier to answer when we have made clearer our attitude towards the General Labour Unions as a whole.

We saw clearly, especially in dealing with Engineering, that there is such a person as a real General Labourer, a worker who is quite unskilled and who shifts easily from one trade or industry to another. Such mobile Labour, if there is much of it, may sometimes need special organisation.[1] Clearly, the

[1] If Trade Unions had a reasonable system of transferring cards and members the problem would largely disappear.

proper function of the General Labour Union is to organise those classes of workers who are engaged in scattered or unorganised trades, till a separate Union becomes possible. It ought to be a sort of Trade Union clearing-house, retaining only such members as could not well be permanently organised in any other way. As soon as a worker came to be permanently employed in some organised industry, the General Labour Union should surrender him to his appropriate Society. This conception would of course involve a great remodelling of the General Labour Unions. At present, when a Union has got a man organised, it shows no willingness to surrender him merely because another Union might put in a more rational claim. The root of the evil is competition between Unions; instead of being linked up in a general organisation in which all could work harmoniously together for the good of the whole, as in Germany, our Unions are always fighting each other for members, and are under no central control whatsoever. A General Labour Union, if it is to keep to its legitimate function, should be a part of the central organisation; its object should be to decasualise and unload its membership on other Unions, and not to retain all the members it can lay hands on. We are far indeed from realising this end; but it may be that the fusion of General Labour Unions will turn out to be a step in the right direction: it may be that, united in one great body, these Unions will learn their true function, and be prepared to hand on their members. But a General Labour Union can in the end work satisfactorily only where it is under the direct control of a strong central Trade Union authority co-ordinating the whole movement.

In fact, the whole problem of industrial solidarity

is essentially bound up with that of central control and direction. Germany, as we saw, was enabled to realise so nearly perfect a form of organisation just because the German Trade Union movement began in the centre and spread gradually outwards, because it was inspired throughout by a consistent policy and a deliberate aim. The British movement is in its present state of confusion because it began with voluntary efforts all over the country, and because there was no force capable of co-ordinating them or influencing their development. It might have been supposed that, by this time, the British movement would have created for itself some influential central organisation, that it would have realised the chaos in which it is, and seen the remedy. That it has not done this is one of its greatest sources of weakness, and its failure can only be explained by the vested interest the officials generally regard themselves as having in the continuance of the present muddle. Central control would at once involve such widespread changes in methods of organisation that the officials, as a rule, will have nothing to do with it.

We saw, in speaking of America, that there is one form of Industrial Unionism which aims, like the Knights of Labour, at organising all workers, irrespective of occupation, in 'one big Union'. We saw, further, how such a scheme, neglecting all differences of interest and environment, is bound to fail. At the same time, we recognised the value of the recurring conception that fundamentally, underneath all differences, and however real those differences may be, the workers have but a single and identical interest in the broadest sense. The method of 'one big Union' is all wrong; but equally wrong is the method which takes account solely of differences, and organises the workers into a number of entirely separate Unions. The differences require to be represented; but they also require to be co-ordinated and reconciled in the greater whole which stands for the deeper identity.

In Great Britain, we have three bodies professing to secure the co-ordination of the Labour movement as a whole. These are the Trade Union Congress, with its standing Parliamentary Committee, the General Federation of Trade Unions, and the Labour Party. It will be seen at once that none of these is a really comprehensive co-ordinating body, comparable in influence with the German General Commission of Trade Unions or even with the C.G.T. in France. The Trade Union Congress has, indeed, nearly 2,250,000 members out of about three millions and a quarter of organised workers.[1] It is, however, a highly academic body; at its annual gatherings the same resolutions are proposed and carried year after year, and practically nothing is done to give effect to them. The Parliamentary Committee is, as its name implies, still mainly concerned with the influence of legislation on Labour: it has survived from the times before the Labour Party, when it was Labour's chief political mouthpiece. Outside politics, its functions are few, though it has recently shown a tendency to take the problem of industrial structure very gingerly in hand. It pronounces its opinion on questions at issue between two Unions; but until the last year or so it has made no attempt to face the difficult problems of Trade Unionism in the industrial sphere. It is a very useful body in its way; but it shows no sign of becoming the co-ordinating force of which we are in search.

The Labour Party, that sad failure of Socialism

[1] Now 3,000,000 out of 4,000,000 (1915).

endeavouring, by a trick, to seem stronger than it really is, naturally cannot perform any functions in the industrial sphere. It seems to spend most of its time trying to persuade the workers that strikes are no use, and even industrial legislation does not usually attract it. Clearly then, the Federation of Trade Unions and Socialist Societies which is called the Labour Party does not concern us here.

The General Federation of Trade Unions is a body of the best intentions; it lacks only power and influence. Its total membership is still less than a million, and the allegiance of some of these is by no means secure. The General Federation set out to unify the Labour movement by the provision of a common fund for use in strikes; each affiliated Union pays in so much per member, and is entitled to so much benefit in case of a strike. Even in the period of industrial peace before 1910 it was possible to see that the Federation was financially weak; the coming of the labour unrest caused such a run on its benefits that its financial position at present gives cause for the greatest uneasiness. It must either raise affiliation fees, or reduce its benefits; and it is feared that either course may mean a heavy loss in membership. The history of the General Federation is the old story of nearly all Federations; the Unions that joined came in very often in the hope of getting something for nothing. Some of them have got it, but others have been badly hit. Naturally, the weakest Unions flocked to take advantage of the chance to get benefits on such good terms as the Federation offered. All went smoothly for a few years; but in 1911 came the uprising of the less skilled workers, and the weaker Unions began to drain the Federation's resources. All through 1911 and 1912 the Amalgamated Society of Engineers, for instance, was handing over large sums of money, through the Federation, to unskilled or semi-skilled workers—in the great Transport strikes especially. Even so, with a few of the richer and more peaceful Unions to draw upon, the Federation was quite unable to make both ends meet. The greatest Unions, the Miners, the Railwaymen and some of the other great Unions, remained outside, and the Federation found itself saddled with the liabilities, without being in a position to command the assets, of the Labour movement. Nor does the situation seem to be in any way improving. The work done by the General Federation under the Insurance Act will certainly secure its permanence as the approved society of many of the weaker Unions; but there seems to be a danger that insurance will become its main function.[1] It has had, all along, to encounter an enormous amount of hostility; time after time it has been saved mainly by the endeavours of its secretary, Mr. W. A. Appleton. So much effort must not be wasted; the Labour movement must come to realise how important it is to have a central organisation that is industrial and not political in character. For the Trade Union Congress is almost as political as the Labour Party; tradition and temperament conspire to make it the organ of the vague and general aspirations of Labour, when what is really wanted for the Trade Union movement is a 'business government' with a revolutionary aim.

It will be seen that, of the three bodies which attempt to co-ordinate the British Labour movement, two only could ever conceivably play any important

[1] Along with banking. It has just completed arrangements for working through the C.W.S. Bank.

part in the co-ordination of Trade Union effort in the all-important sphere of industrial action. Helpless at present, because it has neither the influence nor the membership necessary, the G.F.T.U. is, in form at least, exactly the co-ordinating body required.[1] But securing of the right amount of central control is a matter much more of influence than of determinate powers. There should be some body capable of saying to two rival Unions that their rivalry is a nuisance, and of saying so with the whole moral weight of the Labour movement behind it. Such a body, if it possessed the moral weight, would be better without compulsory powers. Where compulsory fusion would only go to make a bad spirit in the combined Union, moral suasion would create the sense of solidarity, and the fusion would come about as a free and deliberate act of the Unions concerned. This should be the function of the General Federation of the future, which should also have control over the General Labour Union of the future—the Unions' 'clearing-house,' as we have called it. There seems little prospect that such a body will be created at all soon ; but sooner or later the British movement must evolve its central authority, and there seems to be no way of getting this except with the co-operation of the Trades Union Congress and the General Federation. It is of importance that the Federation should pass safely through its present financial difficulties, and particular Unions ought to be ready to make sacrifices to save it. But, as long as two-thirds of the Trade Unionists in this country remain outside, the financial problem will remain unsolved. Membership of the

[1] Mutual insurance against strikes, though it may be best to leave it voluntary as it is now, should be organised through the central industrial body.

General Federation of the future will be regarded as the duty of every Trade Unionist.

It is easy to see, further, what the future General Federation, working along with the General Labour Unions, could do in organising the unorganised. The existing Federation has already done a little; but it is hampered for want of funds, and very often it gets no return for the money it spends on such work. The most remarkable feature of English Trade Unionism is the absence of organised propaganda. More work has been done in this direction by Mr. Tom Mann alone than by the whole of organised Labour. This too arises mainly from the lack of any central body capable of co-ordinating local and sectional effort. There should be, all over the country, properly organised national campaigns on behalf of Trade Unionism, and these should be paid for by the movement as a whole, and directed from the centre.

Again, the Trade Union movement, *as a whole*, has no brains. It has worked out no common policy and makes no attempt to get general Trade Union questions generally understood. The statistical departments of English Trade Unionism do not exist; there is no idea at the centre what is happening anywhere else, and still less what has happened in the past. There is no Trade Union literature, and there is no staff capable of writing it. Soon, it is clear, all these omissions will have to be repaired. Great Britain cannot go lagging behind the rest of the world, allowing the most backward nations to pass her in methods of organisation, and doing nothing to catch them up. This very question of Trade Union structure is the worst of all the instances of our incompetence. In France, the C.G.T., wholly without compulsory powers, has done much to reduce the number of *syndicats* and *Bourses du Travail* (Trades Councils). In Germany, amalgamation has been throughout under central guidance, and there has been the less need for it, because organisation also has been throughout centrally inspired. In Great Britain, where we have the worst possible muddle in organisation, we find no attempt on the part of any authority to make the situation clear, or to work out a policy for meeting it. Amalgamation proposals come, in the main, from a few isolated individuals, and meet with the coldest welcome. The main problem of to-day is to force the Trade Unions to take up the question for themselves.

In studying the future of some of our great Labour organisations, we purposely chose industries or groups of trades in which there seemed a reasonable hope of effecting some change in the near future. When a greater number of industries is taken into account, and especially in the case of some of the smaller or less organised industries, there will be new problems to be faced. These, however, hardly admit of detailed treatment in such a work as the present, and, generally speaking, the foregoing examples may be taken as typical of the whole problem. There is, indeed, one great industry about which nothing has been said, although its organisation presents highly complex and peculiar features. The cotton industry, centred in Lancashire, has developed a system of organisation altogether its own, and any attempt to settle its problems for it on general grounds would be worse than useless. That organisation was admirably described by Mr. and Mrs. Webb in *Industrial Democracy*; but it has changed considerably since they wrote. As opponents of amalgamation very often uphold against it a theory of *federation* based mainly on the example of the textile industry, it is necessary to point out what makes its organisation so peculiar in character.

First, the textile industry is localised. Its concentration in Lancashire makes organisation very easy, and, as Trade Unionism reached maturity there very early, the spirit of craft Unionism is very strong. The independent craft Unions are exceedingly unwilling to surrender any of their separateness, and, under the direction of strongly established leaders of a highly conservative type, are still more unlikely to make any move in a new direction than they would otherwise be. Localisation, therefore, has made it easy for the workers to organise, and has also tended to establish the Unions in stereotyped forms which it is hard to alter. There has been, further, very little difficulty, since 1905, in securing concerted action in the ' manufacturing ' sections; and this too is mainly due to the localised character of the industry.. Living all together, and in no way disturbed by conflicting appeals from various districts, all these sections have found it easy to co-operate in case of need. One of the great difficulties of the national craft Unions is that it is exceedingly hard to reconcile national uniformity with consideration for local differences. A national Union lays down general terms, and reaches an agreement with the employers; but, however good these terms may be in themselves, they very often make concerted action in a district impossible. Some of the Unions, tied down by national agreements, cannot help the rest. These difficulties, for the most part, do not arise in the cotton industry, over the whole of which, broadly speaking, uniform conditions prevail. We are not speaking here of the woollen industry, which is very badly organised and far more scattered; it has its own problems, which make a common organisation far more necessary. In the cotton industry a good deal has been secured by the method of federation, local and general. Even general unity is less important than local federation. The industry being regulated on uniform principles already well established, the Unions have, as a rule, to deal only with particular infringements of the conditions laid down. This is done, in almost all cases, by the Local Federations, which are fighting alliances between local branches of the various Unions. The Unions themselves are often called 'amalgamations'; but this must not be taken as meaning that sectionalism has been done away with. Sectionalism remains and is rigidly preserved; amalgamations are fusions of local sectional Unions into a single great sectional federation for industrial purposes only. The ordinary meaning of the words 'amalgamation' and 'federation' simply does not apply to the cotton industry; its problems are altogether separate, and have to be studied quite by themselves. No doubt, modifications have long been most necessary, and the Northern Counties Textile Trades Federation, now purely a 'manufacturing' body, would be very materially strengthened by the adhesion of the spinners and card-room operatives; but the whole question is far too complicated to be dealt with in this chapter. It is only necessary to speak of it enough to show that arguments in favour of federation as against amalgamation cannot be applied to industry generally merely on the strength of the organisation in the textile trades of Lancashire. The cotton industry is quite peculiar, and the fact that a form of organisation persists in so *localised* a set of occupations is no argument at all for its success in a *scattered* national industry.[1]

[1] This does not mean that Industrial Unionism would not work best in the cotton industry also.

The important point to realise is that the cotton industry is the exception, and not the rule. We have seen, in dealing with other trades and occupations, a difficult problem that is in many respects the same from industry to industry. Concerted action has not, in most cases, been secured, and we have seen reason for believing that it will not be secured until the number of Unions is very greatly reduced. In many trades, a great deal of actual overlapping exists. In the cotton industry, there is practically no overlapping or rivalry. The cotton organisations present order of a kind ; most of the rest present only disorder.

It is, then, on the whole probable that the future industrial organisation of this country will be by no means so tidy and uniform as the advocates of various schemes would have us believe. That the movement towards consolidation is real no one can for a moment doubt : that it will produce real results in the near future is beyond question. But definite, cut-and-dried schemes purporting to cover the whole industrial field only serve the purpose of propaganda : they interest men in the question, but they do not solve it. It is left for the particular Unions concerned, with such outside help as may be forthcoming, to formulate their own schemes and carry them through for themselves. The day of complete and final organisation is far distant, and depends, in many particular instances, on a change both in the conditions of industry and in the spirit of the workers. There is enough to do without going into purely theoretical schemes which have no chance of becoming actual. Those schemes have done good work ; but it is time to recognise that they are academic and theoretical, and to make use, for practical purposes, of the interest that has been aroused by them.

A great many people seem to think, like Mr. F. H. Rose when he debated with Mr. Tom Mann on Industrial Unionism,[1] that, when they have asserted that the only strikes which now have any chance of success are the small ones, they have demonstrated the futility of consolidating Trade Union forces. But, even supposing them to have made good their point—and the great Railway Strike is enough to prove them wrong—they have done nothing of the sort. These small disputes are practically never 'craft' disputes extending over a wide area: they are far more often disputes in a single shop extending to several crafts, or where they are not so at present, they would be far more effective if they could be so extended. As matters stand, sectionalism is nearly as disastrous in small as in great disputes. It is no easier for local branches of different Unions to make temporary agreements with one another than for two great national Unions to co-operate; often co-operation between such branches is impossible because the Unions are involved in national agreements. There is urgent need for permanent working arrangements between the different Unions in particular shops and localities. In particular, with the present craft organisation, local strikes are often crippled by the fact that agreements extending over a wider area than the existing dispute expire at different periods for the various Unions concerned. Wider organisation on the lines of industry or occupation by sweeping away such national or county 'craft' agreements, would make local or shop strikes infinitely easier and more effective. As it is, even when the various sections do combine, a great deal of

[1] A report of the debate fills Number vii. of the *Industrial Syndicalist*.

valuable time is often wasted before they can take action.

The aim of the Greater Unionism is not merely to extend the area of strikes : it is to make strikes, over whatever area they may be fought, more effective and easier to arrange. The end in view is concerted action ; but the aim is to make it easier, and not to enforce it more than is necessary. It is desirable that all the workers in an industry should be in a position to strike together ; but it is by no means always desirable that they should do so. Whether, therefore, we pin our faith to the small or to the large strike—and we shall probably find that small strikes are best in one industry and great strikes in another—it is equally necessary to get the workers organised in such a way as to avoid friction and dispute between different Unions. We shall see this more clearly in the next chapter, when we come to deal with problems of the internal organisation of Trade Unionism.

We have passed in review, as briefly as possible, and with reference to particular industries, the various proposals for amalgamation. In doing so, we have hitherto omitted to consider certain general difficulties which present themselves. It is to this task that we must now turn, in the confidence that, amalgamation being a demonstrable necessity for fighting purposes, no difficulty will be allowed to stand finally in the way.

If the main objects of fusion are clear, the main obstacles are equally so. The first, the reluctance of small groups to merge their individuality in larger units, can only be overcome by argument showing how necessary union is, and by assurances in the rules of the new society, that their interests shall not be neglected, nor their corporate unity disregarded.

TRADE UNION STRUCTURE

If the Unions are to reflect the natural structure of industry, the degrees of individuality recognised by them must be those to which local and occupational unity naturally lead. No natural corporate bond must be neglected, and none must be allowed to grow so strong as to interfere with the free action of the others. These general principles require, in every case, a different application, according to the peculiar structure of the industry concerned.

The second great difficulty, the opposition of officials with vested interests or sympathies, can only be overcome by the action of the rank and file. It will no doubt be necessary to make the dislocation caused by reconstruction as little violent as possible, and as often as may be posts will have to be found for displaced officials; but the Trade Union world cannot afford to be too soft-hearted. In any case this is a matter for Trade Unionists alone.

But we have not yet touched upon the three difficulties which are uppermost in men's minds when they consider the question of Amalgamation, the three which are explicitly discussed, for instance, in the recent pamphlet *A Plea for the Amalgamation of All Existing Trade Unions*. The first of these difficulties concerns contributions. In the Trade Unions at present existing within a single industry, there are naturally found very different scales of contributions and benefits. Men of different degrees of pay and skill naturally require benefits upon different scales. This, the pamphlet points out, need cause no great difficulty. " Already a large number of Unions have several scales of benefits corresponding to the difference in subscriptions ", and it will be quite easy to carry this practice into the new amalgamated Unions. The A.S.E., which has already had to face the problem, has long had various scales to suit varying needs. The general difficulty then can easily be overcome. " In many cases, however, the Unions are paying out far more in one particular form of benefit than is justified by receipts for this special purpose." This refers mainly to superannuation, a growing source of unsoundness in Trade Union finance. This, the pamphlet holds, will have to be rectified by an actuarial revision of scale; and, though this will certainly be a source of difficulty, there seems to be no other way. It is, moreover, desirable that some such revision should take place, if the Unions are to be secured from financial crises in the future.

There is, indeed, the additional difficulty that not only do benefits differ from Union to Union, but the expenses of organisation also vary. There is, however, little doubt that the higher expenditure on organisation is a sound investment, and that the difference is due mainly to the weakness of some of the Unions.

On the whole, then, the question of benefits admits of fairly easy solution. The second difficulty raised is that of the inequality of the reserve funds of the Unions it is proposed to amalgamate. In respect of this a Trade Unionist friend of mine writes to me: " There is one difficulty (which could be surmounted); and that is the one of financial adjustment. I think, speaking without any figures by me, that the A.S.E. have somewhere about twice as much per head in their total reserves as the Boilermakers; but this would weigh very little with any true Trade Unionist ". Probably in many cases there will be no difficulty; but even where there is it can be overcome. As the pamphlet I have quoted points out, it would be possible for the amalgamating Unions to pay in an equal sum per head,

TRADE UNION STRUCTURE

leaving the surplus to provide a separate benevolent fund for the members of the old Union. This is unwieldy and undesirable, but it is a possible method in case a Union should stand out for its pound of flesh.

The third difficulty noticed by the pamphlet is that of demarcation of work. It is quite certain that at present the masters often play off one Union against another in respect of demarcation, and, with the present organisation, there is no adequate method of settling such disputes peacefully. The Trades Councils at present do something of this sort, but their decisions have no compelling power, and they are not strong enough to get them recognised or to prevent ill-feeling from taking concrete form. With an Industrial Union such questions would as a rule settle themselves, or at least would arise only on the marginal ground between two industries. Any job within the industry would be open to any member at the standard rate, and, in cases of doubt, the higher rate should always be exacted. By this means, the Labour Movement would rid itself of what my Trade Unionist friend calls " the standing disgrace of organised labour ".

Yet another difficulty in the way of amalgamation is purely legal. At present, two Unions wishing to join together have to get a vote of two-thirds of their total membership in favour of the proposal. It is well known that it is almost impossible to secure large ballots in the Trade Union world, partly because of slackness, but also because of the shifting nature of employment. In most industries, then, it would be impossible, with the law as it stands to-day, to bring about amalgamation. Of course, the Railwaymen have succeeded ; but their case was comparatively simple, as only three Unions were involved, and it is comparatively easy on the railways to get in touch with the members. Even so, the required majority was only secured with the greatest difficulty ; and it would be, to say the least of it, still more difficult to repeat the success in the case of a less highly organised industry.

Mr. O'Grady has presented to Parliament a short single-clause Bill designed to remedy this anomaly ; but the Labour Party appears to be wholly blind to its importance, and it seems very improbable that it will get through yet awhile. It will be seen, however, that the question is urgent, and it is surprising that the Unions have not pressed it upon Parliament. Unfortunately, the official element in the Trade Union world is still so predominant that it is unlikely that anything will be done, until some great scheme of fusion is actually stopped by the legal difficulty, as the Carpenters and Joiners have been stopped in the past, owing to their 14,000 members abroad. Then no doubt the Bill will pass. Such is the foresight of our legislators.

The question of Trade Union structure has been discussed at such length because the form of organisation adopted must finally determine the powers and policy of the Unions. Function, indeed, determines structure ; and, if we set out with a clear idea of what the function of Trade Unionism ought to be, the first thing to be settled is the structure to be aimed at. We have seen reason to believe that, as we set out with an acceptance of the existing Unions as an essential working basis, this structure cannot be anything like so tidy and uniform as a purely theoretical consideration would suggest ; but we have realised also that, under the diversity of forms which the improved organisation must inevitably include, there may be an essential unity of principle. Even in deciding that the phrase " Industrial Unionism " is not by itself a panacea, we are not abandoning all hope of a reorganisation based on the industrial principle. The ' Greater Unionism ' is not merely a vague phrase, designed to cover the nakedness of an indefinite idea ; it is a general principle of consolidation which, while it has to be applied in many ways, is at bottom uniform. Solidarity is a real aim, and in showing the inadequacy of certain *prima facie* theories we are not denying the principle that Labour must be put in a position to act, as far as possible, as one man. In all the proposals we have made for particular Unions, we have been trying to minimise the chances of friction and maximise the opportunities for co-operation between different classes of workers. Solidarity does not involve the General Strike, but it does involve the fullest possible co-operation of all sections. This is what the Labour movement lacks to-day. Deprived of central guidance, and uninspired by any uniform ideal, the Unions have gone on their own selfish way, and, in doing so, have been blind to their real interests. Their divisions have made them play the employers' game ; instead of standing solidly together against the masters, they have been engaged largely in petty internecine strife and bickering. They have acted, where they have not been too sluggish to act at all, in absolute isolation and with a complete disregard for the more general interests of the workers. This can olny cease when the purely arbitrary divisions at present existing between many of the Unions have been broken down ; and then perhaps we may hope that Labour will secure something like a tolerable standard of life for itself. As long as the present divisions and overlapping are allowed to continue, the industrial movement will fail in its object. Without men and without organisation little can be done ;

the Trade Union movement cannot transcend its members. But the second essential problem, that of control and management within the Union, can profitably be faced only when the actual limits of the organisation have been defined. To this secondary question we may now safely turn.

CHAPTER VIII

TRADE UNION GOVERNMENT—CENTRALISATION AND LOCAL AUTONOMY

THE first purpose of Trade Unions is to fight the employers. Any other activities in which they engage should always be regarded as secondary and, in comparison, unimportant. But, as structure is determined by function, it is clear that the whole system of control and management in the Unions must be so ordered as best to further their main object. In examining the question of control, we shall again be taking into account above all the effect of various methods upon the Union as a fighting body. If some other form of organisation, more suitable to it as a mutual insurance society, cannot be reconciled with full fighting efficiency, that form will have to be discarded. The problem we shall chiefly consider will, therefore, be the control of strikes and wages-movements generally.

Clearly, control may be either central or local, sectional or general. Wages-movements and disputes about the conditions of labour may be kept under strong central control, as in Germany, or a fairly full measure of local freedom may be granted to each locality, as usually happens in France. Again, all power in disputes may be concentrated in the hands of the executive or the members as a whole, or considerable independence may be left to individual crafts and sections within a single Union. In this chapter we shall, as a rule, presuppose the conclusions of the last ; we shall be dealing, in the main, with the problem of control as it would present itself to a movement intent on realising, in spirit as well as in form, the ideal which has been named ' The Greater Unionism '.

In this case, too, we shall find that mere generalisation is useless. The particular forms of control needed in each case will depend, as we saw that Trade Union structure depends, on the nature of the trade or industry concerned and on the present state of the organisations covering it. As, however, control and internal management can be remodelled more easily than actual structure, it is far more possible to get a theory applied and tested in this case. The modification of the system of internal control requires, as a rule, no violent revolution, and, if one form can be shown clearly to be superior to another, there is good hope that it will in time be adopted.

We shall, therefore, in this case also, begin by taking a few typical industries, and finding out what system of internal organisation seems best suited to the particular problems they present. We shall then to some extent be in a position to speak more generally of the tendencies of Trade Unionism as a whole, and to pass a more or less general opinion on the question at issue between centralisers and advocates of local autonomy.

It must be clear, at the outset, that the forms of control that are necessary will vary from Union to Union according to the particular conditions of different industries. For instance, where employers are closely united and have agreed to present a united front to the workers, the greater rapidity with which the employers can act will usually necessitate the placing of very extensive powers in the hands of the central authority of the Union. This is especially the case with the Railways. At the time of the formation of the National Union of Railwaymen there was a great deal of dispute concerning certain clauses in its rules which seemed to certain Syndicalists and to the *Daily Herald* to give far too much power to officials. The crucial clause reads : " The Executive Committee shall have power to inaugurate, conduct and settle all trade movements, and the method of conducting such movements shall be determined by the Executive Committee, as circumstances warrant." It will be seen that nothing could go further ; the Railwaymen have adopted the method of absolute central control.

The opponents of this policy have generally made the mistake of attempting to counter it with indiscriminate denunciations of officialdom and the assertion of the abstract rightness of local autonomy in the barest form. They have often seemed to be asserting the absolute right of every locality or section to do exactly what it chooses, and at the same time to command the support of the Union as a whole. We have seen in the case of Sweden how fatal such a policy must always be. Unless, as in France, the Trade Unions are prepared to fight without funds, the right to call upon central funds must always be accompanied by a right of the central authority to control.

It is significant that even in France, where, as a rule, local autonomy prevails in the fullest sense, the Railwaymen are organised, not in a National Federation, but in one of the three *Syndicats Nationaux*, with a central policy and central control. The close co-operation of the various Railway Companies in this country makes a similar form of organisation absolutely essential. It is, however, possible to have centralisation without making it so rigidly absolute; and already the Knox strike on the North Eastern has shown that, under provocation, the system is liable to break down, In such a case, there is often nothing for the Executive to do but to endorse the illegal act of the section concerned : such irregularities, however, show a weakness in the form of organisation, and prove that there has been an attempt to carry centralisation too far.

It must, of course, be recognised that centralisation cannot be treated as an isolated question. The amount of power that can safely be conceded to the central organisation varies, not only in accordance with the particular conditions of the industry concerned, but also according to the system of representative government adopted. Where a great Union attempts to govern itself on the principles of abstract democracy, by means of an executive elected by general vote of the whole membership, and provides no sort of representation for sectional or local interests, bureaucratic centralisation of the worst kind inevitably results. This is, to some extent, the case with the Amalgamated Society of Engineers. If central control is to work well in a large Union, it must be accompanied and checked by real representative government, which takes differences as well as numbers into account. The recognition of this need by the N.U.R. to some extent makes their absolute central control a workable system. Both the sectional and the local principles are operative in the election of the Executive. The important passages of the rule read as follows (italics mine) :

" The Union shall be subdivided into six electoral *districts* [for the election of the Executive Committee], the various grades *in these districts* being divided into four electoral *departments*, embracing locomotive, traffic, goods and cartage, and engineering shop and permanent-way men. . . . The Executive Committee shall be divided into four electoral *Departmental Committees*, each responsible for the interests of the respective departments enumerated above."

Thus, in the electoral district the local unit is recognised, and, in the electoral *department within the district*, the interest of the sections in each locality, while the Departmental Committees are a recognition that sectional interests are national as well as local. Where the interest concerned is that of the employees of a particular Railway Company, or where for some reason adequate sectional representation is not secured by these provisions, special conferences of those concerned may be called. Thus at every step, the Executive is at least certain of ascertaining clearly the feeling of the sections or localities involved, and, where this is so, it matters less in whose hands the final power is placed. Trade Union Executives are seldom deliberately tyrannical; the muddles they make come mainly from inability to discover the feeling of the workers. The problem, therefore, is largely to provide adequate machinery for the expression of sectional and local opinion : it cannot be finally expressed merely in terms of the actual power vested in the various authorities.

The absolute centralised control of the N.U.R. is, therefore, far less arbitrary in its actual operation than its enemies have tried to make out. It is indeed very unlikely that it would lead to difficulty in any large number of cases. The question is whether all the same advantages might not be secured, and the inconveniences avoided, by a system in form less absolute.

The most obvious modification is, of course, that of balloting the workers concerned before terminating strikes. This, however, need not apply equally to every kind of strike. The first distinction, that between offensive and defensive movements, need not here be taken into account. In either case, central direction is required on the Railways. A second distinction may be made between national strikes, local strikes, sectional strikes, and strikes affecting a particular company. National strikes should be terminable only after national ballot ; in local strikes it should be open to the Executive to take a ballot of the locality before closing the strike ; in strikes affecting a single system, there should be a delegate conference of the men employed on that system before the strike could be closed. Sectional strikes will tend to disappear in favour of local or national movements ; where they occur, they should be terminable by the Executive, acting on the advice of the *Departmental* Executive. Sympathetic [1] strikes should be controlled absolutely by the Executive.

The declaration and conduct of strikes should, in the main, be left, as now, in the hands of the Executive. Such cases as the Knox strike can hardly be provided for in the rules ; but it is quite clear that in such cases, sanction or no sanction, the men will come out, and that they will be right. Possibly a more rapid and summary method of sanctioning such spontaneous movements may be established.

We have seen that, in the case of a highly centralised

[1] Not 'spontaneous' strikes, like the Knox strike, but the calling out of one section to support another.

TRADE UNION GOVERNMENT

industry, which is also a monopoly, it is necessary for the Trade Union organisation also to be highly centralised, and for enormous power to be placed in the hands of officials. We have seen, further, that the safeguard against ' officialism ' in these industries lies in the provision of a good system of representative government, in which sectional and local interests find adequate expression and co-ordination. We shall now turn to an industry which stands, in every respect, at the opposite extreme, and in which the main problem is not simply the strengthening of central control, but the reconciliation of a national policy with a considerable degree of local autonomy.

The Building industry might have been dealt with in the last chapter, when we were speaking of Trade Union structure ; but as the problems that arise in connection with it are rather those of the division of control than structural, it seemed better to postpone all consideration of it to this chapter. Organisation in the Building industry has been going steadily back for the past dozen years or so ; not only has no considered attempt been made to bring in the unorganised, but even the old craft Unions have been losing ground. This has been due very largely to the change in industrial processes ; the old separation of the crafts has been breaking down, and new classes of workers, such as the Faience Fixers, have been taking over much of the work that was once done by other sections. In spite of this, the old Unions have made no attempt whatever to broaden the basis of their membership ; they have gone on in the old way, and, naturally, have fallen behind. The essential preliminary, therefore, to any sort of effective organisation in the Building industry is a broadening of the basis of the existing craft Unions.

This, however, is only a preliminary. A good deal has been heard, during the last year or so, of schemes for the amalgamation of all the Building Unions. Conferences have been held, and a great deal of breath wasted ; but it is quite certain that no amalgamation [1] will result. Only recently, the Carpenters and Joiners have declared their determination to proceed no further with any scheme of amalgamation. They were ready to dally with vague suggestions ; but the production of a concrete scheme at once frightened them off. Their position with a very large number of members engaged in other industries, especially shipbuilding, makes it difficult for them to come into any Building amalgamation.

Certain smaller fusions may make the way smoother for an Industrial Union. All the rival sets of Unions catering for the same crafts (Carpenters, Plumbers, Painters, Bricklayers, Slaters, etc.) could at once be amalgamated ; but, when this had been done, there would remain about half a dozen strong national crafts Unions with a fairly wide basis of membership, and several General Labour Unions. The more difficult problem is to secure effective concerted action among these independent units.

The Building industry is now organised in 67 Unions, local and national, and 13 local Federations. Working for a local market and for the most part on discontinuous jobs, labour in the Building trades must be organised to some extent on a local basis. The locality is the unit which has to be paralysed ; and as the jobs are discontinuous, action has to be taken rapidly. The present state of organisation is exactly the reverse : the national Unions are strongly

[1] Except perhaps fusions of rival sectional Unions, *e.g.* rival Painters', Carpenters', etc., Unions.

entrenched, and act throughout independently, for their own hand; the local Federations are weak, and cannot move without the sanction of the national Unions. All the funds are in the hands of the Unions, and the Federations have to raise all money by means of special subscriptions; no encouragement is given by the Unions to their branches to join the local Federations, nor are the Federation dues paid out of the Union funds. Were this all, the position would be bad enough; but there is worse to come. Success depends, in the Building industry, on the complete paralysing of the 'job' or the locality; all the sections must act together, and there must be some means of controlling all possible blacklegs. But, in the first place, the immense number of non-unionists in the industry generally makes it quite impossible to paralyse a district, and even where non-unionism is comparatively unimportant, the separate Unions generally pull in different directions. Not only do the sections fall out among themselves locally: far more disastrous is the fact that often half a dozen distinct policies are being dictated to them by as many distinct Head Offices. The Unions have different methods of negotiation; they tie themselves up with sectional agreements expiring at different dates, and effective common action becomes altogether impossible. Sometimes, some of the most important sections remain outside the local building Federation, and conclude on their own agreements that are disastrous to the other sections. Moreover, the National Conciliation Board, which includes most of the principal Unions, is probably the most reactionary Labour body in existence. Instead of direct negotiations between a solid body of employers and a solid body of masters, it works by a system of cross-voting.

Often, enough of the workers' representatives seem to vote with the employers to allow of the carrying of perfectly preposterous resolutions. In this case, at least, conciliation has served only to 'dish' the workers.

Even apart from this difficulty, the local Federations are now hampered at every turn. Their objects are to settle questions of demarcation and to secure united action; but it is far from surprising that they have failed in both. The presence of overlapping Unions, and still more the failure of the old craft Unions to open their ranks when old processes gave way to new, have made the demarcation question insoluble. No attempt can be made to solve it until all the Unions are working together in friendly co-operation, and a real effort is made to bring in the unorganised. Demarcation disputes are nowhere so bitter as in the Building industry.

In securing united action, the Federations encountered a further difficulty. Rapid action, we have seen, is always essential to success; but the first requisite, if rapid action is to be possible, is the concentration of power in the hands of a single authority. The problem is in the case not merely that of local as against central control; it arises because the central authority is itself a many-headed monster, or worse. In each Union, the branch has to obtain the sanction of its national Executive before a strike can be declared; this means that every strike requires the permission of a number of isolated and independent national Executives, which there is no attempt to co-ordinate. As these meet at different times, the delay involved often runs into six weeks, and by that time it is generally too late to act. Very often the cause of dispute is particular, and applies only to a single job; but by the time the whole of the workers can come out, the job is finished. If the local Federation takes on itself the responsibility of calling out the workers without the sanction of the Unions, it is in the unfortunate position of having no funds, and of being unable to collect any. A Federation cannot collect funds except through the branches composing it; and these are, as a rule, unwilling to pay twice over—to the national Union and to the local Federation. It is, under such conditions, almost impossible to raise special levies for the support of strikes.

It is therefore absolutely essential to create a single authority with the power to sanction strikes and grant strike pay. Clearly, such an authority can be only a real Industrial Union. We are sometimes told that national solidarity in the Building industry has failed already; but the old Federation, which died of its own futility little more than a year ago, was a *Federation of local Federations*. It linked up, not the strong national Unions, which, by their isolation, now prevent united action, but the weak local Federations, which had themselves no power to delegate to it. Naturally, it reflected their weakness, and, whereas they drag out a miserable existence, died outright. The experiment of a real Building Trades' Federation has never been tried; but it would be hardly less unlikely to succeed. It would have to link up national Unions instead of local Federations, and it would have to surrender complete control of stoppages to the federal executive. In short, it could only be made effective if the Unions sacrificed to it the whole of their power—if, that is, it became an amalgamation in everything but name. This, clearly, is not the kind of body proposed by those who advocate federation in the building industry; they want a powerless body, whose sole use will be to scotch schemes of amalgamation. Building federation is dead and damned.

What is wanted is not so much local control of stoppages as local initiative and local organisation. Stoppages will nearly always be local; but, with strong national Unions in the field, the fighting funds will clearly be centralised. It is essential that the locality should be able to call easily upon the national fund, but it is also necessary to leave the ultimate control in the hands of a national authority. A non-sectional central fund is, undoubtedly, an impossibility, until a real Industrial Union is created by fusion of existing Unions. But failure will continue till there is one central authority to sanction strikes, and so secure the rapid action which, in this industry, is essential to success.

It will have become clear from these instances that the problem of control differs very much from industry to industry in accordance both with the natural character of the industry itself, and with the structure of the organisations covering it. Thus on the Railways there is, if we set aside the Locomotive Engineers and Firemen and the Railway Clerks, a form of organisation at any rate approximating to Industrial Unionism. There is one strong Union, covering most of the industry. This means that central control is very easy to realise, if it is necessary; and as Railway management is, in addition, that of a highly centralised monopoly, the industry has always to be prepared to act as a whole against united employers. Nationalisation would, of course, be the completion of this centralisation on the employers' side, and would involve a corresponding tightening-up of the organisation on the side of the men.

In Building, on the other hand, we have an industry catering for a local market, at present organised by means of national craft Unions. Local solidarity is the first need, and the problem to be faced is therefore that of getting all the workers in a locality organised. Here the locality will nearly always be the unit of action, and here, if anywhere, we should expect to find that local autonomy had its legitimate sphere; but we saw that it is absolutely necessary, where central funds have to be drawn upon, to have central control, and we therefore recommended, along with local action, central sanction for all stoppages. The question of closing strikes in the Building industry is more difficult. It is just this sort of strike that is apt to linger on long after all chance of victory has gone, and it is hard to say how far the local organisations could be trusted to keep their heads. Probably the solution lies in the fixing of a time limit; after a certain number of weeks have elapsed, the national authority should have power, after consulting the local organisation, to discontinue strike pay, though not actually to close the strike.

In the last chapter, we discussed the method of Federation, as opposed to Amalgamation, as the immediate solution of pressing problems in the Transport and Shipbuilding industries. We have now had a very similar discussion in the case of Building. We should, then, by now be in a position to make some estimate of the value of Federation as a method, and, in especial, to address ourselves to the particular problems of control which it presents.

Federation may be defined, roughly, as the linking up of independent Unions for specific purposes, usually for concerted action in trade disputes. We saw in the last chapter that, as a rule, the best test of the real efficacy of a Federation is the presence or absence of a central fighting fund. The absence of such a fund inevitably means that the Federation has no means of controlling the bodies affiliated to it, and is therefore unable to take effective action on any controversial matter. In the case of the Transport workers, we saw good reason to believe that the Federation could only be made effective by the strengthening of its financial basis. Now, it is clear that a strong central fund involves strong central control; federal funds cannot be left at the call of any affiliated organisation, unless the whole has the power of checking and regulating such calls. The government of Federations therefore presents problems of its own; for it is clearly impossible to persuade independent Unions to surrender to a Federation the same powers as branches customarily surrender to the central organisation of their Union. The problem, however, is in the main the same as that which an *industrial* or 'greater' Union has to face; difficulties of adjustment can only be got over by the provision of an adequate system of representative government. Clearly, the governing body of the Federation must in all cases consist of delegates from the affiliated Unions in proportion to their membership; and where the Union contains several different crafts or sections, its delegates should be elected on a sectional basis. Provision should also be made, wherever possible, for the representation, on the federal Executive, of local differences. In practice, however, it will often be found impossible to get a federal Executive representing differences adequately, and this will be most the case where such representation is most essential. It is precisely in Federations of very wide scope, covering an enormous area, that rapid action, in respect of a particular section or locality, is often most necessary. It will, however, be impossible in such cases to summon a general meeting of the various delegates in time to deal with the point promptly.

This is one of the greatest difficulties Federations have to face, as it means either a fatal sacrifice of rapidity in action, or else the handing over of practically all the control to a small and probably misrepresentative executive committee. The Federation, if it is to act promptly, has to create an Executive smaller than its occasional representative Delegate Meeting; but such an Executive can hardly command the obedience of the Unions in anything like the same degree. This may well be fatal; for the need cannot be met by any system of occasional conferences. Particular questions are constantly needing rapid solution. In short, as a rule, a Federation can only do its work effectively by becoming virtually an amalgamation; but when it has gone so far, amalgamation is both an economy and an additional source of strength. Taken as a whole, Federation within an industry is an obsolete method, destined to be more or less rapidly supplanted by complete Industrial Unionism, which alone is suitable to modern industrial conditions.

Federation, no doubt, will continue for some time to be the method of securing concerted action in a good many industries — Cotton being the most obvious instance. In most cases, however, it will tend to approximate more and more to amalgamation—to be, in fact, something very like amalgamation for fighting purposes. As industry becomes more centralised, and as the employers federate more and more closely, Federations of Trade Unions must get more and more power in the control of strikes. Along with this increased control will go the development of stronger central funds; and this must be accompanied by a change in the methods of government, and in the composition of federal Executives. Many of the Federations mentioned in the Board of Trade *Industrial Directory* exist only on paper, or at most consist, for all practical purposes, merely of a Secretary. If they are to do useful work, this must be changed. The day of loose federation, like the day of pure local autonomy, is past; centralisation is the first need in nearly all industries, if strikes are to be brought to a successful conclusion.

Syndicalism, we have seen, is connected, in the minds of many of its supporters, with the demand for more local autonomy. This is especially the case with those Syndicalists who are under the influence of Anarchist-Communism, and, to a less extent, with all those who have caught the fever from France. Industrial Unionists, on the other hand, are for the most part in favour of centralisation accompanied by democratic control; and the movement towards the Greater Unionism in this country has now definitely abandoned the hopeless attitude of those who favour local autonomy, and come to realise that central control alone can meet the needs of modern industrial warfare.

This is seen in its most interesting form in the famous pamphlet issued by a section of the South Wales Miners. *The Miners' Next Step*—the Bible of Syndicalism in South Wales—is a vigorous plea for more complete centralisation. ' The Industrial Democracy League ',[1] founded among others by the authors of

[1] It has just issued a monthly magazine, *Solidarity*.

the pamphlet, exists to put its principles into practice, to secure centralisation over the whole coalfield of South Wales, accompanied by real democratic control. The proposals outlined in *The Miners' Next Step* fall, therefore, under two main heads. They show conclusively that the local strike, supported largely out of local funds, and declared by the will of the locality, fails in an overwhelming majority of cases. They instance the famous Combine strike of 1910–11 and the Aberdare strike. It is quite clear that, save in a very few cases, and those purely defensive, there is very little hope of a strike succeeding unless it has behind it the united force of the district, in this case South Wales as a whole. Centralisation of fighting policy, they make quite evident, is the first essential. This, however, is only one side of their proposals. Almost as much as they fear ' parochialism ', they fear ' officialdom '. They are confident that the carrying out of their policy of centralisation would result, were the government of the Federation to remain as it is now, in bureaucracy of the worst sort. Not only would the policy pursued be peaceful instead of militant ; the rank and file would get still more out of touch with the leaders. The second part of the pamphlet therefore consists of a fierce attack on leadership as a whole : the authors desire, not to change their leaders, but to get rid of the whole idea of leadership. For the present bureaucratic methods, in which the officials always usurp the legislative power that should solely belong to the workers, they propose to substitute control by a monthly delegate meeting representing the coalfield as a whole. The delegates are to be elected by the Lodges, and are to form the sole legislative body. They are to pass all price-lists, and to lay down all general conditions of work throughout the coal-field ;

the officials are only to apply the principles so determined, and are to have, in the strictest sense, merely executive functions. Thus the officials will be deprived of all chance of misrepresenting the rank and file ; and the delegates, being specially instructed by the Lodges on all points, will be in close touch with the feeling of those whom they represent.

This scheme seems to be open to the objection that its system of democratic control is really applicable only in cases where a really broad and general issue is involved, and a clear mandate can therefore be secured from the rank and file. Nothing is more clearly established than that large conferences are highly unlikely to form good legislative bodies, or to deal effectively with questions of detail. The meeting may lay down general principles ; but, in details, all the power will be in the hands of the officials who apply them. Even though the members of the meeting would be delegates and not representatives, though they would be definitely instructed by the Lodges how to vote, it would be found that the important business of the coal-field could not be transacted by a periodical general meeting ; the officials would act on their own responsibilty, and the delegate meeting would preserve only the power of veto. This does not mean that the last stage of the organisation would be worse than the first : power would have passed from the District officials to the centre, and to this extent it would be easier for the rank and file to criticise ; but the administrative power would inevitably still rest with the officials and the Executive.

An interesting corroboration of this view is to be found in the existing organisation of the South Wales Miners' Federation. The constitution now provides for the placing of ultimate sovereignty in the hands

TRADE UNION GOVERNMENT

of a Delegate Meeting representing the Lodges. This meeting is in effective control of general wages movements and negotiations; but in all detailed matters the officials and the Executive are very powerful. Greater centralisation has been secured, and the influence of the Miners' Agent over his own District lessened.

This change is the result of a conflict between three rival parties among the Miners. The old official element stood for the retention of the former system of divided control, in which the Lodge and the District had both a degree of autonomy. This was then found to work out, in practice, as the domination of the official element, local and central. It gave both the central officials and the Miners' Agents considerable power, and left very little to the rank and file. At the other extreme stood the Syndicalists or ' Industrial Democrats,' advocating the system we have just examined. Their reforms involved the abolition of the ' Districts,' and the degradation of the Miners' Agents to a subordinate position. We have seen how their scheme was adopted in some of its leading features, especially centralisation, though it was bitterly opposed by the District officials, whose authority it threatened. The agitation, however, some time ago got far enough to be referred, by general vote of the coal-field, to a committee with orders to draw up a definite scheme; on this committee the official element obtained a majority, and the draft scheme they put forward was decisively rejected. This was the opportunity of the third party, which favoured centralisation, but not the complete subordination of the official element, by which the Syndicalists wished it to be accompanied. The scheme of centralisation and control by Delegate Meeting has already proved itself highly successful, and has meant a great gain in power to the rank and file of the South Wales Miners.

This constitution is indeed a great improvement on the old and should lead to a reconstruction of the Executive. The Executive of the centralised South Wales Miners' Federation should become a body representative of both local and sectional interests. Its members should be elected in electoral districts by various sections of workers. Including all workers in or about Mines, the reformed Miners' Federation would have to pay far more attention to sectional differences, and an Executive elected roughly on the same principles as that of the Railwaymen would exercise a real check on officials, who should, of course, not be eligible to sit on it. This check would be made even more effective by the local character of the industry, and, in fact, centralisation is working less 'bureaucratically' on these lines than it might on those laid down in *The Miners' Next Step*.[1]

We have seen already, in the case of the Amalgamated Society of Engineers, how important it is that a great national Union should get all sorts of interests represented on its Executive. *Abstract* democracy—the bare principle of 'one man, one vote', with its absolute ignoring of differences and shades of value, is a thing of the past; instead of it, we are evolving a new and more real democracy which takes differences into account. It is not aristocratic; for it seeks to represent all differences and interests fairly: it is, in fact, the only true and philosophic democracy. Any great Union that neglects this in working out its system of representative government will fail: it will be driven to centralise; but its centralisation will be a failure, because it will be not democratic, but bureaucratic.

[1] Above this Executive would still be the Delegate Meeting elected by Lodges, with a final power of veto.

The first great problem, then, in Trade Union control is the provision of better systems of representative government. Growing to greatness, in many cases, from small beginnings, the Unions have never paused to set their house in order, or to refurnish with later ideas. Trade Union management is still, in many Unions, decidedly early Victorian, and it is one of the most hopeful signs of the industrial awakening that, in the new schemes that are being formulated, the problem of government is for the first time really being faced. The Railwaymen, for instance, have really endeavoured, with a great measure of success, to get a system of government and control capable of dealing with the greater issues of modern Trade Unionism.

It will be well, before we leave this question of centralisation and government, to corroborate some of the arguments we have advanced in favour of central control by reference to an interview with Mr. W. A. Appleton, Secretary of the General Federation of Trade Unions, which appeared in the *Daily Herald*.[1] He holds that rank-and-file control of strikes merely plays the employers' game; that often the masters, knowing that an organised movement is coming soon, deliberately goad the workers into striking at the wrong time, and so beat them. " Fully half," he says, " of what are termed spontaneous strikes are undertaken at times and under circumstances favourable to the employers." " I wish," he goes on, " to dissociate myself entirely from the demand for full rank-and-file control of strikes. I am as keen as any man on defending the right of the worker to strike at a moment's notice against conditions he finds intolerable, but I hold that the direction of strike

[1] February 12, 1913.

movements must be left to the duly elected officials of the Unions. . . . I am opposed to indiscriminate striking, not in the interests of the officials, but in the interests of the rank and file themselves." Mr. Appleton goes on to point out how little the worker knows of the chances of success, of the condition of his own and the employers' organisation, of the state of the market, or of the chances of a boom or a fall. Success in strikes depends on a correct knowledge of these things, and it is to provide this knowledge that the expert official is required.

People talk so lightly about strikes, Mr. Appleton holds, only because they do not understand what strikes mean. The object of effective organisation is to secure the results without the need for a strike. A trial of strength need not come to the point of a stoppage. Sporadic striking is fatal to solidarity; like the Germans, we must 'organise'. The movement as a whole must be under expert direction, and strikes, be they large or small, must be centrally controlled.

Such a testimony from a man like Mr. Appleton, who in connection with the General Federation, has had more experience of the 'spontaneous' or 'engineered' strike than any other Union leader, cannot be disregarded. Mr. Appleton has shown himself all along more alive than any man to the new situations that have arisen in the Trade Union world. He seems to have been alone in realising the proper attitude for the Unions to adopt towards the Insurance Act;[1] for by doing his best to make the General Federation the common Insurance society of the whole Trade Union movement he gave the Unions their chance really to get something out of the Act—and they rejected it. His opinion on any labour question deserves the most careful

[1] That is, when once they determined to accept it.

attention : on the question of control over strikes it is too strong testimony to be rejected.

Mr. Philip Snowden, in his recent book *The Living Wage*, maintains that nowadays no strikes have any chance of succeeding except small ones, and that these can succeed only when they have public opinion behind them. We are not now concerned with the clear fallacy of this view; we have now only to point out that, whatever the best area for strikes may be, central control and central funds are essential. It is quite certain that the small strike has been crippled more than the large by the lack of such funds, and that the result of centralisation will be 'better times' for the small strike, and greater power for isolated sections of workers.

Along with the consolidation of Trade Union forces, the centralisation of funds and control, and the development of new forms of representative government must go a change in policy on the part of many of the great Unions. With centralisation, the day of agreements is passing away, or, at least, agreements are being so modified in form as to differ wholly from the agreements with which the events of the last century have made us familiar. In particular, there are two classes of agreements which the realisation of industrial solidarity will sweep entirely away. There must be no more 'craft' agreements; the industry or the great 'occupational' Union must negotiate as a whole, on behalf of all its members. In the past, the 'craft' agreement and 'craft' conciliation have been the employer's best weapons against the worker; he has used them unmercifully to set section against section, and, by arranging that sectional agreements shall end at different times, has often succeeded in making concerted action impossible. This difficulty will disappear when industrial solidarity is realised. Workers and masters will stand solidly face to face; and, if an agreement is arrived at, it will be an agreement of all with all.

Secondly, long 'time' agreements must go. In the past, the workers have continually bound themselves down by a long agreement just before a trade boom, and have therefore been unable to take advantage of the period of prosperity. Just when the agreement has expired, the trade boom has ended, and the workers have been compelled either to continue on the old terms or to strike just when a stoppage suited the employer best. As the Unions increase their power, it is probable that the 'time' agreement will tend to disappear: at any rate, it will seldom exceed a year in duration. There is much to be said for the suggestion that all agreements should expire on May 1—Labour Day. But the ultimate settlement of this question is a matter for the particular Unions concerned; it cannot be decided off-hand on general principles.

The last of the great questions of control now confronting the Trade Union movement is part of the general adaptation of administration to function. A comparison of the 1876 Trade Union Act with the rules of any great modern Union will at once show to what an extent the Unions, in their natural development, have taken on new functions unthought of when Parliament yielded to pressure, and gave them their charter.[1] Unfortunately, along with this development of function, there has been no corresponding evolution of their machinery of government.

[1] The whole legal question raised by the Osborne Judgment turned on this point. See Professor W. M. Geldart's admirable pamphlet, *The Osborne Judgment and After*.

In most cases, they are trying to do all the work with a constitution that was meant only to do one part of it. Especially, from the advent of the Labour Party, there has been a lamentable tendency to elect Union officials to Parliament, and to let them try to fill both jobs at once. Inevitably, the efficiency of the work done has suffered in both cases. ' Twicers ' have been bad Union officials and worse Parliamentarians. With the passing of the Insurance Act, the ' twicer ' has, too often, become a ' thricer '. Swamped beneath the mass of conflicting duties, the personnel of Trade Union offices has had no time to think ; it is the fault, not of the officials, but of the system, that matters have been allowed to drift. This hopeless attempt to muddle through will go on, until the Unions address themselves to the task, and set their organisation right. The ' twicer ' must go, and adequate staffs must be maintained, if the Unions are to do really effective work.

Not only must the duplication of jobs be abolished ; the office organisation of most of the Unions requires drastic reform. At present, all sorts of functions are lumped together anyhow ; the Trade Union office is a centre for all sorts of work, and no attempt is made to systematise or to divide. To some Unions this does not apply, and, in particular, the N.U.R. has taken advantage of its opportunity to perfect a system of administrative devolution already begun by the A.S.R.S.[1] The General Secretary of the N.U.R. has under him four Assistant Secretaries, each of whom has under his care a particular part of the Union's activities. Finance, legal matters, trade movements and organisation are now separate departments, and

[1] The Steel Smelters, too, have now an admirable system of office organisation.

the increased efficiency of the administration is already making itself felt.

This question of devolution by function has a further aspect. Not only are Trade Union officials often members of Parliament : the general business of the Unions is hopelessly mixed up with their political activities. Fortunately, the result of the 1913 Trade Union Act will be to necessitate administrative separation, and probably in the end to make the political fund really voluntary. The pig-headedness of the English bench may well turn out to have been a blessing in disguise.

Further, amalgamation will, in most cases, compel the Unions to make a clear separation between ' trade ' and ' benefit ' funds. This, again, will be an unmixed advantage. The use of ' trade ' money for ' benefit ' purposes is an abuse which requires to be swept away, if the Unions are to become real fighting forces.

On the whole, then, the Greater Unionism will turn out to be a movement not only in the direction of consolidation of forces. It will also force the Unions to develop new systems of representative government, and to adopt administrative devolution such as we see beginning, slowly but certainly, in Government departments. It will lead not only to united action, but also to efficient management, and will compel the Unions to bring themselves up to date, and to abandon the conservatism which, in management no less than in structure, has too long prevented them from realising to the full their common interest in face of the common enemy, and, equally, from fitting themselves for the new functions in industry which they are already being called upon to perform.

CHAPTER IX

SOCIAL PEACE AND SOCIAL WAR—CONCILIATION AND ARBITRATION

"The most wretched slavery they call peace."—TACITUS.

IN these 'pacifist' days, the word 'war' has an ugly sound.[1] 'Peace', on the other hand, sounds sweetly on a modern ear : 'peace', 'love' and 'brotherhood' are surely what we are all out to realise. How nice then to realise them here and now ! Social peace ! A country without strikes ! Co-partnership and co-operation of worker and employer ! How delightful, and how soothing to the troubled social conscience !

When all this is hypocrisy, it is bad enough ; when it is mere stupidity, it is even worse. There are, unfortunately, people who really believe in social peace from disinterested motives, and are earnestly engaged in its furtherance. They have been deceived by the nonsensical or hypocritical talk of those who pretend that "the interests of Capital and Labour are identical", and that all that is needed is " a better understanding of economic truths on both sides "—especially on the side of Labour. Let it be understood once for all that the interests of Capital and Labour are diametrically opposed, and that although it may be necessary for Labour sometimes to acquiesce in 'social peace', such peace is only the lull before the storm.

Proposals for conciliation, arbitration, State interfer-

[1] 1913.

ence in Labour disputes and the like, are almost always made in the name of 'social peace'. Strikes affect the public as well as the masters and workers directly concerned; they affect other masters and, still more nearly, other workers. There is on this account a *prima facie* case in favour of all attempts to put an end to strikes and lock-outs, and this *prima facie* case is run for all it is worth by the capitalist press, whenever a big strike occurs. Before, however, we need accept any argument based on this line of reasoning, on the inconvenience caused to the public, the 'consumer', by industrial disputes, there are certain general considerations we may take into account. The employer runs his business for a profit: therefore it is to the employer's advantage to keep his business going, that is, to avoid strikes. It may be answered that the worker lives by selling his labour, and that it must be to his advantage always to find a buyer; but the crucial difference between them is that Capital exploits while Labour is exploited. If both started fair, they would have an equal interest in securing smooth running and avoiding unnecessary friction; but as it is, one starts with everything, and the other with nothing. The worker has gradually to gain, by his own efforts, the position in which he should, in fairness, have been all along. The worker is on the offensive; the capitalist is only trying to keep his place, though he seems, from the rise in profits and the fall in real wages, to be doing rather more than that just at present. The continuance of the *status quo* is, then, the capitalist's constant object, and it follows that a continued state of 'social peace' is just what suits him most, and the worker least. 'Social peace' is a sham and a trick; how far 'social truces' may be necessary in the social war we shall see later on.

What is here being attacked is not the habit of negotiation between the Unions and the employers, but the attempt to represent the success of this negotiation as implying that the interests of both parties are the same. It proves, at most, only the superiority of a disciplined campaign over guerilla warfare. As we have seen, industrial diplomacy, the use of collective bargaining, may and usually does amount merely to a trial of strength, or of estimated strength, between the parties concerned. The avoidance of conflict by such means may be highly desirable, whereas the abandonment of the method of collective bargaining involved in arbitration and in a good deal of conciliation is certainly not so.

In asking, then, whether either conciliation or arbitration is desirable at all, we shall be asking not whether the Labour movement can be drugged into accepting a 'social peace' based on the present system, but whether the recognition of the class-struggle implies war to the death without truce or negotiation. We shall find that, though there is a real class-war, the whole social system does not rest solely upon it, and that, provided the Labour movement keeps its ultimate revolutionary aim clearly in sight, it will get on far better with discipline than without it—far better by negotiating as well as striking than by striking alone. Conciliation, *backed by the threat of a strike*, has a very useful function; conciliation that is disguised arbitration is Capital's latest sleeping-draught for Labour. The arguments for truceless war are very largely arguments really against compulsory arbitration, sectional and long agreements, and veiled arbitration. Get rid of all these, and the residuum of pure negotiation is a useful method of saving strike pay and suffering.

Industrial peace, then, must not be permanent. There is a real class-antagonism, a quarrel that can only be adjusted by the overthrow of capitalist society. The fact that strikes inconvenience the public and are 'brutal' in their effects is an argument, not for prohibiting strikes, but for altering the social system. A public that acquiesces in exploitation has no rights against workers who are up in arms against it : the State has no right to intervene *as an impartial person*. The State should represent the moral sense of the community, and for the moral sense of the community to be 'impartial' in the great war between justice and injustice is for it to forfeit its right as a community. Compulsory interference by the State involves, as we shall see, a moral standard ; the State has only the right to interfere, not selfishly, as the 'organised consumers', but morally, as a social regenerator. At present, it interferes, as a rule, merely to stop the strike at any cost ; its motto is "anything for peace and quietness". But it has no right to peace till it has secured all men their rights—and from the State of to-day, it is more than a little fantastic to expect that.

The whole attitude of the Government, of Sir George Askwith, and of the Industrial Council, as well as all the squealing of the private citizen, assumes that the sole object is to stop strikes ; it would be truer to say that the aim of every right-minded person should be to stimulate and direct them. This attitude is presumably inevitable on the part of a Government engaged in passing legislation to which the people is either hostle or indifferent ; but it is an abandonment of the aspirations of true statesmen, and a surrender of all right. 'Compulsory' arbitration is an appeal to naked coercion ; and coercion is only justifiable in a real democracy.

The Government, admittedly, has no conscience; but the public has one of a sort. The public's chief use for its conscience is to send it to sleep; but a very rude shock will sometimes wake it up. At least a strong minority is alive to some of the worst evils of sweating; and industrial war is made unsafe for the employer in this country, because he does not quite dare, even with the State at his back, to make a habit of " shooting them down ".[1] If he feels really in peril, he is quite likely to try it on; but, at present, the remedy looks more dangerous than the disease.

It is, then, really recognised on both sides that the normal condition of the world of industry is one of suppressed war. Open war all the time, however, does not suit either side. The workers' organisations are often not strong enough to stand frequent conflicts, and they fear to provoke a vindictive and ill-informed public by inconveniencing it too much; the employers, on the other hand, want peace in times of prosperity, in order to reap their profits; and, in times of depression, dare not proceed to the last extremity for fear of waking up the national conscience —which, after all, might turn out to exist.

On the side of the workers, there is a further consideration that makes continual open warfare impossible. The Trade Unions have to take men as they find them, and revolutionary methods only succeed, for long, with revolutionary people. In England, the rebel is a very rare phenomenon. Trade Unionists, as a whole, have very little revolutionary spirit. They will bear the slaughter-house meekly,

[1] Since these words were written, events in Dublin and Cornwall have a little shaken my faith; but if the workers are alive, these very events will give them a chance to make a repetition impossible.

provided the market does not demand the slaughter of too many at once; they will lie down gladly in their thousands in the green pastures of Liberalism and Reform. Meanwhile, profits will go up, and real wages will fall. Capitalism has not yet to die in its last ditch.

The various proposals for the regulation of trade disputes which fall under the head of Conciliation and Arbitration range from something like complete statutory determination of wages to such purely permissive measures as the Conciliation Act of 1896. Compulsory Arbitration, Compulsory Conciliation, universal Trade or Wages Boards, permissive Arbitration and Conciliation, are all methods of interference aiming either at the fixing of the standard of life or at the prevention of industrial warfare. The words Conciliation and Arbitration, as we saw in Chapter II., are often very loosely used, and this looseness may make it easier for a proposal to get passed into law without the workers having realised its true significance. It is absolutely essential that the possibilities should be understood, and that the Unions should get their attitude clear. At present, as the general debate at the 1912 Trade Union Congress [1] revealed, they have the haziest ideas of what the whole subject implies. Generally speaking, there is a vague objection to compulsory arbitration; but the objection seems to be so much a matter of words that it is very doubtful if such a proposal would not be accepted, were it only called something else. Certainly very few even of the leaders realise the nature of all the divergent schemes that are now being proposed, or are at all in a position to pass judgment upon them.

Compulsory arbitration involves the reference of

[1] See *Report of the Trade Union Congress, 1912*, pp. 191-9.

all disputes between employer and employed, in the first or the last resort, to some 'impartial' tribunal with power to decide one way or the other. It prohibits strikes and lock-outs, and substitutes full inquiry into the circumstances; that is to say, it takes the case out of the hands of the parties, and puts it in those of a representative of the community. This is supposed to save the public inconvenience, while securing justice for the disputants.

The best known instance of the actual working of Compulsory Arbitration is, of course, New Zealand, where, though the precise terms of the law are continually being altered, a system uniform in the main has been in operation since 1894. A consolidating Act was passed in 1908, and this was again amended in 1910 and 1911. The peculiarity of the system is that it is open only to registered Associations of employers and workers (at least three employers or at least fifteen workers). It is thus intended to stimulate organisation, but in effect the result of this provision is apt to be that the Act, while remaining voluntary in form, becomes really compulsory. It is always open to workers to declare a strike, provided their Union is not registered, and provided no award applies to them; but it is so easy to form a rival Union of fifteen persons which can get an award legally binding on the whole trade that this safeguard is really illusory. The system is, in fact, generally recognised as being equivalent to compulsory arbitration, and even the recent withdrawal of their registration by quite a number of the Unions will probably not mean for long the right to strike. Strikes occur in spite of the Act; but this is mainly because of the difficulty found in collecting the statutory fines from defaulters.

According to the 1908 Act, which we may take here as representing the system in its developed form, recourse must always, except in the case of State Railwaymen, be had in the first instance to a specially appointed Council of Conciliation, representing the two sides, with an 'impartial' Chairman. Failing a settlement, the dispute at the end of one month may, and at the end of two must, be referred to the central Court of Arbitration, an 'impartial' body, standing for the public, which decides absolutely. The penal clauses for breach of an award or for attempts to bring about a strike or lock-out tend, as in New South Wales, to become more stringent. In the year 1909–10 the Conciliation Councils dealt with 102 disputes, of which they wholly settled 67. In 23 a partial settlement was reached, and only outstanding questions were referred to the Arbitration Court, to which 12 further cases were referred wholly.[1]

Broadly, there is no doubt as to the result of the Act in New Zealand, and in New South Wales and Western Australia, which have Acts largely modelled on that of New Zealand. At first, wages rose considerably in many cases, especially in sweated trades, where they were sometimes nearly doubled. Then the employers, at first hostile to the Act, began to see the advantages of industrial peace, while at the same time the workers, who had at first welcomed it, realised that they had got out of it nearly all there was to be got, and became correspondingly dissatisfied. The better paid workers especially ceased to get rises, and began to cancel their registrations in order to be able to strike. Industrial unrest began to

[1] *Memoranda relating to Strikes and Lock-outs*, etc. [Cd. 6081] Board of Trade, 1912.

spread, and since 1911 at any rate, New Zealand has been very markedly a home of labour troubles. The two hostile sections of the Labour movement, the Federation of Labour, which has a militant industrial policy, and the Trade and Labour Councils, which are mild and political, have united against the Act, and New Zealand has had stormy times. It is no longer what Mr. Henry Demarest Lloyd called it in 1902, ' A Country without Strikes '.

It is hard to say how far this change of front on the part of Labour means the break-up of the system. It will probably bring about a modification, but not any drastic change ; for the whole method of legal regulation of industrial matters is too deeply ingrained in Australia to be rooted out, even were such a change desirable. It is more likely that the system in New Zealand will in time approximate more closely to that of Victoria, which we still have to study shortly. A tendency in this direction was observable in the 1908 Act, and it seems clear at least that the penal element is breaking down, and that New Zealand is approximating to the Minimum Wage legislation of the Victorian Wages Boards. Compulsory legislation against strikes is breaking down all over Australia ; compulsory regulation of minimum conditions is gaining ground. The New Zealand Act provides in form for the fixing of an absolute rate, but in practice the rates fixed are minima, though of course on this system employees cannot *strike* for a rate higher than the minimum.

Could it be shown that compulsory arbitration had worked in New Zealand, it would not at all follow that it could be applied to England. In New Zealand, the total number of workers involved is small, and coercion is comparatively easy to apply.

In dealing with the huge masses of men involved in our great strikes, penal provisions would be impossible, unless they were taken against the Unions; and any attempt to impose such provisions on the Unions would meet with overwhelming resistance. Compulsory arbitration for England is not practical politics[1]; and the Trade Unions would be wiser, if instead of spending all their time denouncing it, they turned their attention to other and more dangerous proposals for compulsory regulation of strikes. If they think only of compulsory arbitration, and waste all their energy on flogging that very dead horse, the State will take advantage of their absent-mindedness to tie them down with something far more dangerous.

Clearly, the Government and the employers have realised this, and are turning their attention to such schemes. In this connection, the recent deliberations of the Industrial Council and, still more, the recent visit of Sir George Askwith and Mr. Isaac Mitchell to Canada are very significant. Canada has adopted, not Compulsory Arbitration, but Compulsory Conciliation, which means, in effect, the compulsory postponement of a strike until the employers and the public are ready for you. This system has spread from Canada to South Africa and the U.S.A., and there seems to be a tendency to adopt it in a good many other countries. As a rule, it applies only to those industries which are vaguely known as 'public utilities'.

Canada began in 1900 with a purely voluntary Conciliation Act on the lines of our own Act of 1896. This was followed by the Railway Labour Disputes Act of 1903, which enforced Conciliation, but did not prohibit strikes, being designed rather to settle

[1] Or was not, until the war made it so.

strikes when they already existed. It was not till 1907, after a long Miners' strike in the West, that the present Industrial Disputes Investigation Act, known as the 'Lemieux' Act, came into existence. According to this Act, no strike or lock-out in the Mining, Railway, Transport or 'public utility' services can be declared till the dispute has been investigated by a special Board of Conciliation and Investigation, appointed by the Minister of Labour, and consisting of one member recommended by the employers, one recommended by the workers, and one either recommended by these two, or, in default, nominated by the Minister. Thus, here again, the 'impartial' person comes in to hold the balance.

Until this Board has issued its report upon the dispute, no strike or lock-out may take place in any of the occupations that come within the scope of the Act. When the Board has definitely failed to effect a settlement, and has issued its report, a strike or lock-out may be declared; but reliance is placed on the influence of public opinion in compelling the parties to accept the 'impartial' award. Any strike or lock-out in defiance of an award may be represented as an unjust stoppage, and the Government relies on public opinion to make such stoppages rare and unfruitful. The prime object is to protect the public from inconvenience, and at the same time to rouse the public indignation against anyone who dares to inconvenience it. Justice is supposed to be done to both parties by Conciliation, and, accordingly, he who refuses to accept an award gets no sympathy.

The fallacy in this view lies in the supposition that a Conciliation Board can decide on grounds of justice. If any Board attempted to do such a thing, there would be an employers' revolution on the spot.

Conciliators and Conciliation Boards of all sorts cannot help being guided very largely by the economic strength of the parties; they plump for the settlement that has most chance of being accepted, whether it is just or unjust; and the sort of settlement people are ready to accept depends on their economic strength. A measure directed merely to the securing of social peace cannot secure social justice as a by-product. This situation is, no doubt, to some extent modified where an enterprise is nationally owned or controlled —that is the main argument in favour of nationalisation—but, in capitalistic industry, where the State steps in merely as a third party, to settle the dispute, ' peace ' will inevitably be the first consideration, and justice a very bad second.

This would fit in well with our profound conviction that, normally, what the worker gets is just what the strength of his economic organisation entitles him to,[1] were not the relative economic strength of the parties itself modified by the Act. In the first place, the striker, if he is the weaker party, is liable to be deprived of the additional strength which he gains from public support: in so far as he is weaker, public opinion is liable to be turned against him, even if he is in the right.[2] Secondly, the delay which must occur before a strike can be declared plays, in very many cases, into the employers' hands. No doubt, this is less the case with ' public utility ' services than with other forms of industry; but even here it may often be fatal to success. The employers have every opportunity to prepare for the struggle; for the workers, no preparation involving delay is necessary.

[1] Except, of course, in sweated trades.

[2] Again we must except sweated trades, in respect of which a section of the public has developed a conscience.

Delay is never to the worker's advantage; often it makes no difference to his chances; but in many cases it is fatal to all effective action.

Sir George Askwith answers this argument with the assertion that, "carried to its logical conclusion, the claim to cease work at a moment's notice, if acted upon, would make business impossible, and in a civilised community business must be made possible." But, in the first place, business should only be made possible in so far as it allows a decent standard of life to the worker; where it fails to do this, it should be made impossible as a means of enforcing redress. Secondly, the claim to cease work at a moment's notice never will be "carried to its logical conclusion," in Sir George Askwith's sense. He is quite right in his assertion that sudden stoppages are not, as a rule, a Trade Union's best way of securing advantages. But the sudden stoppage may be a necessary weapon, without being the normal weapon. It is, for instance, sometimes clearly the best method in the docks, and, in the case of the spontaneous 'discipline' strike, it is absolutely essential. The right to strike suddenly must not be taken away, though the right to strike against an existing agreement may be.[1] The two questions are separate, and should not be confused.

We saw that, even if Compulsory Arbitration had worked well in New Zealand, that would be no reason for supposing it would work well here. Similarly, had the Lemieux Act given universal satisfaction in Canada —and it is far from doing so—we should have no right to conclude that it ought to be adopted here. Canada is a much simpler country industrially, and the number of disputes to be dealt with is comparatively small. The application of the Act to England would necessitate

[1] The solution seems to lie in scrapping time agreements.

enormous machinery, and, as with Compulsory Arbitration, it would be impossible to enforce the penal clauses. Sir George Askwith, in the main, sees this, and does not recommend the adoption of the Act as it stands. He holds that the clauses prohibiting strikes or lock-outs during the progress of an inquiry and imposing penalties for infringement are not really of the essence of the Act, and that its value does not lie in them. " The pith of the Act," he writes, " lies in permitting the parties and the public to obtain full knowledge of the real cause of the dispute, and in causing suggestions to be made as impartially as possible on the basis of such knowledge for dealing with the existing difficulties, *whether a strike or lock-out has commenced or not.* This action on behalf of the public allows an element of calm judgment to be introduced into the dispute which at the time the parties themselves may be unable to exercise."

Turned into human English, this means that the thing is to get the investigation, and not to prohibit the stoppage. Sir George Askwith holds that had the power of investigation existed without the power to prohibit stoppages, the parties would have realised the value of voluntary conciliation, and, in many cases, the stoppage would never have taken place. A good deal of this is certainly true. One of the great difficulties undoubtedly is to get the parties to come together and talk over the points in dispute, and machinery to make such discussions easier is certainly desirable. But there are at least three distinct points mixed up in Sir George Askwith's argument. First, there is the old appeal to the ' impartial ' person, who is supposed to be infallible ; secondly, there is the very wise insistence on the necessity for calm negotiation ; thirdly, there is the inevitable dragging in of public opinion. But 'impartial' persons hardly exist, not because men are knaves, but because they cannot get away from their upbringing—and ' public opinion ', as we have seen, is hopelessly egoistic and contemptible.

Sir George Askwith's points in favour of the Canadian Act therefore reduce themselves to one ; and we shall see, when we come to discuss the actual working of our own Conciliation Act of 1896, what, if any, value his suggestion possesses. It is enough for the present to have learnt that Compulsory Conciliation does not necessarily involve the prohibition of strikes, even for a time. The Canadian Act might be strengthened by becoming solely what it purports to be, an Industrial Disputes Investigation Act.

Before we can proceed to a direct analysis of the situation in England to-day, there is one further form of State interference with industrial conditions which it is essential to study. This is the method of Trade or Wages Boards, generally connected with the Wages Boards of Victoria and now with the Trade Boards set up under Mr. Churchill's Act of 1908.

The Victorian legislation was passed in 1896, with the definite object of doing away with sweating. In certain trades where women were largely employed, the factory-worker had been tending to be displaced by the home-worker, and an inquiry instituted in 1892 showed sweating to exist to such an extent that public opinion—in Australia easier to move and fairer when moved—was stirred to demand Government action. The Act of 1896 set up Wages Boards for four scheduled trades in which home-work largely predominated, and provided for the extension of the system to other trades on the initiative of either House of Parliament. Since 1896, the Act has been several times modified ; but its provisions remain in essentials much the same, though its scope has been greatly widened. The Wages Board consists of an equal number of employers and workers, chosen by the Government,[1] with an impartial Chairman. Their function is to fix the wages and the hours in the trade concerned, and they tend to get control over every possible source of industrial dispute. Their competence has, indeed, been extended to other questions than wages, and the name, 'Wages Boards', is misleadingly narrow. In the sweated trades in which Boards were set up before 1903, there is no limit to the wages which the Board may fix, and, in many cases, they gave women-workers, at the outset, enormous increases, without, it seems, in any way damaging the trade or causing any change save the absorption of home-workers into the factories. Even prices certainly did not rise anything like proportionately to the increase in wages. From 1903 dates a new departure; the Act has been extended not merely to sweated trades, but to the ordinary industries of the country, in which no exceptional sweating existed. In 1907, there were already 51 Boards in existence, regulating conditions in every kind of industrial enterprise. In the case of Boards founded from 1903 onwards, however, a limitation of powers has been introduced. The regulations laid down by the Boards may not exceed the standard rate already paid by good employers. That is to say, in respect of industries that are not sweated, Minimum Wage legislation in Victoria has practically confined its attention to making agreements between sections of employers and workers compulsory over the whole trade. Their effect is similar to that which would follow the adoption

[1] Since 1903. A third of either workers or employers may, by protesting, depose a Government nominee.

of the schemes of which we have heard so much recently for making voluntary agreements legally enforceable.

There is, however, this important difference between the Victorian legislations and a good many of the proposals made for this country. The Victorian system only sets out to fix a minimum standard, and not to prevent the worker from getting more if he can. The Act says nothing about making strikes illegal, and the sole provision imposing any penalty on them is that which allows the suspension of the Wages Board Determination in the trade in which a strike occurs. Thus a dispute on a particular point in the regulations governing a trade may involve the suspension of the regulations as a whole; but such a penalty operates only if the regulations are actually, in the main, favourable to the workers. The Victorian Act has for its primary object, not social peace, but social justice, the securing to the workers of a minimum standard of life.

On the other hand, proposals for making industrial agreements enforceable over a whole trade very often aim at standardising the cost of labour, and at fixing a maximum as well as a minimum. They are often accompanied by proposals for making strikes penal, and are, at bottom, devices for securing a servile ' social peace '. It is necessary to inquire whether, despite its professions, the Victorian Act has shown any tendency to pass over into such a device, or whether it has really preserved throughout its original character of an instrument of social justice.

One of the commonest arguments against the minimum wage is that the minimum inevitably tends to become a maximum. But this argument is robbed of all its force because those who use it apply it quite generally, and take no pains to distinguish case from case. Advocates of the Victorian system generally base their answer on figures dealing with the earlier period of the Act's operation, when it applied solely to sweated trades. They show that the average weekly wages paid in the regulated trades were in every case some shillings above the minimum, and argue from this that the minimum has not tended to become a maximum. Where sweated trades are concerned, this is as a rule the case, though even a tendency of the minimum to become the maximum would not there greatly weaken the value of such regulation.

Where, however, minimum wage proposals are applied to trades that cannot be called, in the same sense, sweated, to large bodies of men earning for the most part a standard rate regulated within limits by custom or agreement, there is very little doubt that statutory regulation of graded minima does standardise rates, and that the minima do tend to become maxima. This happens, of course, to some exent, wherever collective bargaining enforces a standard without legislation; but there is no doubt that statutory regulation tends to standardise the wage still more.

The main point, however, is that, when a wage is standardised by collective bargaining, it is always modifiable by the next act of collective bargaining the Union may undertake. The minimum tends to become the maximum; but the uniform rate so created is not stationary. When, on the other hand, a rate is standardised by statute, it may very easily become difficult, even if the strike is not prohibited, to alter the standard. Such a statutory rate seems to have behind it a public sanction of equity which renders it immutable. It can be altered by the Board, but any attempt of the workers to modify it can easily be made to look immoral. The method of determining wages by a conception of social justice, admirable when it is confined to sweated trades, becomes a reactionary safeguard as soon as it is extended to industry as a whole.

The whole intrusion of the conception of 'equity' into the determination of wages gives rise to very difficult problems. There is a clear and admitted case in equity for the abolition of sweating, and therefore in sweated trades no great difficulty arises; but as soon as any attempt is made to apply the principle of equity to the whole of industry we are absolutely without a common standard. Advocates of the 'right to the whole product of labour' jostle advocates of the 'minimum of civilised life' theory; partisans of equal payment come into conflict with 'rent of ability' economists; "to each according to his needs" is a formula irreconcilable with its rival "to each according to his services." That some labour is robbed every one will admit; but any attempt to regulate wages as a whole raises the pertinent and searching question whether *all* labour is robbed. It stands, in fact, at the parting of the ways of revolution and reform. Those who hold that labour is robbed, not merely where sweating survives, but wherever the wage-system exists, can never accept the principle of State determination of wages throughout industry.

The Wages Board system, then, has a useful sphere of influence in raising the standard of life in sweated trades, and here all parties may reasonably co-operate in furthering it. The Trade Boards Act of 1909 corresponds, in Great Britain, to the Victorian legislation of 1896—only thirteen years behind. It was the result of the inquiry into sweating obtained from Parliament by Sir Charles Dilke in 1906, after the magnificent series of exhibitions organised by the Anti-Sweating League. Applied at first only to four trades in which sweating was notoriously bad,[1] it has recently been extended, and there is no doubt that considerable further extensions will before long take place. Agriculture, for instance, will very probably come within its scope, or be the subject of a new Act on similar lines.

We have seen that, in Victoria, a similar Act beginning as a measure directed purely against sweating, came in time to be extended over the greater part of industry. That, even in non-sweated trades, it secured at the outset considerable advances for the workers cannot be disputed, and, under its operation, Victoria does seem to have enjoyed a very great measure of industrial tranquillity. But it is probable that this tranquillity will not be long maintained. As, in New Zealand, the Act worked smoothly as long as the workers got anything out of it, that is, until the very rudimentary social conscience of the State was satisfied, and then began to break down, it may well be that soon the Victorian workers will reach the point of diminishing returns in State regulation, and begin to strike. The coming of this time may well be retarded by the rather exceptionally developed social conscience of Victoria; but it will probably come in the end. When it comes, the Victorian system will show at any rate its enormous superiority to that of New Zealand; for there will be nothing to prevent the workers from striking, and nothing in the way of their success,—except perhaps public opinion.

It is possible that the application of the Trade Board system in this country to all industries would, in many

[1] Chain-making, Lace-finishing, Box-making, Tailoring. See Board of Trade Report on its Working [H.C. 134].

cases, secure big advances even to workers who cannot be called sweated; but there is not the least doubt that its benefits would be only temporary, and that the dangers to organised Labour would be grave. Organised Labour is just beginning, as the Unions wake up to the need for reorganisation, to put itself into a position for facing the employer fairly; but there is a great risk that any sort of State machinery, once established, would find the task of 'taming' most of the workers only too easy. Fortunately, it would not be anything like so easy to get the machinery going; and this may save some at least of the fighting spirit of 1911. What organised Labour needs is a straight fight with the employers; let real conciliation, that is, the mere bringing of the two sides together, be stimulated as much as possible: let disputes be settled wherever possible without stoppage; but behind every dispute there must still be the organised threat to withhold labour. The workers cannot afford to trust to State regulation, until 'social justice' means, in the mind of the community, something more than a levelling up of the worst-paid workers to the minimum standard of ordinary efficiency.

The Trade Boards Act, then, has its scope merely in the gradual stamping out of home-work and sweating. It cannot solve the industrial problem as a whole, nor should it be extended over organised industry. Indeed, its mission is to work for its own extinction: its greatest service lies in getting the workers whose lives it regulates to organise for the protection of their own interests. As soon as a trade is no longer technically 'sweated', those engaged in it will have to look after their own interests; and the first essential is that workers at present legislated for on humanitarian grounds should organise and make their own demands as soon as 'social compunction' has satisfied its meagre conception of social justice. The organisation of the woman worker and of sweated labour generally is one of the greatest needs of our time; and it is the business of the Trade Union movement as a whole to further to the utmost the admirable work now being done by the Women's Trade Union League and the General Labour Unions.

A great deal of the comparative success, up to the present, of the Victorian, and even the New South Wales, system of industrial regulation lies in the difference of social atmosphere between England and Australia. If such legislation is now beginning to break down over there, we have every reason to believe that it would collapse far sooner here, where the social conscience is unaccountably stunted, and the egoism of the consumer almost unmitigated. Even the Trade Boards Act, great though its benefits have undoubtedly been, has not done nearly so much for the sweated worker as the Victorian Act at once effected. The rises in wages have not, as a rule, been nearly so high, and generally speaking, the Boards have shown a good deal of timidity in exercising their powers. Nor has the stimulus to organisation been so great as might have been hoped; but this is no doubt due to the appalling conditions under which sweated workers were, and, in many cases, still are, living. Even with the best will in the world, the habits of a century cannot be eradicated in a few years; with so weak a will as that behind the Trade Boards Act no very great 'change of heart' can be expected rapidly.

For organised Labour, therefore, the Trade Boards Act has no message. Either no legislation, or other legislation, must be applied to industry generally. We have seen reason to suppose that neither Compulsory Arbitration, as it exists in New Zealand, nor Compulsory Conciliation on the Canadian model will meet the case. We have now to comment upon the actual recommendations made by the Industrial Council in response to a direct request from the Government. The Council was asked two questions:

(1) What is the best method of securing the due fulfilment of industrial agreements?

(2) How far, and in what manner, should industrial agreements which are made between representative bodies of employers and of workmen be enforced throughout a particular trade or district?

The scope of the inquiry was limited to these two points, and in consequence the Report which it has just issued is in no sense a comprehensive survey of proposals for State regulation of industrial disputes; but the limited reference which the Government allowed it showed there was no intention of passing any comprehensive measure. In the course of its answer, the Council raises a great many interesting points: its main care throughout seems to have been to avoid committing itself to anything very drastic, and the result is not a very inspiring document. This shows at least that the Council and the Government realise that they are raising issues which do not admit of trifling, and that any attempt to legislate in a hurry will involve them in a mess from which they will hardly extricate themselves.

The Report is almost unanimous. Though the Industrial Council consists of an equal number of representatives of employers and workers, under the impartial chairmanship of Sir George Askwith, it is difficult to believe that the Report is the result of a real agreement between the two parties. It shows no sign, in any section, that workers have co-operated in drawing it up, though all the representatives of Labour sign it without reservation. It is precisely the sort of document we should expect to be compiled by some mild, 'impartial' authority, intent on 'peace'. That is to say, the employers have left their mark on it, and it seems partial to employers' interests. The phrasing is, of course, strictly impartial. Sir George Askwith probably wrote most of it.

First, the Council practically throws over the idea of making strikes in violation of agreements penal by Act of Parliament. It realises the uselessness of trying to browbeat Labour by these means. Secondly, it rejects the idea of a compulsory guarantee fund to ensure the keeping of agreements. It prefers to leave agreements to be enforced by a moral suasion, which it proposes to back up indirectly in other ways. It repudiates all desire to interfere in any way with the action of existing machinery for conciliation or arbitration; but holds that "in order that the interests of the community may be adequately safeguarded . . . it is desirable that before a cessation of work takes place there should be a period of time (after the existing procedure has been exhausted) sufficient to admit of (a) the further consideration of the position by the parties, and (b) the opportunity of the introduction into the discussion of some authority representing the interests of the community". The Report " does not favour compulsory arbitration, . . . but thinks that before there is a reversion to the method of strike or lock-out, it is important that there should be a pronouncement upon the question at issue by some independent body, or impartial individual ". It therefore recommends that, at some stage, the Conciliation Board should call in an impartial Chairman, with power to *recommend* a settlement. Differences about the interpretation and, possibly, the breach of existing agreements, the Report holds, should be submitted, before there is a strike or lock-out, to some impartial tribunal. Unions and Associations of Employers, it is suggested, should, by a clause in the agreement, be restrained from giving aid to those concerned in causing stoppages contrary to the agreement. But, for the enforcement of these recommendations, the Council is " not at present prepared to hold that in consequence of the rare cases in which agreements are broken "—for, as the Report points out, the vast majority are loyally kept —" a new principle should be imported into industrial arrangements " by the enactment of penal clauses, which would only endanger the work of the great mass of voluntary Conciliation Boards now in existence.

These pious aspirations—for they seem to amount to little more—form the main part of the Council's answer to the first question in its reference. In so far as this answer dispenses with penal clauses altogether, it is not a recommendation of any legislation whatsoever ; it is merely a statement of the Council's view as to the best method of conducting negotiations. The most obvious criticism is that it is far too abstract : it takes no account of the difference between one industry and another. There are no doubt cases in which nothing is to be gained by the rapid strike, and in these cases and, unhappily, in a good many others, some of the Council's recommendations have already for a long time been embodied in established machinery of conciliation. But there are others in which strikes must be sudden to be effective—Building is an obvious instance—and of these the Council seems to have taken no account. Again, there are certain kinds of strikes which must always be rapid in any industry—such as strikes on some questions of discipline and 'principle'—spontaneous strikes and the like, and, above all, sympathetic strikes. Militant Unionism, in arranging any conciliation schemes involving delay in striking, must always insist on exceptions being made of such cases, as the 'political' strike is excepted from many agreements in Sweden. Conciliation machinery, if it be adopted at all, always involves a certain delay; but from the point of view of the worker, the object is to make the necessary delay as short as possible, and certainly not lengthen it by enacting that a period must expire between the breaking-off of negotiations and the declaration of a strike. Such a provision cannot benefit the worker, and is always likely to benefit the employer.

To some extent, these recommendations are bound up with the opinion expressed by the Council on the duration of agreements. "It appears to us," runs the Report, "to be to the advantage of the trade generally that agreements should continue in force for some fixed period." Agreements are of two kinds: "(a) those which have been arrived at for the purpose of establishing machinery for dealing with questions which may arise between the parties, and (b) those which are made as a result of the operation of the machinery established under (a)." In general, the Council holds, agreements of the former class will last longer than those of the second; but "in ordinary cases the period for which an agreement is to last should not exceed three years". It seems clear that, at any rate, agreements of the second class should not last so long, though the Council says little on the point. The Report mentions that the agreement in the Welsh Tinplate trade, which comes up for revision annually, satisfies both parties; and it seems right, on the face of it, that at least as often as once a year, and usually far more often, there should be an opportunity for the revision of terms. Generally speaking, agreements of the first class, which only set up machinery, should not, after the first period of trial, have a time-limit at all. They should be merely terminable on, at the most, three months' notice. Even time agreements of the second class are, at best, in most industries a necessary evil; where a voluntary Conciliation Board is in good working order, and both sides are organised for bargaining, there seems no reason why it should not be open to either party to negotiate at any time. The real object of conciliation is to make such negotiations easy, and not to tie down the workers by long time agreements. If this position were definitely recognised as normal, negotiation would be far easier, and the method of agreements would cease to be open to so much hostile criticism.

So far, on the whole, the Report has appeared a very mild and harmless document; the cloven hoof, however, may be seen to some extent in the Council's answer to the second question referred to it. In advocating the extension of voluntary agreements between representative employers and workers over the whole trade of a district, the Council professes to be merely registering the opinion of a very large majority of the witnesses it examined. In the particular form given to the proposal in the Report, it would certainly not receive so much support. The Council's draft scheme lays down that, on the application of both parties to the agreement, the Board of

Trade may, after inquiry, extend the agreement over the whole of the trade in a district, provided that the agreement lays down that " so many days' notice must be given of any intended change affecting conditions as to wages or hours, *and that there shall be no stoppage of work or alteration of the conditions of employment until the dispute has been investigated by some agreed tribunal, and a pronouncement made upon it*" (italics mine). Further, in considering such an application, the Board of Trade is to take into consideration whether the agreement contains a provision forbidding assistance to be given to persons causing a stoppage in contravention of it.

This is the cloven hoof with a vengeance. The Council, having rejected the idea of making stoppages not preceded by an inquiry illegal, now proposes to produce the same result by refusing to extend agreements over a whole trade where stoppages are allowed. This is clearly directed against strikes; the lock-out is not affected to the same extent by delay. The worker is to be compelled indirectly to surrender what he would not give up were the demand directly made. This idea, whether borrowed from the Victorian withdrawal of the determination of the Wages Board in case of strikes or not, is clearly open to the same objection. The business of the State is merely to declare a minimum, where the State has any business to interfere at all; it should not tamper with the worker's power to refuse his labour as he thinks fit. If the worker chooses to tie his own hands with time agreements, well and good: that is not the State's affair; but the State has no right to bribe him so to tie himself. It may be good or bad to extend voluntary agreements over a whole trade; but the goodness or badness of such a proposal has nothing to do with the worker's right to withhold his labour, and should not be mixed up with it in a single proposal.

The actual desirability of the statutory extension of such voluntary agreements is a far more complicated matter than the Report would lead the reader to believe. The demand first became well known in this country in connection with the Transport Strike of 1912, on the occasion of which Mr. Ramsay Macdonald introduced into the House of Commons a Bill with the object of extending voluntary agreements over the whole of the Port of London.[1] A large section of the working-class certainly favours such a proposal, and there are a good many obvious arguments in its favour. Employers, it is said, are often unwilling or unable to give their workers better terms because, if they do, they will be undercut by 'blackleg' employers not paying the Union rate. Thus the existence of a section of unfederated employers keeps down the whole conditions of the trade, and is, in any case, unfair to the good employer. Moreover, from the point of view of social justice, the extension of voluntary agreements may, in trades that are not specially 'sweated', be the easiest means of securing to all workers a minimum standard of civilised life. There are, therefore, strong *prima facie* grounds for regarding such a proposal sympathetically.

On the other hand, though a Trade Board or any sort of compulsory raising of the standard undoubtedly tends to stimulate organisation in sweated trades, this no longer applies where the majority of the workers are so organised as to be able to meet the

[1] A Bill to make Agreements come to voluntarily between Employers and Workmen in the Port of London legally enforceable on the whole Trade, 1912 [Bill 253].

capitalist in fair fight. In such a case, the extension of the benefits of organisation to the unorganised may tend to perpetuate the class of non-union hangers-on of Labour, and unfederated hangers-on of Capitalism, men who reap the benefits of organisation, but refuse to pay their share. This objection is met by Clause 50 in the Industrial Council's Report:

" It has not been proposed that the Board of Trade should entertain any application for the extension of an agreement unless such application is received from both the parties to the agreement. There is thus no element of compulsion upon either party."

Further, as in Mr. Macdonald's Bill, it must always be open to the parties to withdraw the agreement. Apparently, according to the Bill, one party cannot withdraw the registration without the consent of the other; but it would seem that, in default of any clause in the agreement itself forbidding this, an agreement which requires the consent of both parties for its establishment ought to require the consent of both for its continuance.

With these safeguards, there may be cases in which the power of making voluntary agreements implied conditions of contract over the whole of a trade in a particular district will work well: in particular, there is no doubt that its application to the Port of London would be of advantage to both parties. But, if such a proposal is to be accepted by Trade Unionists, there must be no suggestion of penal clauses in the background; the State must accept the voluntary agreement as it finds it, and not dictate to the two parties indispensable conditions aiming at the securing of ' social peace '. The proposal must stand or fall by itself; if the issue is dishonestly confused, the whole will have to be rejected.

It is clear, however, that such a measure as the Council recommends, even if it were actively administered, would have a very limited sphere of operation. As the Trade Boards Act applies only to sweated trades, such a measure as this would apply only where organised Labour and Capital were feeling the pressure of undercutting from the unorganised, and had a common interest in preventing it. This, clearly, is not the normal situation in Mining, or on the Railways, or with any form of public or municipal service, or in the textile industry. It applies, indeed, mainly where both Capital and Labour are scattered, in the secondary industries of the country, which stand midway between the sweated trades and the great centralised industries. Here such compulsory extension as the Council advises may do good work; but, as in the case of the Trade Boards, any attempt to make a partial remedy apply to industry as a whole will merely end by wrecking its usefulness in its proper sphere. Trade Boards for sweated industries; compulsory extension of agreements for some scattered industries, and at the waterside; for organised industry, economic warfare, whether by means of the strike or of negotiation.

The talk about the necessity for new legislation regulating industrial disputes generally neglects the legislation that is actually in operation. Anyone, however, who even dips into the Board of Trade's *Annual Report of Proceedings under the Conciliation Act of 1896* will at once realise that the normal method of settling disputes in this country is not " the barbaric method " of the strike, but negotiation and peaceful conciliation. The special aid of the Board was invoked, during 1912, 73 times, but only 34 of these cases involved an actual stoppage. During the whole period from 1896 to 1912, the Board has dealt with

597 cases, of which only 292 have involved stoppages. These cases, moreover, are not the sum total of conciliation cases, but the exceptions. At the end of 1912, there were 297 voluntary Conciliation Boards known to the Board of Trade, all existing for the purpose of avoiding unnecessary strikes by means of negotiation. There is a good deal to be said for the view that we have too much conciliation, and that a big increase in the number of strikes would do us no harm.

It is certain that there has been among the workers, during the past few years, a big revolt against conciliation. This is being seen very clearly now, in the case of the Railways, in the repeated demands that are being made for the abolition or reform of the Conciliation Boards first established in 1907, and reformed in 1911, on the occasion of the national Railway Strike. The important thing to realise is that these Boards are really, in the last resort, courts of *arbitration*. They provide, when conciliation has failed, for an award, binding for at least two years, on the part of an ' impartial ' chairman, chosen by the two sections of the Board from a panel drawn up by the Board of Trade. Where the two sections disagree, their differences come, whether they like it or not, before an arbitrator with power to decide.

It is often difficult for an outsider to reconcile the fact that, since the 1911 strike, the men have undoubtedly got quite large advances, with the equally certain hostility of the majority to the Conciliation Boards, which might seem to have secured them these advantages. The present doubt as to the propriety of giving, this October, the required notice to terminate the Boards comes, not from a doubt as to the men's hostility to them, but from the uncertainty of some of the officials, who support the Boards, concerning the safety of standing up against the men's desire.

The chief objections to the Boards fall under two heads. First, it is complained that they are slow, and that the employers use them to postpone discussion as long as they can. This was one of the grievances that led to the modification of the 1907 scheme, and possibly further speeding-up might be accomplished without altering the nature of the Boards.

The second line of objection is more fundamental, and relates to the whole position of the independent Chairman. We saw, in the earlier part of this chapter, how difficult it is to get any really independent person for such a post, especially in a country where the distinction in ideas and outlook between the "two nations" is as marked as in England. The impartial person nearly always comes from the upper class: even if he is really impartial he is suspect; and generally his ingrained prejudices make it impossible for him to be so. The workers distrust the 'impartial' Chairman, and any scheme which rests finally on his decision is bound to break down sooner or later. This applies as much to the Boards set up under the Coal Mines Minimum Wage Act as to the Railway Conciliation Boards.

The use of the 'impartial' person lies, not in his passing a final decision, but in the judicious help he can give to the parties when they are engaged in negotiation. Sir George Askwith's intervention as a mediator is far more likely to produce a satisfactory result than any award of an 'impartial' Chairman overriding the opinion of the parties. It is useless to hope, from legislation, for a means of settling peaceably all industrial disputes; all that the State can do is to facilitate negotiation between the parties. As long as social inequality persists, industrial disputes will go along with it : when inequality has been swept away, we may begin penal legislation in favour of industrial peace—if we then need to do so. Strikes happen because of inequality and injustice ; and until the people realises the depth of that inequality and that injustice, it will be useless for it to apply its miserable standards of social justice in the hope of securing social peace. Social peace is an ideal, as Socialism is an ideal ; and the two will come together, if they come at all.

The State, however, can make negotiation easy. Avoiding all humbug about inquiries before strikes, impartial persons and the rights of the consumer, it can do its best to get industrial disputes settled by the measurement of economic resource, either without actual stoppage, or with as short stoppage as possible. For this, we need no new legislation : the Conciliation Act of 1896 provides all that is needed : let the State but give the working-class reason for a little more faith in the efficacy of its mediation, and let the workers show rather more readiness to avail themselves of the machinery. Let the Board of Trade even be given the power to compel the parties to meet in conference in the presence of its emissary ; but let that emissary have no power to make public any recommendation in connection with the dispute. The 'impartial' person is often a very good conciliator ; but he is generally a very bad arbitrator.

On the whole, then, the result of our inquiry into methods of State interference with industrial disputes is negative. We have decided that there is no panacea, and that the remedy is to leave the two sides to fight it out. At the same time, we have seen that, for particular kinds of trades, there may be valuable methods of State intervention. The Trade Boards

SOCIAL PEACE AND SOCIAL WAR

Act clearly has an enormous value in preventing sweating; compulsory extension of agreements may be useful in certain industries standing between sweated and organised Labour; but for organised Labour no community with as rudimentary a sense of 'social compunction' as ours can hope to lay down rules. Organised Labour must, at all costs, preserve its right to strike; and no boon the State can give it in return can at all compensate for the loss of that supreme and final defence against intolerable oppression. The strike is Labour's expression of free will; surrender that, and the worker becomes the merest wage-slave. The greatest task of the present is the awakening of individuality and spontaneity in the worker: his apathy is the nation's weakness; and the finest thing that can be accomplished by Labour Unrest is a heightening of Labour's sense of being alive, an awakening that will lead men on from mere discontent to the positive striving for a better life. 'Social peace' is the cry of mediocrity striving against 'social awakening'; it is the miserable demand of the narrow-minded egotist to be let alone. But, if the public cannot be made to realise its responsibilities without being kicked into a sense of them, the public has got to be kicked; and strikes and Labour Unrest are the best way. The demand for 'social peace' is an attempt to send Labour to sleep; but Labour is beginning to articulate a new demand, and the morning of a new day is not the right time for a sleeping-draught.

CHAPTER X

LABOUR'S RED HERRINGS—THE FUNCTION OF CO-OPERATION

'SOCIAL peace' is not the only cry raised by those who desire anything rather than a real awakening of the consciousness of Labour. It is felt in many quarters that 'social peace' by itself is not a sufficiently tempting repast, and, consequently, dealers in 'red herrings' are beginning to do a thriving trade. The premium bonus system and the shop piece-work system are spread beautifully beside profit-sharing, tastefully tricked out as 'Labour Co-partnership', on the festive board. The sole drawback is that these red herrings, unlike the honest herring that we love, are not intended to whet the worker's appetite for more.

Often, even in the large majority of cases, the persons responsible for these schemes of 'betterment' are quite honest and well-intentioned. Mr. Cadbury, in upholding the shop piece-work system, is genuinely anxious to forward the best interests of his workers; Mr. Mundy is a really zealous and disinterested advocate of Labour Co-partnership. If, then, hard things have to be said about their schemes, no hard things need be said about the persons themselves; the case is one for reason, and not for denunciation.

The premium bonus system, clearly, has no moral

LABOUR'S RED HERRINGS

pretensions. It is a mere device for speeding-up, for increasing profits, and nothing else. If it claims to increase the workers' wages, it does not pretend to do so except for the purpose of getting more out of the worker. It is a method of getting ninepence for fourpence extra.

This, indeed, would not be enough to condemn it outright, though it might reasonably be urged that the worker himself should receive all the extra profits due to his increased efficiency. The real argument against the premium bonus system goes deeper, and is one with the fundamental reason why all modern attempts at speeding-up, from piece-work to Scientific Management, should, in their present forms, be strenuously resisted by the workers. All such schemes are speeding-up devices, imposed from above, and necessarily directed, in part at least, to the securing of further profits.

The most significant feature of industry during the past few years has been the rapid change in industrial methods and processes. America took the lead in the invention of machinery standardising processes which formerly required great natural and acquired skill. This is leading, as we have seen, to the gradual narrowing of the gulf between skilled and unskilled, and more than at any time since the coming of the Industrial Revolution, machinery is beginning again to oust the skilled artisan. The first result of this change has been the need, on the side of the employers, for some artificial method of speeding-up the semi-skilled and even the skilled machine-worker; the dulness of mechanical processes is such that an artificial stimulus to greater exertion seems to be required. This is found in some sort of bonus system, appealing to the individual cupidity of the worker, and making him do more work than he would do on time rates. In a limited degree, it may seem right to apply such stimuli : men undoubtedly tend to be lazy, and, if such an extra reward makes them less so, it may appear to be all to the good of both parties. The danger is that such methods are not applicable only in a limited degree ; the stimulus is found to be capable of being heightened to a very considerable extent : so that, in the end, the worker, instead of working merely at a proper and normal pressure, is working much too hard for health, mental or physical. The good done by the limitation of hours of labour is thus defeated ; the worker, fagged out by a hard day's work, goes home in the evening fit for nothing, and, instead of an intelligent and educated people, we get a nation of wage-slaves, incapable of profiting by the extra wages they have earned.

Nor is this all ; work at a high pressure cannot go on indefinitely. The worker to whom 'speeding-up' devices are applied grows old sooner, and is thrown earlier into the ranks of the unemployables. If he starves, or comes on the State or his Union for support, it is no concern of the employer's. He has made his profit by speeding-up, and he can always get a new worker to replace one who is worn-out. 'Too old at forty' is the cry, nowadays, largely because men of forty have been worn out in their youth when they ought to have had time and scope for reasonable and intelligent enjoyment.

Unless the Unions can resist this state of things, there can be no remedy until it is realised that the maintenance of the reserve of labour which Capitalism admits to be necessary for its operations is a legitimate charge on profits. At present, the Capitalist wears his worker out, and then scraps him. This has gone much further in America than here; but the great growth of speeding-up in this country is recent, and has not yet had time to make its efforts felt. If an employer wears out a worker he ought to support him when he is 'scrapped'; the 'speeding-up' system is only profitable because the employer reaps the fruits without paying for the damage.[1]

The application of all these systems of 'speeding-up' is, then, a national question, and not merely a matter for the individual employer, who claims to "run his business as he likes." It is as essentially within the scope of real factory regulation as ventilation or lighting, and, if the present tendency in production continues, the Unions will have to step in and make all these devices impossible or unprofitable. Meanwhile, it is the business of the Unions to resist with all their might all attempts to introduce the premium bonus system and the like into their works. The system is bad for solidarity, bad for the individual worker, both morally and physically, and bad for the community as a whole. For the present, at any rate, while masters exploit and workers are exploited, the object of Trade Unionism should be to secure, in most industries, payment purely by time. It is, of course, impossible to sweep away the piece-work system altogether: its general adoption in the coal-mines and the cotton industry put that out of the question. But the object of the Unions should be to work for its reduction, and certainly to resist its introduction where it is not already established.[2]

The premium bonus system is a method of applying piece-work to labour engaged on time rates: it is

[1] Just as motor-bus companies make huge profits because they do not have to pay for the wear and tear of the roads.

[2] In any case, a guaranteed day-rate should be secured.

a particularly bad form of speeding-up, but, in principle, it is essentially the same as all other forms. All are bad; but it is, at the moment, particularly important to resist this new attempt to apply speeding-up to branches of industry which had previously been comparatively free from it. Every strike against such an attempt is a really valuable assertion of the worker's right to control, in such matters, the conditions of his life and labour.

The growth of the premium bonus system, then, is only typical of a wider tendency. Shop piece-work, as described by Mr. Edward Cadbury in its working at Bournville,[1] does not work out so disagreeably. There is even quite a specious case made out for its adoption in that case; but its comparative harmlessness there depends on the general environment. There is no doubt at all that Mr. Cadbury is, according to his lights, a very good employer indeed, on the purely material side. The results he produces savour of priggishness, but that is not for lack of goodwill on his part. The general atmosphere of Bournville, in fact, prevents a speeding-up system from having disastrous results. The worker is artificially provided with leisure, and he would certainly not be encouraged to do himself to death. Moreover, the system of 'shop' piece-work, by which wages are calculated on the output of a whole workroom, is a very different thing from the premium bonus system, which merely speeds up the individual worker. Shop piece-work results rather in a general high average output; it appeals to unselfishness, as well as to cupidity; for everyone in the shop has to suffer for the laziness of one member. Were all employers good employers, such a system might

[1] See his *Experiments in Industrial Organisation*.

produce good results, but in a less 'humanitarian' atmosphere, it might merely result in co-operative speeding-up and bullying of the worst sort, and in a wear and tear of the worker's powers as great as any the premium bonus system could produce.

Such simple devices for speeding-up, however, are insignificant beside the latest American invention. The Industrial Revolution was brought about by the application of mechanical science to industry; the Americans, having discovered psychology, now propose to apply it to a similar purpose. Scientific Management, we are told, is to create a second Industrial Revolution as great, or as bad, as the first. The motto 'The best possible man for the best possible job' is being used to cover a multitude of sins; the speeding-up that aimed merely at exciting the worker's cupidity is to be replaced by a new system which employs every ounce of his capacity—and gives him a slight share in the increased return.

The psychology which is to be applied to industry is, of course, experimental. It takes, in the first place, the form of an examination into 'vocational fitness'. When a boy leaves school, he is taken to the 'psychological laboratory', and told, after a series of tests, physical and mental, tests of power of visualisation, hearing, memory, attention, and the like, for what callings he is, or is not, fitted. Sensibly applied, this system might do good; but psychology is a young, and generally a very stupid, science, more likely to make mistakes from a sublime sense of its own infallibility than to render any valuable help. There are practically no standardised mental tests that can be applied with any confidence in the results. Everything depends on the person who applies the tests; the method, in fact, is not scientific, but individual. Such successes as the system has obtained in America are almost entirely due to the character of its administrators.

The second aspect of the application of psychology to industry is found in Scientific Management. By this new method, the attempt is made, not merely to get the best possible machine, but also to train the man to be the best possible machine. Let us take first a rudimentary instance of the application of physical science to human material. It seems a simple task to load carts with bricks. The new scientist, however, discovers that the process, as ordinarily carried out, is accompanied by great waste of energy. He makes a study of the necessary motions of the body, and reduces the loading of carts with bricks to a science. He then teaches the workers the simple motions required, and they at once begin to load twice as many bricks as before in the same time. The employer then gives them 10 or 20 per cent. on their wages, and makes a very substantial profit on the change. But, he will explain, the result is clear gain to both; the worker gets higher wages, and the employer bigger profits. Unfortunately, it is found after a time that the new method involves enormous wear and tear on the worker. His hours are reduced, and his wages sink to the former level. His position is either worse than before, or at best unchanged; the employer's profit remains. If, on the other hand, the worker goes on working the old number of hours, he is soon 'scrapped', and the employer calls on the reserve of labour. Every time, the employer has it.

It is no use pretending that Scientific Management may not be a valuable asset to the employer, or that, in one form or another, something like it has not come to stay. Both in the physical and, to a less extent, in the mental sphere, an enormous amount of economy of effort might be made by the application of scientific method to industrial processes. But, at present, the application of such methods is wholly in the hands of the employer; what ought to be labour-saving devices are merely ways of raising profits and speeding-up the worker. What, then, should be the attitude of organised Labour to such schemes? Organised Labour has undoubtedly lost enormously by its attempts to resist the introduction of new machinery and its unwillingness to accept inevitable industrial changes: what, then, is it to do in face of this new phenomenon? Labour has resisted in the past because each change has been used merely as a new method of exploitation; if Labour has got any benefit out of the increase in the efficiency of production, Capital has got far more. But in each case Labour has been beaten; the new method has conquered by force of economic superiority, and there is no doubt that, if Scientific Management is economically superior, it too will conquer. No doubt, the danger is not, in this country, anything like so pressing as it is in America; but the worker would do well to be prepared.

To some extent, as we shall see in the next chapter, the danger may be met by an increase in the control of the worker over the conditions of his life. Questions now regarded as in the province of the employer alone, because they are questions of 'discipline' and 'management', will come more and more under the direct control of the Trade Unions. On the other side, the State will tend to step in and extend factory supervision by the prevention of unhealthy devices for speeding-up. With all this, however, there is a real problem to be solved; and no real solution can be attempted until the workers are infinitely more alive to the conditions under which they labour. The dangers of Scientific Management can only be met by stronger organisation and greater alertness on the part of the Unions. If the Unions are really strong, the attempt to apply such a system will be the signal for a great organised demand, on the part of Labour, for greater control over the conditions of the workshop. It will be either Labour's most crushing defeat, or one of the greatest steps in the evolution of the Unions towards an effective control over production.

The schemes we have been examining so far appear definitely, even when they pretend to be to the advantage of the worker also, as profit-earning devices. We come now to a proposal in which the ' business ' and the ' philanthropic ' aspects are more confused, and in which it is difficult to disentangle the one from the other. Co-partnership, as preached by the Labour Co-partnership Association, is, at the same time, a means for securing social peace " by promoting a better understanding between employers and workpeople ", a method of increasing profits by increasing efficiency, a method of raising wages *out of increased profits*, and sometimes, when the employer is not listening, a scheme of social regeneration and reconstruction. We shall have to take all these aspects of its Protean personality in turn.

Those who wish to study the actual working of Co-partnership must be referred to the numerous books and pamphlets dealing with the subject, and to the recent Board of Trade Report.[1] It is not proposed here to deal with its actual working, but merely with

[1] See Bibliography.

the general principles behind it. Anyone who questions the fairness of our estimate will find ample corroboration in the actual history of the various experiments.

The first weakness of Co-partnership is contained in its aim of securing social peace. It is never weary of asserting that "the interests of employers and workpeople are identical", when it is face to face with the greatest class-struggle history has ever seen. In view of the continued iteration of this fallacy, it will be well to see what it really implies. It is, of course, perfectly true that it may often be to the interests of employers and workers alike that industry should work smoothly; but whereas smooth working always suits the employer, it suits Labour only if Labour gets its rights. Labour must always be in a position to upset smooth working, in order to preserve the balance. Any device, therefore, which ties the workers' hands by prohibiting strikes, or giving them "an interest in the business", is fatal to the whole purpose for which Labour is organised—the gradual abolition of capitalist exploitation.

Again, Capital and Labour may, as we saw, have an identical interest in enforcing a voluntary agreement over a whole trade, provided that agreement only sets up a compulsory *minimum*, and there are numbers of other instances in which, on a particular point, the interests of Capital and Labour may coincide. It may be to the interest of both to make the industry efficient, up to the point at which efficiency begins to mean excessive speeding-up for the worker.

All these particular coincidences of interest, however, in no way prove that, fundamentally and generally, the interests of Capital and Labour are identical. As, in a war, it is sometimes to the interest of both parties to call a truce, and even to co-operate in tending the wounded, so Capital and Labour, in their ceaseless warfare, must sometimes pause and act together. This, however, does not destroy the class-war: underlying all these agreements is the essential difference that there are two claimants to the product of industry, and that both cannot have what they want. On the one side, the exploiter, on the other, the exploited; in the middle, but nearer the employer, Co-partnership, with a bee in its bonnet.

We need be at no pains to dispute the claim of Co-partnership that it raises profits. In certain cases, there is no doubt that it does: that is why it has persuaded certain employers to take it up. Where it has not done so, it has failed either from the peculiar character of the industry, or from being a badly drafted scheme, or from the hostility of the workers, or from a combination of these causes. Normally, if the workers accepted it gladly, a well-drafted scheme should raise profits; more employers have not been led to adopt such schemes, partly from conservatism and partly on account of the hostility of Labour.

The claim that Co-partnership raises wages demands more careful scrutiny. In the large majority of cases, it is in effect no more than Profit-sharing under a nicer name, and therefore may be described as a bonus of 5 per cent. on wages. However, even this increase may well be illusory. In the first place, it is generally more than covered by the increased activity of the worker; in the second place, when the time for a rise in wages comes, it may well be that the worker will not get it: his wages with the extra 5 per cent. will then be equal to what his wages alone would have been, and his efficiency will be 10 per cent. greater. This, however, may not regularly happen, and we may grant, for purposes of argument, that the workers really get a 5 per cent. bonus. Even so, their solidarity will have been impaired, their Trade Unionism undermined; so far from being in a better position to control industry, they will be more in the hands of the employer than ever.

It is granted by a leading advocate of Co-partnership that all increases in wages due to its operation must come out of increased profits. The worker adds 10 per cent. to his efficiency, and gets only 5 per cent. of it as a reward.

The accusation will certainly be made that, so far, we have spoken of Co-partnership merely as if it were Profit-sharing. If so, we have spoken of it as it is usually represented, *to the employer*. Co-partnership attempts to distinguish itself from Profit-sharing by the admixture, whenever the employer is not too inconveniently near, of a measure of social idealism. It aims not merely at giving the worker a bonus, or preferential terms for taking up shares in the concern; it aims also at giving him a share in the control of industry. It is, so some of its supporters maintain, the real peaceful Syndicalism, which will, in the end, oust the capitalist and give the workers control. It therefore makes a great point of combining with its profit-sharing schemes provision for the representation of the workers on boards of directors or committees of management. This would be all very well, were not the worker-directors, in practically every case, not only now in a hopeless minority, but also in such a position that they can never hope to become a majority. It may be far worse to have two or three representatives on a board which is completely dominated by hostile interests than to have none at all. Workers who are unrepresented have, at least, a clear fight with their employer; ' safe ' representation merely obscures the issue, and varnishes the class-structure of industry instead of destroying it. The workshop committee that is independent of the management is an admirable institution : the workshop representative in a permanent minority on a board of management is in a hopeless position.

The failure of Co-partnership to give any effective control over industry to the worker would be more easily seen, were not the issue once again artificially confused. The Labour Co-partnership Association concerns itself not only with Capitalistic Co-partnership, which comes from above, but also with Co-operation of Producers, which comes from below. Fundamentally, the two have nothing in common ; their union is in part an accident, and in part a *mariage de convenance*. The Labour Co-partnership Association originated out of the Christian Socialist ideal of the self-governing workshop : it has only become capitalistic since its capture by Profit-sharing, which raised itself to the peerage by the adoption of a nobler name. Against Co-operation of Producers none of the arguments that have been used against capitalistic Co-partnership hold good ; but the idealism which still lurks round the elusive idea of the self-governing workshop should not be used to support the capitalistic device of Co-partnership, *alias* Profit-sharing.

If we examine the alleged success of Co-partnership in recent years, we shall find that it is based mainly on the case of the Gas Companies. Outside them, it has very little solid success to show, and, in these instances, its achievements admit of easy explanation. Gas Companies are not private trading concerns ; they are controlled by the State, in that they cannot increase their dividends as they please, but only in proportion as they reduce the price of gas to the public. Instead, therefore, of reducing the price, they can unload the profits which they are not allowed to divide by means of a bonus on wages. The workers, however, do not get this bonus for nothing. They get it in return for a practical abandonment of the possibility of striking. Strikes in breach of contract or without a long statutory notice are a criminal offence. For the loss of the right to strike the worker is recompensed by a bonus on wages and an illusory share in control. He has no real control over conditions; Trade Unionism is discouraged or beaten down; but in compensation for all he loses, the worker gets a share in profits. There is no social idealism in such a state of things.

Co-partnership is often represented as a pure gift on the part of the employer, and the workers are told that they should not look a gift-horse in the mouth. But such 'gift-horses' are just the horses Labour ought particularly to look in the mouth. They may so very easily prove unsound. Real advocates of Copartnership are perfectly sincere; they do not see the fundamental difference between capitalistic Profit-sharing and working-class Co-operation of Producers. But the capitalist who takes up their schemes does see the difference. They will tell him that he must at all costs not use Co-partnership as a weapon against Trade Unionism; but, if he can, he will so use it. They will regard the election of a working-class director as a first step towards the complete democratisation of industry; he will see in it a way of muzzling his employees. The Trade Unions cannot afford to accept Co-partnership on the strength of the good faith of some of its advocates : in the hands of an unscrupulous employer, it might easily prove too strong a weapon. Solidarity among the working-class is not strong enough to play with ; it requires stimulating, and anything that could in any way be made to undermine it must be rejected absolutely.

As an endorsement of the judgments passed on capitalistic Co-partnership a circular, recently issued by the Labour Co-partnership Association, is, to say the least of it, enlightening. It is intended to catch the employer, and persuade him to adopt Co-partnership. It is entitled *Co-partnership from the Employer's Point of View*. This document seeks to prove that the enhanced profits Co-partnership can undoubtedly bring with it are not neutralised by any real danger that the workers will get control of the business—unless the employer likes. A few working-class representatives on a Board of Directors are quite harmless, and by making long service a condition of such appointments the employer can always draw the workers' teeth. A few nice, mild employees on the Board only strengthen the master's hands, and Co-partnership gives no security to the worker that he will ever get more than this share in control. In matters of 'discipline', the capitalist can remain as securely entrenched as ever, and he will even be the stronger because a strike on a question of 'victimisation' or 'discipline' will have become very nearly impossible. When the Labour Co-partnership Association itself points out that the employer need surrender to the worker no more control than he deems advisable, there can be very little doubt as to the practical outcome of the movement, however sincere its promoters may be.

The following are the most important passages from this interesting leaflet :

" It (real profit-sharing) meets the worker's feeling

that when profits exceed a fair interest on capital he is entitled to a share of the surplus he has helped to create. *It produces that mutual understanding between employer and employed which the rise and reign of the factory system and the joint stock company system have made it almost impossible otherwise to secure.* It shows the worker that he is not regarded as a mere machine, and so lessens the likelihood of any serious dispute between employer and employed. Moreover, by furnishing a moral and monetary incentive to good work, *it tends to the success of the business with which it is allied*. The considerateness of the employer tends to evoke conscientiousness in the employee, and self-interest operates to sustain it. *With men thus interested in their work, management becomes easier, less expensive, and more efficient.*"

So far, so good; but a little later follows this dialogue to give the show away—

"*It is surely a risky thing to admit employees to a share in the control of one's business?*"

"This is another bogey. Co-partnership, in its full development, no doubt seems logically to involve co-operation in management, but *whether a voice in the control be given to the workers under profit-sharing*, and, if so, to what extent, *is matter for decision in each case*. If voting rights are given, the worker shareholders' voting power is naturally very limited at first, and, though it grows as their shareholding grows, their experience is growing at the same time. . . ."

"*But at least a man would have to publish his balance-sheet, and what trouble that might cause!* . . ."

". . . Public companies publish their results without being embarrassed in this way. But if the concern were a private company, *there would be no need to publish a balance-sheet.* . . ."

"... *Is an employer to give his business away?*"

"*That is not in the least necessary.* The principles of profit-sharing and labour co-partnership can be variously applied. . . ."

And so on, the italics being kindly supplied by the Labour Co-partnership Association itself. "Co-partnership, in its full development, no doubt seems logically to involve" all sorts of nice things; this leaflet proves that such logic is not everything.

Co-partnership, *alias* Profit-sharing, gains the whole of its idealistic appeal from its confusion with other movements that have really nothing to do with it. On the one hand, as we have seen, it is confused with Co-operation of Producers, and regards the Garden City Press as one of its most successful achievements. On the other, it is becoming more and more mixed up with what is known as the 'Co-partnership Tenants' movement, which is pure Co-operation of Consumers applied to housing. The co-operative housing movement is outside the present subject; but it must be made clear that it differs absolutely in type both from capitalistic Co-partnership and from Co-operation of Producers. It is a co-operative movement for providing houses on the part not of those who make houses, but of those who live in them; that is to say, it is as much consumer's co-operation as the Wholesale Society and the distributive stores.

It is sometimes urged, in justification of mixing up Co-operation of Producers with Co-partnership, that the one may easily be developed out of the other. But it is quite certain that the employer who takes up with Co-partnership has no intention of bringing about his own extinction; nor is there anything in Co-partnership itself to force his hand. It is a method of perpetuating the present system, and not of ending it.

Co-operation of Producers, therefore, presents a separate problem, which has to be examined by itself. The arguments against Co-partnership do not hold against the self-governing workshop; but it does not follow that there may not be other equally cogent arguments against it. The Christian Socialist ideal of gradually ousting Capitalism by the voluntary co-operation of producers is no nearer realisation to-day than when it was first formulated. The number of self-governing workshops does not grow appreciably, nor do they show any signs of grasping an increasing proportion of the trade of the country. This fact is obscured because, in the Board of Trade reports on Co-operation, the Societies of Producers are lumped together with the English and Scottish Wholesales as 'Productive Societies'. But the Wholesales, which do the bulk of the trade, are federations of distributive stores—that is to say, they are consumers' societies. The success of Societies of Producers must be estimated apart from them.

Briefly, and without going into the evidence, we must here state a bare conclusion. Societies of Producers depend mainly for their custom on the distributive stores, and do not, as a rule, catch the outside market; they are enormously dependent on the personality of the manager, who often bears the whole weight of the business on his shoulders; and they are confined, in most instances, to a few trades. Thus, they succeed especially in the manufacture of boots and shoes and in printing, both comparatively 'small' trades, in which the enterprise need not be on a large scale in order to succeed; but they are non-existent in 'great' industry, coal-mining, textiles, metal work and the like. In short, they may perform a useful function in certain trades which are carried on best on a small scale; but the method of association of producers on the basis of the self-governing workshops cannot hope to extend at all widely. It is no substitute for the present system of production; the revolutionary hopes once based on it have now been transferred to that other form of association of producers, which is the main object of our study, the Trade Union. In the course of the next chapter, the discussion of the ideal aspects of Syndicalism will lead us to pass judgment on the place of this more important factor in the control of industry.

But before we proceed to the discussion of the function of Trade Unionism in the control of industry, there is a rival solution to be considered. Co-operation of Consumers, unlike Co-operation of Producers, has thriven and spread enormously. The bulk of trade done by retail Consumers' Societies all over the world is immense, and the Wholesale Societies also are growing rapidly and launching out more and more into production. Can, then, Co-operation of Consumers ultimately oust Capitalism, and take its place universally as the form of the industrial enterprise of the future?

At the outset, the immense debt which the Co-operative movement owes to the Rochdale Pioneers must be made clear. People often speak as if Co-operative effort began at Rochdale; but as a matter of fact Co-operation had been struggling to obtain a footing long before the Rochdale system was dreamt of. Until the method of selling at market price and dividing the profits was hit upon, the movement had no success. The Rochdale pioneers 'made' the

THE FUNCTION OF CO-OPERATION 339

Co-operative movement by giving it a commercial basis. It became not merely the elimination of the capitalist, but also an excellent way of saving up. It eliminated profit, though at the same time it probably rather increased working expenses; but above all it provided the housewife with an easy means of saving up money for the end of the quarter. Co-operation, then, has succeeded largely as the best known way of compulsory saving. In the process, it has lost much of its idealism; but it has certainly become a 'business proposition'. Very much of the retail trade of this country is now in the hands of the stores. In all the important industrial districts it has won its way; it has conquered, except in the South of England, the majority of the well-paid workers; and it is still spreading. At present, it does not seem likely to conquer the very poor, for whom saving is out of the question, or the rich, who have no need to save; it is a movement of the working-class, and mainly of the higher-paid workers.

It would not be relevant here to go into the question of Consumers' Co-operation as a whole. We are only inquiring how far the Co-operative movement is in itself a solution to the problem of the control of industry; and the answer must be, in spite of the astonishing progress it has made, that it provides no solution. As Co-operation expands, its limitations become more manifest: on the distributive side, it seems to succeed only with necessaries, especially provisions, and as soon as it tries to deal with more out-of-the-way articles, it begins to break down. In production, it clearly cannot extend to any of the greater industries; it may gradually absorb the provision trades and, to some extent, the clothing trades also; but it cannot intrude with any hope of success into most textile work, or into mining or metal work. *A fortiori*, it can have nothing to do with Transport. Certain services are marking themselves out more and more clearly as properly within the sphere of Government or municipal enterprise; and certain others as, at any rate, incapable of being run by societies of consumers. The sphere of co-operation has definite bounds, and it is evident that, though the movement may double or treble the volume of its trade, it will remain, in essentials, pretty much what it is now. It will continue alongside Capitalism; but it will do nothing to overthrow it.

Moreover, even in the sphere to which it undoubtedly applies, it has many unsolved problems to face. Organised, like the State, on the basis of *consumption*, it comes, as soon as it enters into production, face to face with the forces of the producers. The C.W.S., as much as any private employer, and like, as we shall see, the State itself, has to face the problem of the control of industry. The working-class, organised as consumers, come into contact with sections of workers, organised as producers; and awkward questions of rights and functions arise. Co-operation, whatever its scope and its limits may be, whether it is destined to continue in the Society of the future, or to be absorbed in the wider Consumers' Societies of the State and the Municipality, does not and cannot by itself solve the question of the control of industry.

Although, as we have seen, the Co-operative movement has lost a great deal of its idealism, and, especially in the case of the Wholesale Societies, has become commercial in outlook and aim, it has yet enormous functions to perform on behalf of the working-class. Nor should it be forgotten that there is, working upon it from within, a large body of idealists who would willingly recall it to its larger ideals and aspirations. Co-operators like Mr. William Maxwell and the leading members of the Women's Co-operative Guild are doing a magnificent work in making the movement realise its duties, in making the members feel that the stores are not merely excellent savings banks and openings for investment, but also working-class organisations, which should be imbued, through and through, with the spirit of working-class solidarity. The most hopeful sign is the awakening of a section of the women. " Woman ", as Mrs. Billington-Greig says, " is the consumer ",[1] and it is not till women are socially alive that the Co-operative movement will recover its idealism. Then, it may well be, the new spirit in woman will teach the men the idealism they have forgotten. But before Co-operation can take its proper place as one of the three great working-class movements it has much to learn and much to unlearn. The 'dividend-hunting' spirit must disappear, and prices must not be allowed to rise above the market level. The Co-operative movement must make its appeal to the very poor, and constitute itself one of the means of bringing home to them the injustice of their situation and the need for social reconstruction.

Secondly, Co-operation must come into closer touch with other working-class movements. We have heard a good deal recently about proposals for closer unity between the Co-operative Congress, the Trades Union Congress, and the Labour Party. Unfortunately, for the present the whole movement has been side-tracked into a proposal for a political alliance between the Co-operative Union and the

[1] *The Consumer in Revolt*, by Teresa Billington-Greig.

Labour Party. This is unfortunate, partly because political Labour should be independent both of economic Labour and of 'trading' Labour, but mainly because it tends to block useful suggestions with wild-cat schemes that can come to nothing. There is not, at present, the faintest chance of the Co-operative movement as a whole being persuaded to enter the political field.

On the other hand, the stores and the Wholesales might do admirable work by co-operating with Labour in its economic activities. It is a curious anomaly that in England there is no attempt to secure organised help from the Co-operative Societies in case of strikes. In Belgium, the two movements are in the closest possible touch, as was clearly shown in the course of the recent General Strike; and in Germany, though more independent, they work closely together. The workers' power of resistance is enormously strengthened by such help, and no time should be lost in bringing about a similar position in this country.

In the first place, it should be possible for the Unions to increase their power of holding out enormously, if, in case of need, they provided strikers with groceries and the like at cost price from the store, in lieu of a part of their strike pay. Secondly, it should be possible, as in Germany, to get the stores to give their members 'dividends on account', that is, to enable them to buy with dividends not yet due to them; again, the stores should be able to give advances to strikers, to be repaid gradually after the close of the strike; and there are various other methods, commonly employed in Germany, which might well be adopted here. In return for these concessions, the Co-operative Societies might hope to secure the membership of nearly all Trade Unionists,

THE FUNCTION OF CO-OPERATION

and, in addition, to have the Unions, if necessary, as guarantors for the repayment of the sums advanced. The Union would benefit enormously, and the Co-operative Society would have no reason to fear a loss.

Again, might not the Unions, if this closer co-operation in strikes were brought about, reasonably invest a portion of their funds in the Co-operative Wholesale Societies, and do their banking through the Co-operative bank? Both movements would greatly gain from such closer touch, and neither could possibly suffer any damage. Co-operation, by affording the workers a measure of real help in their uphill fight against Capitalism, would regain much of its lost idealism; Trade Unionism would have its economic power largely increased; and the working-class as a whole would gain in solidarity and cohesion. Further, the closer touch established between Trade Unionism and Co-operation would make it possible to face the problem of the control of industry in a more friendly spirit; and, in the microcosm of the Co-operative Wholesales, producers and consumers might begin to work out in amity that future structure of industrial society which will ultimately have to be applied to the macrocosm—the country at large. By means of Co-operation, while it remains an isolated economic phenomenon, the working-class can only hope to save a little money: only where the organised consumer comes into friendly touch with the organised producer is there any hope that we are nearing the solution, for the time being, of the eternal problem of the control of industry.

CHAPTER XI

THE CONTROL OF INDUSTRY—SYNDICALISM AND COLLECTIVISM

HITHERTO, in speaking of Trade Unionism, we have, in the main, been limiting our survey to the immediate future, and considering the Unions as fighting organisations engaged in a ceaseless struggle with the employer for decent conditions and a living wage. Every now and then, and especially in dealing with the Syndicalist movement in France, we have been led to adopt a wider view, and take into account claims made on behalf of the organised producers to a far greater share in the control of industry and even of Society as a whole. These claims we have not yet, save by implication, considered on their merits : we have now to take the plunge and, from the actual working of Trade Unionism in the present, launch out upon the possibilities of its future development. This we shall endeavour to do in this and in the following chapter : here we shall deal with the question generally, as a theory, and in the next chapter we shall try to see how, out of the present organisation of the Unions, may be developed a greater Unionism capable of assuming real and effective control, through its industrial organisation, over the conditions of life and work.

Broadly speaking, there are three alternatives before us, in theory at least, three rival claimants to the

THE CONTROL OF INDUSTRY

control of industry. These claimants are, first, the private capitalist, from the small trader to the trust ; secondly, the consumer organised on a compulsory basis, from the State to the County Council and the Municipality ; and thirdly, the organised producers, the Trade Unions or bodies arising out of them, called 'National Guilds'. It may seem that Co-operation of Consumers falls under none of these heads, and, as it has been dealt with briefly already, it is not proposed to recur to it here : it need only be said that the name of 'a State within a State' will serve, in a certain measure, to guide us in placing it aright. The Co-operative Wholesale is national trading on a voluntary basis ; the store is municipal trading of the same sort : and it is certain that, if the structure of industry keeps on its present line of development, Co-operative enterprise will become more and more like State and municipal enterprise. If, for instance, as the Labour Party's Nationalisation of Mines Bill proposes, the State took over coal-vending, it would at once be faced with the alternative, in many districts, of either duplicating or taking over a Co-operative service ; and it must be clear that, in such a case, the Co-operative Society would, as a rule, have to give way. We may therefore leave Co-operation out of account : we have seen that its sphere is limited, and whether it retains or loses the sphere makes no difference to the general question of the control of industry.

For the moment, then, we may treat the claimants as being three—Capitalism, the consumer, and the producer. It is not proposed to go over again here the well-worn arguments for and against Capitalism. There is nothing to add to the case against Capitalism as is has been stated over and over again : the weakness of its opponents lies in their proposals for reconstruction, and the rival solutions of this problem are the subject of this chapter. Even Capitalism prefers defending itself by picking holes in the schemes of its opponents to presenting a reasonable justification for its own existence. Its only justification is that " it's growed " ; and, in order to remove it, Socialists, Syndicalists, and all sorts of revolutionaries have to come to some sort of agreement about the reconstruction they propose. It will, then, be assumed throughout that the community as a whole has a right to control its own destinies, and that no vested ' right ' or interest has any claim upon it unless it backs up that claim by proof of positive service. We shall consider, not whether the community has a right to take away from those who have, but what, absolutely, is the best means of organising industry in the interests of the whole.

We are, then, coming at last to what is generally regarded as the central doctrine of Syndicalism, the point of its conflict with political Socialism. We are inquiring how far its insistence that industry should be controlled by the producer rather than the consumer is justified by expediency and common sense.

We saw, in our first chapter, that the Socialist movement in Great Britain had tended more and more, as time went on, to lay all the stress on distribution and consumption as opposed to production. Compelled to meet the attacks of opponents by working out a system of State control of industry, it was driven inevitably, by the nature of the arguments it had to meet, into trying to prove that State enterprise could be made more *efficient* than private enterprise, and that the replacing of competition by co-operation would not ' destroy the incentive ' to efficiency, but would, on the contrary, make production better, cheaper and more within the reach of all. Faced with the enormous inequality of wealth, it was driven to insist on a better division of the national income ; and, seeing that redistribution was impossible while industry remained in the hands of the private capitalist, with the control of prices in his power, it laid stress on the essential point that the community must step in and replace the exploiter by some fairer controlling force. Unfortunately, in driving home all these truths, it was inevitably tempted to carry arguments too much to their logical conclusions ; in endeavouring to persuade the world that Socialism was a 'business proposition', it forgot that it must be a 'human' proposition also : it found definiteness and Collectivism, and lost idealism, which is essential to real Socialism.

The great thing, in the eyes of these Collectivists, being to increase the power of the State, by which they meant the functions and operative rights of the community as a whole, they were not careful enough to provide against the abuse of the new power they proposed to confer. Seeing that the democratic State, composed of democratic citizens, ought to have absolute power over all matters that affected the general well-being,[1] they went on to identify their ideal State and their ideal citizen with the State and the citizen of the present, and supposed that a mere extension of the State's sphere of action would bring all other blessings in its train. They forgot that the State cannot, in the long run, be better than the citizens, and that, unless the citizens are capable of controlling the Government, extension of the powers of the State may be merely a transference of authority from the capitalist to the bureaucrat. Nationalisation was presented as a panacea for all ills : it was supposed that, if the State

[1] Such a State, *if composed of active citizens*, might not so readily abuse its powers ; but the wage-system makes active citizenship impossible for the majority.

were given the power, the democracy would rise in its might to control it. We are learning slowly to be more sceptical.

The old argument for nationalisation was largely an argument against competition. We were told, to surfeit, of the twenty milk-carts which Capitalism sent rattling down the street, when one would do just as well. Competition, it was urged, produced overlapping, and this chaos could be remedied by State control. On the other side, we were told that competition was the life-blood of industry; drain it off, and trade and prosperity would perish. To-day, the whole argument seems a little old-fashioned. Competition is dying, but it is being killed, not by the State, but by Capitalism itself. The private trader is being crushed out by the trust, and Socialists are now, in America for instance, attacking monopoly as they once attacked competition. On the other hand, slowly and with pains, capitalist economists are reconciling their consciences to a defence of 'trusts'. Trusts, we are told, pay better wages and secure better services; by eliminating competition, they economise and make production cheaper and more efficient. Time's strange revenges are more than a little amusing.

The case of the Socialist has only become the more overwhelming for the change. Capitalistic development has proved the futility of competition. Unfortunately, this logical triumph eaves him no better off; for private monopoly is a worse enemy than private competition. Capitalism, by accepting Socialist logic, has entrenched itself more firmly: to Socialist ethics it shows no sign of being converted.

It is clear, therefore, that, fundamentally, the Socialist was right all the time. The State, in the

THE CONTROL OF INDUSTRY

interests of the whole community, has got to interfere. Every year it is driven more and more to take part in industrial regulation; and, if the capitalists generally make a good thing out of its excursions into the industrial field, that is merely because of the timidity with which it acts and the weakness and stupidity of the public opinion behind it. The community must interfere in industry, and, ultimately, control; and the question to be examined is what can be shown to be the best method of exercising that control.

It will be easier to see the real strength and weakness of Collectivism when we have looked rather more closely at some of the alternatives that have been proposed. Syndicalism is, on the face of it, and in the mouths of many of its advocates, a claim for the complete control of industry by the producer. It asserts the ambiguous and indefinite doctrine that, as all wealth is created by labour, the worker has " a right to the whole product of his work ". He has a right, not merely to a living wage and decent conditions in the workshop, but to an absolute control over the circumstances of his life and labour.

This fundamental dogma is always modified to some extent when the Syndicalist position is more fully explained; but it lurks to such an extent behind the thought of most Syndicalists that it is worth while to examine what, barely, it implies. First, what is the 'labour' that creates all wealth? It must of course be admitted that it includes 'brain-work', and this the Syndicalists readily grant. But, even so, does labour create all wealth? Clearly, it requires both raw material and instruments to create it with. Does this give labour a right to the raw material in which it works; for clearly the raw material has a 'value', and is 'wealth'. In fact, is it maintained that the miner has a right to the mine in which he works, and the agricultural labourer a right to the land? If so, inequality in wealth will still persist; for all enterprises are not equally productive.[1] The right of Labour to all wealth is not a right of any individual worker or class of workers to any particular object or fraction of the total wealth; it is the right of all the useful to eliminate the useless. It is a right of all those who labour to a fair share of the good things of this life, and not a right of any section to absolute control of the product of a particular industry.

This should not be taken to mean that the producers in a particular industry have no right to any control over that industry: it means merely that their right is not, and is not based on, a " right to the whole product of labour ". Syndicalism can make a far more reasonable demand, if, abandoning abstract economics and leaving the theory of value to take care of itself, it adopts the standpoint of concrete and commonsense ethics, and asks whether, in the name of justice and expediency alike, the producer should have the fullest possible share in the control of the conditions under which he works. It is too little realised, even by Socialists—and especially by Marxians—that the whole question of the control of industry is not economic but ethical. The attempt to found 'justice' on the theory of value merely revives the old conception of individual natural right in its least defensible form. The right of Labour to a life of comfort and self-expression is quite independent of whether it creates all wealth or not.

Leaving aside, then, the economic theory on which

[1] That is if prices are fixed not by cost of production, but by supply and demand.

Syndicalism bases its demand, let us examine that demand solely on its merits. In the minds of most of its critics, and of a good many of its exponents, the actual demand is, unfortunately, vague. Syndicalism, which is, in essence, as its name implies, revolutionary Trade Unionism, varies its proposals according to the form of Trade Unionism on which it is based. Where the Unions are well organised on a national basis, the demand will be for control of conditions nationally by the Trade Union as a whole; where, as in France, Trade Unionism is weak and local, the demand will often take the form of a suggested return to the 'self-governing workshop'. The close alliance, in France, between Anarchist-Communism, with its plea for the 'redintegration' of labour, for complete local autonomy, and for the self-governing workshop, is mainly accounted for by the weakness and parochialism of the French *syndicats*. In Great Britain, where Trade Unionism is a strong national growth, it is safe to neglect all advocacy of Syndicalism which has not the national Union as a basis, and Syndicalism has therefore allied itself, in this country, not with Anarchist-Communism, but with Industrial Unionism. Syndicalism in England is a plea that industry should be controlled, not, as pure Collectivists believe, by the consumers organised in State and municipalities, but by the producers, organised in Industrial Unions. It adopts the 'Greater Unionism' as an essential basis, and is to be regarded as a theory of the future function and destiny of the new Unions which will result from the present movement towards closer unity. In the next chapter, we shall be studying the present and future of Trade Unionism: here, assuming the possibility of developing, out of the existing Unions, bodies capable of controlling industry, we have to discover how far such a system would be desirable.

As Mr. Sidney Webb, Mr. Graham Wallas, and others have pointed out,[1] ' the control of industry ' is a vague phrase, which covers a number of separate problems. It is, on the face of it, improbable that either producer or consumer ought to have absolute control; it is unlikely that either the State or the Unions should take the place of the exploiter entirely; for then either the State would be in a position to exploit the worker, or the worker would be in a position to exploit the community—just as the capitalist exploits both at present. The solution must surely lie in a rational division of functions, allowing both producer and consumer a say in the control of what is, after all, supremely important to both.

The first question usually asked of the Syndicalist is whether he proposes that the workers should actually *own* the means of production. The answer given is practically unanimous: ownership, it is agreed, must be vested in the community as a whole. The difficulty arises when any attempt is made to define ownership. Generally, Syndicalists mean, in vesting ownership in the community, not to surrender any share in control, but merely to do away with the idea of property altogether. Mr. Graham Wallas has pointed out the essential ambiguity of the word ' ownership ', and has advised that it should be dropped out of the controversy altogether. After all, the question is who is to control industry: if absolute control is placed in the hands of the Unions, ' State ' or ' common ' ownership is merely a name.

[1] Mr. Webb in a recent course of lectures on the subject; Mr. Wallas in a paper on Syndicalism in the *Sociological Review*, July 1912.

THE CONTROL OF INDUSTRY 353

The question, therefore, resolves itself purely into one of control. Here we may as well adopt Mr. Webb's threefold distinction as a basis for argument. The control of industry involves, first the decision what is to be produced, when and where it is to be produced, and in what quantities it is to be produced. Secondly, some one has to decide what the processes of production shall be, *how* production shall be carried on. Thirdly, the question of conditions, including all the matters now covered by the Factory Acts, at least some matters of ' discipline ', pay, hours, and the like have to be determined by some authority.

What share can producer and consumer have in deciding all these matters ? The Syndicalist, where he denounces the State and expresses his determination to sweep it away, has to give the producer control in everything. Even the community which owns is, to his mind, merely an abstraction, a convenient way of shelving the vexatious question of ownership. But even the Syndicalist of this type does not propose to hand over absolute control to the particular class of producers engaged in each industry. He suggests that in the adjustment of supply to demand, the Trade Union Congress or its Executive and the local Trades Councils (*Bourses du Travail*) should take the place of the State and tell each section of producers what to produce. But the question what is to be produced is a matter either for the workers who actually produce it or for the community ; it is not a matter for all the producers as producers, no matter what they produce. The Trade Union Congress and the Trades Councils, with their enlarged functions, are in fact merely the State and the municipality in disguise. They are (for this purpose) imperfect organisations of consumers and not real producers' organisations at all.

Thus, we find at the outset a part of the control of industry which cannot be handed over to the producer. Obviously, the consumer, the person *for* whom the goods are made, and not the person *by* whom they are made, must decide what is to be produced, when it is to be produced, and in what quantities. Whether the consumer must also decide where it is to be produced is another matter, and does not seem to be equally evident.[1] This, however, is of less importance, and the solution will emerge as the discussion proceeds.

This answer, however, simple and self-evident as it may at first sight appear, really begs the question. It presupposes the absolute irresponsibility of the producer to the individual consumer as well as to the State. The capitalist of the present day is theoretically in just such a position as this argument tries to prove absurd: he can produce what he likes, when, where, and in what quantities he pleases. Only, the public, on its side, can refuse to buy, and the refusal of the public is the capitalist's loss. The consumer controls the capitalist through his pocket. We cannot, therefore, say how far a Trade Union could safely be given a similar power, until we know what the Trade Union in question would be like. If it were a trading body exercising a monopoly, but selling its goods for its own profit, would not the consumer have on it exactly the check he has now on the trusts? And the trusts are not accused of making the wrong articles, but of charging too much for them. There may be other objections to such a body as the Trade Union would then be, but it would not be in the least likely to make the wrong sort of articles or the wrong quantity, or to manufacture them at the wrong time. Like the trust, it would be out to meet the demand of the market.

[1] If the consumer gets his goods, it does not concern him *where* they are made.

If, on the other hand, the Trade Union is not a trading body, if its members are to be paid at a fixed rate independent of the selling price of their produce, if, that is to say, profiteering is to be eliminated, then clearly the consumer must have some other means of directing their production. They must, in such a case, find out what to make by consultation with a body representing the consumers: they must negotiate with the State, and be guided by the organised, instead of by the unorganised, will of the consumer.

There is, of course, a third possibility. The Trade Union may trade, not directly with the consumer, but with the State. The State may give its order and pay the Union as a whole for the produce, and this might well be in itself a sufficient measure of control. But enough has been said to make it clear at least that not even in this first sphere of control can an immediate answer be given. It will be necessary, then, to return to the question later on.

The second type of decision, according to Mr. Webb's classification, has to do with the processes of production, and it is round these that the dispute really centres. Trade Unions have, no doubt, shown themselves in the past bad and partial judges of new industrial processes. Confronted with an irresponsible employing class, which thrust upon them exactly such processes as it chose, with regard solely to commercial value, and heedless of the effect on the workers, they have come to regard every innovation with mistrust. They resisted the first introduction of machinery, and they have been apt to rebel at every extension of its use. They have tried to bolster up the old system of apprenticeship and to perpetuate out-of-date methods of production ; and they have done all this, not from any deep sense of the value of craftsmanship, but merely from a fear that wages would be lowered and men thrown out of employment. All these reproaches are habitually levelled at the Unions when it is proposed to invest them with any degree of control over industrial methods.

But it is at any rate relevant to ask how we could expect them to do anything else. Clearly labour-saving devices and innovations of all sorts, which should go to mitigate the hard lot of the worker, have been used, in every case, at least in the first instance, for the purpose of raising profits. It may be that in the end the workers have benefited, that finally they have secured part of the increase through enforced rises in wages; but in nearly every case, the first introduction of the new machine has meant a fall in wages and a displacement of the skilled artisan. The introduction of the linotype hit the skilled compositor by enabling more work to be done in the time and making it possible for a lower class of labourer to do his work; and though the skilled compositor gained in the end, he could hardly have been expected to have so much foresight as to see that the volume of work would be so increased as ultimately to increase his earnings. Moreover, an ultimate increase is poor consolation for a period of unemployment to a worker earning normally just enough to make both ends meet. The opposition of Labour to new processes arises from the use to which new processes have been put: where an invention in the hands of a capitalist employer is unwelcome, it will be very welcome when the workers, as a whole, are enabled to use it for the lightening of the daily task. The failure of modern Trade Unionism to accept new inventions is no reason for supposing that, were the danger of exploitation removed, the hostility would remain unaltered.

THE CONTROL OF INDUSTRY

The producer, then, is clearly entitled to a very considerable share in the control of this second industrial sphere. Clearly, the Trade Union of the present, a 'fighting' or a 'friendly' organisation devoted to 'collective bargaining' or 'mutual insurance', is not structurally fitted to take over such control. That is not the question at issue, and the unfitness of actual Trade Unions to control processes will be generally admitted. The question is whether, could Trade Union structure be adapted to the purpose, it would be desirable to place such power in the hands of the producer.

Processes are, generally speaking, decided by experts. Under Capitalism, invention is generally carried on, for profit, by independent investigators, working in the hope of hitting on a success, while the normal work of management, including the application of inventions, is carried on by a salaried manager. But, more and more, great firms are retaining their own inventors and paying them a fixed salary to experiment and give the firm the benefit of the results. The control of industrial processes and inventions may, then, be classed together as functions of 'management'—functions with which Trade Unions organised on the 'craft' basis of the present can, at the most, interfere only occasionally and, in the main, in a negative fashion. The question at issue is not whether 'management' should be conducted by mob-rule, by its transference to the Trade Union as a whole, but whether the managers, who are also producers, should be responsible to, and elected by, the rest of the producers in the particular industry or by an external authority representing the consumers. Clearly, if the consumers elect, the managerial staff will remain independent of the workers, who will be organised over against them as a Trade Union ; if the producers elect, the managerial staff will be absorbed into the Union, which will take on, to some extent, a hierarchical form.

The right to elect the rulers is a recognised principle of democratic political theory. Is there any reason why such a principle should not be applied to industry also ? Indeed, is 'industrial democracy' possible unless it is so applied ? In politics, we do not call democratic a system in which the proletariat has the right to organise and exercise what pressure it can on an irresponsible body of rulers : we call it modified aristocracy ; and the same name adequately describes a similar industrial structure. If democracy can be applied to the workshop, the workers must elect and control their managers, in so far as those managers are concerned with the processes, and not with the what, when and how much of production.

Nor is there any obvious reason why the consumer should usurp the control of such processes. He must get what he wants ; but, provided he gets it, it is immaterial to him how it is made. He need only reserve the power to step in when he is not getting what he wants, or, as we shall see, when he is being made to pay too much for it. Processes, as such, are to him irrelevant.

On the other hand, the producer has an enormous interest in being able to control the processes which are the sum total of his daily labour. Two processes may be, economically, exactly on a level ; but it may make all the difference to the producer that one should be preferred to the other. Not only safety, but also comfort and variety in manufacture, are primarily his concern : to him comes home the joy or the pain experienced in labour, and, therefore, he should be given the fullest possible measure of control. How far such control can be given to him here and

THE CONTROL OF INDUSTRY 359

now, and how far his capacity for it must be gradually developed, we shall try to find out in the next chapter: here we have only to make clear that it is on all grounds desirable that it should be as extensive as it can possibly be made.

On the other hand, it is evident that the consumer may have an indirect interest in industrial processes. As one process may be more pleasant or safer, and at the same time less economical than another, the price the consumer has to pay will be affected as one or other is adopted. He cannot therefore afford to leave the whole control to the producer, unless he can secure that the producer's interest shall be to supply him as cheaply as possible. If the Trade Union is a trading body, dealing with the consumers, collectively or individually, the consumer's interest will be adequately safeguarded by the commercial relation between him and the producer. If the workers are assured of a fixed salary, they may tend to adopt the pleasantest process, whether it suits the consumer or not. A solution becomes possible only if the Union, or Guild, itself becomes the employer, and enters into partnership with the State.

It is often maintained that the producer's interest in these matters will be looked after well enough by the benevolent State, and that, with his organisation behind him, he need not fear the adoption of the more economical and less pleasant process unless it is really just, in the interests of the whole community, that it should be adopted. Such a view would not be tenable in the case of a thoroughly democratic State of democratic men; still less is it true of the State of to-day or to-morrow. For the ordinary individual, the State is so far, and the workshop so near. The strike moves the emotions and Parliament fails to do so just because a man cannot miss the governing class in the workshop, while few even realise its existence in the State. Could the workers elect and remove the governing members of industry, they would begin to exercise a real democratic control.

We may admit, however, that the State must to some extent share in the control of processes. This it can do by preserving an ultimate right to intervene in the control of the management with the producers. Even if the whole personnel of the industry, including foremen and managers of every grade, from the highest to the lowest, be elected, and re-elected at intervals, by the workers, the Guild-Socialist solution, as we shall see, still provides a safeguard whereby the State can secure the community against exploitation. To this also we shall have to return shortly.

The third sphere of control is that of conditions of labour, including the regulation of hours and wages. By those who envisage the Trade Union of the future as a purely independent body, engaged in negotiating with the State in a nationalised industry, much as it deals now with the private capitalist or trading concern, this has always seemed the chief sphere for control by the producers. They have, in fact, regarded the producer's part in control as confined, for good and all, to collective bargaining. But as they have, in many cases, combined this view with an urgent demand for the extension of Trade Boards, dealing with hours as well as wages, over the whole of industry, it would seem that they desire to make the share of the producer in control altogether illusory; for the method of Trade Boards amounts, essentially, to

THE CONTROL OF INDUSTRY 361

determination of wages and hours by the consumer, in accordance with a standard of life laid down by consumers' morality. It would seem, then, that such persons give with one hand only to take away with the other, and that, while paying lip-service to the ideal of joint control by producer and consumer, they still leave all the power and all the authority on one side, and, on the other, only a mere semblance of representation.

The extension of the system of workshop committees is the sop generally thrown to the producer by self-satisfied Collectivism. The workshop committee is, no doubt, a very excellent thing, and industry will, in future, adopt it far more generally; but to regard that alone as an adequate delegation of power to the producer is to misconceive the whole force of the Syndicalistic tendency. In nationalised industry, if not elsewhere, wages statutorily determined as a minimum would certainly tend to become the maximum for which a strike could be declared, though more might in some cases be paid by the State out of its grace and bounty. The power of the Trade Union, as an external organisation, to force up wages would certainly tend to disappear when nationalised industry became the rule; under the State, unless competitive industry remained beside it, wages would be determined by the native goodness of the consumers' hearts, as reflected in their rulers. A strike against a manager on a particular question would still be possible; strikes concerned with wages or hours would be strikes against the moral standard of the community —and, in the community's eyes, the lowness of the standard would in no way condone the offence.

Moreover, it is essential now for the Unions to control wages and hours because their members are underpaid and overworked. The demand for the control of industry is something quite different from a demand for higher wages or shorter hours; it is essentially a demand to control industrial conditions and processes. It is in this sphere, if at all, that the demand must be met, and it is useless to try to get round it by the promise of workshop committees and strong independent Trade Unions under Collectivism.

In fact, at the close of our examination of the three spheres of industrial control, we have come back to what is, in the end, the crucial question. There are two opposing alternatives to Capitalism, which we may call roughly Syndicalism and Collectivism. Is there a third in which they can be reconciled?

A good deal has been heard, in recent years, about the restoration of the Guild System, and there has been, both for and against the proposal, a lot of very loose talk. By opponents, it is urged that the Guilds may have done very well in the mediæval world, but that we have outgrown them, as we have outgrown the City-State. The Guilds, they urge, died of their own rottenness: the system of monopoly and conservatism fell before the onrush of commercial enterprise: the close co-operation and the artificial regulation of prices are not for us. Moreover, they say, the Guilds were associations of masters; and surely it is not proposed to revive such institutions nowadays.

So much talk about nothing raises the doubt whether it is wise nowadays to use the word ' Guild ' at all. Of course, it is not proposed to restore any of these obsolete economic phenomena: what is proposed is a reorganisation of Trade Unionism. The *New Age* and other advocates call the bodies they propose to invest with the conduct of industry ' Guilds ', first, because they are to have a statutory and recognised position in Society; secondly, because they are to exercise a monopoly; thirdly, because they are to be associations of masters in the sense that, in them, every man will be a master; and, fourthly, because the name does stand for a morality in industry which we have lost and which it is important to restore. Further reasons might doubtless be given; but these are among the chief. First of all, then, in discussing 'Guild Socialism' and the system of National Guilds, let us be quite clear what we are talking about, or we shall merely repeat the old argument that the twentieth century is not the fourteenth. In order to avoid confusion, we shall, wherever possible, substitute the words ' Trade Union ' for the word ' Guild '.

The Guild Socialism of the *New Age* is a proposal for the co-management of industry by the State and the Trade Unions. Ownership of the means of production is to rest with the community, but the Unions are to be definitely recognised by the State as the normal controllers of industry. They are to be statutory bodies exercising a monopoly, but admitting of free entry on reasonable conditions. The amount and character of their production are to be determined for them by demand,[1] but the methods and processes are to be left entirely in their hands : they are to elect their own officials, and to be self-governing corporations with the widest powers. In fact, they are to resemble in their main characteristics the self-governing professions, the doctors and the lawyers, of the present. As the Guilds will include every one concerned in the

[1] Demand would be made articulate through the consumers' organisations, national and local—*i.e.* the State and the municipality.

industry, from general manager to labourers, they will be in essence 'Guilds', *i.e.* associations not of *dependent*, but of *independent*, producers.

This scheme, which has been brilliantly elaborated by the *New Age* week by week for the last few years, whether or not it is to be accepted as a whole—and the *New Age* would certainly not claim finality for it—is a very valuable contribution to the theory of Socialism. At last, after many maunderings on the subject of the Guild System, we are presented with an attempt to explain what it really means, and to apply it to modern industry. The *New Age* has realised—what most Socialists are too slow to realise—that the theory of national control of industry has got in a bad way, and that it is not enough to go on saying 'nationalise', unless you know what you mean by it. The scheme of Guild Socialism is, to any one who has read the *New Age* regularly and attentively, at least perfectly lucid and coherent : nor is it merely "up in the air". Its authors have taken every pains to find corroboration of their views in the actual working of industry to-day. Not only have they seized on the cases of the doctors and the lawyers ; they have found a more startling instance in the making of the Panama Canal, which has been conducted by the United States indirectly, by an independent, though by no means democratic, system of control. The State, they hold, has no business in industry itself ; but as it must, in the last resort, share control, it has to delegate its power, and for this purpose it must set up a self-governing authority. Just as the Government does not interfere with the internal discipline of Army or Navy, it must leave the industrial armies to manage their own affairs, while keeping a share in supreme direction, and telling them what it wants made, but not how to make it.

The first fault that is usually found with this scheme is that the Unions are not fit to take over such a charge. This, as we shall see, is perfectly true; but they have never been asked to fit themselves for it. To say that they are incapable of becoming fit is to go further than the evidence warrants.

We may admit at once that the scheme propounded by the *New Age* is faulty in many of its details, and that it is imperfectly linked up with the Trade Unionism of the present. The *New Age*, as Mr. Chesterton has said, is weak on democracy; it is a little too apt to be perfectly satisfied, on the surface at least, with its own ideas, and to resent criticism of every sort. But the scheme which it presents deserves from Socialists a measure of attention which it has certainly not received. The *New Age* has been snubbed for its pains by most of the leaders, and can hardly be blamed for resenting it. The average man must learn to tolerate the eccentricities of genius.

There is no space here to enter fully into the Guild Socialism of the *New Age*,[1] which, indeed, is ultimately less important in its details than in the general ideal illumination which it sheds. Accepting the general idea of 'National Guild' or Trade Union control, let us try to see a little more clearly exactly what it implies. Above all, let us ask ourselves whether the Guild or Trade Union ought to be a trading body or to sell at prices fixed jointly with the State. We have seen that it would be dangerous to delegate absolute control of methods to any corporation which had not an interest in satisfying the consumer's needs, and

[1] See *National Guilds*, edited by A. R. Orage. See also the publications of the National Guilds League.

satisfying them at a reasonable price. Is there not a danger that the 'Guild', if its members have nothing to gain by producing commodities as cheaply as possible, will tend to perpetuate antiquated methods and processes? The doctors are hindered in doing this because they have a high standard of their own, and also because they compete one with another; but can the Guild be relied on to have a similar public spirit and public motive?

Advocates of control by the producers are more than a little apt to give the producer even more than his due, and to make the share of the State in control to some extent illusory. The objections to Union profiteering are as overwhelming as the objections to profiteering generally, and the argument against the trust holds equally when every worker in it is a shareholder. The pay of the members of the Guild must, then, not be of the nature of profit. The State must have a share in determining it, and preserve some control. This it will preserve partly in the right to withhold supplies; but it will be necessary in addition to have some regular means of friendly co-operation. The State and the Unions must not come into contact only as enemies and when they disagree; they must have some common body of general negotiation, in which the heads of the Guilds may meet the heads of the State to arrange the production and services to be demanded of the Guilds. In addition to the National Executive of each National Guild and to the Guild Congress, which represent the producers alone, there must be a joint board, equally representative of both parties. This body must be linked up, on the side of the consumers, with Parliament and with a Government Department; but it must not be directly under a Government Department and a Cabinet

THE CONTROL OF INDUSTRY

Minister. Normally, the Guild must be left to administer its own internal affairs, and to produce, by such methods as may seem to it best, the commodities required by this Joint Board and, ultimately, by the consumer. Producer and consumer together must control ends, while the Guild looks after means.

In reaching this conclusion, which in the next chapter will be made less remote and Utopian, we have allowed a great deal of what the Syndicalists claim. To Syndicalism, regarded purely as a theory of the control of industry, we have allowed that, in the normal conduct of manufacture, the producer must be the dominant partner, though the community as a whole must always reserve an ultimate power to override his will. This, however, pledges us to none of the Syndicalistic theory of the future of Society as a whole; nor are we compelled to adopt the anarchistic views of many Syndicalists. Broadly speaking, Syndicalism, like most theories that have something vital behind them, is right in what it affirms, and wrong in what it denies. The Syndicalist view of Society as a whole is, very clearly, the theorising of a man about what he does not understand—the case of the cobbler not sticking to his last over again. Syndicalism is valuable solely as a theory of the control of industry, an assertion of the producer's point of view. Even as such a theory, it is again right in what it affirms, and wrong in what it denies. It is impossible, as M. Berth desires, to "sweep out of the workshop every authority that is external to the world of Labour"; the State must always preserve a certain right to intervene. For, after all, the producer's organisation is always sectional; even the

Guild Congress represents only all the producers. Producers and consumers together form the ultimate authority. Syndicalism is wrong if it denies the community that final right, if it asserts that the right of the producer to control his industry is absolute and admits of no interference or restriction. It is right if it merely proclaims the immense value of allowing the producer the fullest possible say in the conditions of his life and work. It is not to be accepted as by itself a full or satisfactory theory of the control of industry; it is the other side of the great truth which Collectivism had imperfectly grasped. The true Socialism asserts the ultimate right of the community as a whole; but it lays stress equally on the paramount importance of leaving the control as far as possible in the hands of those who are most directly interested. Socialism cannot afford to neglect either producer or consumer; if, as Collectivism, it forgets the one, it becomes a dead theory incapable of inspiring enthusiasm or bringing about a change of heart; if, as Syndicalism, it forgets the other, it falls into sectional egoism and loses the element of community and brotherhood in individualism and self-assertion. Consumption and production are both important parts of a man's life, and no theory that leaves either out of account can touch the man where he is most alive, in his community with all others and in his daily work.

Collectivism, however, has fought its way and established its position; and Socialism is now, unfortunately, almost identified in the minds of most of its opponents, and even of its advocates, with Collectivism pure and simple. Naturally, then, as Collectivism becomes more a business proposition and less an inspiring ideal, Socialism is suffering; it can only recover and become once more a vital doctrine if it is content to adopt the good that is in Syndicalism and reconcile it with the good that is in Collectivism. This will involve the attribution, in the minds of Socialists, of a wholly new importance to Trade Unions : they must cease to be regarded as a passing phase due to the abuses of Capitalism, and be accepted as corporations which are destined not to extinction, but to a continual growth and extension of capacity. In studying the future of Trade Unionism, we shall be regarding it as the future partner of the State in the control of industry—no longer as a mere fighting organisation, existing only because the employer is there to combat, but as a self-governing, independent corporation with functions of its own, the successor of Capitalism as well as its destroyer.

CHAPTER XII

THE FUTURE OF TRADE UNIONISM

TRADE Unionism exists to-day to carry on the class-struggle. In the economic field, it stands for the workers' claim to higher wages, better conditions and a greater control over their own lives. For the moment, it is essentially there to fight, to fulfil a function in securing the justice which Society denies to its members. Engaged in a ceaseless, uphill struggle against superior economic resources, it is naturally preoccupied with the things of the moment: it is driven to make itself efficient for its immediate purpose, and has no time to look ahead, or take much interest in the remoter future. Just as the individual worker is difficult to rouse to a broad view of his situation because his economic circumstances themselves demand all his attention, Trade Unionism, intent on raising wages at least in proportion to the rise in prices, cannot be bothered with academic matters like the control of industry. It would be idle to expect from the Unions themselves any general realisation of the deeper significance of Socialism and Syndicalism, while economic pressure remains so acute, and, we may add, education so rudimentary and imperfect.

It is, therefore, all the more interesting and significant that, almost without realising it, the Unions are moving naturally and spontaneously in the direction

THE FUTURE OF TRADE UNIONISM 371

in which their theories, if they had any, would be bound to lead them. Continuing to regard themselves as mere ' fighting ' and ' friendly ' associations, they are coming gradually to make more and more demands that have nothing to do with hours or wages. There are the first beginnings, in Trade Unionism to-day, of an attempt not merely to raise the standard of life or to ' better ' conditions, but to change the industrial system, and substitute democracy for autocracy in the workshop.

As we have seen already, the first and most obvious sign of this awakening is the rising demand that membership of the Unions shall be compulsory on all workers. With, roughly, fourteen million persons engaged in industry and only round about four million Trade Unionists, we may seem far indeed from the day on which such a demand can be effectively made ; yet more and more strikes are turning every year upon this point. Although there are eleven million workers unorganised to-day, organisation in some of our great industries has already gone so far that it is becoming possible for the workers to insist on absolute solidarity. In the Coal Mines and on the Railways, in the Textile industry of Lancashire and even among Transport Workers in some ports, the non-unionist is doomed to extinction. The demand may not be granted generally at once ; but it is clear from the recent tendency that in the end it will be granted. Even now, many employers are prepared to accept it ; they realise that the day of the individual contract is gone, and aim instead at building up strong employers' associations to deal with Unions in which all their workers are enrolled.

It would be difficult to exaggerate the significance of this change. Until very recently, even the great employers put their hostility to Trade Unionism in the form of an argument in favour of 'free contract between the individual employer and the individual employee'. They tolerated the Unions, because they could not help it; but they refused, wherever they found it possible, to deal with them directly, and continued to argue that, from the point of view of the community as well as from that of the employer, all forms of trade combination were necessarily evil. Except amongst the very uneducated, this sort of argument is no longer advanced, and it is a sign of the changed times that in the Report of the Industrial Council we find, from employers and employed alike, unanimous acceptance of Trade Unionism. Not only do both sides admit that Trade Unions ought to exist; they actually express their desire that every worker, as well as every employer, should be organised.

Indeed, when once, on either side, organisation has reached a certain point and included the greater number of workers or masters in a trade, the persistence of a small section in remaining out becomes a menace to both alike. Collective bargaining, in all organised industries, is having the effect of standardising wages and conditions, and when the principle of a uniform standard is accepted, it is to the interest of both sides that it should be generally enforced.[1] Compulsory Trade Unionism, then, is accepted by all intelligent persons as being at the least theoretically desirable, whether or no they regard the use of legislation, force or organised pressure to bring it about as either just or admissible.

It will, of course, be a long time before such a state of things can be brought into being by the efforts of the workers themselves. The demand will

[1] See Chapter IX.

THE FUTURE OF TRADE UNIONISM

be made and granted first in a few highly organised trades, and from these will spread gradually outwards to more and more occupations. Every miner, every railwayman and every cotton operative will become a Trade Unionist, and then, as soon as the Trade Unions realise their business and begin a great national campaign among the unorganised, the principle will spread till, at least in all decently paid trades, the non-Unionist will be extinct. He will linger probably among the more scattered, backward and sweated occupations; but such survivals will become the exceptions instead of the rule. The Trade Unions will have established their claim, as a general rule, to include all wage-earners in the particular industries for which they cater.

There is no need, and it would be fatal, to invoke the direct aid of legislation in order to bring about this development. It will come when the time is ripe; but any attempt to make it legally compulsory would do far more harm than good. From the standpoint of the workers alone, a Union including a large minority or even a majority of enforced members would be hampered at every turn. There is all the difference in the world between a true Trade Unionist and a man who merely subscribes to a Trade Union, and, though the influx of a few such nominal Trade Unionists is not enough to weaken a strong organisation, it is only where the Union is already strong that good results can be secured by compulsion. If the Unions are in future to co-operate with the State, they must be strong enough to stand up to the State on equal terms; but bodies created artificially by the State would be so much material in its hands, to mould as it might think fitting. The only way in which compulsory Trade Unionism can profitably be brought about is by the organised pressure of the workers themselves.

This does not mean, of course, that the State should not use other means, short of compulsion, to get as many workers as possible into the Unions. Already, in Chapter IX., we have seen reason to believe that this would be forwarded by making voluntary agreements the compulsory *minimum* standard over some whole trades, and also that one of the best results to be looked for from the Trade Boards Act is the stimulation of Trade Unionism among sweated workers. There is, however, a further instance to which we must draw attention here. Whatever view we may hold on the subject of compulsory contributory Insurance, there can be no doubt that, if we are to have the bitters of it, we may as well have also such sweets as it possesses. With a little common sense on both sides, the Insurance Act might have given an enormous stimulus to Trade Unionism. No doubt, even as matters stand, a good deal of the rapid increase in Union membership is due to the operation of the Insurance Act; but though particular Unions have taken advantage of such opportunities as it offered, the Trade Union movement, as well as the Government, has much to reproach itself with. A great national campaign for members, centrally organised and controlled, just at the time when insured persons were selecting their approved societies, would have made all the difference. By a thorough reorganisation, the General Federation of Trade Unions might have been fitted, as Mr. Appleton saw, to take up the whole Insurance side of the movement, and with such a membership to draw upon, a good financial success might have been made of the venture, in the interests of the workers themselves. Once in

THE FUTURE OF TRADE UNIONISM

control of Government Insurance, the General Federation might easily have begun to oust the private companies from every form of insurance work, and the Trade Unions might have had a great movement, centrally directed, in absolute control of working-class insurance. Against the organised protest of such a body, no Government could long have dared to maintain the contributory principle. As matters stand, the Unions, despite Mr. Appleton's efforts, have failed to realise their chance, and the administration of the Act has passed largely into the hands of private concerns.

This is only partly the fault of the Unions. The crowning treachery of the Government lies in the admission of the private companies to a share in the administration of the Act. Worked through voluntary societies, as the Chancellor of the Exchequer maintained, in order to stimulate the growth of those societies, the Act was allowed to fall into the hands of profiteering companies, operating professedly in the interests of their shareholders alone. Democratic control of approved societies was faked and evaded openly, and the Government has not raised a finger to protest. Still, even with a Government whose tender care for the worker led it to make the Prudential prosperous by Act of Parliament, the Unions might have done much. Instead, when the Act was before the House, they wavered and squabbled and showed not the faintest understanding of its real bearings : when it was once law and past repeal, they relapsed into childish opposition, and refused to touch the unclean thing. However unclean the Insurance Act may be, the Unions have got, for the present at any rate, to make the best of it ; and that they can only do by using it to increase their membership.

One of the great needs, then, of the world of Labour is for more Trade Unionists. If the Unions are to bear any important part in the control of industry, they must stand not for a section, but for all the workers. At the same time, it is clear that this end can be reached only by sectional action; they will come to include all workers in all industries only by first getting into their ranks all workers in some industries. As, in any industry, the number of workers organised becomes really representative of the industry as a whole, it is possible to begin agitation against the continuance of non-Union workers. Refusal to work with non-Unionists should be an integral part of the programme of every Trade Union that is strong enough to enforce it. For not only does the non-Unionist reap the benefit of advances the Unions have won and paid for; he also prevents concerted action, and so stands in the way of further advances being secured. The question of compulsory political action being now more or less out of the way, a man can have no reasonable excuse except stupidity for not joining the Union in which his fellows are organised—and mere stupidity, as well as knavery, has to be coerced, where coercion serves a useful object. Either from stupidity or from deliberate treachery, the non-Unionist in an organised industry is a traitor to his class—and the workers have no use for traitors.

The mere non-Unionist is of course more pardonable than the 'blackleg'. He need only be forced to join the Union; the 'blackleg' should have no more protection than the law is absolutely forced to give him. In especial, the Unions must keep a very wary eye for legislation, such as the employers in the Industrial Council recommend, designed to " afford protection to those who wish to work ", that is, to

THE FUTURE OF TRADE UNIONISM

place the forces of law still more than now at the disposal of the strike-breaker. It is not as a rule wise to offer physical violence to 'blacklegs'; but there is nothing wrong about it, except in the eyes of the law and the middle class. The only argument against it, and also against militancy of other sorts, is that they do not pay.

The enrolment of more members necessitates better organisation. The Greater Unionism is essential to the successful conduct of a great campaign against the non-Unionist. The greatest weakness that now prevents the Unions from attracting new members is the overlapping and lack of co-ordination among themselves. The Unions must include all the workers in industry, and it must include them in as few Unions as possible. We saw good reason for believing that, for the present, Industrial Unionism cannot be complete; it is impossible at once to break down the existing classifications of workers and to re-sort all on the 'industrial' basis. But if, in the remoter future, the Unions are to play the part sketched out for them in the last chapter, it is clear that Industrial Unionism is the right policy, and therefore an ideal to be aimed at. When we have a Trade Union movement embracing all workers in the great industries and at the same time under strong central management and direction, it will become possible to modify their structure universally. Even as long as they remain fighting organisations, confronted with a strong employing class, the 'industrial' basis is for their purposes the best. The next problem before Trade Unionism is a great change of structure, involving widespread amalgamation and the opening of skilled Unions to the unskilled. This transition will be a difficult matter: the attempt to achieve the 'industrial' basis may easily produce fierce conflicts between the great Unions concerned—demarcation quarrels fiercer than before, because they will be not about work, but about men.

Industrial Unions, as we have seen, will be in a far better position than the existing overlapping and rival Unions for achieving the compulsory Trade Unionism which must come in time, if the control of industry is to be in any degree 'syndicalised.' At the same time, it will be realised that even the compulsory Trade Union of which 'greater' Unionists dream is not the 'Guild', the producing unit of which we are in search. It is still an organisation of employees, of dependent and, for the most part, manual workers, faced by the independent heads of production and their immediate staff of management, who remain outside the organisation. While the Union has the employer to fight, it is clear that this division must remain, that the 'Union' cannot evolve into the 'Guild', the association of dependent into that of independent producers. Nor is the position materially changed when the State becomes the employer: under private capitalism and under nationalisation alike the Unions will have to struggle to secure, step by step, a foothold in the control of industry. The way lies in both cases through Industrial Unionism.

It is necessary, therefore, to ask a little more precisely what is expected to happen when the State takes over the great monopolistic industries. The ordinary Socialist, it may be supposed, still expects the State merely to step into the employers' shoes, and run industry, much as the private capitalist has run it, for its own profit. Better wages, he agrees, and better conditions will be secured to the workers by the omnipotent and benevolent consumer-in-chief; but otherwise there will be no change. The worker will still be a 'cog in the machine'; the State will merely take the master's place as skilled machine-minder. This is the state of affairs which is often graphically depicted by its opponents as State Capitalism—a phrase which many Socialists are at a loss to understand, because they utterly fail to appreciate the producer's point of view. The State may not be, in M. Lagardelle's phrase, " a tyrannical master"; but, in the eyes of many advocates of nationalisation, it is certainly to be a 'master'; and a 'master', however benevolent, is not what the producer wants.

It is indeed perfectly true that State Capitalism is the form actually taken by nearly all national industry and trading up to the present time. The British Post Office, Foreign Railway systems, municipal trams and gasworks, all the host of national and municipal undertakings from the German State coal-mines to the street-lighting arrangements of Stow-on-the-Wold, are run on the theory that the public as an employer is merely in the position of a private employer with more or less of a conscience. This is, no doubt, in the main inevitable where public and private enterprises exist side by side, particularly where, as in the shipyards here, the mines in Germany, and the railways in France, a particular service is run partly on Collectivist and partly on Individualist lines; and there is reason to infer from the present position of State enterprise that the State as an employer will always be, at the best, no more than Mr. Cadbury multiplied by several millions—nothing but the good employer writ large. On neither side is there at present either the will or the intelligence needed to create anything better.

If, however, the State, with the open object, not only of commercial success and benefit to the consumer, but also of giving the organised producers more control over their work, and facilitating the formation of a ' Guild ' capable of carrying on industry independently, were to-morrow to introduce a Bill for the nationalisation of some great industry, what could it do to make its will effective ? Not very much, it must be admitted ; but it could make a beginning. First, it should of course recognise the men's Union, and give it every facility not merely for negotiating about wages, hours, and conditions, but also for making suggestions and co-operating, by means of committees, in the routine work of management. Secondly, with an eye to the future, instead of placing the industry directly under a Parliamentary President and a Government Department, it might set up special machinery by means of which the industry might be made an independent unit. The higher officials would, no doubt, have for the time being to be nominated from above ; but they might be nominated in such a way that it would be easy, when the time came, to transfer the whole business of electing officials to the organised industry itself. Throughout, the object should be to set up such machinery as will make easiest the ultimate transfer of control from the State Department to the organised producers, while the necessary safeguards are preserved by the State on the consumers' behalf. This should be the aim no less of the State than of the Trade Unions themselves : the scheme of National Guilds is urged in the interests of producers and consumers alike.

[1] As we shall see in Chapter XIV., Parliamentary control can be made far more effective by development of the committee system.

THE FUTURE OF TRADE UNIONISM 381

Doubtless, the transference of control will be in its earlier stages largely local; and it should be the aim of the Trade Unions to make it so. It is by entrenching themselves securely in the control of the actual business of production, locally as well as nationally, that the Unions will be able to fit themselves for taking over the conduct of the industry as a whole. If the State does not do its part, the Unions will be faced with the task of coercing it.

Within the industry itself, decentralisation of control must be carried as far as possible; every effort must be made to stimulate the sense of responsibility and control in as large a number of workers as possible; instead of a number of 'cogs in the wheel', the State must endeavour to create a body of producers all actively interested in the proper performance of responsible functions. Autocracy in the workshop is wasteful and demoralising, but as long as employed faces employer across an impassible gulf, autocracy is bound to last. The Trade Unionist has no motive for co-operating with the employer; if the State realises its duties, he will have every reason for co-operating with the State.

Moreover, National Guilds imply State ownership and, to that extent, imply nationalisation. If we are to wait for producers' control till the Unions have directly expropriated all employers, and extended their power over all industrial conditions and processes, we shall wait till doomsday—and a little after. Trade Unionists do not, in the main, desire to control industry nowadays, and, unless those who actually control it help them to realise their power, it may be long before they desire it very much more. It is the function of the State, here as elsewhere, to liberate and stimulate energy, to give the worker the fullest measure of control that he is capable of, in order that he may be got to desire more. The State exists not merely to supply, but to stimulate the demand for, the 'good life'.

It is even under nationalisation that we may hope for the greatest stimulation of the workers to a demand for the control of industry. There is, however, a grave danger that, when nationalisation comes, the State will not realise its responsibilities, and industry will merely be run on bureaucratic, instead of autocratic, principles. Nationalisation will so clearly pay the nation that a man need not have enlightened views on the future control of industry in order to be in favour of it. It is well not to put too much faith in the State and the public, and not to rely too much on their acting sensibly except under the influence of fright. It is therefore supremely important that the nascent demand for the control of industry which is springing up within Trade Unionism should not be neglected. Control can only come when, inspired from within or from without, the Unions have made themselves fit for it; and if they are even to move any appreciable distance in the direction of such fitness, they must take up a far stronger attitude than they have done in the past on important questions of principle. There are signs that the Unions are making demands for the enlargement of their sphere of control; but there are no signs that the meaning of those demands is being realised.

'Discipline' and 'management' had till quite recently been supposed, by masters and men alike, to be spheres in which the employer's authority was unquestioned. Yet recent strikes have proved over and over again that the workers are no longer prepared to submit to injustice merely because it shields itself under these names. Autocracy in these spheres is breaking down; and, as the Unions grow in strength, the collective voice will be heard more and more raising its protest against any abuse, no matter whether the master plead privilege or not. In some cases, this will no doubt lead to awkward problems. In learning to suspect the autocracy of management, the workers will very likely learn to be too suspicious; they will sometimes see injustice where no real wrong has been done, and, if they become really strong, discipline in the good sense may become difficult to enforce. But when this situation arises, it will not prove the necessity of a return to the old autocracy: for a reasonable alternative will then have presented itself. Instead of autocracy checked by insurgence, it will then be possible to set up real democratic government: instead of the official, manager, and foreman appointed from above, industry will begin to be governed by rulers appointed from below. The workers, having learnt how to interfere in control, will then assume actual government, just as modern democracies have begun by enforcing concessions by insurrection and have then gradually forced their way to recognition and habitual control. Instead of unconstitutional government, the workers will rule by constitutional government, and industrial democracy will be well in sight.

It is sometimes said that the most tyrannous rulers the working-class can have are those who have been promoted from the ranks, and that if you gave the ruled governors from his own class he would ask to have the aristocracy back the next day. There is much in this argument, and there will always be much, while the class structure of Society continues.

In the main, this difficulty in producers' control can be conquered only by education : voluntary adult education, especially in the case of the Workers' Educational Association, is gradually producing a type of man who would not be a petty tyrant, but a sympathetic leader, capable of understanding the working-class, and remaining of it, even if his standards rose higher than those of his fellows. But the difficulty will be conquered by education of another sort also: the extension of Trade Union demands will gradually produce a type of man more capable of exercising control at once over others and over himself. The Trade Union will change little by little from an association of dependent producers to a 'Guild' of independent producers, in which all degrees of skill and intelligence will be found harmoniously co-operating. The Trade Union will come ultimately to include the 'management' as well as the employees because it will itself evolve managers.

In the case of the 'checkweighman' in the mining industry, there is an official elected by the Union and recognised by the employer, and the office of the checkweighman in the pit is often very much more than his name implies.[1] There is no reason whatever why, as education spreads, and the Unions extend their demands, this principle of an elected management should not be carried very much farther, and such an extension would be made easier if the State took over an industry and the capitalist ceased to control. For there would then cease to be two classes in permanent opposition within the industrial sphere ; the State might learn to run industry, not autocratically for profit, but to get it run as well as possible in the interest of the community in general.

[1] The right, now legally established, of the checkweighman to be also an inspector of mines has added greatly to his power.

THE FUTURE OF TRADE UNIONISM 385

A particularly interesting example of the growing share of the Unions in actual control may be taken from the present position in the South Wales coalfield. The South Wales Miners' Federation will no longer allow any pit to get to work until the price-lists of the wages to be paid have been passed by the Federation as conforming to the standard rates of the district. The owner may do the preliminary work of preparing the pit and opening up the shafts; but before he can take out a ton of coal, or begin to recoup himself for his outlay, the Union intervenes and dictates, within limits, the conditions he is to observe. Applying mainly to wages, this system does not involve any new principle; but it is a significant instance of the growth of power and solidarity among the workers. Where formerly the standard rate would have been secured, if at all, by a strike when the pit was actually working, it is now impossible for the pit to get to work without making the concession in advance. In the old sphere of control over wages, the Unions are getting more power and more recognition; the Union rate is being recognised as the standard rate.

We may expect, then, that, alike under Capitalism and where an industry is publicly owned and directed, the future will show the Union developing gradually the powers and the faculties necessary for control. First will come the stage of mere recognition, in which the capitalist, public or private, will negotiate directly with the Union, as an external body. The Union will still be a fighting organisation, engaged in industrial warfare; but it will have made the first step towards an actual share in Government by securing the recognition of its right to protest, just as the political rights of democracy are derived from the first recognition of a negative right of the Commons to protest. Nominally, the decision will remain at this stage with the capitalist, and the Union's share in control will depend mainly on the amount of external pressure it can bring to bear; but really the worker will have secured a footing in control, and made the way easier for the second step. Then will come a number of stages, in public enterprise at any rate, where the Union is being taken more and more into partnership, and the system of dual management will be developed. The officer elected by the Union will meet in the middle the officer nominated by the State, and will drive him gradually out of the lower posts till the process culminates in the extinction of the State official, in the realm of actual industry.[1] Finally will come the stage where the Union will be a 'hierarchical' body, including all workers actually engaged in production or transport, whether their labour is manual or managerial; the control of the State being limited, from this point, to that part of management which is outside production and has to do with the regulation of supply and demand and the like, and with the harmonising of the interests of producer and consumer. This last stage will be what the *New Age* writers call Guild Socialism, which is being represented here merely as the logical outcome of the Greater Unionism.

If this view of the future control of industry is adopted, it is clear that many difficult problems arise, at the present day, in connection with the attitude to be adopted by the State towards the Unions and, still more, by the Unions towards the State.

The State of the present, for very incompetence and short-sightedness, is in the main unaware of the problems it has to face. Its policy is opportunism,

[1] This will be accompanied by a similar growth of control in privately run industries.

the muddling through accompanied by loose thinking which are what the Englishman calls ' common sense '. It therefore settles each question as it arises, without consideration of wider issues : it takes the Unions as it finds them, and is wholly unconcerned with their possible or proper functions in the society of the future. As a result, it congratulates itself on its own failures, and regards the record of its wasted opportunity as a clear demonstration of the eternal rightness of the ' practical man '.

France, on the other hand, sometimes lets an idealist climb to power. Waldeck-Rousseau, the Premier who passed the Trade Union Act of 1884, faced, before they had become at all clearly defined, the difficult problems of the relation between the Unions and the State. And it is at least arguable that, by trying too soon to take the Unions to some extent into partnership, he produced the violent revolt of the Labour movement against all forms of State control which gave birth to the C.G.T. If the State, while the Unions still mistrust its sincerity, attempts to take them into partnership in any way that involves a sacrifice of independence to compensate for an increased authority, it will merely drive them into revolt and put back once again the possibility of that real co-operation which will come only when both sides are ready to enter into it willingly. The present need is for the State as employer to do its best to foster the growth and independence of the Unions by giving them recognition ; they must learn to deal with the State in industry as external bodies before they can learn to come in and join the State in actual management. The view that ultimately the Unions will become real and recognised organs of the community by no means involves the view that they should sacrifice their power or their autonomy. In order to be able to co-operate, they must be able to negotiate on equal terms.

The Trade Union has harder problems to face, and here again the situation is complicated by the tendency to muddle through and consider only the questions of the moment as they arise. Feeling quite rightly that their associations exist above all to fight the capitalist, as the instruments of collective bargaining and the assertion of working-class solidarity, Trade Unionists are always fearful that any sort of co-operation with the State means emasculation. They hear politicians talk glibly about ' social peace ', and, realising that artificial social peace is the modern substitute for the Bastille and the *lettre de cachet*, they naturally suspect that the State will be equally unfriendly to all their aspirations. They are therefore determined to preserve, above all, an absolute isolation from governmental functions, " to resist to the death ", as a French writer puts it, " all attempts to draw the working-class into the capitalist sphere ". You cannot, they maintain, at once fight the enemy and co-operate with him ; and the State is the corner-stone of the edifice of Capitalism.

This argument is difficult to answer, and there is a great deal of truth in it. The Unions must at all costs preserve their independence, and any advances made by the State must be rejected instantly, if they involve any sacrifice of independence. But just as the State is being driven, against the will of the rulers, to interfere more and more with industry, the Unions are being driven, and will in the future be driven far more, to co-operate in the task of Government. The Insurance Act is not an isolated phenomenon : it is a typical instance of the modern tendency. Hating the Act and wishing only to abolish it or at least drastically amend it, the Unions are forced all the same to administer it, if they wish to retain and increase their membership. A group of Unions as strong as the Miners' Federation may be able to say it will have nothing to do with the Act—though such a policy may well prove to have been short-sighted and choleric— ; but the majority of Unions certainly could not afford to allow offended dignity so much latitude. Willing or unwilling, they had to come in and do the Government's bidding. They realised this: what they failed to understand was that, having to toe the line, they had better toe it with the best grace they could. They might, by collecting the crumbs the Act threw them, have taken up seven baskets full—in the sense that they might have doubled their membership. Their preference for a policy of splendid isolation lost them their opportunity, and failed to preserve for them their isolation: they are in the Act, but they are in it as subordinate partners to the Prudential.

No one can say what will be the next question in connection with which the same problem will arise; but it is certain that, more and more, the Unions will find themselves called on to decide between co-operation and uncompromising hostility. But the Unions, as the C.G.T. has found, cannot afford to tackle two enemies at once; they have their hands full with the capitalist, without taking on the State in addition more than they can help. They will be forced, indeed, to show the State a strong front on many occasions, especially when the State acts the part of strike-breaker; but they will do this none the less efficiently for realising that the State need not be throughout, the capitalist dodge they are apt to represent it as being. The State represents the consumer—

imperfectly indeed ; for it represents him only in the distorting-mirror of a powerful governing class—but it has, at least sometimes, to act up to the standards of the community as a whole. There is much that the Unions can gain, even from a ' capitalist ' Government ; and their object should be to get all they can without sacrificing their independence. Let them think less of isolation, and more of independence ; and they will find, in the State, the means of strengthening their position against Capitalism—and, if need be, against the State itself.

When, therefore, the State sets up semi-public bodies such as the Port of London Authority—to take a particularly bad instance—it is useless for the Unions to say that the Port of London Authority represents the employers—though that is true in the main—and that they will have nothing to do with it. They gain more by using even the inadequate representation given them than by standing altogether outside. What little good work the Authority has done has been due very largely to the efforts of the two representatives of Labour—Mr. Gosling and Mr. Orbell. If again, in a Bill for the Nationalisation of Railways, they are offered representation on the governing body, let them not refuse it ; let them use it to put their case before the State authority. Even such inadequate grants of participation in government are of immense value, and may well be the starting-point for a general transfer of the normal control of industry to the organised producers. Let them come in and cooperate ; but at the same time let them strengthen their independent organisations and bring to bear all the pressure they can. The power of the Unions alone can turn the inadequate concessions of the present into the real working partnership of the future.

THE FUTURE OF TRADE UNIONISM

Syndicalism then, or whatever we choose to call the growing assertion of the producer's point of view, turns out, on closer inspection, to involve a far less violent and antagonistic attitude on the part of the Unions to the State than has generally been supposed. As long as the employer can raise prices to cover an increasing wages-bill, it will be impossible for the Unions to put in practice the direct expropriation of which they dream, to make industry actually unprofitable to the capitalist. The consumer pays; and the producer, though he may extend his sphere of control and improve his relative position, does not eliminate rent and profits. This elimination, indeed, cannot and should not be accomplished sectionally, by a single body of producers acting for themselves alone; it is essentially the business of the State—a general problem affecting all and demanding general treatment. Nationalisation may be a half-way house to producers' control. As we shall see in the next chapter, the adoption of this view necessitates a revised estimate of the value and importance of political action: the general strike is a wild dream, and even Mr. Tom Mann, is his recent book, seems prepared to throw it overboard. Expropriation is the State's business; and the development of the new forms of industrial control must be coupled with the growth of State ownership. Nationalisation retains all the importance assigned to it in Socialist theory; but it becomes a means, and not an end in itself.

The future of Trade Unionism accordingly depends on the spirit in which it approaches the task of working out for itself a status in Society, of changing gradually from a fighting to a producing body, as the conditions of Society are modified. The class-structure of Society necessitates the class-struggle; but the class-struggle is, by virtue of its object, only a phase. What, then, is to be the function of the Trade Unions when there are no private employers left to fight ? Is it then to seek out another enemy and wage a new war against the State ? If it does this it will fail : for the State is far stronger than the employer, and might crush the Unions if it were left uncaptured. It is a poor theory of Society that regards industrial warfare as permanent ; such warfare is presumably directed to the securing of justice, and will cease when justice has been secured. The Trade Unions will then have a higher function than mere industrial soldiering to perform : they will be engaged in a task which arises, not out of social antagonism, but out of social solidarity. The Greater Unionism involves not merely conscription of the workers for the class-war, but the enrolment of every worker in that industrial army which exists fundamentally not to foment revolution, but to produce wealth. The Unions have to fight sham social peace and shoddy patriotism ; but they have to work for the realisation of that real peace which can come only with the dissolution of the capitalist system and the substitution for it of a Society dominated throughout by the producer's point of view, which is the spirit of social service. If the Unions can be made strong and intelligent, there is no need to fear the 'Servile' State; service is not servility, and the man who is doing the work of the community will not need either to touch his hat to any master or to be always on the look out for a fight. The Trade Unions must fight in order that they may control ; it is in warring with Capitalism that they will learn to do without Capitalism ; but they must realise their freedom in partnership with, and not in opposition to the State.

CHAPTER XIII

ECONOMICS AND POLITICS

To a great extent, the conclusions that will be reached in this chapter have been presupposed in all that has gone before. We cannot be clear in our own minds about the structure the Unions should develop, or about the attitude the State should adopt towards them, unless we are already in possession of a theory on the more general question of the relation between economics and politics, between economic and political action, both in the present and hereafter. If we hold that the destiny of the State is to be merged in the institutions of the producers, our view of the sphere of economic action in the present will be profoundly altered; if, on the other hand, we believe in the permanency and necessity of the State, we shall take a different view alike of the present and of the future of Trade Unionism. The 'Sovereignty' towards which we wish to see the Unions moving will be in the one case a 'political Sovereignty' coextensive with all common action that requires co-ordination and control, and in the other a purely 'economic Sovereignty', aiming solely at the control of industry and recognising in other spheres the paramount right and authority of the State. It will have become clear in the preceding chapters that the latter view is that which has been adopted in this book, and that, on the view that is here maintained, it is possible to remain a Socialist while recognising the value of Syndicalism.

The whole problem of government is essentially bound up with the control of industry. Whether the economic interpretation of history be true or false, or a bit of both, no one will deny the paramount importance of economic considerations in the modern State. Even those who criticise the world of Labour for testing legislation by its influence on the economic position of the workers generally apply an equally rigid standard, and ask, of each proposal, whether it is " good for trade ". Both sides are primarily interested in economics ; only their economic theories differ.

When, therefore, Mr. Balfour attacks the Labour Party on the ground that it is a class-party, representing not the will of the community as a whole, but the organised interests of a section, he is guilty either of perversion or of narrow-mindedness. The existence of a class-party is bad, but the existence of the class-structure of Society is worse ; and as long as the class-structure survives, political organisations, in so far as they have any reality at all, will inevitably reflect that structure. Sweep away classes, and there will be no more parties representing a class ; sweep away the class-party, and the class will remain, but will be unrepresented. It is easy to see which alternative involves the greater injustice.

If, then, politics are to possess reality, there must be a party standing definitely for the dispossessed. Whether it be ' Socialist ', or ' Labour ', or anything else by name, it will be distinguished from the capitalist parties by the fact that it is out to give expression to a theory, to vindicate the rights of Labour not merely to slightly improved conditions of villeinage, but to actual independence and control, both political and economic. This must be the distinctive mark of any party that is to have the right to call itself a ' Labour ' or ' Socialist ' Party, or to make a third in the ' flat-catching ' of General Elections. A party that stands for none of these things has no right to call itself by any such name, even if it gets its members elected. It is ' capitalist ' in theory and outlook, and therefore incapable of representing the real will of Labour.

To attack the Parliamentary Labour Party nowadays may look rather like flogging a dead horse. If a General Election came to-morrow, there is not the least doubt that ' Labour ' would lose many seats,[1] and that those it retained would belong to it by Liberal favour and sufferance. The party consists of about thirty Liberals, often of the mildest type, and six or seven Socialists. It is led by a man who quite honestly believes in independent Labour representation, but believes also in the Liberal alliance. It consists largely of men who do not believe in independent Labour representation at all, and of a small section that does not believe in the Liberal alliance. That is to say, it is under a strong personality who is both a Liberal and a Socialist—of sorts ; but it consists of Liberals or Socialists, and not of hybrids. The philosophic outlook which has enabled Mr. Ramsay Macdonald to span the impassable gulf is not intelligible to the simpler souls he has to lead. They do not detect the finer Hegelianism in a party that is both ' independent ' and ' not independent ' ; they can only scratch their heads in bewilderment when they are asked to be Liberals most of the time, and then suddenly told, on a spectacular occasion, that they have to demonstrate to the world their absolute independence of the Liberal Party. Mr. Macdonald threads his

[1] 1913.

way cunningly; but his party is not sophisticated enough to follow him, and it looks as if the united Labour Party were about to "pass into otherness", and become many, if we may speak of Mr. Macdonald's poor little party in his own Hegelian language.

Certainly to the man in the street, and to some extent even to Socialists, recent events at by-elections have been very perplexing. First we had Leicester : a vacancy occurred in the Liberal half of a two-member constituency returning a Liberal and Mr. Macdonald. The Labour Party decided, against the wish of the I.L.P., not to contest the seat, whether from lack of funds or from fear of endangering Mr. Macdonald's position at the next election. After some delay, an independent Socialist candidate was brought forward, and the Liberal nominee seemed in danger. A curious passage then happened between the Labour Whip, Mr. Roberts, and Sir Maurice Levy, a Leicestershire Liberal member ; in consequence of a communication made by Mr. Roberts, a message seeming to come officially from the Labour Party was used everywhere on Liberal platforms to get the workers to support the Liberal against the Socialist. Until the election was over, no denial of the message was issued ; and the denial then made was promptly refuted by Sir Maurice Levy. Finally, Mr. Roberts offered a formal apology, and nothing more was said. The impression, however, remained in everybody's mind that the Labour Party was not so independent as it pretended to be.

Then came Chesterfield. The Derbyshire Miners put forward a candidate in place of their late leader, Mr. James Haslam. Mr Kenyon was adopted by the Trades Council and seemed to be an accredited Labour candidate. The next that was heard was that he had been officially adopted by the local Liberal Association.

and the suggestion was made that Mr. Macdonald and Mr. Ure should speak for him from the same platform. Such dependence was far too open to be tolerated : Mr. Kenyon got a strongly worded letter from Mr. Macdonald, and was repudiated by the Labour Party. Subsequently, the Chesterfield Trades Council reversed its decision. Mr. Scurr was put up by the extremists or 'rebels' as a Socialist candidate. In the sequel, Mr. Kenyon was elected by as big a majority as Mr. Haslam had got in 1910, and Mr. Scurr polled only a trifle over 500 votes. The withdrawal of official Labour support, in a Trade Union constituency, had no effect whatever upon the result.

After the event, Mr. Macdonald [1] has explained that his strongly worded letter meant nothing. He and his friends of the Labour Party, we are told, did nothing to embarrass Mr. Kenyon, and we are given to understand that he views with enthusiasm the return of a Lib.-Lab. whose chief tenet appears to be an almost theological reverence for the Chancellor of the Exchequer. Very wisely, Mr. Macdonald wishes those Labour members who are pure Liberals to clear out of the Labour Party; the curious thing is that he should seem so anxious for them to get elected. The Labour Party falls between two stools : it is neither professedly a wing of Liberalism nor in any sense a really independent party. Such a policy must be fatal in the long-run; seeing that Labour in effect runs in alliance with Liberalism, its supporters will return to that section of the Coalition which is in a position to give them what it pleases; the Labour Party as a 'dependent-independent' party is doomed to ultimate extinction.

[1] In an interview quoted in the *Daily Citizen* of August 25, from the *Aberdeen Free Press*.

In this connection, considerable interest attaches to the views of Mr. James Holmes, the recent unsuccessful Labour candidate for Crewe. Mr. Holmes is in favour of accepting and professing the Liberal alliance, of securing a working arrangement about seats, and campaigning jointly at the next election all over the country. If we are to have a dependent party at all, this is clearly the right policy; by becoming openly a wing of Liberalism, Labour may retain nearly all its seats, and even gain more in the industrial districts. The position would then be one that even Labour leaders could understand; and Mr. Walsh, Mr. Hancock, Mr. Kenyon and the rest would cease from troubling. After all, Mr. Keir Hardie is getting old, and there are very few others who would make a fuss.

But what, in Heaven's name, is the use of a Labour Party of this sort? The Parliamentary Committee of the Trades Union Congress, with the organised workers behind it, could do far more by bartering working-class support at elections for real concessions in the economic sphere. That is how the Trade Union Act of 1876 was won; and there is much to be said for the method. The policy of a purely dependent Labour Party is fit to be supported only by Liberal working-men in search of safe seats.

There is another policy, which Mr. Philip Snowden has been putting forward tentatively in recent articles in the *Labour Leader*. Is it not worth while to chance the consequences and go out for real independence? It is true that the Labour Party would probably be reduced by such a policy to about a quarter of its present strength; but, as Mr. Snowden holds, it is at least arguable that such a small, fighting group would be of far more service to Labour than the present party with an appearance of strength far beyond what it really possesses. Mr. Keir Hardie, Mr. Snowden, Mr. O'Grady, Mr. Thorne, Mr. Jowett and one or two others form a nucleus for the growth of a real Socialist Party capable of voicing the wider aspirations of the workers in the political field. Such an independent Labour Party would undoubtedly have a hard fight, especially for funds; but if it succeeded in holding its own, it could do far more valuable service than the present party, which only serves as a means of catching the Socialist vote in the country for Liberal measures in Parliament.

One other solution has been proposed—independent Socialist representation. Such representation is, of course, what is really wanted; but with the Socialist movement in its present state, it is impossible to look for the co-operation needed to build up a strong party. The failure of the B.S.P. and of the 'industrial' Lansburyites shows clearly enough that it is impossible, as yet, to build up an independent political force outside the Labour Party. The solution lies, then, rather in purging the Labour Party itself, and the Chesterfield by-election gives hope that the process is already beginning. Trade Unions raising funds for political representation on a voluntary basis must have the way left open to them for coming into the Party; and out of them, the Independent Labour Party and the Fabian Society, with, ultimately, the B.S.P. and the 'rebel' Heraldites, it may be possible to build up a really strong Socialist Party, whether it call itself 'Socialist' or 'Labour'.

What then, in our view, would be the function of such a party? Even the Syndicalists of the South Wales Miners' Federation declare themselves in favour of revolutionary political action; but what exactly is meant by this word 'revolutionary'? It is sometimes said that Labour in politics should confine itself to "furthering economic emancipation", that it should regard itself as "merely auxiliary to the industrial arm". Such a position is put forward by M. Lagardelle in France,[1] and by the *New Age* in this country. But before we can say how far it should be endorsed, it is necessary to look into it more closely. Is political Labour confined to this auxiliary function, not merely to-day and to-morrow, but essentially and for ever? Or is it only urged that the sole useful service a Labour Party has it in its power to do at the present time is to prevent legislation against strikes, and to call the attention of Parliament to the pressing economic problems that confront the working-class?

Clearly, if we have been right in our theory of the future of industrial society, Parliamentary Labour, or Socialism, will have, in the future, an immense part to play. Nationalisation, we have seen, does not become unimportant because the importance of the producer is recognised: it becomes far more important. As the control of industry cannot be assumed in a day, the State will have its part in the process of transition, and it is of the first importance that the power should be in the hands of a strong, democratic Government capable of appreciating the working-class point of view. Parliament will have, in future, not merely to clear the ring for the industrial struggle, but to intervene more and more, and to take over control from the capitalist, while on their side the workers are assuming control.

If, however, the insistence on the subordinate

[1] *Le Socialisme Ouvrier*, passim.

ECONOMICS AND POLITICS

function of Parliament has reference only to the present, it is still, indeed, exaggerated; but it is broadly right. Labour cannot hope, within a measurable space of time, to command a majority: it is condemned to perpetual opposition, and, consequently, has to rely on the weapon of organised protest. Such a Labour Party as was advocated above would not, as a rule, be important by virtue of its actual voting strength; it would depend for its power on the organised force behind it in the country as a whole. It would therefore be concerned mainly with urging upon the attention of Parliament the economic demands of the workers it stood for; and the concessions it obtained would vary with the power of the Trade Unions to make themselves a nuisance if their demands were refused. It would, in this sense, be merely seconding, and registering the fruits of, economic action or power.

Broadly speaking, therefore, we may admit that, for the present, the task of the Labour Party is secondary, and that, in a House still dominated by class-interests, it can only hope to get listened to in so far as it has organised force behind it. At this point, however, the advocate of political action as to-day the strongest weapon in the workers' hands generally turns round upon his opponent with a *tu quoque*. "You say," he urges, "that political action is impotent; but what about industrial action? The strike fails far more regularly and far more fatally to accomplish what it promises. For every rise in wages, prices go up threefold; and, even so, it is becoming more and more impossible for the workers, however organised, to face the organised employers on equal terms. The strike is played out; instead, we must convince men of the need for stronger political action, by which alone the expropriation of the ruling class can be brought about."

This argument, coupled with the sentimental objection that the strike is 'barbarous', is so often advanced that something has to be said about it. In the first place, it is quite true that the strike is barbarous and horrible; but if it succeeds, it is a necessary evil which pays on the whole. The worker cannot afford to have too many feelings for the community till the community develops feelings for him: till then, it is even good that the consumer should sometimes suffer for the injustices he allows to go on. The consumer is not the innocent third party he is often represented as being; he is the exploiter's accomplice before the fact.

If, then, strikes do or can succeed, what we want is more strikes. If they do not and cannot succeed, we must give up our antiquated weapon, and forsake the blunderbuss of economic action for the scientific precision of the parliamentary repeating rifle. Should we find, however, that the blunderbuss, awkward as it is, contains real shot, while the rifle is provided only with blank cartridges, we may prefer to retain the older and more cumbrous weapon. The difficulty is to find any means of testing the two on their merits. Clearly, Labour has often missed its enemy with the blunderbuss; but whether the parliamentary rifleman has aimed crooked and missed, or aimed straight with a blank cartridge, it is a trifle difficult to determine.

In the past, strikes have often failed and often succeeded. Political action on the part of Labour has achieved nothing at all, since the passing of the Trade Disputes Act. This year,[1] every section of the Coalition has driven its bargain with the Govern-

[1] 1913.

ment, except the Labour Party ; Labour alone has got only kicks for its ha'pence. On the other hand, since 1900, prices have risen out of all proportion to the rise in wages, and the worker was undoubtedly, in 1910, far worse off than he had been ten years before. Four years of Liberalism, with quite a strong Labour group in Parliament, had done nothing to raise the worker's standard of life. But neither, it is urged, had industrial action done anything. The answer is that from 1900 to 1910, the workers allowed their economic organisations to go to sleep. The rediscovery of political action, after a preparatory period, brought a strong Labour Party into being in 1906, and round this the hopes of the workers were centred. By 1910, the Unions, if they had not lost their illusions about the Labour Party, had at least realised the need to supplement it, and the Labour Unrest followed. We must judge of the success or failure of economic action, not by its achievements over the whole period from 1900 to 1913, but by what it has done since 1910.

During these three years, at any rate, the strike has shown its power. Though there have, of course, been failures, it cannot be disputed that, as soon as the workers began once more to apply the industrial weapon, wages began to go up and conditions to be improved. Both the national Transport strike of 1911 and the national Railway strike brought the workers in those industries large advances, and the recent strikes in the Black Country were also, in the main, very successful. It has been demonstrated clearly that the strike is not played out, and that, on the contrary, real wages can be made to keep pace with the rise in prices only if Labour is ceaselessly active in the economic sphere. The instances of failure, the London Transport strike of 1912 and the Leith strike of 1913, admit of other explanations. They failed, not because strikes must fail, but because they were declared at the wrong moment, and because the organisation behind them was weak. Those who refuse to believe that strikes *must* fail are far from thinking that strikes always succeed.

Indeed, the successes that have been recorded are far more surprising than the failures. Politically, Labour is a co-ordinated movement, capable of united action and possessed by a common policy: yet it has achieved nothing. Economically, Labour is hopelessly divided. The various Unions are almost without co-ordination and wholly without a common method and policy. There is no central authority, and there is no common brain. If results have been got with such an instrument as present-day Trade Unionism, there is every hope for the future. For the use of the industrial weapon is already teaching the workers that better organisation is necessary: they are seeing that strikes fail, where they fail, largely because the forces of Labour are not united, and succeed, where they succeed, in spite of the Unions' weakness and disunion. The Greater Unionism will add enormously to the economic power of the workers; it will make successful strikes far more frequent, and will often make strikes unnecessary. The Railwaymen have already found this out; since they won their national strike in 1911, they have achieved the fusion of three out of the four Railway Unions; and it is easy to see, from the temper generally displayed among them, that they realise how enormously unity has increased their strength. The day of small Unions is past; but the day of strikes has by no means gone with it.

The contention of Mr. Snowden [1] was that the only strikes that have any chance of succeeding nowadays are the small strikes, by which he seemed to mean the scattered and almost unorganised uprisings of sweated workers. No strike, according to him, can succeed nowadays without the support of public opinion. These contentions have been proved to be false by the events of the last three years. Small strikes have succeeded, but so have big strikes, and there have been less failures in the case of large than of small stoppages. Naturally, the unrest has tempted a good many workers who are very badly organised and very weak in economic resource to try their luck along with the others; and it is true that such strikes have succeeded, as a rule, only where plenty of public support has been forthcoming. But, without any real public opinion either for or against, other great upheavals have succeeded; and if we are to draw any moral from recent events, it should be that organised strikes have every chance of success where the Unions behind them are really strong. The sectional strike and the local strike, unsupported by the national organisations, have proved their weakness; but the moral is not that the strike weapon should be thrown aside as useless, but that the workers should improve their organisations to secure full solidarity. Not statutory regulation of wages, but the Greater Unionism, is what the experience of the last three years ought to teach.

When, however, we go on to ask whether industrial action can, by itself, bring about the social revolution, the same answer will not suffice. Even if strikes can succeed in raising real wages and in bettering conditions, it does not follow that they can ever,

[1] In *The Living Wage.*

by themselves, bring about the expropriation of the capitalist. Nor does it follow that, even if they could, they would be the best means of doing so. For if, as the Industrial Democracy League recommends, the South Wales Miners could, by a series of encroachments, actually make industry unprofitable for the capitalist, and so succeed in taking it over for themselves,[1] they might still remain, from the point of view of the community as a whole, a profiteering body, with economic interests quite likely to conflict with those of the whole mass of producers and consumers. They might have acquired, by direct action, the valuable property which now belongs to the coal-owners; but, if that property is to be used in the interests of the whole people, it must belong not to a section, but to the community. Guild profiteering may be better than the private capitalist; but it is not Socialism, and there is no guarantee of its acting equitably. The object of Socialism is to sweep away profiteering altogether, and to use the work of all in the interests of all; the object is emphatically not to entrench the coal-miners in the place of the coal-owners.

Even then, if direct action could bring about revolution, there would be dangers involved in its use. Expropriation is a matter for common, and not for sectional, action; the control of the producer over industry ought to act as a co-ordinating, and not as a disintegrating force. In speaking of the General Strike, we saw that, if it were possible, it would be unnecessary, because the community could do its work far better.[2] But we also saw that there is very

[1] See *The Miners' Next Step*, and cf. Chapter VIII. of this book.
[2] Cf. Chapter VI.

little chance of the General Strike becoming possible : it presupposes such a standard of education among the workers that bureaucracy would have lost all its dangers. A democracy so educated would be perfectly capable of controlling its rulers ; and it will hardly be disputed that, in such a case, political and industrial action would go hand in hand, and national ownership would be realised together with producers' control.

Similarly, it is inconceivable that, even in a single industry, the workers should reach such a stage as to be ready and fitted to take over the control of industry before the State has actually stepped in and nationalised that service. To make such encroachments on Capitalism, the Union would have to be enormously strong ; but, having reached such strength, it would have to make its demand of the State. There is this further difficulty. The theory that industry will be syndicalised by gradual encroachments on the employers always assumes that the private employer will still exist. But it is absolutely certain that, long before the Miners are in a position to make any complete demand for control, the mines will have been nationalised. It is of the State that they will have to make their demand, and it will suit their purpose far better to persuade the State to grant it than to fight the State for it. Political action will go hand in hand with economic action in developing the new method of control.

Of course, this does not mean that the method of gradual encroachment is not right up to a point. The Unions will fit themselves for their partnership in control with the State by strengthening their organisation and making increasing demands upon the capitalist. They may well have a firm foothold in control before the State takes over the industry. But this does not alter the essential nature of the process : sooner or later, they will find themselves face to face with the State, and, for both parties, friendly co-operation will be far more advantageous than internecine warfare. If nationalisation is to mean a change of heart as well as a change in business methods, the State and the Unions must co-operate in bringing about the new commonwealth of industry.

The Unions, therefore, will have need of the State when they address themselves to the task of democratising industry. But will not the State, equally, have need of the Unions ? It is not difficult to see how real this need, too, will be. Nationalised to-day, no industry could help being run, in the main, very like any capitalist enterprise. The Unions have neither the character, nor the will, to co-operate in management. They have evolved neither the structure, nor the government, nor the men required for such a task. Before the State can hope to relieve itself of the industrial burden, the Unions must have become far stronger, more cohesive, and more self-reliant. It is all to the State's interest that the Unions to-day should exercise every possible pressure upon the capitalist and upon itself, if by so doing they may develop the new powers which are essential to their proper functioning in the future.

It is still the accepted theory among politicians that the less the State interferes with industry the better. Like the demand for ' social peace,' this view has a solid foundation of common sense. Social war has no business within the State, and the State has no business in industry. But in both cases it is mere wilful hypocrisy to blink the facts. If the State has no business in industry, neither has the capitalist—

and the State must help to turn him out. If there ought not to be a class-war, neither ought there to be classes—and the State must help to sweep them away. The State has to go into industry to set it in order ; and then it has to come out. *Laissez faire* is only justified when things are going well; for the present muddle and injustice, drastic interference alone is adequate.

This view, of course, is directly in conflict with the expressed theory of most Syndicalists. The State, they tell us, must be destroyed root and branch ; it must not only be cleared out of industry, but abolished altogether. The producers, organised in Industrial Unions, Trades Councils and in a General Federation of Trade Unions and Trades Councils, are perfectly capable of carrying on the whole work of the nation.

The view has been already expressed that, generally speaking, Syndicalism is right in what it asserts, and wrong in what it denies, and that, in the industrial sphere, it has hold of the valuable truth that industry should be run by the producer for the consumer, and that the consumer should not perpetually stand over the producer with a whip giving his orders. But Syndicalism tends to neglect the equally important truth that industry should not be run by the producer for the producer, and that the producer should not perpetually present a pistol at the consumer's head, and proclaim that unless the consumer pays his price, no commodities will be forthcoming. Even in industry the consumer has a function; for he consumes the fruits of industry, and has a right to get them at a just price. Outside industry, in the general business of government, the case against Syndicalism is overwhelmingly stronger. The modern world has got industry on the brain, and can think of nothing else; when it has asserted that the

State has no function in industry, it believes that this involves denying the State any function at all. But the preoccupation of the State with industrial questions is a mere phase in its development, caused mainly by the Industrial Revolution and the advent of machine-production. As the State gets clear of the meshes of industrialism in which the nineteenth century caught it fast, new State functions will emerge, and it will be seen more clearly that politics are wider than economics. Industrialism has stunted the State's growth : it has fed it on the unwholesome diet of the class-war, and let it into a premature decay. But if once the incubus of industrialism could be removed, the State would recover its health, and begin once again to give expression to the spirit of community and nationality which pervades every people whose national life is sound. Could the control of industry be handed over to the producers, and could all profiteering be eliminated, the State would be set free to work for the deepening of national life, for the realisation of a greater joy and a greater individuality. It would be liberated to work for the liberation of energy, instead of being preoccupied with the sordid task of patching up a false social truce and concealing the bankruptcy of the national life fund.

Two examples must suffice. The lot of a Minister of Education at the present day is not a happy one. Everybody knows that the nation is under-educated, and that, if Great Britain is losing ground, it is because the minds of her citizens are not allowed to develop. Yet no Cabinet and no Parliament is prepared to provide the money needed for making our national education worthy of a great people.

There is no Minister of Health ; but this is not

because the people is too healthy to need one. It is generally admitted that the greater part of the misery, the poverty, the drunkenness and the crime that poison our national life can be directly traced to disease and underfeeding. Yet no Cabinet and no Parliament will stir a finger to alter all this. It would cost too much. Instead of a great measure for the prevention of disease and destitution, we have the miserable Insurance Act passed to make the worker pay for patching him up when his ailments impair his industrial efficiency.

This sort of neglect is enough to account for the attitude of Syndicalists towards the State. The State has done nothing to deserve their respect; and no very encouraging answer can be given when they ask what prospect there is of its reformation. But the one state of mind that, however intelligible it may be, is never pardonable is social despair; and the attitude which the Syndicalists have taken up is, in effect, an abandonment of the problem. We must have the State to carry on crusades for the improvement of public education and public health; and, however scandalous the State's neglect of these things may be, the remedy lies, not in abolishing, but in reforming it. The Syndicalists are right in thinking that the Trade Unions are the most powerful instruments for the education of the people; they are wrong in thinking that they will end by destroying the State.

Economic action, then, is the first thing now, in order that political action may become the first thing hereafter. Educated in the Unions, the workers must learn to conquer the still greater association of which all, men and women alike, are members. They must not despair of the problem, or seek to sweep away the State, merely because it has strayed from its proper purpose. They must realise that it is the State's business to distribute wealth and to arrange services, to provide for the well-being of the whole, and to afford every individual full means of self-expression. Economics will then be seen as only a branch of the true politics, by means of which the people co-ordinates and controls the whole life of the body politic, while it leaves to every part full freedom to express itself in the service of the whole.

CHAPTER XIV

HOPES AND FEARS

IT is sadly easy to grow sceptical of the future. Weary of idealists who refuse to consider the present because their eyes are fixed upon a distant goal, most men refuse to believe that it is even possible to say anything sensible about the remoter future. They bid us stick to facts, because facts alone offer solid ground. It is indeed true that what we have to say of the future can only be worth saying if we link it up with the present, if we show it to be at least a possible development of Society as we actually know it: mere idealism is not of practical value. But surely it is impossible to see the brute facts of the present in their true order and import, unless we somehow arrange them for ourselves, as links in a long chain of development of which the present is but a fragment. Seen in this light, great things will often grow small, and small things great; and we shall find, in some little fact, some cloud the size of a man's hand, the promise of the ' great change '.

It is a duty, as well as an impulse, to refuse to believe that the present system can continue for ever, that the future will go on being like the past, that the capitalist will eternally exploit, and Labour be eternally exploited. Such a view is the last ' despair of the republic ', a despair which we may forgive, but cannot approve. For after all education *is* spreading, and Labour *is* slowly waking up to a sense of its power and its responsibilities; and with enlightenment must surely come at any rate the will to sweep the present system away. Its continuance is a matter of will, or rather of its absence; we cannot hope to shake off the burden of profiteering until we have shaken off our lethargy and, with clear heads, willed the substitution of something better. The State cannot be more advanced than the citizens: its General Will is but the reflection of their wills, and as their wills are good and lofty in aim, the State will realise a higher good for all its members. You cannot make men good or happy by Act of Parliament; but it is equally certain that men can make themselves happy by such Acts: the goodness and happiness of the State depend on the goodness and happiness of its members. Will is, in the last resort, the basis of the State, which can succeed only if there is an organised goodwill behind it.

If, then, we are asked what chance there is of Trade Unionism undergoing such changes of heart, function, structure and power as we have outlined, we shall dare to answer that there is every hope. The signs of an altering and an increasing demand on the part of the Unions may be small, but they are unmistakable: at present mostly unrealised, they are bound to become conscious and deliberate. The sphere of Trade Union action cannot permanently recede; every inch of footing gained in the control of industry is gained for ever. The Unions are bound to go on widening their demands, whether under the influence of a conscious theory or not; new disputes will arise, and, in a particular quarrel, a general principle will be established before either side has realised its full significance. This is what happened in the Knox strike of 1912 on the North-Eastern Railway: it was a strike, not for the 'right to get drunk', but for the right of the workers to stand by one another in case of injustice, for their right to reject the verdict of authority in the workshop on a question of 'discipline'. It was by no means the first strike of its kind; but it focused public attention, and established the principle: its influence can be seen in the large number of similar strikes that have followed it.

Mr. Alexander Siemens, one of the employers on the Industrial Council, presenting a short memorandum of his own which is, in effect, a minority report, said very wisely that, on questions of principle, it is no use to call in an 'impartial' tribunal to decide between the two parties. Questions of principle at least will never be settled by arbitration; they are material for a fight to the finish, and the State must either settle them by legislating in favour of one side against the other, or must leave the two to fight it out. The readiness of Labour to fight in just such cases as these is the most hopeful indication that there really is something positive behind the Labour revolt. It may have begun merely because the shoe pinched—its first aim may have been merely to bring real wages back to the old level; but there are signs that, now Labour has tasted blood, it will not go quite calmly to sleep again. It is the business of idealists to make the most of all the unrest there is; and, by this means, there is hope that the seed they sow will bear fruit, and that Labour will at last set its feet steadfastly on the road that leads to the control of industry.

It is generally possible to tell a 'practical idealist'

from a 'practical man' by his view about the 'abolition of the wage system'. For the idealist, the phrase sums up perfectly what he is after, the destruction of the system whereby one man buys the life and labour of another for his own profit. The practical man thinks the idealist is answered when he has told him that men must always be paid for services done and must always draw their pay periodically; whether then it be called wages or something else seems to him indifferent. The whole argument he regards as beating the air; he prefers to concentrate on 'a more efficient distribution of wealth' to talking 'airy nonsense' about the wage system.

Two persons as sane as Mr. and Mrs. Webb have fallen into this fallacy in their pamphlet *What Syndicalism is*. To them it appears not to matter a jot what you call the money you receive for service done, provided you get the money. Presumably, it would be equally indifferent to Mr. Webb if his weekly allowance were called 'hush money', or to Mrs. Webb if she were paid entirely in 'blackmail'. But a wage is a wage, not because it is paid weekly, but because of a determinate relation between him who gives and him who receives—a relation which makes it emphatically more blessed to give than to receive. The cry for the 'abolition of the wage system' is a cry for the destruction of the whole idea that labour is a commodity, to be bought and sold like any other commodity, that labour has its market price, settled by supply and demand, by the higgling of the market, or what not, and not by any idea of human need or social justice, or even of service rendered. It is not denied that, nowadays, labour is treated as a commodity, and bought and sold with regard only to the advantage of the purchaser and the economic need of the seller; but it is maintained that this state of things is wasteful, degrading and preventible. Capitalism buys in the cheapest and sells in the dearest market; and it buys its labour on exactly the same terms as its non-human commodities. But essentially Labour differs in nature from commodities, not merely because, if it is not used, it is being wasted—that applies equally to a machine—not merely because it may be made more or less efficient as more or less is spent on it—that too would apply to a factory as a whole, and not merely to the labour in it—but because it is human, and the value of humanity is not a market value, though humanity may have, in a bad social system, a market price. The wage system must be abolished in the sense that it must be made impossible merely to buy labour as cheaply as possible, irrespective of its need or service; instead, Labour must share fairly in what the community produces, on a basis partly of need and partly of service, but never of market price.

The abolition of the wage system was really the question round which Mr. Bernard Shaw and Mr. Belloc spent so many wingless words in their famous debate last year. There was the spectacle of an old idealist tamed by the 'practical men' of the Fabian Society meeting an unpractical man who had despaired of the State. The debate centred round the meaning of the word 'service.' When Mr. Belloc said that we were moving towards the Servile State, Mr. Shaw rejoined that exactly what he wanted was to be allowed to 'serve' the community. Mr. Belloc extolled the virtues of freedom, Mr. Shaw those of ministration. But on the real point the two disputants never came to grips; they never really got down to discussing what makes the essential difference between service and servility, between a ' servant of the public ' and a slave of the State. Mr. Shaw pointed out, very rightly, that the Servile State is with us here and now : Mr. Belloc retaliated that nationalisation would not abolish it. Both, in fact, were out for the abolition of the wage-system ; the public slave is a commodity, the public servant a man. The slave is absolutely in the power of his master ; the servant of the public is free to serve, within limits, on his own terms, and to do the State the service for which he is most fitted. He takes his pay as a partner in the enterprise ; he shares in its prosperity and suffers when it fails ; his service is rendered not to a human superior, but to the great family of which he is a member. The wage-slave, on the other hand, has no share in the enterprise ; his standard of life is fixed, and does not vary with the national prosperity ; his service is sold to a superior, who uses it for his own benefit and not for that of the community at large.

It is easy to see what a difference the substitution of a personal for a purely financial relation throughout State service would bring about in the whole complexion of the workers' lives. The ' incentive to labour ' is an incentive to bad labour ; the relation between employer and employed is purely a ' business ' relation, and in ' business ' the practice " is giving too little and asking too much ". Both sides inevitably try to get as much as they can and to give as little as they can for it : it is only the accident of situation that makes the egoism of Labour just, and the egoism of the employer unjust. The everlasting continuance of the wage-system would mean the impossibility of substituting a nobler motive. Mr. Shaw is as keen for the abolition as Mr. Belloc ; he goes farther, and demands equal payment for all. Ultimately, he is clearly right; as long as unequal payment continues, the wage system continues to a certain extent; but an enormous step would have been made towards its entire abolition were payment made according to need and service, and not according to market-value. Standards of life are still too various for equality; they are not too various for a greater measure of justice and equalisation.

Since the industrial system began, reaction has always sheltered itself behind the demand for an incentive to Labour. There has been no sadder spectacle in the world than that of William Morris, an almost isolated figure in the Socialist movement, pleading for a nobler conception of human nature. Where work is bad and done for an unworthy master, there can be no incentive save gain; where work is noble and joyous it is its own incentive. But, we are told, all work cannot be like that. Most men are bound to mind machines, and do dull labour for hire; the few, the artists, the craftsmen and the skilled brain-workers, may indeed find a joy in labour which comes from the sense of successful self-expression; but such joys are not for the many. It must not be forgotten, however, that there are two sides to the gospel of joy in labour; the work may itself be so obviously fine and stimulating that no man who takes to it can lack an incentive to do his best; but even where the task is not so thrilling, there is a noble stimulus to good workmanship that comes from the sense of co-operation and responsibility. Co-partnership of the better sort is possible in private industry only because even an illusory sense of responsibility works wonders. A man who feels that he is not merely so much raw material to be used up in the process of manufacture will put his back into his work because he is conscious that it is *his* work. Not the sense of ownership, but the sense of responsibility, is the secret of the success of the small agriculturalist in Denmark and Ireland. The sense of being owned is deadening ; the sense of possession means, not so much that a man desires to have the title-deeds of his estate, as that he desires to work for himself and the community and not for a private master to whom he is nothing and who is nothing to him.

Morris, therefore, was fundamentally right in appealing for the restoration to the worker of his ' joy in labour ' as the sole means of bringing about ' the great change '. But the joy is not impossible without the abandonment of machine-production : a man may take a joy in his machine, if he is its master instead of its servant. The ordinary tasks of the ordinary man can in great measure be brightened and made happy by the influx of a new spirit of co-operation ; but the new spirit cannot come unless every worker can be made to feel, in some degree, responsible for the work he has to do. The Syndicalist movement has produced no more inspiring document than a little pamphlet issued by M. Gabriel Beaubois about the time of the great French Postal Strike. *La Crise Postale et les Monopoles d'État* is a plea for the extension to all the workers in every grade of the service of just that sense of responsibility for which bureaucratic management allows no room. In the postal service, the Government has to do, for the most part, with men of a high standard of intelligence ; yet, in practice, even the details of management are highly centralised, and red tape trammels the action of every grade of actual workers. Local initiative is crushed out ; rule and method are carried to ridiculous extremes, and dictated absolutely by the central office. No one, except the high officials who pull the red tapes, is allowed a chance of expressing his individuality in his daily work. M. Beaubois shows how, in a thousand and one ways, the actual worker could economise time and effort and make the service more effective, and he has shown how little national enterprise does to encourage individual enterprise on the part of those whom it employs. Much of what he says would apply equally to our English Post Office, though it is said that here an attempt at some measure of devolution is already being made.

It is no wonder that many thinkers turn away from nationalisation in disgust when they see how little national enterprise differs, as a rule, from private enterprise. But those who oppose nationalisation on the ground that it will bring about the Servile State make two mistakes: they regard the State of the present as something fixed and unalterable; and they reckon without the Trade Unions.

The badness of the State to-day is easily explained by the weakness of the popular will behind it. But if the State can be captured by one side it can be captured by the other also. The State of the future will not be the centralised bureaucratic mechanism of to-day; it will be the alert and flexible instrument of the General Will. New methods of democratic government will be evolved, and, instead of the abstract democracy of the ballot-box, there will be a real democracy aiming not at increasing continually the absoluteness of its control, but at delegating functions to self-governing bodies within itself, and at the same time harmonising their activities with the good of the whole. Parliamentary devolution by means of the Committee system, administrative devolution by the granting of wider powers to local and *ad hoc* authorities, and industrial devolution, making the Trade Union a self-governing producing unit, will go hand in hand. Even the few first steps that are being made in this direction, the growth in the functions of the Estimates Committee of the House of Commons, the establishment of bodies like the Road Board and the Development Commission, and the beginnings of friendly co-operation with the workers in some Government dockyards, are enough to remove much of the terror that is often felt by Socialists lest they should only entrench State Capitalism and bureaucracy. Until the workers are themselves captured for progress and until they set about the task of really moulding the political machine to suit their fancy, the danger will remain; but every sign of awakening on the part of the workers makes it less. Instead of the reformist Labour Party, there is hope that some day we shall have a revolutionary party imbued, not with the spirit of blind revolt, but with a real consciousness of what the State must be made.

In the task of educating the workers up to this point, as well as in preparing themselves for the control of industry, the Trade Unions have, as we saw, a great part to play. Nationalisation will be barren, save as a business proposition, unless the Unions see to it that they are given a share in control. But it is equally true that, unless politically the Unions help to frame the nationalisation policy of the State, they will find it very hard to secure the consideration of their claims. Through political action, the workers have to secure that the Government shall grant the demands of the Unions, as fast as the Unions fit themselves for the functions of control. The worker will strike with his companions, when he will not vote with them; and the strike has to be used as a method of political conviction. The Trade Unions must convince their members of the functions the State has to perform in relation to them; before a political party subsidised by them can get any real strength, it must have behind it the effective backing of the Unions. A Labour Party at present ought to regard its function as subsidiary to that of Trade Unionism; and it should be always on the alert for a chance of helping the workers in their economic struggle. As soon as, in becoming political, it ceases to be mainly economic in outlook, its hold over the workers is gone, and it loses touch with the rank and file. On such terms no political party can hope to increase and multiply and replenish the earth.

We have followed up the main lines of thought that are now stirring the Unions in this country, because in them, far more than in any recent legislative enactments, is to be found the key to the future development alike of our industry and of our national life. It is only important, in conclusion, to emphasise once more the essential unity of the problem. The history of foreign Labour movements is important to us because France, America, Germany, and Sweden have been facing problems largely similar to our own. In studying their theory and practice we are learning useful lessons to guide us in the understanding of the Labour movement in Great Britain. We passed then to a survey of the pressing problems of Trade Unionism at the present day, and saw how essential to their success in the daily struggle against the employer is reorganisation of the Unions, in respect both of structure and of internal government and control. We then turned to the relation of present-day Trade Unionism to the State of to-day, and saw the danger lurking in specious proposals for immediate social peace and justice. We laid stress on the fact that the class-war is real, and that no solution which ignores or denies it can be accepted by those who are trodden beneath the cloven hoof of Capital. In the light of this view, we rejected certain false proposals for social reconstruction.

We then took a leap into the future, and, throughout the remainder of the book, discussed more general problems of the future function of the State and the future control of industry, in the light of what we had said of the present, but with the object of taking a wider outlook upon it than our merely practical consideration had afforded us. Especially in the chapters on ' The Future of Trade Unionism ' and on ' Economics and Politics ', we tried to bridge the gulf between the present and the future, in so far as it can be bridged without the useless elaboration of prophecies that are sure to come false. And, at the close, we reaffirmed our faith in the future of the State as the expression of the General Will of the people, and in the Trade Union movement as the great force by which almost alone, for the present, progress can be truly furthered. The Unions, we saw, reorganised and co-ordinated, cannot indeed supplant the State, but may become the instruments of the State's reformation and the controllers of the processes of industry in the future Above all, we have seen that, if Trade Unionism is to accomplish its purpose, it must not be content to appeal to the blind ' instinct ' that is urging it forward. That ' instinct ' is present ; but if it is to achieve anything, it must gain consciousness and intelligence. The intelligent capitalist can make short work of the *élan vital* of the workers, unless it is translated into

HOPES AND FEARS

a definite will. The State is, at best, only as good as the citizens; and the citizens, would they but realise their power, can make it what they will. The 'sleeping giant' needs waking up; but when he wakes up he will need intellectual quickening as well. The present muddle in the world of Labour comes partly from lack of intellectual opportunity, but partly from intellectual indolence; the slave can only throw off his chains by showing himself a better man than his master. Education and the Greater Unionism have the task before them of making the worker realise his position and the remedy. If they can do this, they will not merely destroy Capitalism; they must not cease

> "Till they have built Jerusalem
> In England's green and pleasant land."

BIBLIOGRAPHY

The most important books are marked with a star (*).

CHAPTER I

BELLOC, HILAIRE	The Servile State. 1912. 1s.
CADBURY, EDWARD	Experiments in Industrial Organisation. 1912. 5s.
CHESTERTON, G. K.	What's Wrong With the World. 1911. 1s.
HOLMES, EDMOND	What Is and What Might Be. 1912. 4s. 6d.
KROPOTKIN, PETER	Fields, Factories and Workshops. 1s.
,,	Mutual Aid. 1s.
,,	The Conquest of Bread. 1s.
LAGARDELLE, HUBERT	Le Socialisme Ouvrier. 1911. 3 fr. 50.
MARX, KARL	Capital. 3 volumes. 31s. 6d.
MORRIS, WILLIAM	A Dream of John Ball. 2s.
,,	News from Nowhere. 1s.
,,	Hopes and Fears for Art. 5s.
,,	Architecture, Industry and Wealth. 6s.
,,	Signs of Change. 5s.
,,	A Factory as it Might Be (pamphlet). 1d.
,,	Useful Work versus Useless Toil (pamphlet). 1d.
*PAUL-BONCOUR, J.	Le Fédéralisme Économique. 1902. 6 fr.
,,	Les Syndicats de Fonctionnaires. 1908. 80 cent.
ROUSSEAU, J. J.	The Social Contract. 1s.
RUSKIN, JOHN	The Nature of Gothic, with an Introduction by William Morris. 1s.
*SOREL, GEORGES	La Décomposition du Marxisme. 80 cent.
* ,,	Réflexions sur la Violence. 6 fr.
WARE, FABIAN	The Worker and his Country. 5s.

CHAPTER II

Daily Citizen	1912–15.
Daily Herald	1912–15 (now the *Herald*).
Daily Mail	What the Worker Wants (reprinted articles). 1912. 6d.
HENDERSON, FRED	The Labour Unrest. 1912. 2s. 6d.
HYNDMAN, H. M.	Socialism and Labour Unrest (pamphlet). 1912. 1d.
MANN, TOM	*The Industrial Syndicalist* (12 pamphlets). 1911. 1d. and 2d. each.
,,	From Single Tax to Syndicalism. 1913. 1s.
MONEY, L. G. CHIOZZA	Riches and Poverty. 1910. 1s.
New Age	Weekly. 6d.
New Statesman	Weekly. 6d.
New Witness	Weekly. 6d.
SNOWDEN, PHILIP	The Living Wage. 1912. 1s.
TILLETT, BEN	The 1911 Transport Workers' Strike. 1912. 6d.
Times	Labour and Industry (reprinted articles). 1913. 1s.
WATNEY, J., and LITTLE, J. A.	Industrial Warfare. 1912. 5s.

CHAPTERS III–IV

ANTONELLI, L.	La Démocratie Sociale devant les Idées Présentes. 1911.
BERTH, E.	Les Nouveaux Aspects du Socialisme. 1908.
BIÉTRY, P.	Le Socialisme et les Jaunes. 1906.
BOUGLÉ, C.	Syndicalisme et Démocratie. 1908.
BUISSON, E.	La Grève Générale. 1905.
CHALLAYE, F.	Syndicalisme Révolutionnaire et Syndicalisme Réformiste. 1909.
DELESALLE, P.	Les Bourses du Travail et la C.G.T.
DILIGENT, V.	Les Orientations Syndicales. 1910
*GRIFFUELHES, V.	Voyage Révolutionnaire. 1910.
,,	L'Action Syndicaliste. 1908.
GUESDE, J., LAGARDELLE, H., et VAILLANT, E.	Le Parti Socialiste et la C.G.T.

BIBLIOGRAPHY 429

Hoffmann, L.	La Grève. 1912.
Jay, R.	La Protection Légale des Travailleurs. 1910.
,,	Qu'est ce que le Contrat Collectif de Travail ? 1908.
*Jouhaux, L.	Le Syndicalisme Français. 1913.
Kritsky, Mlle.	L'Évolution du Syndicalisme en France. 1908.
Lagardelle, Hubert.	La Grève Générale et le Socialisme. 1905.
*	Le Socialisme Ouvrier. 1911.
Leroy, M.	Syndicats et Services Publics. 1909.
,,	Le Code Civil et le Droit Nouveau. 1904.
*Levine, L.	Syndicalism in France. 1912. 7s. 6d.
Lewis, A. D.	Syndicalism and the General Strike. 1912. 7s. 6d.
Louis, Paul	Histoire du Mouvement Syndical en France. 1907.
,,	Le Syndicalisme Contre l'État. 1910.
Mermeix	Le Syndicalisme Contre le Socialisme. 1908.
Millerand, A.	Le Socialisme Réformiste Français. 1903.
Naquet, A.	L'Anarchie et le Collectivisme. 1904.
Pataud, E., et Pouget, E.	Comment Nous Ferons la Révolution.
,,	Syndicalism and the Co-operative Commonwealth (translation of above). 1913. 2s. 6d.
*Paul-Boncour, J.	Le Fédéralisme Économique. 1901.
* ,,	Les Syndicats de Fonctionnaires. 1906.
*Pelloutier, F.	Histoire des Bourses du Travail. 1902.
Pouget, E.	See Pataud.
,,	La C.G.T. 1908.
,,	Le Sabotage. 1910.
Proudhon, P. J.	Idée Générale de la Révolution.
,,	De la Capacité Politique des Classes Ouvrières. 1865.
,,	La Révolution Sociale.
Sorel, G.	L'Avenir Socialiste des Syndicats. 1901.
* ,,	La Décomposition du Marxisme. 1908.
,,	Les Illusions du Progrès. 1911.
,,	Introduction à l'Économie Moderne. 1911.
,,	La Révolution Dreyfusienne.

*SOREL, G.	Réflexions sur la Violence. 1910.
ST. LEON, E. M.	Le Compagnonnage. 1901.
STODDART, JANE T.	The New Socialism. 1910.
VAILLANT, E.	See Guesde.
WEBB, S. and B.	What Syndicalism Means. 1912.
YVETOT, G.	ABC Syndicaliste. 1911.
ZÉVAÈS, A.	Le Syndicalisme Contemporain. 1912.

CHAPTER V

ADAMS, T. S., and SUMNER, H. L.	Labor Problems. 1909.
BARNETT, G. E.	See Hollander.
BOHN, FRANK	See Haywood.
BROOKS, J. G.	American Syndicalism: the I.W.W. 1913.
*CARLTON, F. L.	History and Problems of Organised Labor. 1911.
COMMONS, J. R.	Races and Immigrants in the United States. 1908.
* ,,	A Documentary History of American Trade Unionism.
DEBS, E. V.	Industrial Unionism (pamphlet).
DELEON, D.	Marx v. Mallock (pamphlet). 1908.
ELY, R. T.	The Labour Movement in America. 1890.
FAGAN, J. O.	The Autobiography of an Individualist. 1912.
FOSTER, W. Z., and FORD, E. O.	Syndicalism.
GILMAN, N. P.	A Dividend to Labour. 1899.
HAYWOOD, W. D., and BOHN, F.	Industrial Socialism.
HOLLANDER, J. H., and BARNETT, G. E.	Studies in American Trade Unionism. 1906.
HUGHAN, A. E.	American Socialism at the Present Day. 1912.
I.W.W.	Report of First Conference. 1905.
*LAWRENCE	Report of Strike of Textile Workers at Lawrence. 1912.
MAROT, HELEN	American Labour Unions. 1915.
ST. JOHN, V.	The I.W.W. (pamphlet).
SINCLAIR, UPTON	The Industrial Republic. 1907.

BIBLIOGRAPHY

SOMBART, W.	Socialism and the Social Movement (tr.). 1909.
SUMNER, H. L.	See Adams.
TRAUTMANN, W. E.	Why Strikes are Lost, etc. (pamphlet).
WALLING, W. ENGLISH.	Socialism as It Is. 1911.
,,	The Larger Aspects of Socialism. 1913.
,,	Socialist Labour-Unionism and Labour-Union Socialism.
WASHINGTON, BOOKER T.	The Man Farthest Down in Europe. 1912.
WILLIAMS, B. H.	Eleven Blind Leaders (pamphlet).
ZIMMERN, A. E.	American Impressions (*Sociological Review*). July 1912.

CHAPTER VI

*ANON.	Neunter Internationaler Bericht über die Gewerkschaftsbewegung. 1912.
ANON.	Statistisches Jahrbuch des Deutsches Reich. 1912.
BERNSTEIN, E.	La Grève et le Lock-out en Allemagne. 1908.
BUISSON, E.	La Grève Générale. 1905.
LAGARDELLE, H.	La Grève Générale et le Socialisme. 1909.
LANZILLO, A.	Le Mouvement Ouvrier en Italie.
*LEGIEN, K.	Die Deutsche Gewerkschaftsbewegung.
MANN, TOM	From Single Tax to Syndicalism. 1913.
MICHELS, R.	In 'Syndicalisme et Socialisme' (H. Lagardelle).
MORRIS, WILLIAM	News from Nowhere.
PATAUD, E., et POUGET, E.	Comment Nous Ferons la Révolution.
POR, ODON	Syndicalism in Action (pamphlet). 1912.
,, and ATKINSON, F. M.	Syndicalism (*English Review*). July 1912.
SANDERS, W. S.	The Socialist Movement in Germany (pamphlet). 1912.
* ,,	Industrial Organisation in Germany (New Statesman Supplement). o.p.
*SWEDEN	La Grève et les Lock-out en Suède en 1909, 1912.

CHAPTERS VII–VIII

ANON.	A Plea for the Amalgamation of All Existing Trade Unions (pamphlet). 1912.
* ,,	The Miners' Next Step (pamphlet). 1911.
*BOARD OF TRADE	[Cd. 6109]. Report on Trade Unions, 1906–1910. 1912.
,,	Industrial Directory. 1913.
,,	[Cd. 7733]. Seventeenth Abstract of Labour Statistics. 1915.
KENNY, ROWLAND	Men and Rails. 1913. 5s.
LLOYD, C. M.	Trade Unionism. 1915. 2s. 6d.
MANN, TOM	*The Industrial Syndicalist* (12 pamphlets). 1911.
REGISTRAR OF FRIENDLY SOCIETIES	Report on Trade Unions. 1913.
Solidarity	Monthly. 1913–1914.
Syndicalist	Monthly. 1912–1914.
TRADE UNION CONGRESS	Report. 1912. 6d.
TRIDON, A.	The New Unionism. 1914. 1s.
*WEBB, S. and B.	History of Trade Unionism. 1894–1911. 7s. 6d.
* ,,	Industrial Democracy. 1897–1911. 9s.
,,	Problems of Modern Industry. 1907. 5s.

CHAPTER IX

*BOARD OF TRADE	[Cd. 6603]. Report on the Industrial Disputes Investigation Act of Canada, 1907, by Sir George Askwith. 1912.
,,	[Cd. 6081]. Memoranda prepared from information in the possession of the Labour Department relating to the text and operation of certain Laws in the British Dominions and Foreign Countries affecting Strikes and Lock-outs with especial reference to Public Utility Services. 1912.

BIBLIOGRAPHY

BOARD OF TRADE	. [H. C. 38]. Tenth Report of Proceedings in 1912 under the Conciliation Act of 1896. 1913.
,,	. [Cd. 6472]. Report on Strikes and Lockouts and on Conciliation and Arbitration Boards in the United Kingdom in 1911. 1912.
,,	. [H. C. 134]. Memoranda in Reference to the Working of the Trade Boards Act. 1913.
* ,,	. *Labour Gazette*, monthly.
BRODA, R., and DEUTSCH, E.	. La Fixation Légale des Salaires. 1912.
*INDUSTRIAL COUNCIL.	[Cd. 6952]. Report on Enquiry into Industrial Agreements. 1913.
KNOOP, D.	. Industrial Conciliation and Arbitration. 1905.
LLOYD, H. D.	. A Country without Strikes. 1900.
*MÉTIN, ALBERT	. Le Socialisme sans Doctrines. 1910.
PIGOU, A. C.	. Principles and Methods of Industrial Peace. 1905.
,,	. Wealth and Welfare. 1912.
REEVES, W. PEMBER	. State Experiments in Australia and New Zealand. 1902.
TAWNEY, R. H.	. Minimum Rates in the Chain-Making Industry. 1914. 1s. 6d.
,,	. Minimum Rates in the Tailoring Industry. 1915. 3s. 6d.

CHAPTER X

AVES, E.	. Co-operative Industry. 1907.
BILLINGTON-GREIG, T.	The Consumer in Revolt. 1912.
BOARD OF TRADE	. [Cd. 6045]. Report on Industrial and Agricultural Co-operative Societies in the United Kingdom. 1912.
* ,,	. [Cd. 6496]. Report on Profit-Sharing and Labour Co-partnership. 1912.
CADBURY, E.	. Experiments in Industrial Organisation.
FABIAN RESEARCH DEPARTMENT	. Co-operative Production and The Co-operative Movement (1914) (New Statesman Supplements).
FAY, C. R.	. Co-partnership in Industry. 1913.
,,	. Co-operation at Home and Abroad. 1908.

LABOUR CO-PARTNER-SHIP ASSOCIATION	Pamphlets, leaflets, etc.
LLOYD, H. D.	Labour Co-partnership. 1898.
MÜNSTERBURG, H.	Psychology and Industrial Efficiency. 1913. 5s.
PEASE, E. R.	Co-partnership and Profit-Sharing, a Fraud and a Failure ? (pamphlet). 1913. 1d.
*SCHLOSS, S. D.	Methods of Industrial Remuneration. 1907. 3s. 6d.
*WEBB, BEATRICE	The Co-operative Movement. 1899. 2s. 6d.
WEBB, CATHERINE	Industrial Co-operation. 1910. 2s. 6d.
WEBB, SIDNEY	The Place of Co-operation in the State of To-morrow (pamphlet). 1913. 1d.
WILLIAMS, ANEURIN	Co-partnership and Profit-Sharing. 1914. 1s.

CHAPTERS XI–XIV

BEAUBOIS, G.	La Crise Postale et les Monópoles d'État. 1908.
BOOTH, C.	Industrial Unrest and Trade Union Policy. 1914. 2d.
CLAY, Sir A.	Syndicalism and Labour. 1911. 1s.
DAVIES, EMIL	The Case for Railway Nationalisation. 1913. 1s.
,,	The Collectivist State in the Making. 1914. 5s.
FABIAN RESEARCH DEPARTMENT	State and Municipal Enterprise (New Statesman Supplement). 1915.
HARLEY, J. H.	Syndicalism. 1912. 6d.
LEWIS, A. D.	Syndicalism and the General Strike. 1912. 7s. 6d.
MACDONALD, J. R.	Syndicalism. 1912. 1s.
MANN, J. E. F., SIEVERS, N. J., and COX, R. W. T.	The Real Democracy. 1913. 5s.
MANN, TOM	From Single Tax to Syndicalism. 1913. 1s.
MARX, KARL	Capital.
ORAGE, A. R. (editor)	National Guilds. 1914. 5s.

BIBLIOGRAPHY

PATAUD, E., et POUGET, E.	Comment Nous Ferons la Révolution.
,,	Syndicalism and the Co-operative Commonwealth (translation of above). 1913. 2s. 6d.
PELLOUTIER, F.	Histoire des Bourses du Travail. 1902.
PENTY, A. J.	The Restoration of the Guild System. 1906. o.p.
,,	The Restoration of the Guild System (articles in *New Age*). 1913.
PRATT, E. A.	The Case against Railway Nationalisation. 1913. 1s.
*RENARD, GEORGES	Syndicats, Trades Unions et Corporations. 1909.
,,	(English translation in preparation.) 5s.
ROBINSON, M. F.	The Spirit of Association. 1913. 5s.
SHADWELL, A.	Syndicalism (in Nelson's Encyclopædia of Industrialism). 1913. 1s.
SNOWDEN, PHILIP	Socialism and Syndicalism. 1913. 1s.
WALLAS, GRAHAM	Syndicalism (in *Sociological Review*). July 1912.
*WEBB, S. and B.	Industrial Democracy. 1897–1911. 9s.
,,	What Syndicalism Means. 1912. 2d.

INDEX

ABC Syndicaliste, by G. Yvetot, 112.
Ablett, Noah, 277.
Action Syndicale, L', by Barthou, 59, 117.
Agitation, 37.
Agreements, 77, 79, 153, 193, 216, 267, 281 ff., 301, 307 ff., 310 ff., 329, 374.
Agriculture, 40.
Allemane, 64.
Amalgamated Society of Engineers, 210, 214, 221, 226 ff., 244, 253 f., 262, 278.
Amalgamation, 161, 215, 217, 219 ff., 236, 252 ff., 273.
America, 57, 95, 96, Ch. V., 202, 211, 241, 294, 321, 325 ff., 348, 423.
American Federation of Labour, 135, 136 ff., 141, 151, 158 ff.
American Impressions, by A. E. Zimmern, 131.
Anarchism, 4, 89, 90, 95, 124, 199, 200, 203, 274, 351, 367.
Anti-militarism, 91, 120, 196.
Anti-patriotism, 91.
Anti-sweating League, 304.
Appleton, W. A., 244, 279–80, 374.
Arbitration, 40, 48, 49, 56, 285 ff., Ch. IX.
Askwith, Sir G., 49, 288, 294, 297–8, 307 ff., 317.
Associations of Employers, 185 ff., 290.
Atkinson, F. M., 167–8.
Australia, 40.
Avenir Socialiste des Syndicats, L', by Sorel, 67, 87.

Balfour, A. J., 20, 394.

Barthou, Louis, 59, 117.
Bataille Syndicaliste, 118.
Beaubois, Gabriel, 124, 420.
Belgium, 43, 122, 195, 342.
Belloc, Hilaire, 4, 14, 417.
Bergson, Henri, 4.
Berth, Edouard, 90, 93, 97, 200, 367.
Billington-Greig, Teresa, 341.
Black Country Strikes, 47, 403.
Blacklegs, 55, 108, 133, 376.
Board of Trade, 35, 60.
Bohn, F. See *Industrial Socialism*.
Boilermakers, 218, 221, 227, 254.
Bottle-blowers (Italian), 168.
Bournville, 324.
Bourses du Travail, 62, 64–7, 69, 71, 73, 80, 81, 98, 109, 111, 114, 115–9, 154, 246, 353.
Bourses du Travail, Fédération des, 65–6, 68, 117.
Boycott, 97.
Briand, 201.
British Socialist Party, 399.
Brooklands Agreement, 209.
Brousse, Paul, 64.
Building Unions, 265 ff., 270, 273.
Burns, John, 40.

Ca' canny, 95.
Cadbury, Edward, 12, 320, 324–5, 379.
Canada, 49, 294 ff., 307.
Capitalism, 345–6, 348 f.
Carpenters and Joiners, 228, 266, 267.
Centralisation, 176-182, 241, 246 ff., Ch. VIII.

INDEX

Chapelier, 62.
Chartism, 21.
Chasse aux renards, 108.
Checkweighmen, 384.
Cheminots de l'Est, 62.
Chesterfield election, 396 f., 399.
Chesterton, G. K., 14, 365.
Christian Socialists, 9, 332, 387.
Christian Unions (Germany), 170 ff.
Class-representation, 21, Ch. XIII.
Class-struggle, 21, 88, 125, Ch. IX., 370, 391–2, 394, 424.
Clynes, J. R., 235.
Coal-strike, 1.
Collectivism, 3, 5, 7, 8, 10, 13, 17, 54, Ch. XI., 378 f.
Comité d'Union Syndicaliste, 90.
Commune, Paris, 63.
Communism, 124, 200, 274.
Compagnonnage, 23, 63.
Competition, 348–9.
Compulsory arbitration, 287, 288, 290 ff., 308 ff.
Compulsory Conciliation, 294 ff.
    ,,   Trade Unionism, 371 f.
Conciliation, 48, 104, 153, 216, 267, 281 ff., Ch. IX., 305.
Conciliation Act, 290, 294, 315 f.
Confédération Générale du Travail, 60, 61, Ch. III.–IV., 129, 148, 246, 387, 389.
Confédération Générale du Travail Income, 81.
Confédération Générale du Travail Statutes, 69.
Confédération Générale du Travail, Strength of, 71.
Conseils du Travail, 67.
Consumers, 6, 7, 340 ff., 353 ff., Ch. XI., 409.
Contributions, 253–4.
Control of Industry, 7, 56, 340, 343, Chs. XI.–XII., 394, 406 f.
Co-operation, 6, 29, 80, 109, 122, 201, 206, 210, 337, 338–43, 345.
Co-operation of Producers, 168, 332, 336, 337 ff.
Co-operative Union, 341.
Co-operative Wholesale Society, 7, 336, 337, 338, 340, 342 f., 345.

Co-operative Wholesale Society Bank, 343.
Co-partnership, 285, 320, 328–37, 419.
Co-partnership from the Employer's Point of View, 334 ff.
Co-partnership Tenants, 336.
Cornwall, 289.
Cotton industry, 216, 218, 247 ff., 273, 323, 371.
Cradley Heath, 47.
Craft Unionism, 47, 56, 111, 135, 139, 212 ff.
Crise Postale et les Monopoles d'État, by G. Beaubois, 124, 420.

Daily Citizen, 50, 221, 397.
Daily Herald, 3, 4, 51, 221, 261, 279–80, 399.
Daily Mail, 53.
Debs, Eugene, 151.
Deleon, Daniel, 142, 162.
Demarcation, 218, 255.
Denmark, 420.
Development Commission, 366, 380, 421.
Devolution, 24, 380, 421.
Diligent, V., 59.
Dilke, Sir C., 303.
Direct Action, 85, 93.
Discipline, 54, 327, 334, 382.
Disputes, Trade, 8, 54.
Dock Strikes (1889), 40.
    ,,   (1911), 41, 107.
    ,,   (1912), 107.
Doctors and Insurance Act, 364.
Dublin, 289.
Dyson, Will, 51.

Economic Federalism, 28.
Education, 16–19, 384, 410, 425.
Eight Hours' Day, 78, 85.
Élan vital, 4, 424.
Eleven Blind Leaders, by B. H. Williams, 140.
Employers' Associations, 6.
Engineering, 227 ff.
    ,,   Federation, 218.
Engineers' Journal, 40.
English Review, 167.
Ettor, Joseph, 148.
Experiments in Industrial Organisation, by E. Cadbury, 12, 324.

INDEX

Fabian Society, 2, 3, 4, 5, 8, 399, 417.
Factory Acts, 353.
Federalism in the C.G.T., 70.
Fédéralisme Economique, Le, by J. Paul-Boncour, 59.
Federation, 40, 137, 215 ff., 235, 247 ff., 271 ff.
Ferri, Enrico, 88.
Fields, Factories and Workshops, 12.
Ford. See *Syndicalism*, by E. C. Ford.
Foster, W. Z., 141, 157, 161.
France, 26, 31, 57, Chs. III. and IV., 128, 179, 211, 259, 261, 274, 344, 351, 379, 387, 423.
Free Contract, 273.
French Revolution, 22, 58.
From Single Tax to Syndicalism, by Tom Mann, 41.

Garden City Press, 336.
Gas Companies, 332–3.
Geldart, W. M., 282.
General Federation of Trade Unions, 72, 120, 198, 243 ff., 279, 374.
General Labour Unions, 220, 222, 226, 231, 234 ff., 238 ff., 245, 266, 306.
General Strike, 77, 80, 93, 94, 106, 179, 193–204, 342, 406.
General Will, 23, 29, 414, 421, 424.
George, D. Lloyd, 375, 397.
Germany, 61, 105, 121, 169–82, 197, 202, 232, 238, 247, 259, 280, 342, 379, 423.
Giovanitti, 149.
Gompers, S., 136, 159, 160.
Gosling, H., 390.
Greater Unionism, 47, 56, 73, 176, 179, 214, 257 f., 260, 272, 274, 284, 351, 377, 392, 404, 425.
Griffuelhes, V., 67, 74, 77, 85, 89, 101–2, 107, 113.
Guérard, 75.
Guesde, Jules, 64, 72, 86, 91, 121, 173.

Guild Socialism, 51, 362 ff., 378, 380, 386, 406.
Guild System, 12, 362.

Hancock, J. G., 398.
Hardie, J. Keir, 196, 398.
Hartshorn, Vernon, 277.
Haslam, James, 396.
Haywood, W. D., 129, 134, 138, 149.
Health, Public, 410.
Hegel, 396.
Hirsch-Duncker Unions, 170 ff.
Histoire des Bourses du Travail, by Pelloutier, 124.
Holland, 197.
Holmes, Edmond, 16.
„ James, 398.
Humanité, L', 75.

Immigration into U.S.A., 130.
'Impartial' persons, 288, 295, 309, 317 f.
Independent Labour Party, 2, 396, 399.
Individualism, 5.
Industrial Council, 307 ff.
Industrial Democracy, by Mr. and Mrs. Webb, 53, 247.
Industrial Democracy League, 274, 276, 278, 406.
Industrial Disputes Investigation Act (Canada), 295 ff.
Industrial Organisation, 56.
„ Peace. See Social Peace.
Industrial Socialism, by W. D. Haywood and F. Bohn, 129, 134, 138.
Industrial Syndicalist Education League, 41, 156.
Industrial Unionism, 56, 111, 113, 118, 128, 135, 142, 153, 160, 162, 163, 166, 176, 179, 211, 212–3, 221, 223, 227, 234, 236, 241, 256, 272, 274, 351, 377.
Industrial Workers of the World, Ch. V., 128, 135, 139 ff., 143, 153, 161, 162, 211.
Industrial Workers of the World, Preamble of, 143.
Insurance Act, 16, 33, 244, 280, 283, 374, 388,

INDEX

Intellectuals, 2.
International Trade Union Conference, 92.
Internationalism, 42 ff., 90–2.
Invention, 357.
Ireland, 420.
Italy, 167 ff., 202.

Jaurès, Jean, 88.
Jouhaux, L., 61, 67, 95, 104, 105, 112, 114, 118, 119, 120, 128.
Jowett, F. W., 399.

Kenyon, Barnet, 396 f., 398.
Knights of Labour, 140, 241.
'Knox' Strike, 262, 415.
Kropotkin, Peter, 12, 13.

'Label', 97.
Labour Leader, 398.
Labour Co-partnership Association, 328, 332, 334 ff.
Labour Party, 5, 8, 13, 14, 15, 31–2, 36, 72, 182, 207, 211, 242, 283, 341, 345, Ch. XIII., 423.
Labour Unrest, 1, 14, Ch. II.
Lagardelle, Hubert, 67, 69, 74, 77, 78, 85, 86, 87, 88, 89, 90, 91, 109, 113, 114, 125, 126, 200, 379, 400.
Lansbury, G., 399.
Lassalle, F., 170.
Lawrence Strikes, 142, 144 ff.
Leadership, 275.
Leicester By-election, 396.
'Leisure' State, 10.
Leith Strike, 404.
Lemieux, 297.
Leroy, Maxime, 59.
Lever, Sir W., 169.
Levine, Louis, 61, 62.
Levy, Sir M., 396.
Liberalism, 15, 290, 395, 396–7, 398, 403.
Living Wage, The, by P. Snowden, 281, 405.
Lloyd, H. D., 293.
Local Autonomy, 108, 114–6, 137, 180 ff., Ch. VIII.

Macdonald, J. Ramsay, 20, 313, 395, 397.
Machinery, 10 ff.

Maisons des Ouvriers, 117.
Man Farthest Down, The, by Booker Washington, 131.
Management, 327, 357 ff., 382.
Mann, Tom, 40, 41, 202, 246, 251, 391.
Marat, 63.
Marx, Karl, 2, 5, 19, 64, 86, 88, 91, 125, 167, 170, 204, 350.
Maxwell, W., 341.
Metal Workers' Union (Germany), 176 ff., 232.
Millerand, A., 67, 79, 84.
Miners' Eight Hours' Act, 46, 224.
  ,,   Federation, 43, 55, 75, 218, 223, 323, 371, 389, 407.
Miners' Minimum Wage Act, 46, 224, 317.
Miners' Next Step, The, 274 ff., 406.
'Mines for the Miners', 124.
Mines Nationalisation Bill, 345.
Minimum Wage, 46, 198, 300 ff., 329.
Minorities, Rights of, 75.
Minority Report, 33.
Mitchell, Isaac, 294.
Money, L. G. Chiozza, 35.
Morning Post, 3.
Morris, William, 9, 13, 200, 203, 419.
Munday, W., 320.
Municipal Trading, 345.
Mutualité, 83.
Myths, Social, 123.

Napoleon III., 63.
National Union of Railwaymen. *See* Railwaymen.
Nationalisation, 7, 13, 28, 271, Ch. XI., 378 ff., 381 f., 390, 391, 400, 407 f., 422.
Nationality, 27, 45.
New Age, 2, 51, 132, 362 ff., 386, 400.
New South Wales, 292, 306.
New Statesman, 51.
New Witness, 38.
New Zealand, 40, 290 ff., 304, 307.
News from Nowhere, by Morris, 200, 203.
Niel, L., 76, 89, 106, 120.
Nietzsche, 4, 86, 95.

INDEX

Non-Unionist Question, 8, 54, 371.

Occupational Unionism, 212, 229.
Office du Travail, 60.
Officials, 52, 56, 109, 205 ff., 261, 265, 273, 275, 279–80, 283.
O'Grady, J., 256, 399.
On the Firing Line, 138, 144, 159.
Orbell, H., 390.
Orientations Syndicales, Les, by V. Diligent, 59.
Osborne Judgment, 20, 282.
Osborne Judgment and After, The, by W. M. Geldart, 282.
Ouvrier Textile, L', 75.
Overlapping Unions, 175.
Ownership, 352.
Oxford, 18.

Panama Canal, 364.
Parliament, 4, 19, 26, 47.
Parliamentary Committee of the Trade Union Congress, 120, 242, 398.
Parti Ouvrier Français, 64.
Pataud, 'King', 98, 106, 124, 200.
Paterson Strikes, 142.
Paul-Boncour, J., 59.
Pelloutier, Fernand, 59, 66, 67, 90, 98, 99, 124.
Piece-work, 321.
Placement, 85, 106.
Plea for Amalgamation, 253.
Poincaré, Henri, 92.
Political action, 47, 90–1, 376, Ch. XIII.
Por, Odon, 167.
Port of London Authority, 313, 390.
Port Sunlight, 169.
Post Office, 379, 421.
Pouget, Emile, 67, 70, 73, 74, 76, 78, 83, 84, 89, 93, 94, 98, 105, 119, 121, 124, 200.
Premium bonus system, 320–1, 323–4.
Pretence, House of. *See* Parliament.
Prices and Wages, 35, 401 f.
Producers, Ch. I., Ch. XI., and *passim*. *See* Trade Unionism.
Production, 353 ff.

Production and Distribution, 5, 7, 346 f.
Profit-sharing, 320, 331, 332, 335.
Proudhon, 73.
Prudential Insurance Co., 375, 389.
Psychology, 325.
Public opinion, 34, Ch. IX., 405.

Radicalism, 5.
Railwaymen, 51, 55, 221, 222, 226–7, 261 ff., 269–70, 283, 371, 390, 404.
Railway Strike, 251, 403.
Redintegration of Labour, 12, 13.
Réflexions sur la Violence, 4, 67, 85.
Réformistes, 62, 72, 75–7, 80, 84, 89–90, 101, 106, 110, 111.
Renard, V., 86, 90.
Riches and Poverty, by Chiozza Money, 35.
Right to the Whole Product of Labour, 349 ff.
Rights, 346.
Road Board, 366, 380.
Roberts, G. H., 396.
Rochdale Pioneers, 338.
Roosevelt, Theodore, 161.
Rose, F. H., 251.
Rousseau, J. J., 23, 29, 63.
Ruskin, 9.

Sabotage, 77, 80, 94, 108.
St. John, Vincent, 154, 163.
Sanders, W. S., 177.
Scientific Management, 321, 325 ff.
Scurr, J., 397.
Self-governing workshop, 332, 337 ff.
Semi-skilled workers, 232–3.
Servile State, 4, 11, 13, 417.
Shaw, Bernard, 417.
Shipbuilding, 132, 227 ff., 273.
Shipwrights, 228.
Shipyard Agreement, 228.
Shop piece-work, 12, 320, 324–5.
Sidneywebbicalism, 3.
Siemens, A., 415.
Simons, A. M., 159.
Snowden, Philip, 281, 398, 405.
Social Contract, by Rousseau, 23.

INDEX

Social-Democratic Unions (Germany), 170 ff.
Social peace, 77, 84, 104, 125, Ch. IX., 328 f., 388.
Socialism, 5, 14, 31, 55, 346 ff., 393–4.
Socialism of Institutions, 70.
Socialisme Ouvrier, Le. See Lagardelle.
Socialist, The, 142.
Socialist-Labour Party, 142.
Socialist Party in France, 84, 85–6, 88, 102.
Socialist Party in Germany, 173 ff., 182.
Socialist Party in U.S.A., 159–60.
Sociological Review, 131, 352.
Solidarity, 274.
Sombart, W., 162.
Sorel, Georges, 4, 67, 85, 87, 93, 97, 98, 107, 123, 127, 167, 194, 200.
Sou du Soldat, 92.
Soupes Communistes, 80, 118.
South Africa, 294.
South Wales Miners, 218, 224–5, 274 ff., 385, 399, 406.
Spain, 203.
Speeding-up, 320 ff.
Spencer, Herbert, 5, 14.
State Capitalism, 6, 378, 422.
„ Interference, 25, 28, 408 f.
„ Monopoly, 6.
Steam Engine Makers, 222.
Steel Trust, 129.
'Stop-in' Strike, 96.
Strike against War, 196.
Strikes, 15, 30, 33, 46–7, 56, 163, 191, 261 ff., 269, 275, 279–80, 295 ff., 312, 333, 401 ff., 405.
Suffragists, 95.
Sweated trades, 292, 299 ff.
Sweden, 182–90, 197, 208, 310, 423.
Syndicalism, 1, 3, 4, 7, 9, 11, 13, 14, 17, 22, 24, 25, 26, 31, 37, 45, 46, 52, 55, 59–60, 67, 77–8, 98, 110, 124, 126, 156, 165, 166, 168, 194, 199, 201, 204, 274, 331, 338, Ch. XI., 391, Ch. XIII., 399, 409, 420.
Syndicalism, by E. C. Ford and W. Z. Foster, 141, 157.

Syndicalisme Français, Le, by L. Jouhaux, 60, 104, 105, 112, 115, 118, 119.
Syndicalist, 157, 161.
Syndicalist League of North America, 156–7.
Syndicalist Unions (Germany), 172.
Syndicat National des Chemins de Fer, 76.
Syndicats, 58, 60, Chs. III., IV., 66.
Syndicats de Fonctionnaires, Les, by J. Paul-Boncour, 59.
Syndicats, Fédération Nationale de, 65.
Syndicats jaunes, 60, 73.
„ *mixtes,* 60, 83.

Tacitus, 285.
Taff Vale decision, 20.
Tammany Hall, 141.
Tariff controversy, 25.
Taxi Strike (London), 80.
Thomas, J. H., 221.
Thorne, Will, 399.
Tillett, Ben, 40, 234, 235.
Trade Boards, 104.
„ „ Act, 15, 48, 299, 303 ff., 306, 318.
Trade Disputes Act, 36, 402.
„ Union Acts, 20, 255–6, 282, 284, 398.
Trade Union Congress, 72, 75, 242, 244, 290, 341, 353.
Trade Union government, 52, 56, Ch. VIII.
Trade Unionism, 5, 6, 8, 11–7, 20, 24, 26–8, 31, 32, 46–7, 51, 55, 111, 112, 121, 172, 175, Chs. VII.–VIII., 327–8, 331, 338, Chs. XI.–XIII., 414, 422 ff.
Trade Unionism and benefits, 72, 121.
Trades Councils, 353, 409.
Transformations de la Puissance Publique, Les, by M. Leroy, 59.
Transport Workers' Federation, 43, 217, 234 ff., 272, 273, 371, 403.
Trautmann, W. E., 141, 155, 159.
Travailleur du Bâtiment, Le, 96.
Trusts, 129, 138, 348, 354.

INDEX

Tutorial Classes, 17.
Twicers, 283.

Unions de Syndicats, 117. See *Bourses du Travail*.
Unions Départmentales, 117.
Unions Régionales, 117.
United Machine Workers, 222.
Unrest, Labour. *See* Labour Unrest.
Ure, Alexander, 397.

Value, theory of, 349 ff.
Victoria, 293, 299 ff., 304, 306.
Voyage Révolutionnaire, by V. Griffuelhes, 74, 101, 107, 113.

Wage System, 31, 90, 152, 416 ff.
Wages, 8, 15, 38, 44, 330 f., 361, 391, 401.
Wages Boards, 48, 290, 299 ff.
Wages in America, 135.
Waldeck-Rousseau, 59, 63, 67, 84, 116, 387.
Wall Street Journal, 159.
Wallas, Graham, 352.
Walling, W. English, 156.
Ware, Fabian, 4, 27.
Washington, Booker, 131.

Webb, Sidney and Beatrice, 2, 3, 8, 33, 53, 118, 247, 352, 416.
Wells, H. G., 53.
Western Australia, 292.
Western Federation of Miners (U.S.A.), 140, 152, 158.
What is and what might be, by E. G. A. Holmes, 16.
What Syndicalism Is, by S. and B. Webb, 118, 416.
What the Worker Wants, 53.
Why Strikes are Lost, by W. E. Trautmann, 141, 155, 159.
Williams, B. H., 140.
Wilson, Havelock, 79.
Women's Co-operative Guild, 341.
Women's Trade Union League, 306.
'Work' State, 10.
Worker and his Country, The, by Fabian Ware, 4, 27.
Workers' Educational Association, 17, 384.
Workers' Union, 231.
Workshop Committees, 12, 331, 361.

Yvetot, Georges, 112.

Zimmern, A. E., 131.

Printed by
MORRISON & GIBB LIMITED
Edinburgh

Notes to the Text

1. p.4, 1.7.
Hilaire Belloc (1870–1953). A prolific writer, Belloc was a passionate Catholic in revolt against industrialism. He believed that true freedom for the mass of the population could only be attained through the widespread distribution of small property, and he thus advocated a return to the 'medieval' system of peasant proprietorship, workshops and guilds. In some respects Belloc's outlook was not so far removed from that of the Guild Socialists, and he was in fact on friendly terms with Orage and often contributed to the *New Age*. G. K. Chesterton (1874–1936), another celebrated Edwardian writer to whom Cole refers, occupied a position rather similar to Belloc's. The latter was drawn into the centre of the 'intellectual unrest' of the period by the passage of the National Insurance Act in 1911 (see note 3 below). Belloc saw this measure as indicative of a tendency in contemporary society whereby men would increasingly be persuaded by the state to exchange freedom for security, thus bringing into being a regime which he characterised as the Servile State—the title of his book on this theme published in 1912—which he defined as 'one in which a portion of the inhabitants of the State, dispossessed of the means of production, are secure in sufficiency, without the dispossession of the capitalist or means-of-production-owning class'.

2. p.12, 1.8.
Prince Peter Kropotkin (1842–1921). A Russian aristocrat forced to leave his native country in 1876 as a result of his revolutionary political views. He spent some time in Switzerland and France, but in 1886 settled in England where he remained until after the Russian Revolution of 1917. His last years were spent in Russia. Kropotkin was a geographer and geologist of some note, but it is on his political writings that his fame rests, for he was the leading exponent of the doctrine of Anarchist-Communism. His most important works—*The Conquest of Bread* (1892), *Fields, Factories and Workshops* (1898), and *Mutual Aid* (1902)—were written during his stay in England. Kropotkin envisaged the emergence of a society based upon small, self-organising rural communities, where individuals would combine industrial with agricultural pursuits, thus achieving a 'reintegration' of life. He had much in common with William Morris (1834–96), but differed from the latter in his affirmation of advanced technology, which he saw as a means to the desired social ends. The advent of electric power for example would, he argued, make possible the decentralisation of industry into the countryside.

3. p.16, 1.1.
Social Insurance. Compulsory unemployment and health insurance was introduced for certain categories of workers in 1911. This measure was part of a package of social reforms introduced by the Liberal government which took office in 1906. Although the trade unions co-operated in the implementation of the insurance scheme, the latter was bitterly opposed by the socialists within the Labour Party, who objected to the contributory principle upon which the scheme was based: see G. D. H. Cole, *A Short History of the British Working Class Movement* (1948 edn.), pp.306—10.

4. p.35, 1.20.
Board of Trade statement. Cole refers presumably to the *Report of an enquiry by the Board of Trade into Working-Class Rents and Retail Prices* (1913), Cd. 6955. The report showed that in London retail food prices had risen by 11.4 per cent between 1905 and 1912.

5. p.40, 1.2.
Tom Mann (1856—1941) *and Ben Tillett* (1860—1943). The two most famous leaders of the mass unionism of the unskilled—the former an engineer by trade and the latter a seaman and docker. Both were actively involved in the upsurges of Union activity in the periods 1888—90 and 1910—14. During the latter period Mann was a forceful advocate of syndicalism, and edited the *Industrial Syndicalist* in the years 1910—11 (see note 6 below).

6. p.41, 1.26.
Industrial Syndicalist Education League. A loosely organised body founded in 1910 by those who subscribed to the doctrines expounded in the *Industrial Syndicalist*—the doctrines in question being derived from both Syndicalism and Industrial Unionism. Tom Mann was the leading spirit in the League, which for a brief period attracted a wide measure of support amongst the extreme left-wing elements in the Labour Movement. The League's existence came to an end in 1913. During its life it was above all pre-occupied with the immediate issues arising out of the great industrial unrest of the time; once this unrest began to wane the organisation disintegrated.

7. p.46. 1.34.
Eight Hours Act and Minimum Wage Act. These two pieces of legislation were secured by the Miners' Federation in 1908 and 1912 respectively. The Minimum Wage Act was in a very real sense a result of direct action, since it was rushed through Parliament by the Government during the great national coal strike which began in February 1912. The passage of the Act brought the strike—by far the largest Britain had known—to an end in April the same year.

8. p.47, 11. 3—4.
Strikes in the Black Country. After the great strike wave of 1910—12 there came a lull in the early months of 1913. The relative calm was, however, disturbed by the sudden upsurge of strike activity in the Midlands area around Birmingham and the Black Country. This new strike wave was triggered off by some girls at Dudley, and spread to include about 50,000 workers in a wide variety of industries. The episode was typical of the spontaneous, unorganised and confused character of much of the industrial unrest in the 1910—14 period: see Lord (G. R.) Askwith, *Industrial Problems and Disputes* (1920).

THE WORLD OF LABOUR

9. p.50, 1.16.
Sir George Askwith (1861–1942). Became Lord Askwith in 1919. Controller-General of the Labour Department of the Board of Trade, 1909–11. Chief Industrial Commissioner, 1911–19. Askwith was the great industrial conciliator of the pre-1914 period, and there were few major disputes in which he was not involved, trying to bring the parties to a settlement. His experiences in industrial relations, including the Canadian visit which Cole mentions, are set out in his book, *Industrial Problems and Disputes*, (1920; new edition, with introduction by Dr. Roger Davidson, 1973 The Harvester Press, Brighton).

10. p.53, 1.26.
'What the Worker Wants'. In May 1912 the *Daily Mail* invited people of all shades of opinion to contribute articles on the subject of the causes of the contemporary labour unrest. The invitation did produce a considerable response. Contributors included H. G. Wells, John Galsworthy, Philip Snowden, H. M. Hyndman, Seebohm Rowntree, Sir Walter Runciman, and various aristocrats, businessmen, labour leaders, public school headmasters and churchmen. The articles were later published by the *Daily Mail* in book form.

11. p.54, 1.27.
Brooklands Agreement. This agreement ended the 1893 general stoppage in the cotton spinning industry. It became well known nationally because it established an elaborate procedure for the settlement of future disputes in the industry without resort to a stoppage. In January 1913, however, the Cotton Spinners' Amalgamation gave notice to terminate the Agreement.

12. p.136, 1.24.
Samuel Gompers (1850–1924). Gompers was born in London, son of a Jewish cigarmaker. He migrated with the family to the United States when he was thirteen. He was one of the founding fathers of the American Federation of Labour, formed in 1886, serving as its first president, and remaining in that office—with the exception of one year—until his death. During his union career he became strongly anti-socialist and focussed the attention of the American trade union movement upon short-term goals to be attained within the existing capitalist system. Under his influence the American Federation of Labour became a bastion of job-conscious craft unionism.

13. p.180, 1.27.
'It is from the employers, rather than from the workers, that attempts to extend the area of disputes habitually come'. Cole was describing the situation in Germany, but a similar process had been at work in Britain, where in the period before 1914 employers' associations had played the predominant part in building up industry-wide bargaining procedures, thereby extending the potential area over which disputes might take place. The engineering industry, with its national lock-out in 1897, forms a good example of this. For the role of employers' associations see also Cole's comments on Sweden (p.187).

14. p.193, 1.5.
'What is contended is that Sweden presents in miniature the inevitable future of industry in greater countries'. Although Cole's prophecy proved to be rather wide of the mark, it certainly has been the case that

the Swedish system of industrial relations has continued to fascinate outside observers, and has often enough been held up as an example to other nations. See, for example, Michael Shanks, *The Stagnant Society* (1961), pp.127—36.

15. p.198, 11. 1—3.
'In this country, it is clear that, for a long time at any rate, we shall not have a labour movement prepared to call a general strike in support of any one section'. In this view Cole was, of course, to be proved wrong. He himself was to play a not inconsiderable part in the reform of the TUC, leading to the creation of the General Council in 1921, and it was this General Council which called for a sympathetic general strike on behalf of the Miners in 1926.

16. p.221, 1.20.
J. H. Thomas M.P. (1874—1949). Engine-driver by trade, assistant general secretary of the Amalgamated Society of Railway Servants (National Union of Railwaymen after 1913) 1910—17, general secretary 1918—31. Thomas, one of the foremost trade union leaders and Labour Party politicians of his day, was a leading member of the TUC. General Council and held office in the first two Labour Governments. His ties with the Labour movement were, however, severed when he joined MacDonald's National Government in 1931. Always on the right wing of the movement it was somewhat ironic that he should have been the leading figure in the NUR, a union formed in 1913 on an 'industrial' basis and hailed by the left as a model for the whole union movement to follow.

17. p.222, 1.4.
'As soon therefore as the NUR attempts to touch the skilled workers in the "shops" it will come into direct conflict with the ASE and other craft unions'. The various problems confronting organisation on the railways were the subject of a special study by Cole and R. Page Arnot—*Trade Unionism on the Railways* (1917)—produced under the auspices of the Fabian Research Department. The issue of the 'shops' was dealt with in chs. XV and XVI of this work.

18. p.235, 1.33.
J. R. Clynes (1869—1949). Originally an operative in the cotton textile industry, Clynes made a Union career for himself as an official in the Gasworkers' and General Labourers' Union, one of the general unions created at the end of the 1880s. He was president of this organisation (and its successor the National Union of General and Municipal Workers) 1914—37. Like Thomas, Clynes was also a prominent figure in the Labour Party, holding office in the first two Labour Governments, and also in the Coalition Government of World War I. He was very much a moderate, and had little sympathy with those of the left who placed their reliance on industrial rather than political action as a means of social transformation.

19. p.244, 1.21.
W. A. Appleton (1859—1940). Secretary of the Lace Makers' Trade Union 1896—1907, Appleton became secretary of the General Federation of Trade Unions in the latter year, an office he held until 1938. Although Cole speaks approvingly of Appleton in 1913, it became clear during World War I that the latter was very right-wing in his attitudes. He was in fact a friend of Samuel Gompers (see note 12 above), and

when Gompers died continued to maintain contact with other leading figures in the American Federation of Labour. See H. Pelling, *America and the British Left* (1956).

20. p.282 n.
Osborne Judgement. A decision given in the House of Lords in 1909, in the Osborne case, which prevented the trade unions from spending money for political purposes. The decision struck a considerable blow at the Labour Party, but was reversed by the Trade Union (Amendment) Act of 1913.

21. p.288, l.24.
Industrial Council. This body was set up by the government in 1911 as a result of the mounting tide of industrial unrest. It was composed of an equal number of employers and trade unionists, and was chaired by Sir George Askwith (see note 9 above). Its purpose was to hear disputes and recommend terms on which they might be settled. In this task the new body failed completely and after a year's existence it was wound up. During its brief life, however, it did conduct a general investigation into industrial agreements; this investigation is discussed by Cole on pp.307ff.

22. p.289 n.
Events in Dublin and Cornwall. So far as Dublin is concerned, Cole is referring to the bitter stoppage involving the Irish Transport Workers' Union, an extremely militant organisation founded in 1908. This stoppage lasted from August 1913 to January 1914, and represented an all out effort by the Dublin employers to crush the union. As to Cornwall, the reference here is to a strike of china-clay workers in August 1913.

23. p.321, l.13.
Scientific Management. This term came into use in this country in 1910 to describe the movement among industrial managers which aimed at a more systematic and efficient use of manpower. The new approach entailed such devices as time and motion study and incentive systems of payment. It was essentially an importation from America, where its great advocate was the engineer and inventor F. W. Taylor (1856—1915).

24. p.399, l.18.
B.S.P.: The British Socialist Party, formed in 1911 as an explicitly left-wing socialist party in open opposition to the Labour Party. It embraced, among a number of other groups, the old Social Democratic Federation which had been formed back in the 1880s. The BSP did not, however, attract much new support. After World War I it merged with other left-wing fragments to form the Communist Party of Great Britain.

25. p.415, l.2.
Knox strike. A strike on the North Eastern Railway in 1912. The objective of the 6,000 strikers was to secure the reinstatement of engine-driver Knox, who had been reduced in rank by the company as a result of alleged drunkenness while off duty. Knox was reinstated after a Home Office enquiry. The significance of the episode was that it seemed to indicate a willingness on the part of labour to use industrial action for other than purely economic ends, and so to present a challenge to managerial prerogatives.